THE DIARY

OF

JOSEPH FARINGTON

edited by

KENNETH GARLICK and ANGUS MACINTYRE

VOLUME II

JANUARY 1795 — AUGUST 1796

Published for the Paul Mellon Centre
for Studies in British Art

by

YALE UNIVERSITY PRESS
NEW HAVEN AND LONDON
1978

Designed by John Nicoll.
Set in AM747 Times by Preface Ltd, Salisbury, Wilts.
Printed in Great Britain by Biddles of Guildford.

Published in Great Britain, Europe, Africa, and Asia (except Japan) by Yale University Press, Ltd., London. Distributed in Australia and New Zealand by Book & Film Services, Artarmon, N.S.W., Australia; and in Japan by Harper & Row, Publishers, Tokyo Office.

Library of Congress Cataloging in Publication Data

Farington, Joseph, 1747–1821
    The diary of Joseph Farington.

    (Studies in British art)
    CONTENTS: v. 1. July 1793-December 1794.--v. 2. January 1795-August 1796.
    1. Farington, Joseph, 1747-1821. 2. Artists--England--Biography. 3. Arts, English. 4. England--Civilization--18th century. 5. England--Civilization--19th century. 6. London. Royal Academy of Art.
    I. Garlick, Kenneth, 1916-   II. Macintyre, Angus D.
    III. Paul Mellon Centre for Studies in British Art.   IV. Series.

N6797.F37A2 1978   759.2[B]   78-7056
ISBN 0-300-02314-6

CONTENTS

LIST OF PLATES

STUDIES IN BRITISH ART

8. Henry Singleton R.A. *Joseph Farington*, detail from *The Royal Academicians in General Assembly* (Plate 12). The Royal Academy of Arts, London.

JANUARY 1795

Thursday — January 1st.

Yenn, I called upon this morning, and staid with him some Hours. — He had misunderstood the terms of the subscription to the Rivers. — It was settled that He should return one of the vols He subscribed for and only complete his set of the Thames.

Yenn told me of his dispute with Soane at the Architects Club. He said the frequent abuse of the Royal Academy & its members caused him to adress Soane, after He had mentioned to Holland what He thought of *his* repeated disrespectful language with regard to the Royal Academy. — Holland had held that Painters & Sculptors were of no comparative account as members of society when compared with Architects. — Yenn shewed me a very angry letter written to him the same evening by Soane. — in which He states, "that He never wishes to belong to a Society of which such a man is a Member".

Yenn said that a few days after West delivered his last discourse, Yenn happened to be at the Queens palace. The King asked him if He was at the Academy on Wednesday the 10th. — Yenn said He was. The King replied "I suppose you had a good deal of Hack, Hack, Hack" alluding to Wests pronunciation of the word Academy which He pronounces *Hack*ademy. — The King further said West had given tickets to several persons abt. the Court. — The whole expressed the smile of the King at Wests pretending to turn Orator.

West, recd. £1300 for his large picture in the Chapel at Greenwich, and 5 guineas each for 25 drawings which He made. — On finishing the work West gave a dinner at Greenwich to many gentlemen belonging to the Hospital &c. Yenn was there. — West spoke of the Royal Academy & himself in such a way as to make it appear as if he was, under the King, the principal cause of the institution. — Yenn, jealous of the honor of Sir Wm. Chambers, his old master, asserted that He was the great mover of that business.

On the 4th. of June 1793 Yenn attended at the Queens palace, along with many others in the morning out of respect to the King. Copley was there. — The King mentioned the Exhibition of that year & said it was the worst that had been made since the foundation of the Royal Academy. — He said Hoppner & Beechy had distinguished themselves, but that Lawrence was fallen of.

Hoppner, I called upon. — Giffard was there. — Hoppner only slightly hinted at the ensuing election. I said He must remember the opinion I gave him sometime since.

Hoppner has 4 children. The eldest is 10 years & half old. — Offleys, I dined at with Susan & Bob. — Mrs. Offley, Mrs. Salisbury, — Mr. & Mrs. Harris, 2 Miss Arbouins, — Mr. Arbouin, — Miss Harris, Minet, Philips there. L. Salisbury to supper.

Friday Jany 2d.

D. Bell & Mr. Lindoe came to consult me as to the wishes of Mr. Lindoe to practise in painting. Mr. Lindoe, brought several specimens in oil. I told him there was a very good intention shewn in some of them, and that He wanted principles & regulation. — That I thought He might receive as much instruction in twelve months as wd. be necessary, and that being properly introduced among professional men, after that period He wd. be qualified to avail himself of their Society, and might proceed in his practise with all the advantage required. — That I had no doubt of his obtaining necessary instruction for that period, on terms that cd. be no object to him. — I advised him and Mr. Bell to take into consideration what I said and to call on me again when I wd. give them answers to any other questions they might desire to put.

On commencing this conversation before I saw the pictures, I reccomended to Mr. Lindoe not to relinquish the situation in which He is now placed, as I could not advise him to run any risk of failing in the profession. — He said He meant to retain his present employ & devote his extra time to painting. They fixed to call on me again on Wednesday next. — The Academy Club, I went to, — Hoppner told me, that His Father & Mother were Germans. His Father was a Surgeon. Hoppner was recommended to the King as a Lad of Genius, and the King had him placed to board with Mr. Chamberlains family. Mr. Chamberlain who is now in the Kings Library, and was one of the pages. — Hoppner was allowed 3 shillings a week pocket money. — He was acquainted with Mrs. Hoppner (the daugr. of Mrs. Wright the modeller in wax), several years before they were married. — Hoppner has been married upwards of 12 years. — On his marriage being known, He recd. a message from the King that His Majestys allowance wd. be withdrawn. Hoppner was during several years subjected to great difficulties. — He had Lodgings, a two pair of stairs floor, in Cockspur street. When He took a House in Charles St., St. James's Square, He painted three quarter portraits for 8 guineas a head. In this time He contracted a heavy debt, & had relatives besides his wife & children to provide for. — During some years while in Charles St. He did not get near £400 a year. — Lord Hampden, has been a continued friend. — He had bad health owing to a weakness of the bowels. He has been cured of this complaint by taking pepper corns, crushing them in his mouth & swallowing them. Doctor Darwin reccomended them originally, and Hoppner was advised to try that which had answered.

Mrs. Hoppner assisted all in her power to relieve him in his difficulties. She herself made *his cloaths* as well as those of the Children.

Copley told me that Wilton had offered the rooms, formerly occupied by Moser, for the accomodation of Mrs. Hadriel, as House-keeper. — Nollekens, said He was apprentice to Scheemaker, the Statuary. He went to *him* at Eleven years of age, and continued with [him] as Apprentice and Journeyman twelve years. Nollekens went to Rome and was in Italy 9 years. The last new years eve completed 24 years since He returned. He has been married 20 years, and is about 56 years old. — He studied at the Duke of Richmonds gallery abt. two years.

Wyatt, told me that He dined yesterday at the Architects Club, when Hatfield was balotted for. There were present:

Cockerell – Soane
Westall – Brettingham
Yenn   – Bonomi
Jupp

There appeared one black ball against Hatfield which excluded him. — Wyatt says it is certain that either Soane or Brettingham, put in the Black ball. — He speaks highly of Hatfields manners and promising abilities. — Wyatt was mortified at the rejection & told the members that He wd. Black ball any Candidate that should hereafter be proposed, as He found a *reccomended* person was rejected witht. a reason being assigned. — Holland, proposed Hatfield & Wyatt reccomended him.

Wyatt spoke highly of the abilities of Dance, & particularly of Newgate as a specimen of true taste in design. But He thought Dance in some instances has quitted grammatical art for fancies. — He said that in the new front of Guildhall, Dance had substituted for true gothic, something taken from the prints of India Buildings, published by Hodges.

Saturday — Jany 3rd.

This morning the glass was at 23 in my painting room. window had been open.

Dance, I called on. —, Soane brought a set of designs intended for altera-tions to be made for the accomodation of the House of Lords, — Soane said He could complete the whole in 4 years.

Singleton, I sat to for the last time, and reccommended the introduction of *the Architects* in a proper place, which He agreed to. — Burch caused the derangement. — Miss Singleton, his cousin, was painting in the same room.

Humphry, I called on. Singleton, his former pupil, has engraved a few small heads from his pictures of Sir George Baker &c at ten guineas a plate.

Boswell, I recd. a letter from dated at Auchinleck. If Dr. Gillies is elected to succeed Mr. Gibbon Boswell writes that he must with regret withdraw from the Society. If not He desires me to read a letter to the Club, expressive of his regard & that He shall join them at the end of this month. He reccomends that they substitute Saturday January 31st. for *January 30th.* for the next dinner day, and supposes the latter day was proposed accidentally.

Mrs. Offley, Mr. & Mrs. Salusbury, — John & Wm. Offley, and Carey dined with us.

Mr. Salusbury says Lord Beverly is much pleased with his situation at Orwell Park.

Sunday, Jany 4th.

Baker, Hearne, Edwards and Humphry dined with me.

Poggi called on me today. Lady Inchiquin has given the sale of Sir Joshuas Prints to Christie.

Monday — Jany 5th.

The Shakespeare gallery & Cheapside I went to, and took an acct. of the expenditure of monies on acct. of the publication of Rivers, and of the monies recd. — The Alderman told me it was a bad acct. — Mr. Burbridge at the gallery, said Captn. Rattray would not take them & that others had complained of the colouring particularly.

Mr. Lodge of the Heralds Office was there. He told me Mr. Paulett who succeeds to the Marquisate of Winchester, had abt. £6 or 7000 a year. He is about 58 years of age and a respectable character. His great, great grandfather was Brother to the great, great, grandfather of the late Duke of Bolton. He will inherit little of the *Ducal* estate.

Tuesday Jany 6th.

G. Steevens, told me at the Shakespeare gallery, that notwithstanding Dr. Johnson had given such enthusiastic praise to Milton, He did not believe the Dr. really felt as He wrote, and that He rather did it in compliance with the opinion of the world. Steevens does not think the Dr. had any high relish for works of imagination.

G. Nicol, told us He had much trouble with Hayley while the latter was writing the life of Milton. Hayley first produced a life written in so strong a spirit of republicanism that Nicol told him He could not print it. Hayley made alterations, but said He would print the [life] at a future time as first written. — Hayley is a violent Republican.

Offleys, I dined at. — Mrs. Offley & Mr. & Mrs. Salisbury there. Mr. Salisbury, told me Sir Charles Morgan of Tredegar has £25,000 a year. — 12,000 of which is in Monmouthshire. The Duke of Beaufort has abt. the same value of estates in that County.

Wednesday — Jany 7.

D. Bell, called on me. — We conversed abt. Mr. Lindoe who prefers studying in the Landscape line. — Bell mentioned Freebairn, and said He was told Freebairn is a violent Republican & talks of going to America. — I shewed him a list of the Members of the Royal Academy, and mentioned Ibbetson. — At last He told me that delicacy had prevented their proposing anything to me but it was the earnest wish of Lindoe, as well as *his*, that I could make it convenient to give him instruction. I had before asked him what they had an Idea of paying for a years instruction. He said that £100 wd. be no object. I said I thought that considering Mr. Lindoe's situation I thought that was too much. He said they had indeed thought of from £50 to 100.

In reply to the proposal made to me, I told him I had now a pupil whose time of engagement was expired. He had pd. me £200 for 3 years, & that I was so well pleased with him as to desire him to continue studying though I had no compensation for it. — I said that in his case as well as in Mr. Lindoes I had satisfied myself that they were so situated as not to run a desperate risk, but that each had a resource if the profession should not answer. I told him that association with the best Artists was of great consequence to such as proposed following the profession, and that in my private opinion some of those we had mentioned had no great opportunities of giving a pupil that advantage. — We concluded by agreeing to meet again on Monday next when I told him I wd. give my final answer. Mr. Lindoe called on me while Mr. Bell was with me, but at Mr. B's desire went to the Percy Coffee house while we had the above conversation. — Opie, I called on in the evening. — He told me Mr. Booth gave his daugtr. Mrs. Ford £7000. Ford is a reserved man, and is said not to be good tempered. — Mrs. Ford has been in a very nervous state since her marriage.

I told Opie that Fuseli was wrong in encouraging the hopes of Marchant too much, and inducing him to believe that if certain persons exerted themselves He wd. gain his election. — I said I had no doubt that Hoppner wd. have 20 votes.

Opie expressed his surprise at Beechy having raised his price to 30 guineas a head. He said that his pictures were of that mediocre quality as to taste & fashion, that they seemed only fit for sea Captains & merchants:

whereas Lawrence & Hoppner had each of them a portion as it were of gentility in their manners of painting.

Thursday Jany 8th.

Fuseli, I called on in the evening. Marchant came. Fuseli having written to the Council in favor of Mrs. Lowe at Cipriani's desire was a little mortified that she was not elected Housekeeper. — We conversed on the approaching election. I told Marchant that I was convinced Hoppner was now certain of 17 votes, and that 18 wd. be a majority. — I said this before Fuseli, to shew my opinion fully.

Friday, Jany 9th.

Sir G. Beaumont, I called on. — He shewed me the pictures He has brought from Essex. He had been so many months out of practice that it is only lately that He began to feel himself tolerably certain in his execution.

Great indignation is felt at Wilberforce having joined the opposition or rather at his having moved the amendment. Pitt had some notice of his intention, but Wyndham knew nothing of it, previous to his speaking. Wyndham expresses his opinion strongly, & says if miscarriages take place Wilberforce will have been in a great degree the cause. He has by his conduct encouraged our enemies & discouraged our friends.

Sir George dined yesterday with Lord Mulgrave who He says has an uncommon vein of humour.

We went together to Waltons, who has painted a head of Lord Cornwallis. — There we met Mr. Thos. Walpole, the Minister to Munich, who returned abt. three weeks ago.

Carey, I spoke to this afternoon on the subject of Mr. Lindoe studying with me. I told him that want of room obliged me to propose to him to paint at his lodgings in Rathbone place, a second floor, for which He pays half a guinea week. — That I hoped he would still consider himself as equally connected with me as before, and consider himself as much at home in my house as if He lived in it. — That I wd. superintend his studies as usual. — I reccomended to him to endeavour to get two pictures ready for exhibition, which I wd. take care of there. Marchant, came in the evening. Playfairs gesses & drawings are to be sold at Christies tomorrow and Wheatleys goods on Monday next.

Saturday Jany 10th.

Playfairs sale I went to. — Many professional men there. Six or seven sketch Books in which He made his Italian studies were put up to sale. They were much admired, but were bought in by Soane at 90 guineas, as Mr. Playfair told him they should not be sold for less than £100. — Lord Warwick, Ld. Powis, & Dr. Munro expressed a wish for them, but wd. not go to that price. — The Plaisters which Playfair bought at Rome, Flaxman said sold for £10 more than they cost him, freight included.

Dance, I called on. Chalie the wine merchant some time ago told him that Mr. Pitts Major Domo, said that He was weary of denying creditors, that Mr. Pitts Hatters Bill was £600.

Sunday Jany 11th.

Wyatt, I called on this morning. He is confined to his room owing to falling from a ladder which broke under him on Monday last by which his left arm is much bruised, and it is not yet known whether a bone is broke, though it is rather believed not. — I went at Horace Hamonds request but did not see him.

Baker & Hearne called on me. Baker desired to have the sketch of the Town Hall at Lynn. I told him I owed him a drawing for favors recd. which shd. come with the other if He wd. chuse one. — He said Dr. Munro desired to be introduced to me.

Hearne & Baker sat to Dance for profiles. We afterwards dined at Bakers. — Hearne, Dance, Edwards, — Marchi, — Revd. Mr. Guard & Richd. Baker & Marchant there.

Marchant had been to Sir Robt. Ainslies to see a set of drawings made for Sir Robt. by a german Artist, of the Pyramids, in the Holy Land &c. — Marchant says they are not only better than Revelys but superior to Du Croiz.

Monday — Jany 12th.

Baker, Dance, Charles Webb & Hearne dined with me.

Captn. Meyer, 2d. son of Meyer, the late Academician, died at Salisbury, yesterday. — Being sensible of his approaching end, with the leave of his Colonel, He sold his Commission the day before his death. — He was a very well disposed young man, & had served in India under Lord Cornwallis. — Mrs. Meyer has now one son & 4 daughters living.

Burke it is stated in the papers is now attended by Dr. Willis.

Lord Inchiquin, called, but I was out. — Marchi told me yesterday that he is 73 or 4 years of age.

Tuesday — Jany 13th.

Revd. Mr. White, breakfasted. — Glover was born in Leicester in the lowest line of life. Shewing a disposition to draw He met with some encouragement and taught drawing at a school at Appleby in Leicestershire from whence He removed to Lichfield where He taught at two or three schools and in private. — White, feels that He is conceited and that He rather endeavours to conceal his having had any instruction.

Wheatleys, drawings and pictures were sold today. The pictures sold low. a large picture of Plough Horses in a frame which cost 20 guineas sold for £17.10. — A picture of the 25 guinea size in a frame sold for £14.10. — Two of a smaller size sold in frames for £24.3. – .

Marchant, came in the evening. — Fuseli has recommended to him to desire me on the night of the election to state to the meeting the obligation due to Marchant for his active service towards procuring the indulgence to British Artists of bringing their studies from abroad duty free; and to read the letters from Rome to Marchant on that subject. — I was surprised at the impropriety of this request but told Marchant only that I wd. speak to Fuseli on the subject.

Wednesday — Jany 14th.

Smirke called. Hickey the Sculptor died yesterday after an illness of 3 or 4 days only owing to having lain in a damp bed. — Rossi is desirous of obtaining the commission to execute Garricks monument which Burke had procured for Hickey. — Smirke thought Mr. Wyndham might be applied to for his interest with Burke, but I said it was reputed that Burkes health is such as to make it unlikely that an application cd. be made to him.

Thursday Jany 15th.

Wyatts, I called at. He is better. — weather very severe.

Friday 16th.

G. Steevens, told me at the Shakespeare gallery that Mrs. Garrick has nothing to do with the monument ordered from Hickey. An old friend of Garricks proposed to be at the sole expence which was proposed as He understood to be abt. £600, and Hickey was recommended by Burke as one well qualified and wd. do it on reasonable terms.

D. Bell, called on me. I told him I wd. instruct Mr. Lindoe for a year for £63. He expressed his satisfaction & said it was what Lindoe wd. rejoice at and He thought my proposal liberal. I told him as to payment that I payed Wilson at the commencement of the year but Mr. Lindoe might suit his convenience and pay me half on commencement and half when half a year had expired.

Saturday — Jany 17.

Smirke called & I told him the conversation I have had with G. Steevens. He said Albany Wallis is the person who gives the monument. I proposed speaking to Lysons who probably cd. through some Channel make an interest with Wallis.

Lysons called in the eving. He is acquainted with Mr. Froward, partner with Mr. Wallis & will speak to him.

Smirke has ordered the Queens Birth day dinner for 35. 26 tickets only are ordered.

Sunday — Jany 18th.

G. Dance, I called on. He says Mrs. Fitzherbert complains that she has expended £8000 in entertainments &c provided for the Prince of Wales, and that if He wd. pay that sum, & trouble her no more she wd. be contented. She says she has lived the life of a Galley Slave for 4 years past.

N. Dance, thinks Pitt no War Minister.

Ld. Inchiquins, I dined at. Dr. Lawrence of the Commons, & Mr. Trevanion, Member for Dover there.

Ld. Inchiquin mentioned as a proof of want of feeling in the Royal family, that Mrs. Ewart, widow of Mr. Ewart, minister at Berlin, & who has been the companion of the Duchess of York, by the fire at Oatlands Her apartment was burnt and her Cloaths &c. Everything proper was said & promised on the occasion, but nothing has yet been done, and her pension is 18 months in arrear.

The King & Royal family at Windsor go twice a week to the Play house there to see a miserable set of performers. What an insensibility it shews at times like these. — The Etiquette is that no Lady is to go into the Boxes with a Cloak on, though the family are cloaked as they please.

Dr. Lawrence has a poor opinion of the abilities of Mr. Hastings. A man of talents not adequate to his situation. Of some parts but no judgement. Of no real feeling but the affectation of it. In short the semblance or imitator of a character rather than possessing the substance — The accts. of the health of Burke are false. He is in possession of himself, and now only feels as a man of sensibility may be expected to do.

The Primacy of Ireland is worth abt. £10,000 a year with vast patronage. The Duke of Portlands interest procured it for Dr. Newcome.

Will Burke is in a very nervous state of Health. He is upwards of 60 years of age. — Edmund Burke is abt 64 or 5.

January 19th.

Queens Birth day kept.

Bob went to Oxford. He told me there wd. be plenty of accomodation room in their College in the summer.

At the dinner at Freemasons Tavern there were — persons.

	Academicians present		Associates
Messrs.	West	Smirke	Hoppner
	Cosway	Bourgeois	Tresham
	Wilton	Farington	Marchant
	Bartolozzi	Richards	Bigg
	Yenn	Zoffany	Rooker

Tyler	Burch	Edwards
Banks		
Dance		

Among persons invited were

Messrs.	J. Taylor	—	Bowyer	—	Giffard
	Heriot	—	Batty	—	Chalmers
	Daniel	—	Porden		
	Soane	—	T. Dance		

I staid with Dance &c till past 12.

Soane, called on me this morning, to state the dispute between him & Yenn at the Architects Club. — He said He was speaking of foreign Academies & Yenn applied what He said to the Royal Academy. — I told him I thought He wd. have stood a good chance if the election had taken place in November, & reccomended to him to cultivate the acquaintance of the members when opportunities offered.

Yenn, invited me to dine with him on the 8th. of February.

Soane, invited me to dine with him on Friday next.

Bowyer, told me Valentine Green pays him 200 guineas a year for the use of a room to exhibit Loutherburghs pictures in.

Tuesday — Jany 20th.

J. Taylor called on me. — Heriot has purchased his poetic compostions and is now printing them. — He gives Taylor 40 guineas for them. — In the poem called the Stage is the character of Kemble as an Actor. Taylor read it to him and Kemble said He only wished he merited such a description. Taylor was at the funeral of Hickey yesterday along with Tresham, H. Webber, Kean the Miniature Painter & Hickeys brother. He says Hickey was a very sensible man and had a talent for writing.

Wednesday — Jany 21st.

The Frost continues intense. At noon 4 degrees below freezing point in my painting room with a fire in it.

Thursday — 22d.

Smirke, called and showed me an anonymous letter inclosing an "Ode to a Young sculptor", which was on Monday sung by Malton and not much noticed. — Smirke believes it to have been written by Porden, the Architect.

Prince of Orange landed on Tuesday at Harwich, slept that night at Colchester, and came to London yesterday at noon. — with him came the Princess his daugr. and his second son. — He came in a Bye Boat and before he got on board his situation was critical from the disaffection shewn by the poeple.

The Princess of Orange landed at Yarmouth on Monday. She was accompanied by the Hereditary Princess & Her Young Child. They arrived in town last night. — They escaped with difficulty from Holland. — The Zuyder-Zee was frozen over the night before they embarked, which made their escape more difficult.

January 23rd.

The glass, this morning in my painting room stood at 10 oClock a fire in the room & the window down - at 21 degrees & a half. — on the stair case at 28.

Boswell, called on me. He returned from Auchinleck on Monday last. Auchinleck near Kilmarnock in the County of Air. — He told me Mr. Malone has been in Cheshire to see Miss Bover and has offered himself to her, but is not accepted. Lord Sunderlin has seen Miss Bover & is much pleased with her. His Lordship is married but has no children, He is the elder Brother of Malone & has £6000 a year which will come to Malone if He is the survivor. Malone has £800 a year to spend. — Boswell says though Malone is obliging in his manners, He has never been a favorite of the Ladies, He is too soft in his manners.

Boswell has often met Lord Spencer at the Literary Club but never observed any vigour of mind in him. — Soanes, I dined at. Dance, Smirke, Cosway, Hodges, Hoppner, J. Taylor, Marchant there. — At Eleven oClock we left Soanes, & Smirke, Hoppner & myself went home with Dance & staid till 4 o'clock in the morning. Dance drank to Hoppners election.

Saturday — Jany 24th.

At home alone.

Sunday 25th.

Hoppner, called to remind me of his having engaged Dance, Smirke & myself to dine with him tomorrow.

Revd. Mr. Este, called & with him Gandons eldest son who is lately arrived from Dublin. His Father talks much of returning to England. Este, prognosticated that in 3 years the monarchies of Prussia & Austria will be destroyed. — He says if the war lasts 12 months longer there will be an insurrection in England.

He says the Prince of Orange gets drunk every day. In Holland He was accustomed to dine at ½ past 12 and from that time was seen no more. — The Princess of Orange is devoted to political intrigue. — The Hereditary Prince and his Brother are manly & promising. The Dutch have detested the Prince of Orange since the Prussians were called in by him to keep them in order, and had He staid in Holland there is little doubt but He wd. have been tried for his life.

At Guildhall on Friday Este says that 4000 persons were assembled and that there were not more than 100 but what voted for peace.

The Frost, is still more intense. The Glass in my painting room, with a fire and window down, stood at 19 — 13 degrees below freezing point. — on the stair case it was at 27.

A Collection from House to House has been made in the South Division of this Parish. £228-15. has been given. 762 families have been relieved with Coals, bread & money &c. A second collection is proposed to be made on acct. of the continued severity of the season. Marchant called in the evening, & Smirke.

Monday — Jany 26th.

Batty, called and said the Thermometer stood on Saturday night at 4 which was lower than had ever been known in this country since that instrument had been made use of 50 or 60 years ago. Hoppners, I dined at with Smirke & Giffard. Dance could not go. — Giffard told us Lord Grosvenor is about 64 years of age. Lord Belgrave 27 — Lady Belgrave 22 — Lord Belgrave has a very bilious constitution being seldom well 2 days together. He has been better since He married. Giffard says Lord Grosvenor has been a great loser by the turf. He never knew how to bet judiciously. He has been a moderate drinker of wine and observed early hours in going to bed.

Chamberlains, father, Hoppner told us, was originally a Life Guards Man. It was through the interest of old Lord Ligonier that He was brought to the notice of the King.

While we were at dinner at Hoppners, Mrs. Hoppner was delivered of a Boy. She had been indisposed the whole day.

Brettingham, the Architect wrote a silly letter to Hoppner a few days ago on acct. of Hoppner having put off his sitting for his portrait.

Hodges, pictures, Giffard told us, were this day taking away from Bond Street.

A Thaw, began this afternoon..

Tuesday — Jany — 27th.

Messrs. Pepyss & Forster called for a second subscription for the poor.

Lysons called. — He was in company a few nights since with the Mr. Hopes of Amsterdam. — They spoke of the poeple of Holland as being divided into parties, and though not eager for the French coming, yet ill inclined to associate for a general defence. — They said Holland abounded in Naval Stores belonging to the public & to individuals, & that 20 sail of the Line might soon be fitted out. — It was not doubted but that Admiral Kingsbergen who commands 6 sail of the Line in the Texel would be glad to bring them to England, but it is not probable that He will be able to influence the sailors. Mr. Hopes, say, there are not so many Dutch sailors among them as might be expected, a great number of Swedes, Danes &c being employed in the service. — The Mr. Hopes have brought to England their fine collection of pictures, & have removed so much of their property as they said as to have left only chairs and tables behind them. — It is supposed Mr. Hopes have realised in this country half a million, & that the Stadtholder has secured as much while the storm has been brewing.

Lysons told me Sheridan has been very busy in fomenting a disposition in the City to adress for peace. One Reid has been a busy agent for him. — Dr. Hodson who was committed to Newgate for seditious expressions made use of in the London Coffee House has also been an active agent. — Not one out of 50 it is said of the Crowd assembled were really Livery men.

Mr. & Mrs. Molyneux dined with us: Also Carey. — Mr. Molyneux said the white Ladies in the Island of St. Kits, will not sit at a table with any Mulatto by descent though scarcely tinted with Colour. — This extends to men & woemen.

Mr. Molyneux first prevailed by his example on the Gentlemen of that Island to drink Port Wine, which they had been accustomed to think too strong for the climate. It is now drank commonly. The Glass, the Thermometer, at Mr. Cavendishs, at Clapham, stood on Saturday night at 4 degrees below 0, when it is 10 degrees below 0 in Russia it is reckoned extreme cold. — The Glass today is 45 upon my staircase.

Lord Howes, fleet is unfortunately prevented from sailing by the sudden change of the weather, & the French fleet may return to Brest.

Mr. Grey, when at School was of a restless and mutinous disposition, Molyneux says He has been told by Greys school fellows.

Dick wrote to me today that last week Tom Walker obtained abt. 80 signatures to a requisition to call a Town meeting in Manchester for the purpose of adressing for peace. Not 12 of the persons named were known. — A counter requisition was immediately proposed & signed by 130 of the most respectable persons in Manchester, which crushed Walker's attempt. — Trade is now very brisk in Manchester.

Wednesday — Jany 28th.

John Kemble, the Actor, this day published in several papers the following advertisement.

"I John Philip Kemble, of the Theatre Royal Drury Lane, do adopt this method of publickly apologizing to Miss De Camp for the very improper & unjustifiable behaviour I was lately guilty of towards her: which, I do further declare her character & conduct had in no instance authorized; but on the contrary, I do know and believe both to be irreproachable".

Thursday — Jany 29th.

The Turkish Ambassador, this day made his publick entry. He went to Sir George Howards, Governor of Chelsea Hospital, in his private carriage, & there met Lord Jersey who attended as Master of the Ceremonies, — From thence they came to St. James's together. — At half past 12 they arrived there, I saw in the Coach, the Ambassador, Lord Jersey, — Sir Clement Cotterell, — and Mr. Pissani, the interpreter. It was a Coach of the Kings drawn by 6 Horses with Ribbonds &c. — Other Royal Coaches followed. In the 2nd. Coach was a Turk who appeared to hold Credentials. — Before the first Coach several horses, richly caparisoned, were led by Turks clothed in silks. — 2 Turks in silks, walked on each side of the first and second coaches. — The Day was very fine. — Dr. Wharton, of Winchester, the Bishop of Landaff, and Mr. Burgess of Oxford were at the Shakespeare gallery. — Dr. Wharton looked over the new edition of Milton and remarked upon the prejudice of Johnson against that great man.

Geo: Steevens, came to the gallery. He told me the Bishop of Landaff had £25,000 left him by the late Mr. Luther, Member for Essex and was in good circumstances, though the Bishoprick of Landaff is of little value, £700 a year. Mr. Burgess, He says, is an eminent scholar, particularly in the Greek language. He is nephew to Dr. Lowth, late Bishop of London.

Mr. Steevens had just heard the cause of Kembles advertisement. — He attacked Miss De Camp, in the green room, at the Play House. — Her screams caused poeple to break open the door which prevented His attempt from succeeding.

Knights, poem, is reprinting. Bulmer told me the first Edition of 750 is disposed of. abt. 20 pages will be added. — Knight, proposes to publish another work, in which He will introduce etchings from the pictures of Old Masters & etchings of examples of modern gardening, and will point out the errors in both.

Fuseli called in the evening.

H. Hamond came to town.

Friday — Jany 30th.

Smirke this morning looked over my sketches in oil and pictures laid in, and reccomended to me to finish the upright picture of Windsor Castle and part of the Bridge, — and the view of St. Pauls taken from under Black Fryars Bridge, — as subjects for the Exhibition. He seemed particularly to reccomend to me not to over finish them in certain parts. — If I have time, He next reccomended to me to finish the view of Bridgnorth Bridge *in shade,* and the upright study of a waterfall.

Humphry called. — The Stadholder dines with the King today for the first time.

The Frost, has returned. The Glass in my painting room this afternoon was at freezing point.

Saturday Jany 31st.

Lord Inchiquin I called upon. — Malone has reccomended Hutchins to sell the prints, He says Christie sells such articles in too careless a manner. Poggi has paid in £450 on acct. of the drawings. Lady Inchiquin privately told me she cd. not but be uneasy about that property — with regard to disposing of the pictures I told them they must either now resolve to bring them forward the ensuing Spring or determine to keep them 4 or 5 years for they could not expect better times sooner. — Boswell came in.

The Academy Club today consisted only of Eleven persons. West is at Windsor and Tyler confined by cold. I was in the Chair. — At Boswells request we staid after Tea till 2 in the morning. — The following the Company left. — Boswell, — Lawrence, — Hoppner, — Burch, — Garvey, — Hamilton, — Smirke — Rooker.

Kemble, Bourgeois, said, appeared on the stage a night or two since. A party of friends went there to support him. In the course of the Play at a certain passage, an attempt at hissing began, which was outnumbered by clapping and no farther notice was taken of Kembles late behaviour. — It is said it was not in the green room but in a passage room that He attacked Miss Decamp.

Boswell, brought me an invitation to dine at Lord Inchiquins on Wednesday next. Malone & Kemble are to be invited.

FEBRUARY 1795

Sunday February 1st.

rain all day.

Lysons, dined with me. — He dined yesterday at Mrs. Montagus. Mr. Rose of the Treasury was there. He said that the commerce of this country had never been higher than in the last year except in 1792. — That the sum insured at Loyds last year amounted to 80 millions, — of course the *Customs* must have been very great.

Sir Jos: Banks, I went to with Lysons. — Duke of Leeds, — Lord Morton, — Lord Mountmorres, — Sir George Shuckburgh, — General Mordaunt, — Dr. Ingenhouz, — Honble. Mr. Peachy, — Arthur Young, — Dr. Russell, — &c &c there. — Mr. Dryander told me Sir Joseph Banks has given cards of invitation to more than 200.

Monday Feby 2d.

Frost again.

Wyatt, I called on. — Mr. Penn, the representative of that family, came in. Wyatt says He is a remarkably shy man. — He has £4000 a year from the British Government, and large estates in Pensylvania. — The Government of that Province gave him £100,000 for the Royaltys He held.

Wyatt told me his terms for travelling to see Houses & receive orders are half a Crown a mile, — *his time included*. He said for making a drawing of Alterations and delivering in an estimate of such a work as H. Hamond seemed to want wd. be about 25 or 30 guineas.

Wyatt asked me who was likely to be taken up by the Academy at the election, and that He was disengaged. — I said I thought Hoppner had the best chance. He said He thought Hoppner had the best claim.

D. Bell, wrote me that Mr. Lindoe had communicated to a friend in the country his scheme & his wishes, and they being approved Bell wd. call on me to settle what is necessary.

Major Le Marchant called on Carey, I had some conversation with him on the subject of his practising drawing in Smiths manner with which He is captivated.

300

Opies, I went to in the evening. — Mrs. Gillies, Mrs. Ford, Miss Booth, — 2 Miss Hickeys, — Mr. Mullings, — Mr. —, Opies pupil there.

Mrs. Gillies told me Lord Hopetouns affairs are put in trust for the benefit of his creditors. — His estates are called £30,000 a year, and they allow him 6 or 8000 a year.

Tuesday — Febry 3d.

Marchant called in the evening. — He was at Cosways last night. They told him Miss Hatfield was married to Coombes on Wednesday last. She wrote them a letter the day before acquainting them with her intention which was the first notice they had of any attachment subsisting between them. She has been in the country a month.

Hayley, the Poet called on Marchant yesterday & said He had been with Hodges who was very low spirited in consequence of having heard the Duke of York was at his Exhibition & that his having chosen for subjects *Peace & War* it is supposed proceeded from Democratic principles.

Lady Spencer told Marchant on Sunday that Wyndham grows thin being over harassed in his situation. She expressed Her wish to be again settled at Althorpe and said nothing but the public good would have induced Ld. Spencer & Wyndham to hold places.

Humphry came in. Bowyer, the miniature painters Father was a ship-wright. Bowyer was clerk to a merchant in the City. Middleton the Colourman introduced Bowyer to Humphry some years ago. —

Pitt was against the Duke of Richmond resigning but the King would have it so. — From a conversation with Malone Humphry thinks Ld. Amherst will be superseded.

Parsons, the Player, died this morning at his house in Lambeth. — aged abt. 51 or 2.

Wednesday Febry 4th.

Lord Inchiquin, I dined with. — Mr. Boswell and his 2 daughters, Mr. Malone, and Mr. & Mrs. Kemble there.

Malone related that Sam Irelands son is said to be in possession of some manuscripts of Shakespeare and a whole play entitled Vortigern. — The story He told does not engage confidence when a man of Sam Irelands character is to support it, yet it is said that Dr. Wharton &c &c have seen part of the manuscripts and give credit to them.

Malone says Mr. Wyndham suffers much from his exertions and is grown very thin. — He has too much sensibility for a publick situation. — Malone hinted that Oxford was likely to return Wyndham to Parliament if Norwich did not.

Thursday, 5th.

Lawrence I called on. — He has not recd. notice to attend the meeting next

Tuesday. I told him I wd. speak to some of the Council to write to West who is the cause of the delay.

Sir G. Beaumont called on me. — He thinks Wilberforce has done much mischief by his conduct in Parliament, and that it certainly appears as if the solicitation of the Dissenters has operated on his mind. His motion cd. do no good as he was sure to lose it.

Sir George wishes Wyndham had remained out of office, as with his abilities at the head of the country Gentlemen at this crisis He might have had great effect against the opposition. It is believed to have been much the wish of the Duke of Portland to have Wyndham in office.

The Duchess of Gordon desired Sir George to call on Lawrence to see the Portrait of Lady Louisa Gordon. Sir George does not think it like. — He thinks Hoppner has a decided superiority over Lawrence.

Friday — Febry 6th.

Glass, in my painting room witht. fire — 29.

Tyler, I called on who thinks it best for Lawrence & Westall to apply personally or write to West at Windsor on the subject of their not having been summoned for Tuesday next. — This I told Westall who said He would go to Lawrence.

Hamilton called on me. — He never spoke to Fuseli abt. Marchant and the ensuing election but to Martin who Fuseli desired to speak to him. — Hamilton gave no answer and said He wd. talk with Fuseli. — He thinks Hoppner ought to be elected. He spoke highly of young Flaxmans drawings. Flaxman told Hamilton He thought the works of Banks equal to those of Canova.

Carey I told today I should require his room on Monday next.

Mrs. Offley called and told me she had agreed to board with Lynch Salisbury who has given £1500 for a House at Hitchin. Mrs. Offley is to give £200 a year for herself, maid & Coachman, and to pay for her Coach separate.

Saturday — Febry 7th.

Westall, I called on. He & Lawrence sent a letter of remonstrance to West at Windsor this morning, on their not having been summoned to attend on Tuesday next to receive their Diplomas.

The Duke of York, and Prince William of Gloucester, went to Hodges Exhibition, and abused his pictures as being of a political tendency expressing their surprise that such pictures should be exhibited.

Major Le Marchant called. I recommended to him to apply drawing *forms* as well as *effects*. He was at the House of Commons last night when Grey made his motion relative to the government of France as fit to make peace with. — He said Grey spoke unequally sometimes with force but when heated lost himself, so did Whitbread. Sheridan spoke pointedly and forced a reply from Pitt which He did not intend to the others.

Carey took his painting things away today. — Macklin, the player, died on Thursday last aged 95. N.B. This acct. was not true.

Sunday — Febry 8th.

Hoppner called. — We talked on the ensuing election. — I told him Tyler, Hamilton & Wyatt wd. certainly vote for him. — I told him my situation has been disagreeable as Fuseli had given Marchant reason to expect He wd. succeed if I and some others wd. exert themselves. That I had been acquainted with Marchant 26 years & considered him an able Artist and shd. be sorry any prejudice shd. rise in his mind: that to prevent it I had told him before Fuseli that Hoppner wd. have 17 votes certain & 18 would be a majority of the whole Academy. I added I hoped Marchant wd. be second as that wd. be some consolation. — I recommended to Hoppner to say little on the subject as it wd. only create Heartburnings. — He said He was not at all addicted to repeat things. — I concluded by telling him if no accident, owing to members thinking him certain, prevented his being on the second balot, — I considered him sure of his election. — From the jokes which passed, He concluded He was to provide a supper on Tuesday night & asked me who He shd. invite. I told him by no means provide a supper or invite persons. If anybody called give them a glass of wine and a bit of anything that happened to be in the way.

Fuseli I called on. I told him Marchant had proposed as from him that I shd. read the proofs of what Marchant had done to procure the indulgence to artists to import their studies duty free. — He said Marchant had misunderstood him, that He only insisted that it wd. be of little advantage if I read them only in Council, but that He had told Marchant He was sure if I read them on Tuesday night it wd. do him harm.

Thaw this day. Glass up to 46 on stair case.

Monday — Febry 9th.

Thaw continues with rain. Glass 52.

Hoppner called on me this morning. I recommended to him not to call on Bacon & Russell as I thought He wd. degrade himself by unnecessary solicitation. — I also observed how prudent it wd. be not to allow any prejudices to rise in his mind against such as might not support him. That Fuseli was induced by a feeling of obligation to Marchant. He said He was ready to make any allowance and nothing wd. stick on his mind.

Will, came to town with George who went to school.

Tuesday — Febry 10th.

Lawrence called on me & brought a letter which He had recd. from West at Windsor in answer to that sent by Lawrence & Westall claiming their admission to the Academy this day. — G. Dance came in and with us was surprised at the nature of the apology.

Marchant I called on & spoke to him on the subject of his having as from Fuseli proposed to me to read tonight at the Academy the letters sent to him from Rome thanking him for his services in having contributed to procure the indulgence to British Artists to import their studies duty free. — I told him I wd. not on any acct. bring forward such a matter at such a time, and that I had told Fuseli so yesterday. — He said on considering it He was already satisfied it wd. be improper.

I told Marchant that I understood that Fuseli had given him false hopes of succeeding and that Hoppners prospect must be very fair from what passed last year. — He said He did not expect to succeed & was only sorry for the trouble his friends had taken.

Humphry dined with me. Westall came in indignant against West. Marchant came to tea. Humphry & I went to the Academy and took up Dance & Tyler.

Present at the meeting
Mr. West.

Wilton	—	Cosway	—	Rigaud
Bourgeois	—	Yenn	—	Bartolozzi
Smirke	—	Fuseli	—	Bacon
Farington	—	Tyler	—	Russell
Wyatt	—	Banks	—	P. Sandby
Burch	—	Hamilton	—	Northcote
Opie	—	Garvey	—	Humphrey
Copley	—	Nollekens	—	Dance

The minutes having been read, Mr. West called the attention of the members to the business of the evening, which He said was to elect an Academician in the room of Newton. I then rose and expressed my surprise that the Academicians elect were not admitted, as their pictures had been delivered 3 months. — West was confused and made lame excuses. The principal one was that He had been afflicted with gouty complaints for 3 weeks past which had prevented his being in Town. — One circumstance was strong against him, viz: the King having *signed* an approval of the election of the President & Officers for the present year, about 3 weeks ago yet the Diplomas were not signed.

I then proceeded to state that another business was improperly suspended, viz: "the election of a student to go to Italy". — I said it was a hardship to keep the Candidates in a state of suspense.

This conversation concluded by West promising to call a Council soon, which should be followd by a general meeting to elect a student and to admit the Academicians elect. — The Balot for an Academician then took place. Three letters were produced. From Loutherburgh *expressly for Marchant*, — from Catton and from Mrs. Loyd, — and Wheatley.

First Balot
Hoppner 19 — Marchant 7 — Tresham 2 —

Second Balot

Hoppner   18
Marchant   6
————
24

Dance — Yenn — Smirke — Bourgeois & myself supped with Hoppner & staid till past 12.

Febry — 11th.

C. Offleys I dined at. Barroneau & Dr. Roberts there.
    Glass 57.

Thursday — Febry 12th.

C. Offley I called on & assisted him in selecting pictures to be put up.

    Humphry drank tea with me. — I went to the Antiquarian Society for the first time this Season, — Salisbury Brereton in the Chair. Hodges was balotted for and elected. — From thence I went to Lysons in the Temple. — On my return home found Marchant who is well reconciled to his disappointment. George James, Lysons told me, died of the gout sometime since in prison in France, where He went to reside with his family from oeconomical motives. — He was the son of a Barrister in the Temple, and was educated in Art under Pond. — He married Miss Boisseur, sister to a Mr. Boisseur, a Swiss merchant. She had £15,000. — James was a bad painter, but a good mimic, and very entertaining in society by singing humourous songs &c. He had also a talent for drawing caricatures. — He returned from Italy abt. 35 years ago.

Friday — Febry 13th.

Heavy snow last night. — Glass today 43.

    Will went to Hoddesdon.

    Royal Academy Club I went to. — Thirteen present. Tyler in the Chair.

    Hoppner told me Mr. Nares had mentioned to him that what I said at the Royal Academy on Tuesday is stated in a newspaper.

Saturday — Febry 13 [14th].

Bowyer, called on me on acct. of the picture of Charles 2d. — He is desirous it shd. be ready for the opening his Exhibition abt. the 24th.

    Captn. Molloy, called on Bowyer yesterday. — He told him He had such evidence in his favor as would make those repent who had made it necessary for him to be brought to a court martial. — It is remarkable that Molloy & Albemarle Bertie, two of the *shy Captains* each get £25,000, by the capture of the Spanish Register Ship and Lord Hood and Admiral Gell each £50,000. Note — The above statement is contradicted as to the sums.

Sunday — Febry 15th.

Hearne, I breakfasted with. — Baker & Byrne came. Watts the engraver of the Book of small views has lost 3 or £4000 which He gained by that publication, by lending it to persons, and is now working for Byrne.

Baker, I dined with. Hearne & Richd. Baker there.

Monday — 16th.

C. Offley, dined with me. — Dick & Eliza arrived at dinner time. — Will Boardman is in the Kings Bench.

Joe Green called this morning.

Tuesday 17th.

Sir George & Lady Beaumont called. — Sir George yesterday in company with Ld. Mulgrave, visited Brothers the Prophet announced by N. B. Halhed. — Sir George says he is evidently mad, but probably used as an instrument by democratic persons. — He recommended to them to submit to the French as it wd. be in vain to resist.

G. Dance called. Soane has informed him that Wyatt told him He had never applied for the Comptrollership of the Board of Works, — to the King, Queen, or princesses Dance has exerted himself since this notice.

Ld. Lansdowne told Dance yesterday the Empress of Russia is dead.

Banks Jenkinson is in love with a daughter of Lord Bristol to the great concern of Ld. Hawkesbury.

N. Dance told G. Dance that the Duchess of Dorset had sat 10 or 12 times to Hoppner who had not succeeded in making a picture from her. — Dance was surprised at Hoppners want of power in drawing.

Wednesday — Febry 18th.

At Home.

Thursday — Febry 19th.

Lord Inchiquins, I breakfasted at. — Lady Inchiquin desired me to speak to Sir George Beaumont requesting him [me] to offer Sir Joshuas prints to him, in which case after a valuation some hundred pounds would be deducted to make the offer a bargain to him. — Mr. Hope of Amsterdam has declined the same offer, as He has never collected Prints or drawings. — Sir Joshuas drawings would be offered to Lord Abercorn on the same terms.

Speaking of gaming Lady Inchiquin said Sir Joshua had a strong passion for it, as He himself allowed, — and He was convinced it was inherent in human nature. He said that the principle of it appeared in a variety of instances. — Offer a beggar as much per week to work moderately as He wd. confess He obtained by soliciting Alms, & He wd. refuse it. — In one case certainty would preclude hope. — Tell a man of 50 that His life shd. be secured to 90 but then it must terminate, He wd. rather take his chance.

Sir Joshua though He had a passion for gaming kept it within bounds. — He once won 70 guineas at a sitting which was the largest sum He ever gained. — If He went into a Company where there was a Pharo table, or any game of chance, He generally left behind him whatever money He had abt. him.

Miss Pelham, Lord Inchiquin mentioned as an extraordinary instance of suffering from the passion of gaming. She has lost £70,000, yet carries every guinea she can borrow to the gaming table, where she will weep & lose. — When she has lost what money she has abt. her she will solicit a loan of a few guineas from any person near her, even from a stranger. Sometimes gentlemen will subscribe a few guineas and give them to her on such occasions.

Lord Inchiquin told me he won at one sitting from Sir John Bland £34,000. The last throw at Sir John's desire was for £12,000, £6,000 a side which Sir John won, leaving *Lord Inchiquin winner on the whole* of £34,000. Sir John gave Bonds &c for the money, but went to France, where He put an end to his life.

Febry 20th.

Foster Bower, Kings Council, died at his chambers in Lincolns Inn, on Wednesday last, aged 48.

Smirke called on me. Sharp has rudely refused to engrave from a picture painted by Smirke for Bowyer, of Edwd. 6th. refusing to sign when pressed by Cranmer.

Snow, today Glass 31.

C. Offleys I dined at with Smirke & Dick.

Saturday Febry 21st.

Poggi I called on, who this day opened his Exhibition of Clevelys pictures. — He desired me to speak to Boydells to induce them to come there & hoped they wd. take in subscriptions for him.

Sir G. Beaumonts I dined at. — I told him Lord & Lady Inchiquin wished him to speak to Lord Abercorn who probably might be induced to purchase collection of prints on advantageous terms. — much below a valuation.

Sunday — Feby 22d.

A Cold Thaw. Wind S.E. Glass 40.

Mr. Baker called and looked over my Blue Book of loose drawings and preferred the view of Worcester Cathedral & Prebendal buildings, which I gave him. He paid me 3 guineas for the drawing of Guildhall, Lynn. I refused 5 guineas which He offered me.

Hearne, I called on who told me He did not get more than half a guinea a day by drawing.

White of Deptford dined with me. — The Builders of the private Dock Yards proposed to the Commissioners of the Navy to build 74 gun ships at £20 a tun, — which terms were refused. £17 was the price usually paid. — The wages paid to workmen in the Yrds. are very great. Caulkers & Shipwrights who understand their business well can get 20 shillings a day. — In peaceable times they can earn when paid by the piece, half a guinea a day.

White says the French ships sail better than ours not from the superiority of their form only but because they are not so filled with timber, being lighter in this respect they have an advantage.

Robert Clevely, the ship painter when young was bred a Caulker but not liking the business quitted it. Admiral Vandeput has been his great friend. He was Clerk to the Admiral when Captn. of a Yacht & on other service. — He is abt. the age of White who will be 49 in March next. — When Clevely was a Caulker He was laughed at for working in Gloves.

Sir Wm. Rule of the Navy Office was a Shipwright and has rose by degrees. — He was removed from being Builder at Woolwich to be 2d. Surveyor of the Navy. He is abt. 52 years of age. — He is an active man & much liked in his situation.

Monday — Febry 23.

At home. — Dick went to the House of Commons to hear the Budget opened.

Tuesday — Febry 24th.

Hearne, I breakfasted with and carried my Blue Book of Drawings to have his opinion as to prices I shd. ask. — I desired him to make choice of one for himself. He laid out three to choose from viz: Upright York Buildings, Entrance to Warwick Castle, and Hearnes Oak. — I think He considers the last as at least equal to any for characteris[tic]k penning. — He said He thought them worth five guineas each.

Dick went down to Gravesend in the Exeter with Captn. Wilson.

Eliza dined with Lady Hamilton who told her that Richd. Brothers, who calls himself the Prophet, she remembers at Exeter a few years since when He was considered as a little disordered in his senses. She understood He had been Lieutenant of a Man of War.

Wednesday — Febry 25th. — 1795.

at Home.

Thursday — 26th.

Sir George Beaumont I breakfasted with. I mentioned to him the wish of Lord & Lady Inchiquin that He wd. assist them in their sale. Sir George said He had never bid even for himself.

Mr. Pitt & his friends are indignant at the conduct of Lord Fitzwilliam in Ireland. — The general and unusual dismissal of persons from places is reprobated.

Boydell I called on. — He was lately with the King two Hours. — The King talked much abt. the Royal Academy. He said He had always considered the period for electing Associates as improper as it clashed with the time allowed to Academicians elect.

He said West had attributed to him that the Diplomas of the Academicians elect were not signed before the 20th. of February, but that was not the fact. They were never proposed to him or He wd. have signed them either at Windsor or in Town. — He asked Boydell what He supposed cd. be Wests motive for the misrepresentation. Boydell said He cd. only suppose West might keep back the Diplomas to prevent the new Academicians from having Votes. — The King said *that* probably was the case, but He wondered after their long enmity that West shd. take an interest in Hoppners election.

The King rather wondered at the Academy electing Hoppner who had made himself obnoxious by abusing the Members.

Offleys, I dined with. The Company — Dick, — Messrs. Evans, — Barroneau, — Crump, — Wye, — Smirke, and a son of Mr. Sealy.

Friday Febry 27th.

Tyler, I called on with Dance. We drew up the following requisition to call a meeting of the Council, in consequence of Richards having issued cards of notice for the reception of pictures for the ensuing Exhibition, and having fixed a *Good Friday* to be a receiving day, witht. a Council having been called to authorize a Card & determine the days of receiving. —
    Copy of letter to West.

"To the President of the Royal Academy

"We the undersigned Members of the Council request the favor of you to call a meeting of the Council as we have some matters to communicate which require to be stated without delay".

We are, Sir,
Your most obedt. Servts. &c.
Wm. Tyler
Geo. Dance
Jos: Farington
Robt. Smirke

London
February 27th. 1795.

The letter I sent to Wests House in Newman St. by James who brought me information that West is at Windsor.

The Academy Club I dined at & was President. — 12 present.

Boswell told me that Captn. George Wynyard, and Captn. Sherbroke being at Nova Scotia and seated in a room together, — There appeared a figure before them which Captn. Wynyard said it is the appearance of my Brother, who is in London. When told to the Officers the story was laughed at, but 4 months after an acct. came from England that at the time of that appearance the Captns. Brother died in London. — Boswell related the story last night at the Mount Coffee House before Captn. Wynyard who supported the truth of it.

Lysons & Joe Green I found at home in the eving.

Saturday [28th].

Ld. Inchiquins I breakfasted at. — Offley I dined with in Thornhaugh St. — Dick, John & Wm. Offley.

MARCH 1795

Sunday, March 1st.

Sir Geo: Beaumont I breakfasted with. — At one went with him to Sir Robt. Ainslies, Princes St., Hanover Square, to see the drawings of Meyer. The company, — Lady Susan Bathurst, — Lady Beaumont, — Mr. Bankes of Corfe castle, — George Dance & Marchant. — General Ainslie came in — I gave him my direction.

The drawings consisted of views on the Nile, — of Grand Cairo, — the Pyramids, — Alexandria, — Rodes, — Jerusalem, Bethelem &c. They appear to be very correct. Meyer, attended 3 English gentlemen on this Tour. Mr. Graves, Mr. [blank] & Mr. [blank]. Meyer was present to shew the drawings.

Ld. Inchiquins I dined at — Christie & Marchi there.

Christie proposed to sell Mr. Fitzmaurices plate while the pictures were on view, which I said I thought very improper, & He then said He wd. sell it in a lower room. — Christie recommended to sell all the pictures of the first day *without reserve.*

Monday, March 2.

Sir George Beaumont I breakfasted at, and at the desire of Ld. & Lady Inchiquin requested him to meet them at Christies room on Thursday next to look over the collection when arranged in order to set a value on certain pictures, to be bought in if not reaching a proper price. Sir George agreed to meet them. — Meyer [*recte* Ainslie] was yesterday elected a member of the Dilletanti Society.

Ld. St. Asaph yesterday voluntarily resigned his situation as Gentleman of the Bedchamber to the Prince of Wales.

Church & King, Manchester Club dined today at the Free Masons Tavern. — Dick dined there. — 24 in number, a guinea each.

Tuesday — March 3d.

Ld. Inchiquin I called upon. Mr. Hope of Amsterdam told them yesterday at Poggis that their prospect of disposing of their pictures was as bad as possible, the value of money was so great &c &c. Loutherburghs exhibition of Ld. Howes Victory I went to with Hoppner. We thought the picture ill coloured & I think not so ingeniously designed as I shd. have expected from Loutherburgh. The picture of Valenciennes appeared to me much worse than I thought it the last year. — When the novelty is over these pictures appear very defficient.

Wednesday March 4th.

Boswells, I dined at. The Company Ld. Delaval, — Count Casteneau, — Sir Wm. Wolsely, — Col. St. Paul, Mr. Osborne, formerly Minister at Dresden, Major Wynyard, Mr. Malone, — Captn. Lee of the Life guards. — Two Misses Boswell [*added later, in margin*: the eldest, miss Veronica, died in October, following] and Young Jas. Boswell.

Major Wynyard confirmed the story to me of his having seen the apparition of his Brother Jack as it proved afterwards in the hour of his death which happened at Kensington Palace in General Wynyards appartments. The major was at that time in Nova Scotia, in Barracks at Halifax, and not being very well, He in company with Col. Sherbroke, who was also an Invalid, declined going to the Officers Mess & dined alone. The Doors of the room were shut. — The figure of his Brother appeared at his elbow. He cried out "there is my Brother". Col. Sherbroke saw the figure and was equally surprised, and described it identically as it appeared to the major. — They each wrote down the remarkable particulars and four months after when the Ice broke the packet from England brought an acct. of the death of John Wynyard, of the guards as above stated.

Col. St. Paul said He was much acquainted with the late Lord Strange & was at Knowsley in the year 1747. — He now resides in Northumberland, abt. 10 miles from the Tweed, and 50 beyond Newcastle.

Thursday — March 5th.

Mr. Champernowne called on me. He proposes to make views in Devonshire & to publish them. Ld. Inchiquin & Lady and Sir George Beaumont, I met at Christies large room and was employed with them till 5 in settling prices at which the pictures shd. be bought in if no person bid higher. I dined with Sir George Beaumont.

Friday — March 6th.

Yenn, I breakfasted with., who shewed me his designs for completing two rooms in Windsor Castle.

Ld. Inchiquin & Lady- and Sir George Beaumont I met in Christies, old Royal Academy Room where we were employed till past 3 in settling prices.

Saturday 7th.

Sir Geo. Beaumont I breakfasted with, and at 10 we went to Christies little Room & met Lord & Lady Inchiquin and marked prices for some of the remaining Lots & concluded this part of the business. — Sir George concurs with me that it will be prudent for them to reduce the sums set against most of the pictures as there is a great probability of their being bought in.

Sunday — March 8th.

Lord Inchiquins I went to at 2, and finally settled the prices at which pictures were to be bought in. — Lady Inchiquin had previously lowered many of the prices.

Tylers I dined at. G. Dance, Hodges, Garvey, Richards, and Humphry there. — We talked about the Academy. Richards said He had issued the notice for the Exhibition pictures being recd. contrary to precedent witht. an order of Council, but *no Council having* been called and the time drawing near, He ventured to do it.

After the others were gone Tyler, Dance determined on a letter to be sent to West at Windsor & in town that He might not have the plea of not receiving it. Dance wrote the two letters. It differs from one I had prepared. — Copy. "Sir, We the undersigned Members of the Council of the Royal Academy, having on the 27th. of February last, addressed a requisition to you in writing to call a Council without delay for the purpose of considering business of importance to the Royal Academy and not having been favored with any attention to our request, anxious that no further procrastination may take place We beg leave to repeat our desire that a Council may be immediately summoned.

We are, Sir,
Your most Humble Servts.

Geo. Dance
Wm. Tyler
Jos: Farington
Robt. Smirke

March 9th. 1795"

Monday — March 9th.

West, I sent the two Letters to. One to Newman St, the other to Windsor, his servant saying He was not in Town.

Ld. Inchiquins I dined at. — Christie & Marchi there. — Wm. Hardman wrote to me desiring to call on me on Wednesday for my opinion of some of the pictures which He had marked in Sir Joshuas sale.

Tuesday — March 10th.

Champernowne called on me & selected 5 of my drawings.

Smirke told me this morning the injury the collection would sustain if more days of viewing were not allowed. — I went to Lord Inchiquins at 12 & finding him & Lady Inchiquin at home I stated strongly the above opinion & recommended that they shd. gain at least two days, & let the sale begin on Friday and end on Tuesday next. — They immediately drove to Christies.

Champernowne I called on and went with him & Simpson the picture dealer to see a large Parmegiano which belongs to Mr. Christies Father. — Simpson said West had declared it to be worth £1000. — I do not wonder at it as it is painted in the manner in which West executes but is better. — From thence went to Christies & found the room full, *all* concurring in admiring the collection.

Fryers, I dined at, wither I went with Hughes who I met at the sale. — Mr. Watts, Mrs. Watts spinster, — Mrs. Hughes, — Miss Telfair there. — Fryer said He wished for two or three pictures to hang in the dining room at Taplow but would not wish to exceed 20 guineas, each.

Wednesday — March 11th.

Ld. Inchiquins I went to this morning.

Hearne I called on. He has hung up my drawing of York Buildings waterworks, and says it is much liked — Baker has bought the drawing of Hearnes Oak.

Hardman called on me at noon to ask my opinion of his purchasing certain pictures at Sir Joshuas sale.

Hughes called on me. — I told him I found Mr. Fryer wanted 2 or 3 pictures of a certain price & size, and that I had by me 3 or 4 which He might look at. If it was his opinion they wd. suit He might mention them. He said He had intended to speak to me this morning to let him have a picture for himself. — On looking them over He chose the little Landscape with an effect, and the upright Westminster Bridge & Abbey.

Christies I went to with Hughes, — found Hardman there & marked several pictures. — Advised him only to buy *good* pictures as they are always of value.

Cox was at the sale and asked my opinion.

Ld. Inchiquins I dined at. Two Miss Hickeys, Mr. William Burke, — Sir Edmund Nagle, Major Wood — Major Dodd there.

Sir Edmund described the action in which He has been engaged with La Revolutionaire of 44 guns, while the Artois had only 38. He took the French man.

Not being very well I came home early.

Thursday — March 12th.

At home all day, very indifferent from over exertions & cold — wrote to Lady Inchiquin my fears that I shd. not be able to attend tomorrow.

Bowyer wrote me for his picture.

Friday — March 13th.

Marchi came this morning from Lady Inchiquin with marked catalogues inclosed.

Hardman called & I went with him to the sale & met Hughes. — The Offleys & the Younger Daniel bid for Lord Inchiquin.

Saturday — 14th.

Ld. Inchiquins went to in the morning. — settled prices for the day. — Hughes called — I had sent small effect picture to Fryers who desires to have it & a Companion.

Hardman called. settled prices for his purchase of today. — Went to Christies.

Sunday — [15th].

Dances I went to & met Tyler & Smirke. We agreed on certain motions to be made on Friday next at the Royal Academy Council.

Ld. Inchiquins I went to, and with them to Christies great room, where Lady Inchiquin and I again looked over the prices for the pictures.

Lord Inchiquins I dined at. Honble Miss Jefferys, — Lady Beaumont, — Lord Scarborough, — Lord Wentworth, Sir George Beaumont, — Mr. Malone, Mr. Boswell, Mr. Ranby and Mr. Obrien there.

Lord Wentworth said He wd. lay 100 to 20 Mr. Hastings wd. be acquitted. — Lord Scarborough said He would lay 100 to 1 on the same.

Monday — March 16th.

Sir George Beaumont I breakfasted with, and we went together to the sale. — Sir George bought The Descent from the Cross by Rembrant for 41 guineas.

Hughes I dined with. — Cookson, & Mr. & Mrs. Watts — there.

Lord Inchiquins I called at in the evening.

Harry came to town.

Tuesday, March 17th.

Sir George Beaumont I breakfasted with. We went together with Hardman to Hughes to look at his Battle picture, and from thence to Christies. — After the completion of the sale I dined with Lady Inchiquin & went with her to the Play at Covent-Garden.

Wednesday — March 18th.

Lord Inchiquins I breakfasted at, and went from thence to Christies & sorted the Lots bought in under different names.

dined at home.

Thursday — March 19th.

Ld. Inchiquins I went to in the morning, Lady Inchiquin expressed a desire to have some of the principal pictures which have been bought in sold. She accordingly fixed the following prices:-

			Guineas.		Sir Joshuas valuation.
Afterwards	Susannah	—	120.	—	350.
altered to	Vision of Daniel	—	160.	—	600.
220. —	Rubens designs for White-hall ceilings	}	130	—	
	Wisemens offerings Poussin	}	500	—	800 gave
350	Sorceress, Teniers. —	}	395	—	600
100 —	Sampson & Dalilah, Rubens	}	150		300 gave
	Raphaels Holy Family		100		300
	Negros Head Paul Veronese	}	70	—	sold to Mr. Whitbread for 110.

Lady Inchiquin called on Susan & Lord Inchiquin on Dick. Dined at home. Harry with us. In the evening Tyler & Smirke came and we settled the plan of proceeding at the Academy tomorrow. — Dance did not join us.

Friday — March 20th.

Hardman called on me to settle for his pictures.

Lady Inchiquin wrote to me to desire I wd. look over pictures bought in. I then told Her Ladyship as she had offered me the Carrach head I wd. propose in the room of it to take the 3 little pictures bought in at

G. Poussin	10–10–0.
Carrach	4. 4. 0.
Artois — called	6. 16. 0
	21. 10. 0.

She expressed great satisfaction at my selecting these in preference to their choosing for me.

I offered her for a friend £240 for the Delilah & Susannah but told her in my opinion it was too little. She declined the offer on consulting Lord Inchiquin.

Lady Inchiquin called on Susan.

Lady Inchiquin then altered her card of prices and added

			Sir Joshuas valuation
Good Samaritan – Bassan.	40.	–	100.
Titians head by himself	30.	–	200.
Silenus. Rubens	– 35.	–	80.

Royal Academy Council I went to with Dance, Smirke & Tyler. — Tyler spoke on the inconvenience of having a Council at so late a period of the Spring season. — The days for receiving the pictures were changed to the first & second of April, *Wednesday & Thursday,* instead of Thursday 2d. and *Good Friday.* Saturday the 4th. for examining pictures, and Monday the 6th. for Arranging Committee commencing business.

I then proposed adressing the King on the subject of signing Diplomas of the 3 Academicians elect. West now informed us He had spoken to the King on the subject and His Majesty expected the pictures and Hoppners also.

A letter from Hoppner was read. He had sent a picture which He hoped wd. be recd. & admitted by the Council & by His Majesty, and He trusted in the course of the summer He shd. be able to execute something more *within the limits of his abilities.*

The picture He sent was his sea piece exhibited last year. His letter was judged improper, on the score of his proposing a change of his picture which was considered a bad precedent; but the picture being much approved it was admitted, as the Council will not be bound to allow a change & no notice was taken of that circumstance in the minutes.

I strongly pressed the necessity of having Academical business trans-acted with His Majesty in a more direct & becoming form than it is at present — That a President ought to be attended by the Secretary on such occasions, and carry a *document* of the resolutions or wishes of the Council. — Bacon doubted whether He shd. not oppose the Idea, but West approved the intention if it cd. be carried into execution in a manner satis-factory as to etiquette. — Smirke strongly supported the Idea, — Dance spoke for it and Tyler.

Letter from Sir John Call was read desiring the Academy wd. proceed with the business of settling how the statue in honor of Lord Cornwallis should be carried into execution. Two Thousand pounds have been subscribed in India for the purpose. Resolved to call a General Meeting on the 4th. of April to elect a Student to go to Italy.

Sir Wm. Chambers sent a letter recommending to the consideration of the Council Oeconomy in making out the Catalogues by which £300 a year might be saved.

I notified the death of Mr. James, Associate.

Council present
Messrs. *West*

Tyler   —   Bacon
Dance   —   Zoffany
Smirke   —   Farington

Saturday — March 21st

Mrs. Townley called on me on acct. of Daniels vision.

Sunday — March 22d.

Lord Inchiquin I paid 280 guineas to. 120 for Rembrants Susannah — and 160 for Daniels Vision — for C. Offley.

Harry, Smirke & I breakfasted with Dance. Harry sat to have his portrait finished more.

Dr. Monro and Mr. Henderson called & looked over my drawings. The Dr, bespoke two to be made.

Lord Inchiquins I dined at. — Lord Powiscourt, Mr. Malone, Boswell, Captn. Brice, Dick, Charles & John Offley, and Mr. & Mrs. Kemble there.

Monday — March 23d — 1795.

Lysons I breakfasted with.

Lord Grey de Wiltons, I dined at with Dick. — The Company, Lord Curzon, Lady Bromley, Lady Arden, Lord Belgrave & Young Mr. Bootle.

Tuesday, March 24th.

Dick went to Captn. Wilson at Gravesend. — I recd. the pictures of Susannah and Daniels vision from Lord Inchiquins.

Lord Grey de Wilton called.

Westhall called in the evening. — He wished to purchase the Marriage in Canean at Sir Joshuas sale.

West said at the last Club that the picture of the Negro when Sir Joshua bought it had a dark drapery sketched in and a dark back ground. Sir Joshua painted the present drapery & background.

Wednesday — March 25th.

Westall I called on to look at his pictures &c intended for Exhibition. — He shewed me two of his Poetical Compositions. An Ode, the subject "Orpheus entering Hell" and an Ode on the effect of Impudence when united to Pride.

N. Dance, called on me.

Sir Wm. Erskine of Torry, acct. of his death in yesterdays paper.

C. Offley I dined with, and cleaned the picture of Ouse bridge.

Thursday — March 26th.

Harry, dined with us.

Friday — March 27th.

Revd. Mr. Gardner called on me to desire my interest in procuring a reception for two pictures and a drawing which He has prepared for Exhibition. Royal Academy Club I dined at. — Bourgeois spoke to me for Northcote who wishes to have two half length portraits placed one on each side of the Chimney piece. — I said I wd. do anything I cd. to oblige him consistently with propriety. — Yenn spoke to me in consequence of Holland, the Architect, having requested that a Crayon portrait of him might be well hung. — Bourgeois also recommended the Crayons of a French emigrant a Mr. Lacoste. — Hamilton desired me to take care of two portraits by Mrs. Bell. — Nollekens mentioned to me that Sir Wm. Chambers has withdrawn the Academy subscription to Maltons Views of London, and requested me to move in Council that the subscription may be continued.

Humphry mentioned to me that Hodges is said to propose leaving London, and residing somewhere in the Country. Marchant said Mr. Trevelyan had told him somewhere in the neighberoud of Southampton.

Boswell told me that He had serious intentions of writing the life of Sir Joshua Reynolds, — but that He hesitated a little abt. Lady Inchiquin as in describing the dispute with the Academy He must acknowledge Sir Joshua to have been to blame.

Saturday March 28th.

Hardman sent from Calonnes sale to desire I would come there to give an opinion. The pictures sold so high as to be above his purchase. — Offley I dined with.

Royal Academy Council I attended.

Present
Messrs. West

Zoffany	—	Tyler
Dance	—	Bacon
Bourgeois	—	Farington

Smirke

Passed a resolution to regulate ourselves "that whoever does not attend the Council by ½ past 7 shall forfeit his pay".

Recd. the Minutes relative to Sir John Calls adress from gentlemen at Madras, for the Academy to appoint an Artist to execute a Statue of Ld. Cornwallis.

Agreed to request Sir John Call to meet the Council on Wednesday next.

I read a motion which I proposed to make in Council "That when in order to expedite the publick business of the Academy any four Members shall adress a requisition to the President to call a Council the President shall direct the Secretary to summon a Council to be held within Six days, from the day when such requisition shall have been made".

A long conversation took place on the subject. West said He wished such a regulation had been made when the Academy was instituted, but He did not like to have the privileges of the President infringed while He was in the Chair as it might be future cause of complaint.

Bacon doubted the propriety of the measure, as infringing on the given power of the President to call meetings.

I agreed to postpone the motion as Bourgeois & Zoffany were gone.

I mentioned Sir Wm. Chambers having withdrawn the Academy subscription to Maltons views of London. — It was agreed to receive them as some numbers had been recd.

Council sat till near 12 — no supper.

Sunday — March 29th.

Dance I breakfasted with. — Smirke there. They agreed firmly to support my Motion to oblige the President to call a Council if required on business by 4 Members.

Monday 30th.

Carey I called on & gave him advice abt. finishing his 2 pictures for the Exhibition.

Westall I called on to see his large picture & drawings prepared for exhibition. He wrote to me this morning for that purpose.

Mr. Bowles sent me a large picture for the Exhibition, subject to Sir George Beaumonts opinion & mine.

Offleys I dined at. The Company Mr. & Mrs. Hardman, 2 Misses Hardman, young Hardman, — Dick, Eliza, — Susan, John & Wm. Offley.

Tuesday 31st.

Sir George Beaumont called & agreed with me that Mr. Bowles picture must be exhibited. — I wrote to Mr. B. — Went with Sir George to see his large Cottage landscape which He is doubtful abt. exhibiting. — I advised him to exhibit it.

Smirke called. The medal Committee sat last night & accepted his Model. Nollekens brought a drawing & a model, the impropriety of which measure was felt, as competition is now out of the question.

Craig I called on. He had called on me. I looked at his drawings intended for exhibition, and made a remark on his large one.

Byrne & his 2d. daugr. called on me. She has made a miniature of Lady Beaumont from Sir Joshuas picture which she desires to exhibit. I could not positively inform her whether miniature Copies from large pictures are admissible.

APRIL 1795

Wednesday — April 1st.

Council at the Royal Academy. Sir John Call attended, and said He had recd. £2000 from the Committee at Madrass to defray the expence of a statue of Lord Cornwallis, to be erected in the square of the inner fort at Madrass. — The Statue to be abt. 8 feet high. — Minutes were made and read to Sir John who engaged to advance such sums to the Artist employed as He shd. be authorised to pay by the Council of the Royal Academy.

Sir John, told us He had a Cataract forming over his eyes which had nearly blinded him, though externally the sight did not appear to be affected. It commenced in Novr. last and Mr. Wathen told him He hoped as it rapidly encreased it wd. in a short time be fit for correcting.

Therlock, had applied to me in favor of a young man of the name of Pastorini to be admitted a Student in the Plaister Academy — tonight He was admitted.

The Council agreed that whoever did not attend by half past 7 shd forfeit *his pay*.

Council present

Mr. West
Bacon — Smirke
Bourgeois — Tyler
Farington

Thursday April 2d.

Sir George Beaumont I breakfasted with. — Sir George still in doubt abt. exhibiting. — Offleys I dined at, — The Company, — Boswell, Tyler, — Humphry, — & Dick.

Friday [3rd].

Hamilton I called on to see his pictures. Also upon Hoppner & Lawrence for the same purpose.

Sir George Beaumont I dined with. He is now determined to Exhibit two pictures. The Cottage in the Wood, & an upright founded on a picture of Fouquier.

Saturday — April 4th.

Royal Academy I breakfasted at with the Council, read the letters to the Council & afterwards reviewed the pictures which we finished examining abt. 4 oClock. — On acct. of General Meeting to be held in the evening we postponed examining the miniatures to another day.

Council present at dinner
West

Bacon	—	Tyler
Loutherburgh	—	Dance
Bourgeois	—	Smirke
Zoffany	—	Farington
Wilton	—	Richards

Rose — Secretary

Dined and drank tea in the Council room.
    At the general meeting in the evening, present

West

Wilton	Burch	Rigaud	Fuseli
Dance	Barry	Farington	Yenn
P. Sandby	Nollekens	Opie	Wheatley
Tyler	Bacon	Northcote	Humphry
Catton	Loutherburgh	Russell	Smirke
Zoffany	Garvey	Hamilton	Bourgeois

The Academicians elect were introduced and recd. their Diplomas in the order of election.
    Stothard
    Lawrence
    Westall
    Hoppner

The new regulation proposed by the Council was brought forward viz: To change the time allowed for producing specimens of their ability to Academicians elect to Octbr. 1st. ensuing their election. — Barry & Rigaud spoke against it. It was referred to Council to reconsider the regulation, and to allow the usual time, and to prevent inconvenience to change the day of election to the month of *March* ensuing the expiration of that day.
    A Student was elected to go to Italy. The Candidates were, — Artaud, Howard and Joseph.

Dance made a motion that previous to the election the Candidates shd. produce specimen[s] of his [their] present ability that the Academy might be able to judge precisely of their respective merits. — This motion had been *privately* agreed to by Bourgeois a voter for Artaud & by Opie. — It was violently opposed by Barry & Fuseli particularly both of whom were for Howard. — The question being put only 5 or 6 voted for it. — The election then commenced when there appeared on scrutinizing the lists that Artaud had 15 votes and Howard 13. — Joseph had none. It was contested by Barry &c. that a Balot in the Box shd. take place, but it was overruled as the third candidate had not a single vote. — Sometime afterwards Barry said He had been informed that there were specimens of the works of Artaud & Howard up stairs sent for Exhibition which were said to have influenced the votes of certain members. He now *changed his ground* and expressed a desire to have those pictures brought down and examined, and that the vote shd. be reconsidered. Bacon now said that though He had voted for Howard & thought highly of his merit, He cd. not consider the Academy as acting unbecomingly if Mr. Barrys motion shd. be attended to. — The Motion was overruled.

Among the voters for *Artaud* were:

	For Howard
Catton	Garvey
Dance	Rigaud
Tyler	Bacon
Hamilton	Russell
Bourgeois	Nollekens
Smirke	Lawrence
Opie	Westall
Northcote	Fuseli
Wheatley	Barry
Hoppner	
Stothard	
Loutherburgh	
Zoffany	
Yenn	

Smirkes model for the medal was produced and examined. — I moved that the Academy do adopt Mr. Smirkes model which passed unanimously. — Tyler moved that it be referred to the Council being a matter of expence, to carry it into execution. The motion passed.

Sunday — April 5th.

Hardman called. — Princess of Wales arrived.
  Byrne called abt. his daughrs. works for exhibition.
  At home all day.

Monday — 6th.

Arrangement of pictures commenced. — I and Dance attended. — John, the Porter of the Academy, was born in the year 1729.

Wilton told us that Russell who wrote "letters from a young painter in Italy", married an Italian woman, who when Dance was in Italy was esteemed imprudent in her conduct.

Tuesday — 7th.

On Committee of arrangement. — Dance attended.

J. Boydell applied to me by desire of Pope the Actor in favor of Shee, and in favor of Barrows drawings.

Dance wrote to Dupont signifying to him that unless He sent a picture to the present Exhibition He would not be qualified to put his name as a Candidate to be an Associate, — He added that I concurred with him in mentioning this. — Dupont did not return a written but a verbal answer "that He would send an answer".

Humphry called on me in the evening.

Wednesday — April 8th.

On Committee of arrangement. — Tyler there.

A Council met to examine the miniatures. — Hughes called at the Academy at the request of Cooper, the drawing master, to desire me to hang his black lead pencil drawing in a particular direction. — At my request Cooper came to us, and I told him as one of the Committee I wd. do all I could to oblige him.

Smirke & Bourgeois dined with us.

Prince of Wales married tonight at 8. — Illuminations general.

Byrnes daugrs. miniature copy from Lady Beaumont by Sir Joshua refused. — No copies but in *Enamel* admitted.

Thursday. 9th.

On Committee of Arrangement. Tyler there. Dance & Charles Webb dined with us.

Sir George Beaumont I called on in the eveng. & mentioned some remarks I had made on his picture which He might alter for the better. — He agreed to have it out and that I shd. make chalk marks as notes.

Mr. Barrow wrote to me on acct. of his drawings being rejected. — Boydell is his friend — Rossi applied to me for permission to paint his groupe — granted.

Malton, requested me that his inside of a Library for Sir Christopher Sykes may be hung in the plaister academy.

Dupont called at the academy. Richards only saw him. He apologized for being late with a picture but will send one.

Coombes told Bourgeois that He had been complimented by Burke on His History of the Thames & that had he not *been cramped* he shd. have made it a compleat work.

Friday — April 10th.

At arrangement Committee. — Tyler there.

Sir George Beaumonts Landscape I touched on with Chalk & He sent for it. In the afternoon He sent me a note positively demanding both His frames. — I wrote an answer which I shewed to Wilson & Richards who approved it. — Hoppner called in the eving and we went together to the Club to Tea. — There I shewed Sir Georges note & a copy of my answer to Tyler & Dance who approved the latter. *They* wrote a letter to Sir George expressing their concern at his withdrawing his frames & requesting him to reconsider his intention.

Offleys, Ball I went to. Hardman & his daughters there. I staid till ½ past 12.

Lady Beaumont called this eving on Susan, & expressed Sir Georges concern on supposing his note to me was too strong. — He proposes sending his upright, and will write to the Committee tomorrow morning. West is to dine with him on Sunday & He wishes me to meet him.

Saturday April 11th.

At arrangement Committee, Tyler there.

Sir George Beaumont wrote a letter to me in which He expressed obligation to me & compliments to the Committee. He desires to have the large picture back & to leave the upright. He invited me to dine tomorrow, — West is to be there.

Garrard called for a picture which He is to keep till Thursday next. A note from Gilpin who wishes to keep his large picture till Monday. Dupont called, to apologize for not sending His pictures sooner. He will be content wherever they are hung. — Craft left an enamel picture and a note requesting I wd. get it into the Exhibition. I took it down to the Academy. — Boswell & Bourgeois dined with us. Boswell was out of spirits and had no appetite.

A Council in the evening. Invitation settled. Sir Wm. Chambers sent a note recommending a diminution of invitations — leaving out Music & a limitation of Champaigne.

We left out 17 names of last year & added abt. 20 new ones. — West proposed 4 or 5, — Sandby 2, — Garvey 2, — Bourgeois 2, — Dance 1, — I 2, — Boswells Brother at his request, invited.

Sunday — April 12th.

Academy I went to & painted on my picture of Windsor Castle. — Carried the dead colour of Bridgnorth Bridge.

Offleys I dined at. West & Daniel dined with Sir G. Beaumont.
Lysons came to Charlotte St. in the evening.
John at the Academy was born in 1729.

Monday — April 13.

At Arrangement Committee. — Tyler there 3 Hours. — In afternoon
Dance. — Completed great room, if no alterations are required. Richards
made out Catalogue of Head of room. He made out first side on Saturday.

Tuesday 14th.

Daniel I called on at ½ past 7. — Afterwards on Opie & Hamilton. The 2
latter sent their pictures to the Academy which were fixed and the pictures
there. At Arrangement Committee. Dance there, Tyler dined. — Banks
called on the Committee at Tea. — Boswell this day attended the Literary
Club, and went from thence too ill to walk home. — He went out no more.

Wednesday — April 15th.

Opie I called on early, and recommended to him to polish up his ¾ portrait
of a Lady, which He said He wd. do.
    at Arrangement Committee Tyler there. — Bourgeois dined with us. His
picture came today. — We have nearly completed the Great Room and
Anti-room, and might easily have done it had not Banks taken of our men
to make a frame for his model to stand on. — West drank tea with us. I
proposed to send an invitation to the Margrave of Anspach, which was
agreed to.
    This day I painted a good deal on my small pictures. — On filling the
Great room this day there were *30 frames empty*. — Bourgeois says many
more than last year at this period of arrangement.

Thursday — 16th.

at Arrangement Committee. — Dance & Tyler there. — finished the Great
Room & the Anti room.
    Wilton told me that Lady Chambers is 38 years old. Miss Chambers
near 19. Sir Robt. Chambers abt. 60. — He says so strict has been the conduct of Sir Robt. as to many affairs that He wd. not now return worth
more than £40,000, & that 10 years ago He was not worth £10,000. Sir
William Jones had saved £60,000, — and Sir Elijah Impey £100,000. Sir
Wm. by rigid oeconomy.

Friday — April 17th.

at Academy Arrangement. Tyler & Dance there.
Sir William Chambers wrote to me to request a good situation for the
whole length portrait of the Turkish Ambassador by Breda. — It is the

opinion of the Committee it cannot be removed into the great room witht. detriment to the exhibition.

Dance formed a design for an arrangement in the Council room.

Bourgeois dined with us. — Hoppner came to tea. This morning He recd. a message to attend the Prince of Wales. He went at Eleven and at ½ past 2 saw the Prince, who told him that the King desired to have a whole length Portrait of the Princess of Wales in the Robes in which she was married. The Prince desired His Majesty wd. name an Artist. The King said Hoppner. The Prince said it was agreeable to Him, as He would have proposed Hoppner had He not waited His Majestys pleasure. The Queen said Hoppner was a good young man.

Dick recd. a letter from Harry, who on Wednesday bought Parrs Wood for him. He gave £6450 for it, including fixtures &c. worth £150. — Dick called on Will Boardman in the Kings Bench who said it cost him more than £12,000.

Lindoe & Bell called while I was at the Academy.

R. Payne Knight, was lately black balled at the Literary Club. Two Balls were against him. — A second balot took place as it was supposed a mistake might have occasioned the Black Balls, and much said of his claim. — Two Black Balls again appeared. — One Black Ball excludes.

Saturday — April 18th.

At Academy arrangement. — Tyler & Dance there. Sir George Beamont wrote me a note desiring to keep his picture till Monday, I answered till Tuesday. — Paye came with a picture and desired to have His picture of [blank] back as He had not time to finish it. Dance & I told him it must be finished, or sent in as a sketch, as the arrangement was completed. — We gave him till Wednesday next.

I wrote to Sir Wm. Chambers in the name of the Committee informing him that we could not witht. detriment to the Exhibition remove Bredas picture of the Turkish Ambassador from the Anti-room.

Humphry called at the Academy. I told him his portrait of the Archbishop of York is much approved.

Sir F. Bourgeois brought a letter in the evening from West which He had this day recd. from Mr. Brown, one of the Kings pages, — signifying that on acct. of the Ball to be given at the Queens House on Thursday next, it would not be possible for the King to come to the Exhibition on Friday: but that if the Opening cd. be postponed witht. inconvenience His Majesty wd. come on the Friday following. — Dance, Tyler, Richards, Bourgeois, & myself. concurred in opinion that the opening must of course be delayed. Sir Francis said West thought the dinner might take place as proposed, and the Exhibition open on the Monday following & be *shut for the day* when the King proposed to come. This we thought very improper and disrespectful to His Majesty, and that the dinner & opening shd. be postponed till after the Kings visit.

Sunday — April 19th.

Dance, I called on. On reconsidering the matter He is fully of opinion that it was by no means necessary as a matter of etiquette to hang the picture of the Turk at the Head of the room on acct. of his being in a Diplomatic character.

Hardman, called. He goes out of town tomorrow.

I staid at home till dinner, being much fatigued by academy attendance and the effects of a Cold.

Offleys I dined at. Dick, Eliza, Susan & Minet there.

Smirke, is indifferent in health, and was bled yesterday.

Bensley, the Player sat to Dance today for a profile.

Mrs. Mackenzies children came with their grandmother to Offleys. She has been married abt. 11 years and is now abt. 29 years old.

Monday — April 20th.

at arrangement Committee. Dance there. Tyler came after.

A Council held at 10 this morning when Mr. Brawns letter was read, and an answer was written by Mr. West drawn up by him and corrected by the Council, signifying that the Exhibition wd. not be opened till Monday the 4th. of May.

I mentioned the subject of placing the picture of the Turkish Ambassador and observed that if it once became a rule to place Diplomatic characters at the *head* of the room, an Artist had only to procure a sitting from one to secure him the best place. — It was finally agreed that a Committee must use their discretion.

The Council present were
Mr. West

Zoffany — Bourgeois ⎱ an adjourned
Dance   — Farington ⎰ Council

J. Boydell sent me a letter inclosing one from Mr. Breda, wishing for a place in the great room for his picture of the Turk.

J. Taylor wrote to desire me to supply him with the names of the portraits.

Hoppner I called on in the eving. — Saw Mrs. Hoppner & told Her if the portrait of the Duke of Rutland is in the room on Thursday evening it will do.

Tuesday — April 21.

At arrangement Committee. Dance there, Tyler dined.

Humphry sent his two last pictures. — Hoppner called in the evening.

He desired me to come to see his picture of the Duke of Rutland tomorrow — Humphry called.

Marchant came to Charlotte st. in the eving. — Richards told me today He was acquainted with Mr. Herring, nephew to Archbishop Herring, who castrated himself, in consequence of his wifes having had a severe labour.

I took in a frame of miniatures this eving. which had been rejected, beloning to a Dumb young man of the name of Arrowsmith.

Gainsborough, did not leave his nephew Dupont anything which was thought hard. Mr. Harris of Covent Garden Theatre considering Dupont as wanting employ commissioned him to paint portraits of the Actors of that Theatre and only to proceed with the commission when He had no others.

Wednesday April 22.

At Arrangement Committee. — Dance there, Tyler dined.

Sir George Beaumonts picture came. — Cards of 2d. invitation were sent out, form as follows:— "Their Majesties not honouring the Exhibition with their presence till Friday May 1st. The Dinner is deferred to Saturday May 2d. when the Honor of Lord &c &c."

Hoppners I called at with Dance and drank Tea. Made some remarks on his picture of the Duke of Rutland, and gave him till Tuesday next to finish it.

Duke of Rutland sent a drawing for Exhibition. Pays candle light picture came not finished carefully. We gave him till Tuesday next. Garrick when at Rome sent £50 to Brompton the Painter who was distressed in circumstances and told Dance to draw upon him, if He wanted money, which Dance afterwards did for £50.

Bensley the Actor has seen Irelands Shakespeare manuscripts and says there is nothing but what might be imitated. — Chalie the wine merchant, told Dance that he has had £15000 at Bourdeaux under the care of agents, and that it is perfectly safe, which shews there is a difference in parts of France as to security.

Sir George Beaumont called.

Thursday — April 23.

At arrangement Committee. A little after eleven went to Westminster Hall where in Yenns Box, I had two places for Dick & myself given me by him. — The Lords came into the Hall at ½ before one oclock, and Mr. Hastings acquittal was pronounced to him exactly at two oClock. — The Lords who voted were in all 29. — There were 16 charges.

The following Lords voted Mr. Hastings *guilty* on the first charge.

The Lord Chancellor — Duke of Norfolk

Earl of Suffolk — Earl Fitzwilliam
  — Radnor — Carnarvon

The following Lords voted, Not guilty.

The Archbishop of York	Bishop of Bangor
The Duke of Bridgewater	— Rochester
— Leeds	Viscount Sidney
Marquiss Townshend	Lord Middleton
Earl of Coventry	— Boston
— Dorchester	— Thurlow
— Beverley	— Sommers
— Warwick	— Walsingham
— Falmouth	— Sandys
— Mansfield	— Hawke
	— Moira
	— Fife
	— Morton

Thus ended this long protracted trial which has lasted Seven years, two months, and Eleven days, having begun February 12th. 1788.

In one of the galleries there was a slight disposition to applaud on the conclusion but it instantly subsided, and nothing cd. exceed the order and striking appearance of the audience assembled.

at half past two I returned to the Academy with Dance who had been in Sir William Chambers Box with Susan & Eliza, Sir William having given me two tickets. Completed the Plaister Academy & Council room arrangement.

Bourgeois came to tea and I read to him Bredas letter to Boydell abt. his picture of the Turk.

Boswell has been very ill, attended by Dr. Warren twice a day. He is now pronounced out of danger. His excesses have brought his constitution to a crisis which has alarmed him much.

Marchant came to Tea. — The Court today was crowded almost beyond example. The Prince of Orange & family were in the Kings Box. The Turkish Ambassador & Suite, were in the Foreign ministers Box.

Harrisons & Knyvets Concert at Willis's rooms I was at in the evening with Dance, Dick, Eliza & Susan there.

Lord & Lady Inchiquin sent an invitation for me & Susan to dine there on Monday next.

Friday — April 24th. 1795.

at Academy arrangement. — Tyler there. Completed the arrangement.

9. Sir Thomas Lawrence P.R.A. *Mary, Countess of Inchiquin*. R.A. 1795 (175). Private Collection.

10. Sir Thomas Lawrence P.R.A. *Lady Louisa Gordon*. R.A. 1795 (?55).
The Hon. Robin Neville.

Time employed.

Farington	17 days	Last year	
Tyler	10	Smirke	16 days.
Dance	9	Bourgeois	16 days
	—		—
	36		32

Lawrence, the Committee wrote to. — Letter signed by Richards. — Lawrence has three pictures out, and has made no apology for not sending them yesterday evening as promised. Miss Pope's Benefit at — The Rivals, & Spoiled Child by Mrs. Jordan.

Saturday — April 25th.

At Academy painting on my pictures. Lawrence called to apologize for not sending his pictures.

Offleys I dined at. — Messrs. Campion & nephew, Wye, Parke, Balantyne of Aberdeen, Minet, Dick, — Harris — & 3 Offleys.

Sunday — 26th.

Lawrence I breakfasted with, to look at his pictures of Lady Inchiquin & Lady Louisa Gordon.

Academy I went to and painted on my pictures.

Dined at Home. — Dick, Eliza & young Livesay who is going to the East Indies.

Monday April 27.

At Academy painting. — Smirke came down and advised a little scumbling to take of the soapy clearness of view near Windsor.

Viscount Hampden called at Academy & wrote a note to the secretary requesting the President & Council to invite Mr. Hailes Envoy to Copenhagen — to the dinner — as a lover of the Arts & a *student*. — Lord Inchiquins I dined at with Susan. The Company, — Captn. & Mrs. Hartwell, — Mr. Drew, the Solicitor, — the Revd. Mr. Totty & Mrs. Totty, Mr. Gwatkin, & Old Mrs. Gwatkin, and Lawrence. — Lord Inchiquin came from the House of Commons, where had been warm speaking on the Kings message relative to the Prince of Wales's debts. — A call of the House was moved by Mr. Stanley & so supported that Pitt gave way & it is fixed for next Monday week.

Tuesday — April 28.

At Academy painting. — West there. His two pictures of Lord Clive & Moses with the sacrifice, were brought. — I dined at home but returned to the Academy to Tea. — Hoppner sent the Duke of Rutland, — Lawrence,

Lady Inchiquin and Lady Susan Gordon, — Danloux — his half length.
An adjourned Council in the eving.

Bacon — Bourgeois
Tyler — Farington

Examined the answers to cards of invitation and Bourgeois proposed to
fill up vacancies.

Lord Hawke — Sir Wm. Dolben
Sir James Wright —
Mr. West — Mr. Hopes of Amsterdam
I — Sir George Baker
and Dr. Reynolds
which were agreed to.

It was proposed that the Council shd. dine together at Richolds on
Thursday viz. to taste the wines as usual, and agreed to. — Owing to Sir
Wm. Chambers oeconomical proposals the last year it was given up.

Wednesday April 29th.

At Academy painting. — West there touching on His pictures. — Dance
came & dined with us. — In the evening Bourgeois came, when it was
stated by Mr. West how much the Academy Exhibition suffered by the
general abuse of newspapers and that it wd. be prudent to prevent it if
possible. we all, including Richards, concurred in the same thing and Bourgeois mentioned J. Taylor of Hatton Garden as a proper person to manage
such a matter. The expence to be borne under the article advertisements,
and that a council shd. commission Richards, to defray the expenses. — I
proposed that the *True Briton* shd. be adopted instead of the *Fashionable
World,* as one of the two papers for the common advertisements of the
Academy, which was adopted.

Mr. West said He had been much reflected on in the *True Briton* sometime since but Heriot had inserted a contradiction and said the other came
in from authority or it shd. not have been inserted. West said a Scotchman
was at the bottom of the attacks which had been made on him.

West told me it was a pity I had not finished the Bridge at Bridgnorth as
that He thought was the best arranged effect.

George Hardinge wrote to West today inviting himself to the dinner. A
card was sent him, and through my means, one to Mr. Thos. Walpole,
which *I* inclosed to him.

Thursday — April 30th.

At the Academy painting. — West completed his retouching. Dined at
Free Masons Tavern with the Council, present.

West
Bourgeois — Dance
Smirke — Farington
Wilton

Ordered the Dinner at 12s. a head including the Desert. — The last year it was 10s. 6d. but owing to the dearness of provisions Richold said He cd. not give us so good an entertainment. — We ordered for 126. Richold said He wd. provide for 130 & take his chance.

MAY 1795

Friday — May 1st.

Sir George Beaumonts I breakfasted at. The picture He has painted for the Exhibition has been much praised by Lord Carysfort, Captn. French &c. Went with Sir George to Lord Inchiquins. Lady Inchquin & Lady Orkney desire to go to the Exhibition at 12 on Sunday instead of today. Went with Sir George to the Panorama of Bath. Met Lady Beaumont & went to the Exhibition at ½ past 12. The King, Queen, Duke & Duchess of York, Princess Royal, Elizabeth, Augusta, Mary &c had left the place after staying two Hours. — They expressed their satisfaction in warm terms. The King said the Room was a picture.

The Duke of Gloucester & Duchess, Prince William & Princess Sophia came immediately after.

We joined Susan, Eliza, Dick & Dance in Mr. Wiltons appartments where we had a little collation.

After the Dukes party left the Academy, Mrs. West, Mrs. Brounker & two other Ladies Came.

The King & Royal Family after leaving the Academy walked on the Terrace before Somerset House. The people assembled applauding.

Saturday — May 2d.

Royal Academy I went to at noon, and with West put names on plates for a considerable number of invited persons.

[*See facing page.*]

The Company which dined were as follows.

[*See over page.*]

334

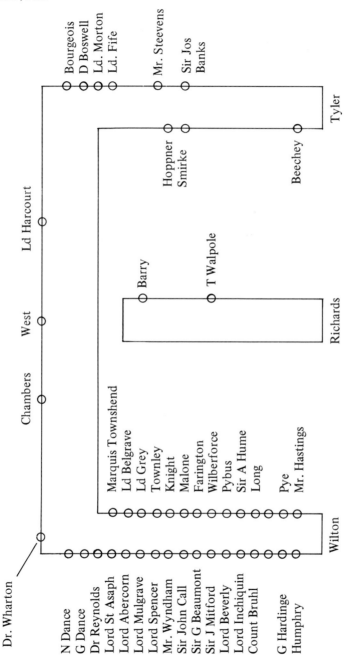

The Lord Chancellor.

Marquiss Abercorn
Townshend

Earls Suffolk
Harcourt
Hardwicke
Beverley
Inchiquin
Mansfield
Fife
Carysfort
Morton
Spencer

Lords Grey de Wilton
Mulgrave
Sheffield
——
——
Count Bruhl
Baron Noloken

Viscounts Hampden
St. Asaph
Belgrave

Foreign Ministers
Marquiss del Campo
Le Chevalier de Engestrens
Compte de Wedel Jarsburgh
Count Pisani

Bishops London
Lincoln
Salisbury
Norwich

Honble Chas. Greville
— Robt. Greville

Sir John Call
Sir H. Englefield
Sir Joseph Banks
— George Beaumont
— Abraham Hume
— Nigel Gresley
— William Dolben
— John Mitford
— George Baker
— Wm. Young

Messrs. Wyndham
| Wilberforce
| Pierrepoint
| Lambton
| Hailes
| Pybus
| Smith
| Knight
| Townley
| Hastings
| Steevens
| Malone
| Chas. Long
| Geo: Hardinge
| Thos: Walpole
| Mann Godschall
| D. Boswell
| Revd. D. Wharton
| Dr. Reynolds

Dinner was on table complete a little before 6. Wilberforce & Sir George Beaumont thought Musick *at* Dinner wd. add much to the general effect.

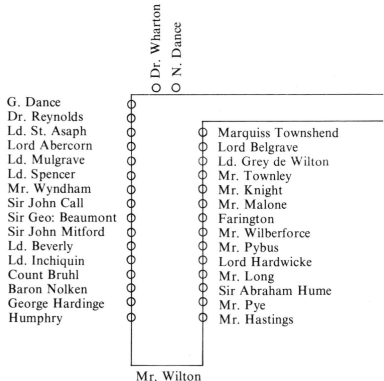

The Company in general staid later than usual. Most till 9 oClock. — Ld. Spencer & Mr. Wyndham till half past 9. — Lord Hardwicke went afterwards next to West & with Smith of Clapham & Mr. Langton staid till past 10. — abt. ½ past eleven I went to Holylands Coffee House with G. Dance, Smirke, Beechy, Rooker, Rigaud & Bourgeois. Drank tea & staid till past 12.

Nollekens expressed displeasure at the disposal of Pelegrinis pictures.

Northcote said He was convinced the Committee were determined not to have him considered as having a claim to Portrait Painting. The exhibition in general pleased much. Many compliments on the arrangement. — Ld. Harcourt, N. Dance, Sir H. Englefield, &c. complimented me on my pictures.

Ld. Suffolk gave as a Toast 'The President of the *Royal Academy'*. No notice taken of the *body* which Bourgeois said was owing to a mistake of Lord Suffolk.

Malone told me Lord Ossory said this morning that He had been 19 years successively at the Academy dinner before this year. — He said Hoppner had abt. 5 years ago painted a portrait of Miss Bover for the Prince of Wales.

Boswell very ill of a strangury.

Sunday, May 3d.

Sir George Beaumonts I breakfasted at.

Lady Inchiquin, Lady Orkney & another Lady I met at the Academy at 12. Lady Inchiquin thinks it a poor Exhibition.

Taylor called on me at the Academy & I took him through the rooms. I gave him a list of the portraits.

Humphry called on me to thank for the situation of his pictures.

Offleys I dined at. Dick, Eliza, Susan & Mrs. Evans there.

Sir Joseph Banks, I want to at ½ past 8, Duke of Leeds, Lord Morton, Lord Fife, Lord Mountmorris there.

Sir Joseph Banks told me & Dance He thought we had better have a man behind the President to call the Toasts. — He said West shd. not have *named* him, but have given "The Royal Society": as a Toast. — He said He had always thought it a defficiency that we did not take places for distinguished persons, as the neglect of it caused inconvenience.

Dr. Warren said Boswell might recover, — Mr. Earle the surgeon, said He was as bad as possible, and that He wd. never again if He recovered be able to pass urine in a natural way. — G. Dance, Lysons, & I went to Parks Coffee House, I told Lysons if Boswell dropt he wd. make a proper Secretary for Foreign Correspondence.

Monday May 4th.

The Academy I went to in consequence of having been applied to by Hone to change the situation of his frame of miniatures, which I did, and removed them nearer the light.

Downman thanked me for arranging his drawings.

Underwood thanked me for the arrangement of his drawings. — Beechy do. for his & Mrs. Beechy. — Bigg do. for his pictures.

Mrs. Wheatley asked my opinion of her teaching to draw.

Gilpin I talked to on the subject of the Academy, and of making him a member. He said after having been many times disappointed He would not put down his name in the common way. At last we settled it that if it shd. be resolved by a vote of the Council to put down his name, He would be justified to His friends to whom He had said He would not again subject himself in the common way to disappointment. It then might be reported to the publick that

"Mr. Gilpin was proposed by an unanimous vote of the Council and elected a member of the Royal Academy".

Dick & Eliza went to Hoddesdon.

Taylor dined with me. — Heriot makes at least £2000 a year by the True Briton & Sun.

Taylor told me it was remarked that in my small pictures now exhibited I had entirely changed my manner & that the pictures were much approved of.

Lysons came in the evening.

Tuesday — May 5th.

Lord Inchiquin I breakfasted with. — Poggi has told her if the Prints of the naval engagement do not answer He shall be ruined. — He proposes to leave the House in Bond St.

We looked over some of the Pictures by Sir Joshua. I advised to cut out single Heads and have them framed as studys before brought to sale. Also to frame His sketches of the Russia picture & Oxford window.

Mrs. Fryer wrote to me. She is pleased with Hones portrait of Mr. Fryer but others condemn it. She wants my opinion previous to its being set. The setting is to cost at least £300. — Hone had 12 guineas for it. — The papers today praise the arrangement of the pictures highly. — In the True Briton & morning Advertiser my pictures are handsomely spoken of.

Westall I called upon. He thanked me for arranging his pictures & drawings. He commended my view of Windsor.

Carey called on Susan and told her my pictures were much admired, and it was observed how much my manner is changed.

Hoppner called at Tea. He this morning waited on the King to know the size and situation of the Princess of Wales's intended picture. The King condemned Hoppners red and yellow trees, particularly the picture of Lady Charlotte Piercy, said Beechy was first this year, Hoppner second, liked His pictures of the Duke of Rutland, and Lady Yonge, but concluded He had not made up his mind about the picture of the Princess. — Said when He saw Lawrence's picture of Lord Mountstuart He started back with disgust — All this passed before Pages & others. Yenn was present.

Hoppner is at a loss abt. calling on the Prince of Wales. I told him I thought He might do it with propriety on a point of duty and respect to express to His Royal Highness that He had waited on the King who had not determined on the subject, and to express to His Rl. Highness, his readiness to obey any commands which He might receive if his services shd. be required.

Jeffries, the Jeweller told me today that the Bank to be established at Dartmouth is to be under the firm of Seale, Gretton & Hodges. — He said Hodges had for several years past urged *him* to engage in a Banking scheme with him.

Dick returned from Hoddesdon.

Wednesday May — 6th.

Steers called on me.

Fryers I dined at. — Mr. Jones, Marshall of the Kings Bench, Young Goad, Robarts, Miss Telfair, Miss Peters &c dined there.

Mr. Fryers alterations at Taplow cost him upwards of £4000. — In the first instance Brettingham stated the expence at £1600 not to exceed £2000, & the Bills He sent in were upwards of £3000. — Taplow stands Mr. Fryer in upwards of £14000.

Young Robarts, a son of Mr. Parry the Director, — a son of Williams, do. — young Fitzhugh, — and another are going to China as writers in the Cirencester Indiaman.

Mr. Jones said, Lord Kirkwall will inherit after the death of his mother upwards of £10000 a year. — Lady Orkney has an income for life of £3000 a year. — Her estate is between 2 & 3000 a year, charged with a debt of £30,000 — The Taplow estate is abt. £1000 a year, and belongs to Lord Inchiquin for life.

Thursday — May 7th.

G. Dance called. Waldron, the Shoemaker, who has quitted business, and is a collector of Prints, told him this morning that Yenns father who died lately, was a Whig maker, & Barber, in King street, Cheapside.

Revd. J. Gardner called to thank me for arranging his pictures. — Hamilton has begun the picture of the marriage of the Prince.

Lysons, called. He told me G. Hardinge had mentioned me to his Brother as having seen me at the dinner.

Smirke sent the picture of Charles to Bowyers Gallery this morning.

Comyns, I called on. He asks 450 gs. for the Murillio bought of Lord Dundass. Etching of Lysons, frontispiece I finished.

Friday — May 8th 1795.

Sir George Beaumonts Landscape has been much praised in the Morning Chronicle & Morning Herald.

My pictures have been commended in the Morning Advertiser and in the True Briton. — In the Morning Chronicle it is said "Mr. Farington has changed from his first stile and not adopted a better, His pictures have more *smoothness* than formerly."

The arranging Committee have been much commended in the True Briton, & more in the Morning Post, and generally in other papers.

Lawrence asked Tyler why young Lock was not invited to the dinner. Tyler said because some circumstances of his behaviour last year induced the Council to omit him in the invitations.

Gilpins proposal of having his name put down by the Council I have mentioned to Smirke Dance & Tyler who are inclined fully to proceed in that manner.

Beechy told me the other day, that Mrs. Beechy only began to paint miniatures in May last. She proposed it as a resource in case of any accident happening to him. They have Six Children.

Sir George Beaumont wrote to desire that Lord Beverlys family may see the Exhibition on Sunday next.

Sir Alexander Hamilton & His Nephew, dined with us. Tyler to tea. — Marchant in the evening. — Wm. Lock says Lawrences portrait of Lady Louisa Gordon is the best portrait in the Exhibition. — Susan, Dick & Eliza went to Ranelagh with the Offleys.

Saturday — May 9th. — 1795.

Smirke called. — Bowyer desired him to tell me He was delighted with the picture of Charles under the Oak.

Lindoe called and is desirous of commencing his studies with me. — I told him I shd. be obliged to go out of town in the course of the summer, but I would allow for that time by giving him when I was in Town so much time as wd. make up his twelve months. — He expressed his satisfaction.

Sir George Beaumont called.

Mr. Bowles called.

Bedford Coffee House I dined at. A Wager of Charles Offleys to John. — Waters, Outram, Garrard & Dick there.

Lawrence published a letter in the Oracle on acct. of his Father, as I suppose, having yesterday puffed him in that paper. — I think his letter injudicious.

Mr Wilberforce wrote to desire me to dine with him on Monday.

Sunday — May 10th.

Kershaw called on me. Mr. Daulby has desired him to lend Him some drawings of mine for His Son to copy. I told Kershaw I wd. send Mr. Daulby a set of Drawings for his son to copy which He might return to me when done with.

Kershaw desired to take charge of them, and wished me to give him a *private list of the prices*, as He was convinced many of them would be disposed of.

Lord Beverly, Lady Beverly, Lady Charlotte & Lady Susan Percy, The Duchess of Hamilton & Miss Muir, Mr. & Mrs. Bennett & Miss Bennett & Captain Bennett, I met at the Royal Academy whither they came with Sir George & Lady Beaumont. — I afterwards dined at Sir Georges with the above Company excepting the Duchess of Hamilton & Miss Muir. Sir John Mitford the Solicitor general, also dined there, — and the Revd. Mr. Du Tong.

Captn. Bennett has been a prisoner in France from the time of relinquishing Toulon into which place He went by mistake Eleven days after. He left Paris the 10th. of April last. He heard Barrere make part of his defensive speech. Barrere spoke remarkably well & daily made converts of some of the national convention. He had the appearance of a gentleman. Captn. Bennet knows Talien, who is a gentlemanlike man. He writes a great deal but seldom speaks. The French people as far as He could judge are sick of the war and of the changes that have taken place. They were disposed every where to treat him very well.

The Prince of Wales' debts were talked of, & the company seemed little inclined to discharge them or to encourage such profligate expences.

Lord Beverly is much disatisfied with the Shakepeare prints. Lady Beverley subscribed but has discontinued the work.

Monday, May 11th.

Lady Inchiquin I called on & staid 3 or 4 hours, sorting Sir Joshuas portraits & studies into classes as a preparation for sale next Spring. Wilberforce I dined with at three. Sir Pepper Arden, Master of the Rolls, — Sir John Mitford, — Lord Muncaster, — Mr. Banks, — Mr. Danby, — Mr. Richd. S. Milles, — Sir George Beaumont, — Mr. H. Duncombe, — a Clergyman and a French emigrant gentleman dined there.

Sir John Mitford seems to think Captn. Molloy is unjustly charged. — Sir John is related to Mrs. Molloy.

Captn. Molloy is a natural Son of the late Admiral Sir Thos. Pye. Mrs. Esten, the Actress, is a natural daughter of Sir Thomas by a Mrs. Bennett. — Sir Georges I went to in evening.

Knight has published a second edition of his landscape, with a strong advertisement against Repton & others.

Will came to town.

Tuesday — May 12th.

Revd. Mr. Lysons called on me. — Mr. Lindoe called. He is invited on a party to Devonshire and returns the end of the month.

Carey called. — I recommended to him to go to Wales for a month or 6 weeks, then return, and I wd. inspect his studies, after which He may go to some other place for study for the remainder of the season.

The Shakespeare Gallery I went to. — I told Boydell the 2d. Vol: of Rivers wd. not be published before August. He said if it wd. be better executed it was best to postpone publishing.

Bulmer I called on. — Coombes has issued proposals for a History of the Reign of His present Majesty. Bulmer thinks He may publish the whole in two years.

Lysons called in the eveng. — He dined at Sir Joseph Banks. Lady Inchiquin commended my pictures. Others had done so, He said.

Will dined with us.

Wednesday — May 13th.

Westall called. — His price for the Shepherd in a Storm is a hundred guineas.

Lysons brought me one of his plates to etch in a few trees. — Mrs. Smyth died on Sunday last, which event I am informed of by Horace Hamond in a letter.

Susan is appointed Executrix with Mr. Henley.

Comyns I called on & bought the picture by Wilson.

Mrs. Gilman dined with us.

Sir Francis Bourgeois drank tea. He is much irritated by the abuse of Williams (Antony Pasquin) in the Observer. — I advised him not to mind it. — Hoppner has told him what passed in conversation with the King.

Thursday — May 14th.

Mr. Bell of Lynn called. — Mr. N. Dance called. — He has broke up his last exhibition picture, He says it appeared in the Exhibition too much of a colour.

Mr. Bowles called. — They both think the Tomb of the Horatii one of Wilsons first performances. — Sir Alexander Hamiltons I dined at, with Dick. Lady H & Mrs. Dickson there.

Lysons called in the evening. — I had etched some trees for him in one of the plates for his Brothers 3d. Vol. — Lysons brought me the second Volume.

Friday — May 15th.

Dick & Eliza left London at ½ past 8 to dine at Oxford and sleep at Chapel-House.

Lord Fife I called on. He was out, He leaves London next Monday week.

Carey dined with me. — Lysons called in the eving. — also Westall.

Saturday May 16.

Left London this morning at ½ past 9 with Susan, dined at Harlow, tea at Bo[u]rn Bridge, evening at the Ram at Newmarket.

Sunday 17th.

Lynn we got to at 3 oClock, to Mrs. Richd. Hamonds. — Mrs. T. Bagge & Mr. Wm. Bagge dined. H. Hamond came in the evening. — Mr. T. Bagge & Tom supped.

Monday 18th.

Jas. Case I called upon. He had a paralytick stroke in Febry last at Mr. H.

Morewoods at Alfreton Hall, Derbyshire. — He has lately had a second. His speech very imperfect.

Mrs. Astley & Col. Astley there.

Dined at Mrs. R. Hamonds. H. Hamond and Mrs. T. Bagge.

Mrs. Smyths funeral. Mr. Wm. & Thos. Bagge went to it and were Bearers.

The Bagge family supped again at Mrs. Hamonds this evening.

Tuesday, May 19th.

Poor Boswell died this day, — at his House in Tichfield Street.

Sandringham I went to with Susan. Mr. & Mrs. Henley only there. He told me this eving. how happy He shd. be to see us there whenever it suited us, for that He attributed his reconciliation with his mother after marriage to Mrs. Faringtons mediation.

Wednesday — 20th.

At Sandringham. — Henley told me that Mrs. Henley had said to him yesterday that she was confident nothing of the Cloaths was intended by Mrs. Smyth for her as Her name was not mentioned in the Will.

Thursday — 21.

Mrs. Henley I told at Susans request that any part of the *Laces* or Cloathes, which she fancied, Susan requested her to take.

Massingham we went to, to dinner — Mr. Thos. Bagge & daugtrs., Mr. Wm. Bagge, Mrs. Richd. Hamond, Mrs. T. Bagge & Mr. Carr dined with H. Hamond. — Mr. Thos. Bagge spoke to me abt. a young man who is deaf, son to Mr. Lane, Collector of Lynn, who has an inclination to drawing. — Cliefden House burnt this evening.

Friday — May 22d.

At Massingham — Susan, Horace only.

Saturday 23d.

At Massingham. — Horace dined at Sandringham.

Sunday 24th.

Massingham I left in the evening and went to the Crown at Swaffham.

Monday 25.

London I came to at 10 at night having left Swaffham at 5 in the morning. — Fare of the Coach one guinea Six passengers.

Lord Harcourt, — Sir George Beaumont, — Mr. Bowles, — Kershaw, the Offleys, — Garvey to invite me to dinner, called during my absence, — Also N. & G. Dance, Humphry. — Marchant.

Tuesday — 26.

Sir George Beaumont, I breakfasted at. — He told me he had returned Bromleys second volume.

Lady Inchiquin having wrote to me from Taplow I called on her. Cliefden House was burnt owing to a maid servant having carried a basket of Linnen upstairs with a Candle in her hand. — A spark had lodged among the linnen. The House was destroyed in less than four hours. — The wings only saved. — Great quantities of most valuable furniture belonging to the late Lady Shelburne &c &c was destroyed. — The Country people plundered during the fire.

The Prince of Wales saw the fire from the Terrace of Windsor and said it must be either Taplow Court or Cliefden, and they would have no water. — His regt. of light Horse were there, no part of which did He send or any message or further enquiry. This, considering the personal regard He has pretended to have for Ld. Inchiquin, is a strong trait of his Character, Want of feeling. — Lord Inchiquin the next morning sent to the Col. for some assistance & the Prince sent Compts.

The *King*, on the contrary, the next day on coming to Windsor, sent a most handsome letter to Ld. Inchiquin, & Lady Orkney on their misfortune.

Dr. Joseph Wharton & a Clergyman came in.

Sir George Beaumonts I dined at. Mr. Bowles & Mr. Hearne there.

Wednesday — May 27th.

Lord Inchiquins I went to with Spiller the picture liner. Mr. Drew came. Much difficulty in getting in money for pictures painted by Sir Joshua. — Sir John Honeywood pleads limitation of 6 years. Mr. Musters will not take his picture. Lord Lisburne offers 50 guineas for Lady L's portrait.

Mr. Norris of Manchester I met at Christies. He desires to have the scene at Lodore now exhibiting.

Mr. Baker called to desire I wd. procure him a large paper copy of Mr. D. Lysons "Environs of London".

Lysons called in the evening. He says it will be years before his Brother will receive any profit from "Environs &c".

Thursday — May 28.

Batty called. I gave him the large drawing of Bridgnorth Bridge and Town.

C. Offley called. William had a terrible fall from his Horse on Saturday last at Enfield. The Pole of a postchaise drove into the chest of his horse, which died in 20 minutes. — William was projected, it was said 15 yds. from the Horse. — He was taken up senseless, but recovered after being bled. dined and eving. at home alone.

Friday May 29th.

Shakespeare Gallery I called at. Copley I met. Sharp has engaged to finish the plate of Gibraltar in four years. — Copley says the Plate of Lord Chatham only yielded 2500 impressions, and is so worn it will not bear retouching — Josiah Boydell replied it ought to have borne 2 or 3 retouchings. — The defect of the plate is owing to its having been so often beat up.

Ld. Inchiquins I dined at. — Lady Orkney, Lord Kirkwall, Mr. — Obrien, and Marchi, at dinner. — Boswell has left his 4 younger Children, one Boy and three Girls, £100 a year each, an annuity on the family estate, which is about £1700 a year. Mr. Malone, Mr. D. Boswell, a half Brother, — and [blank] are executors. [*The named executors were Boswell's widow and Sir William Forbes of Pitsligo, Bt., and the named literary executors, Sir William Forbes, Malone and Rev. William Johnson Temple.*]

By the will, Boswell desires to be interred at Auchinleck, the seat of his ancestors. — It will cost £250 to carry the Body there.

Boswells papers are put into Mr. Malones possession. — No preparations for a regular work appear. — quantities of parts of newspapers are tied up together probably intended for some purpose He had schemed.

Lady Inchiquin thinks the character given in the True Briton is drawn with great exactness of knowledge of Boswell.

Lord Inchiquin told me the difference between the Duke of Portland & Lord Fitzwilliam is in no degree made up.

The Prince of Wales is at this time in a state of animosity to the Duke & Duchess of York. — They do not speak.

The Duke of Yorks conduct as Commander in Chief is much approved of. — He is attentive and accessible.

Saturday — May 30th — 1795.

Christies I went to and met Mr. Norris of Manchester, who bought three small pictures for £4.10.0. He paid me for the picture Scene at Lodore £7.7.

Copleys Exhibition of "Charles demanding the impeached Members", I went to. — Only 4 people in the room while I was there. — The picture struck me as rather glaring, & as being very much injured by a frame over charged with mouldings, looking like gilt lace work round the picture. — very carefully finished.

Marchant came in the evening. — Copley appears much disappointed in his pursuits.

Sunday — May 31st.

Kershaw called this morning. — Mr. Daulby has written him a letter of thanks to me for proposing to lend Mr. D's son some of my drawings to copy.

Dr. Mathews, & his son called. — He has employed Smirke to paint three subjects in imitation of Bass relief for a drawing room.

Coombes told Mr. Price that *He* wrote the answer to Mr. P., from Repton.

Sir Alexander Hamilton called. — He thinks the first question for the payment of Mr. Hastings law expences will be carried. — but doubts the annuity being carried. — Mrs. Hastings vain expences and appearance has prejudiced many.

JUNE 1795

Monday — June 1st.

Coombes called. — We looked over some of the views for the second Volume of Thames. — I lent him my sketch book in which I have written observations made during my Tour on lower part of Thames & Medway.

Mrs. Cosway has dismissed the monk she brought from Genoa. Cosway paid demands made by him to the amount of 160 guineas.

Coombes made up the Book of Eneas Andersons account of the Embassy to China. Anderson had kept a minute daily journal in small pocket Books and appears to have been very attentive to circumstances. — He was servant to Lord Macartney, in a capacity called "Courier", — and went with him to all places.

Coombes regulated and corrected Reptons letter to Price, but the *matter* was entirely Reptons. — Coombes has also assisted him in the work preparing for publication. — Repton has strong fears of the consequences of Knights enmity & Prices report, which checks him in answering them.

Mr. J. Livesay, called with his Son, to thank me for civilities shewn him.

Sir Alexander Hamilton called.

Steers called. He has sold the picture of Bridgnorth Bridge for 15 guineas. — He desired to know for a friend the price of my nunnery small picture in the Exhibition. I fixed it at 12 guineas witht. frame, 15 with.

Dr. Steevens bought in his evening by Wilson. He had *privately* put 50 gs. for it — It was knocked down at 48.

Tuesday, June 2d.

Steers, I breakfasted with.

Lysons I called on, & went with him to Cadells the Bookseller. Not a single copy of Bromleys 2d. Volume has been sold.

Offleys I dined at. — Barroneau, — & Outram there.

Wednesday — June 3d.

Hearne I breakfasted with.

Offleys I dined at. — Kershaw, — Campion, — Outram, — Sealy, Harris, — his Brother in law, & 2 other gentlemen there.

Bowden, the singer receives 8 guineas a week from the Playhouse and a benefit. — His last benefit produced him abt. £150. — He is abt. 41 years old.

Thursday — June 4th.

G. Dance, I called on. — He is to go to Ireland to the Lord Lieutenant towards the end of august with Lady Elizabeth Pratt.

Smirke drank tea with me. — The East India Company (Directors) subscribe for 30 sets of Daniels views, which, coloured, He sells at 30 shillings a pair. — Twelve pairs will make a work.

I have been employed three days in drawing on small Canvasses select subjects, as I am induced to think pictures of a small size will be saleable, being convenient for many. — I also propose & Smirke thinks it a good scheme, to paint upon some of my drawings begun on paper, by which I shall save the troubling of outlining.

Turner, whose drawings are in the Exhibition, was a pupil to Malton.

Friday — June 5th.

The Prince of Wales, a letter to, on the subject of paying his debts I bought today. It appears to me to be the strongest in expression I ever saw to a Prince. It proves the temper of the times.

Sir Alexander Hamilton I dined with.

Lord Courtney has secured to Mr. Obeirne £1000 a year for his life for £10,000.

Mrs. Hastings was maid of Honor at the court of Mecklenburgh Strelitz, married Mr. Imhoff in consequence — as it is said of the effects of a former intrigue. — Mrs. Schwelenbergh obtained from Sir Wm. James an appointment of Cadet for Imhoff, and He & Mrs. Imhoff happened to take their passage to Madrass in the Grafton Indiaman, when Mr. Hastings was also a passenger going out as 2d. in Council to Madrass, — from whence He was removed to Bengal. — His attachment to Mrs. Imhoff commenced during the passage. A regular Divorce according to the rules of a german Court between Imhoff & his wife, after which Mr. Hastings married her. — It does not appear that a known criminal connection was formed before. The divorce was under pretence of some personal ill usage, received by Mrs. Imhoff from Mr. Imhoff.

The Kings Birth day dinner yesterday was thinly attended. — Bartolozzi & P. Sandby, Stewards. — Eleven Academicians were present.

Malone, I met today. — Boswell was not apprehensive of his approaching end, and died without pain or effort.

Saturday — June 6th.

Tyler I called on and engaged to go to dinner at Mr. Mathias on Sunday June 14th.

Compositions I have been arranging and drawing outlines this week, collected from my various studies.

Sunday June 7th.

G. Dance I breakfasted with. — Heriot called and sat for his profile. — Mr. Miles is the Author of the letter to the Prince of Wales & the letters signed Legion & Neptune.

Baker called on me. — Mrs. Opie is said to have left Opie.

Steers called. I went with him to Bryants Gallery. — The long Claude with the Castle near the Sea, Coxe has bought for abt. £700. Lord Berwick the other long Claude for abt. £600. — Mr. Hamilton the Bacchanal Poussin for abt. £1200. — G. Dance I drank tea with and we went together to Sir Joseph Banks's. — The last night will be Sunday 21st. Lord Morton, Lord Mountmorris, 2 Lysons, Dalrymple &c &c there.

Monday — June 8th.

Mr. West I recd. a note from. — The acct. for Wolletts monument is to be closed tomorrow. My name is down for 3 guineas, also Webbers. I sent my money with a note to him signifying I wd. mention the claim on Webber to Mr. Baker & Mr. H. Webber.

Mr. Bowles I dined with. — Mrs. Bowles, Miss Bowles, & Miss Emma, and Sir George Beaumont there.

Sir George Beaumont subscribed Ten guineas towards Woolletts monument & Hearne subscribed five guineas.

Melcher [Malchair] of Oxford is a devoted admirer of the pictures of Wilson. — So great was the respect for Melcher at Oxford, that on his publishing a print of a Gateway sometime since the opportunity was embraced by his friends and subscriptions were made sufficient to purchase an annuity of £150 a year at least. He is towards 70 years of age.

Lord Guildford has an interest in the Borough of Banbury equal to 10 votes out of 15 or 16; yet such was the dislike to have *Adam* forced upon them that Ld. Guildford was obliged to give way, and Mr. Holbech as a Country Gentleman was proposed.

Meuxs Brewhouse in Liquor Pond St. — A vessel is now finishing there which is 65 feet diameter and 27 feet deep. — It will hold 20,000 barrells of porter and will cost £10,000.

Tuesday — June 9th.

G. Dance I drank tea with.

Mr. Dryander, sat for his profile this evening. "Jonas Dryander, born a

Gottenburgh March 8th. 1748 — Came to England July 10th. 1777. — His Father was a Professor at Gottenburgh". — Sir Wm. Chambers was born at Gottenburgh. — It is computed that the population of Sweden amounts to about 2 millions 9 hundred Thousands. That was the last estimation.

It is customary in Sweden only to execute one in a case of murder though *many* might have been accessory. The rest are imprisoned for life. In that state, if people [are] of an *inferior degree*, they are obliged to work.

Mr. Dryander remarked that no Foreigners learn to pronounce the Swedish language so well as the English do. — The Swedes bear an inveterate hatred towards the Danes, much stronger than appears in the English towards the French.

The population of Denmark is about 3 millions and a half.

Sheridan settled £15,000 in the 3 percents on Miss Ogle as a marriage settlement.

Wednesday — June 10th.

Hearne I called on. — Many of the subscribers to Woolletts monument have objected to the ridiculous & vain inscription of the word *Wolfe* upon it, which has been directed by West.

Sir George Beaumont I dined with. Mr. Bowles, Hearne, and Mr. Barrow who went to China with Lord Macartney there.

The population of China, as appears by the Emperors books amounts to three hundred millions and a half.

The great wall which separates China from Tartary is abt. 1500 miles long and passes over mountains of great heigth. — It is 15 feet wide at the top. — It is said to have been completed in 5 years. — It has been built above 2000 years.

Barrow is giving Lady Beaumont lessons in Euclid. — Eneas Anderson who has published an account of the expedition to China, was formerly a private in the footguards.

Thursday June 11th.

Hamilton I called on. — He has been lately employed in painting small portraits of the Nobility who were present at the Princes marriage, for the picture intended to represent that subject. — He told me the Princess Elizabeth first suggested the idea of having a print of the subject to Tomkins the Engraver.

The Duke of Dorset and the Marchioness of Bath are the two persons who have hitherto refused to promise to set for their portraits — The picture is to be 12 feet wide.

Friday — June 12th.

Bryants Gallery I went to.

Captn. Hamilton called, I was out. He left a letter from Captn. Fairfull and wrote himself that Rev. Dr. Robertson of Calendar, has heard that Mr. Peter Graham of Aberfoil, is to be mentioned as having contributed much to the History of the Forth, and He thinks He ought to be noticed as I perused papers of his writing on subjects connected with that river &c.

Smirke drank tea with me. I told him I had been lately employed in digesting landscapes & drawing them on Canvass.

Easterly winds have prevailed several days and Monday & Tuesday much rain, and since little sunshine. — Humphry called in the evening.

Saturday — 13th.

Captn. Hamilton I called on. I told him Mr. Graham of Aberfoil had rendered me very particular service by accompanying me to the source of the Forth, and that I was obliged to Dr. Robertson for lending me a copy of the Statistical account which He had sent to Sir John Sinclair, but that it was an obligation of much less importance than what I owed to Mr. Graham, or even to him (Captn. Hamilton) who had accompanyed me to Loch Lubenaig &c. — That He might inform Dr. Robertson I am not the compiler of the *Historical part* of the Rivers, but certainly am disposed to recommend such notice as may be proper to be taken of each person who has contributed to the stock of information.

Captain Hamilton of Leney, is now in Lord Elgins Fencibles and is going to Ireland.

Singleton I called on to see the Academician picture which is on shew at his house No. 4 Haymarket. Barry on seeing the picture consented to set for his Portrait which He had before refused thinking the distribution of situations not sufficiently equal.

G. Dance I dined with and afterwards sat for a profile.

Sunday June 14th.

Steers I breakfasted with.

Bryant the picture dealer, married a sister of Lord Shrewsbury by whom He has several Children. Steers has seen Lord & Lady Shrewsbury at Bryants.

Rossi went to Windsor this afternoon, with a petition to the King which He intends to present tomorrow morning the object of which is to be appointed by His Majesty to execute one of the monuments ordered for St. Pauls or Westminster Abbey to memory of Officers. — Smirke drew up the Petition & I proposed some alterations, which He adopted.

Mr. Mathias, Deputy pay-master of his majestys privy purse I dined with at his house at Ealing, in company with G. Dance, Tyler & Richards. — Mr. Ball, a surgeon, who married one of Mr. Mathias's daugtrs. and Miss Mathias were there.

Mr. Mathias was bred a portrait painter, and was under Ramsay in

1739. — In 1745 He went to Italy and returned in 1748. — He was 75 years old last December.

Mr. Mathias was very intimate with Vernet while at Rome. Vernet married there a Miss Parker, daughter of an Englishman who had formerly been in the English Navy but settled in Rome & became an Antiquarian.

Mr. Finney, of Fulcheth, is now about 76 or 7 years of age.

Ramsay was a man of cold & narrow mind and possessed so little professional ardour that He has said He never painted but two pictures that were not for money.

Richards told us that on closing the Exhibition acct. last night it appeared that £830.9.0 had been recd. this year more than the rect. of last year. — The whole rect. £2032.

Easterly, cold winds still prevail. — Glass 56.

Monday June 15th.

Christie I called on. Mr. Bryant & Mr. Slade have not yet settled their accts. for the purchase of Sir Joshuas pictures. About the first week in July the money will be required.

G. Dance I dined with & He afterwards finished my profile.

Dr. Haydn, we called on at his lodgings No. 1 Bury St., St. James's. He was dressing to attend the Prince of Wales. He engaged to dine at Dances on Wednesday next. Lady Elizabeth Pratt & a party of her forming are to dine there.

Deval, the mason of Mortimer St., lately deceased, contracted to build Newgate at 2 shillings & sevenpence a cubical foot for the *stone & working* it (plain work & mouldings included). This was in the year 1770. — Such is the rise on this article that three shillings & six pence a cubical foot is now paid for the stone before it is worked. It may now be averaged when worked out at Four shillings a foot.

Morland, Senior wrote to me again to be considered when the Charity of the Academy is distributed. He is 76 years old.

Tuesday June 16th.

Lady Beaumont wrote to inform me Mr. West had called there today and subscribed three guineas towards the maintenance of poor Cozens and would subscribe a guinea annually. — She desired me by Wests direction to adress a letter to the Council to recommend Cozens as an object of the charity.

Miss Harriet Hardman wrote to me that Her Father had authorized her to purchase a small landscape of mine in the exhibition.

Byrne called. — Lady Beaumont will take His daughters miniature copy of Sir George[s] portrait by Sir Joshua, and Lady Beverly has employed Her to make a copy of *her* portrait by Sir Joshua. — His eldest daugrs. drawing of flowers has been admired in the Exhibition & Mrs. Davies of the Boarding School has called to ask if she will teach drawing, which she has offered at 5s.3d. a lesson.

Eames, the engraver, is about to quit his profession, and become a partner in a Silversmiths house in the City. — This He is induced to as the times are unfavorable for publications.

Wednesday — June 17th.

Breakfasted Andertons Coffee House and looked over files of Newspapers for Criticisms on the Exhibition. The following *I found on myself.* *Criticisms* Ledger & London Packet.

82. View near Windsor.

"Eminently distinguishable for all that strength of effect & sober truth of colouring for which the Landscapes of this Artist have been so long celebrated. The pencilling, however, though brilliant & solid, is not free."

136. A small landscape.

"The manner of Mr. Farington in his larger pictures is usually bold & forcible, rather than locally precise & laboured. The contrary however is the case in this Landscape which is finished up with great nicety, and we can very well account for this. Mr. F. has lately been in the habit of drawing much from nature in a small scale, and for the sake of dispatch as well as superior correctness, He has had recourse for his outlines to the aid of a Camera. The filling up of those of course requires all that kind of execution which eminently distinguishes this production".

General Observations in the Ledger & London Packet.
"Royal Academy".

"The Exhibition of this year opened this morning at 12 oClock with 735 paintings, sculptures, and drawings. It is but justice to state generally before we proceed to particularize that of these there are more good and fewer bad than we have had to notice for several years; at the same time their distribution is much better than heretofore".

"The smaller productions have the advantage of the larger — among the most conspicuous names are those of Messrs. West, Westall, Lawrence, Dance, Sandby & *Farington*".

On concluding the Criticisms He observes.

"In Landscape painting the English Artists approach nearer to perfection than in any other department of the profession, and are not equalled by any of their continental neighbours of the present day".

Criticisms. True Briton & Sun.

No. 82 View near Windsor.

"The merit of this Artist is so well known, that our eulogium can add nothing to so well earned a reputation. This is an excellent picture, as well as a faithful representation of the Scene. The buildings in front and the Bridge are as spirited as anything we ever saw. There is a pleasing

impression of tranquility, resulting from the whole and altogether we can hardly say more than that it is worthy of the pencil from which it came."
No. 136. A small Landscape.
"It has been observed that Mr. Farington has displayed a considerable change in his manner this year. The observation is just and it is strange that, having originally struck out a good manner, He should change without deviating into one less commendable, in ways totally distinct, and yet with no abatement of excellence. — The picture before us, is, to use the language of Auctioneers, "a beautiful Cabinet Gem". The Scenery is romantic & interesting; the Trees, the rocks, and more particularly the water, are all touched in a very exquisite style, and through the whole there is what has been called "the poetry of Landscape".

St. James's Chronicle.

No. 82. View near Windsor.
"The light and Shadow have great force; the buildings are accurate, and the colouring good throughout.
No. 136-139. Small Landscapes.
"The colouring is harmonious and the finishing high; but it wants the effect generally produced by this Artist."
Lysons I called upon. He has got the three volumes of his Brothers work on large paper for Baker.
Miss Hardman I called on at Mr. Waughs, Dowgate Hill.
Baker I called on & met Henry Webber and went to the Bank where Baker & I transferred the stock which stood in John Webbers name to Henry Webber. It amounts to £96 a year long annuities. — Henry Webber has as much more as makes £150 a year, and has property in Houses, it is said, at least equal to that sum. — I told H. Webber that it was customary for each Academician when He had been in Council the first time to present a piece of plate. That for 10 years past the elected members had each given a plate value abt. £7. — and of course it wd. be a respect to his Brothers memory to have that memorial left in the Academy. — In answer He declined it at present. I told him that His late brothers goodness having furnished him £3000 I thought He might pay the compliment of £7 to his memory. He said He had lately sustained losses of more than £100.
I told him also of the demand for 3 guineas towards Woolletts monument his brother having subscribed towards it but had not paid. — This He did not oppose.
Captn. Henry Roberts, Mr. Baker wrote to at H. Webbers desire, and Mr. B. and myself signed the letter. He stated a demand on Mr. Roberts of £5 which H. Webber had informed us Captn. H. Roberts had promised to pay. — H. Webber took away the letter to deliver it at Captn. Roberts house.
West at the final meeting of the Committee for settling the acct. of

Woolletts monument was obliged as Chairman to put the question "That the word *Wolfe* be erased from the monument". This word had been chisselled into it in several places, by the private direction of West to Banks. Tomkins the writing Master proposed the question & was seconded by Eames.

C. Offleys I dined at. Minet there.

Thursday June 17th [18th].

Sir George Beaumont I breakfasted at. — £33 has been subscribed for poor Cozens this year. — Lady Beaumont applied to N. Dance but He refused.

Lord St. Asaph has offered to Lady Charlotte Percy and is accepted. Sir George B., proposed the offer at desire of Lord St. Asaph. — He is 34 years old she 19. — He has 4 Children 2 sons 2 daugtrs. The eldest abt. 9 years old.

Mr. Markham eldest son to the Archibishop of York, who has been in India is to be married to Miss Elizabeth Bowles, 5th. daugtr. of Mr. Bowles, He is 36 she is 18.

Charles Lock to be married to Miss Ogilvie daugtr. of the Duchess of Leinster.

Charles Offley called. We had some talk abt. Mr. Harris.

Copley has sent Offley proposals for a disposal of the picture of Lord Chatham by Lottery. Tickets 5 guineas each and to be 500 in number, first drawn ticket in State Lottery to determine it.

Wyatt wrote to me from Ely, that if required He would go over to Hamond. I wrote to Wyatt & Hamond.

Smirke to tea with me. — He sent the picture of a "Citizen and his family" to Guildhall this morning.

Friday June 19.

Weather very wet yesterday & this morning. For a fortnight past Easterly winds and now rainy & cold. Fires necessary. — Wind still easterly. Great coats necessary.

Hughes called (Mr. Fryer impatient for his pictures). Went with him & Dance to Singletons to see the Academy picture.

at home dinner & eving.

Hadyn, has attended the King & Queen, and at other times the Prince of Wales, at least 40 times, and been kept up, contrary to his usual hours, till one or two in a morning, and yet never had the smallest pecuniary recompense from any of them.

Saturday — June 20th.

H. Hamond wrote to me, desiring me & Susan to make use of Massingham whether He is there or not.

Richards informed me this morning that He paid Mr. Roberts, Brother in law to poor Cozens, Ten guineas last year on the Academy account.

Lady Beaumont called and I informed Her of the above.

Sir George Beaumont called. — I shewed him the three little pictures by Smirke. He almost wishes Smirke could never paint larger.

G. Dance, I dined with. Mr. & Mrs. & Miss Katencamp, Mr. Drew, Mr. G. Smith, and Tyler there. Lysons came to tea.

Lord Harewood, (the late) left a fortune of at least £50,000 a year Mr. Drew said. — He had £16,000 a year in Yorkshire, at least £25,000 a yr. in the West Indies. £200,000 in the 3 pr. cents besides a variety of property in different situations. He has left Lady Harewood abt. £4000 a yr. for life and she will have £20,000 to dispose of. — To General Lascelles, £2000 a yr. for life and £10,000. — The bulk of his fortune He has bequeathed to his cousin E. Lascelles elder Brother of the General.

Lysons recommended to me the Medals of Bolton of Birmingham & thought He would do the Academy medal well.

Sunday — June 21st.

Mr. Berwick called on me. — He thinks it probable he shall quit business in 4 or 5 years & by that time have £100,000. — He proposes to pass some time in travelling.

Baker, Hearne, & Marchi dined with me. — Lysons called in the evening.

Woolletts Monument. The motion for expunging the word *Wolfe*, was made by Tomkins, the Writing Master, and seconded by Eames. — It was carried unanimously. — The meeting was at the Crown & Anchor. — West being in the Chair, put the motion *officially*. — In a few days the word was expunged, — as West proposed having it inserted after the monument was advanced towards finishing Bankes only marked it in black letters, instead of cutting the letters in the stone.

Monday — June 22d.

Marchi came and assisted in varnishing &c. Hardmans pictures. He dined with me.

Tuesday 23d.

Weather became warmer. Glass 63.

Lysons I breakfasted with.

Coombes, I met at the Shakespeare Gallery. He is this day removing his goods from Knightsbridge to a House He has taken near Harrow. — Bulmer told me He is to give £40 a year for it and some land.

Nicol gave me Marshalls review of Knights Poem.

Jeffries, this eveing. told me Hodges had sold to him his lease of the house in Queen st. for £700. — The lease is for 21 years. — Hodges has advertised his pictures &c. to be sold by Christie contrary to the advice of Jeffries who advised to keep them till a more favorable season. — Mr. Seale is not to be in the Banking partnership. It is to be Gretton & Hodges only. — Jeffries has had great anxiety abt. the Prince of Wales's debts which is now over.

Wednesday — June 24th.

Lysons I called on.

Mrs. Siddons has performed lately several nights in Edinburgh. She recd. for her share £800. — Her Brother Stephen Kemble, the proprietor of the Theatre got £1600. — From Edinburgh she went to Newcastle, — from thence to Birmingham.

Thursday 25th.

Wet weather.

Mr. Berwick, Lysons & I breakfasted with G. Dance this morning & Mr Berwick sat for a profile.

Antiquarian Society I went to. Sir H. Englefield in the Chair. — The last meeting of the season. The next meeting will be Thursday Novr. 5th.

Friday 26th.

Hardmans first case I sent of, with Rubens Tygers, — Imperialis Birds, — De Wits, inside of Church, — and Garrards, Brewers Yard. — Also a case to Mr. Daulby, with Rembrants half length, belonging to Mr Hardman.

Hodges pictures, and paintings in water colours, were this day on shew at Christies.

Mr. Berwick, G. Dance, — Lysons, — and Smirke, dined with me. — Dined at 5. — staid till 11.

Saturday 27th.

Lady Beaumont I breakfasted with. — The Parliament it is likely will be dissolved immediately. Sir George remains in town on this account.

Lindoe, called today. He is desirous of commencing his studies on Monday next.

Offleys I dined at. Outram there. — News came of Lord Bridport having taken off L'Orient, The Alexander, — Formidable, and Tigre, French Men of War, part of a Fleet of 12 sail of the Line.

Also of the Scorpion Sloop of 16 guns, having engaged the Hyena of 26 guns and taken her. All the officers of the Scorpion to the Boatswain were killed.

Sunday — June 28th. — 1795.

Wet weather, and fires.

Offleys I dined at. No company.

Sir George Beaumont left Town.

Monday — 29th.

Lindoe, came and began drawing from my large drawing of a rock & fishermens huts at Hastings.

Hodges sale I went to with C. Offley & Outram. — Davenport bought several lots, — Cockerell two, Caleb Whitfoord two, and I two for C. Offley.

The pictures sold at very low prices. The large picture of *Peace* which had been exhibited sold for 19 guineas, — that representing the effects of War, for 19 guineas and a half. — Each frame cost Hodges 30 guineas. The Drawings sold better than the Pictures. One of them for 35 gs. — The Harvest picture exhibited two years ago sold for 10 gs.

Very few persons were present at the sale. — Lord Ossory, — Lord Clanbrassil & Lady Lonsdale the only persons of rank. Lady Lonsdale bought two lots.

Offley, I dined with, Outram there.

Mr. Berwicks drawings & Shakespeares &c I sent to him today in Cornhill.

Tuesday 30th.

Carey dined with me. He returned from a 6 weeks excursion to N. Wales yesterday. — He went by Shrewsbury to Lanroost, — to Conway. — Carnarvon, Bethgellert, Harlech Castle, Barmouth, Dolgelly, Bala, Corwen, Langollen, Chester, Liverpool, — in the mail to Coventry, — Kenilworth, Warwick, — Stratford on Avon, Oxford, — London.

The weather in general dull, cold & unfavourable, which prevented his ascending Snowden, — Cader Idris, or any mountain of distinguished height. — In this excursion he trusted to accidental conveyances. The expence attending it something less than 20 guineas. — At Carnarvon & Barmouth He was suspected to be a Spy. — Careys annual expence is now about £150. — Fires today and wet weather.

JULY 1795

Wednesday — July 1st.

Hughes, I breakfasted with, and proposed a frame for the picture of Westminster Bridge instead of that I have provided as He did not approve it.

Lindoe commences his year on this day. — He came & was employed in drawing.

Westhall called on me. Old Lawrence has written him a very insolent, abusive, letter, which Westall has answered in a spirited manner.

Outram I dined with at the Freemasons Tavern. C. Offley & William there.

Fires, and wet weather.

Sir Joseph Banks this day made a Knight of the Bath.

Thursday — 2d.

Shakespeare Gallery I went to. — Repton has given me his Treatise on gardening. Steevens, Revd. Mr. Douglas, and Hoole, at the Gallery.

Weather rainy and gloomy.

Drank tea at Percy Coffee House with C, J, & W. Offley & Outram.

Friday 3d.

Baker, I breakfasted with, on acct. of a Bill from Kershaw.

Offleys I dined at. — Outram there.

Saturday, July 4th.

A very wet morning.

Sir Alexander Hamilton called early to invite me to the launch of the Lascelles today at Deptford. He is come to town on purpose to be there.

Hughes called on me & we went to Lysons Chambers. Mrs. Hughes, Mrs. Watts and Lawrence drank tea there.

Cooksons income is at this time near £1100 a year. He has now four children, with a prospect of another.

Mr. Powis, who delivered the Irish Bishoprick, is said to have agreed with Dr. Langford to receive his Canonry of Windsor, if an Irish Bishoprick is offered for Dr. Langford.

Mr. Bolton of Birmingham this [day] sent 3 medals to Lysons as specimens of his capability to execute the Academy Medal.

Dr. Horsley, Bishop of Rochester, was of Cambridge, but went afterwards to Oxford, & was private Tutor to Lord Aylesford, who afterwards gave him some preferment. Lord Thurlow happening to visit Lord Aylesford on leaving him desired a Book to look at in his carriage. Lord Aylesford gave him Horsleys controversy with Priestly, with which Lord Thurlow was so much pleased, that He determined to promote him & ultimately obtained the Bishoprick for him. — Horsley appears to be a man who disregards money, but loves power & bustle.

Sunday — July 5th.

Fuseli I called on. — Charles Moore there.

Baker I dined with. Hearne, — Marchi, — Marchant, Edridge and Richd. Baker there.

Carter died a few months since.

Wet evening.

Monday — July 6th.

London Bridge picture for Mr. Fryer, I finished.

Mrs. Jodderick applied to me to recommend her for the Academy Charity.

Tuesday 7th.

Mr. Malone I called on relative to settling with Christie, who has not yet given in any account of the sale of Lord Inchiquins pictures. Mr. Drew, the Solicitor, by direction of Mr. Metcalfe has written to him.

Lord Inchiquin on his marriage with Miss Palmer recd. of her property £20,000, which He paid to his creditors, the dividend which it made being accepted by them as compensation for their whole demand. A few who had annuities stood out. These annuities amounting to about £1000 a year continue to be paid. — Before the compensation with the other Creditors was made Lord Inchiquin had given up the income arising from his estate to them out of which they allowed him £1200 a year. — The £20,000 of Lady Inchiquins is to be repaid and funded for Her future use out of the profits of his Lordships estates now restored to him which Mr. Malone thinks will be done in three or four years. That payment completed His Lordship will have for the remainder of his life the whole income arising from his estates (the £1000 a year annuity excepted) and the interest of Lady Inchiquins £20,000, — making in the whole £6 or 7,000 pr. annum. — On the marriage it was also settled that £5000 of Lady Inchiquins money should be given him witht. reserve of which He has already recd. abt. £3500.

The present income of His Lordship may be abt £2500.

Christie I called on who told me He wd. give me a few days notice when the settlement of Lord Inchiquins sale wd. be made.

The weather fine today. Glass 65.

Wednesday — July 8th.

Garvey called on me this morning to desire me to assist in procuring some relief for the widow of Carver from the Royal Academy.

He told me Hodges said to him sometime since He shd. not be able to realize more than £300 a year to retire to the Country upon.

Lysons I drank tea with. The Abbe Courayer, a Portuguese, was there. He left Portugal from an apprehension of being persecuted by the Inquisition for having communicated his opinions freely. — He has been in England some months, and visits Sir Joseph Banks's frequently.

Abbe Courayer talked of Spain, in which Country He has travelled much. — He said the English travellers had been very favorable in their descriptions, much more so, than would be justified by those who might follow them. He mentioned the country of La Mancha in which he had travelled 100 miles without seeing a tree. — The upper Nobility he said are *physically* degenerated. From inter-marrying with each other (abt. 50 families of them), they have from generation to generation united the hereditary diseases of both sides, and are distinguishable from the other Citizens by their insignificant, exhausted appearance.

The Duke of Alcuida, the present Minister of Spain, is abt. 35 years of age. Ten years ago He was only in the situation of one of the Body Guard, a private gentleman with little or no fortune. To the Queens passion for him is imputed a rise so rapid & high. In addition to his rank He has the Blue Garter of Spain.

H. Hamond came to tea.

Thursday — July 9th.

Bread was ordered on Tuesday by the City Magistrate to be raised to *one shilling the quartern loaf*, in consequence of the scarcity of wheat, — and on that day a motion was made in the Court of Aldermen & Common Council to discontinue the wearing Hair Powder which was carried by a majority of 12.

Mr. Malone I called on. — He invited me to dine with him on Sunday next.

John Offley I dined with at Freemasons Tavern. Barroneau, — Garrard, — Outram, — Hamond, Minet, Harris & C. Offley the company.

Friday — July 10th.

Miss Atherton called I was out.
Bob came to town this evening.
Council at Royal Academy this evening.

Present.

Mr. West — Smirke
Tyler — Dance
Bacon — Zoffany
Bourgeois — Farington

Sir Wm. Chambers attended & with him Rose as the annual accts. were to be audited. — Sir. Wm. told us if we went on so expensively we should be ruined. — That our Exhibition dinner was an idle expence &c &c. — This language of despondency was not founded on any reasonable ground as the academy has encreased its capital on an average of even the last 5 years if we add the interest of our money in the funds to our Exhibition rects. — as appears by the following statement

Exhibition rects.			Annual Expences.		
		£			£
1791	—	2126	1791	—	2576
—92	—	2602	—92	—	2396
—93	—	1932	—93	—	2429
—94	—	1902	—94	—	2294
—95	—	2132	—95	—	2232
		£10688[10694]			£11825[11927]

We have now in the funds

			pr. annum
			£
Charity Fund	£4000 in 3 pr. cents	—	120
General Fund.	£9800 in 3 per cents	—	294
			414.

which interest added to the rects. will amount to more than our expences.
Dance & Tyler were appointed to examine the Book of Academy accts. deposited by Sir. William Chambers.

The Annual Charity was voted as follows:-

		Last year.
	£	£
Mrs. Barrett, widow of Geo. Barrett R.A.	10-10-0.	10-10-0.
Mrs. Baker, widow of – Baker R.A.	10-10-0.	6- 6-0.
Mrs. Tomkins do. of Wm. Tomkins associate	7- 7-0.	4- 4-0.
Cozens	10-10-0.	10-10-0.
Morland, father of – Morland.	10-10-0.	—————
Mrs. Pine, – widow of – Pine	10-10-0.	—————
Mrs. Carver, widow of – Carver, Scene painter.	7- 7-0.	5- 5-0.
Mrs. Riggs *Children*, – she died lately	10-10-0.	—————
Mrs. Lowe, widow of – Lowe.	6- 6-0.	5- 5-0.
Mrs. Jones	5- 5-0.	3- 3-0.
Mrs Fournier, widow of Fournier, drawing master.	5- 5-0.	4- 4-0.
Mrs. Jodderick.	5- 5-0.	4- 4-0.
Mrs. Picot, daugtr. of Ravenet.	4- 4-0.	4- 4-0.
Mrs. Eichel.	3- 3-0.	3- 3-0.
Mrs. Verdussen.	3- 3-0.	3- 3-0.
Mrs. Seest.	4- 4-0.	4- 4-0.
Mrs. Zeeman	4- 4-0.	3- 3-0.
Mrs. Kitchener.	3- 3-0.	3- 3-0.
Mrs. Roberts.	4- 4-0.	4- 4-0.
Mrs. Vispre.	4- 4-0.	4- 4-0.
Mrs. Smith, Fabers daugtr.	4- 4-0.	3- 3-0.
Mrs. Roper.	3- 3-0.	3- 3-0.
Mrs. Sheridan	3- 3-0.	3- 3-0.
Mrs. Beasell	4- 4-0.	4- 4-0.
Mrs. Foldstone	—————	—————

Sir William Chambers & Rose went away early. The Council remained till past eleven. No supper.

The expence of the Annual dinner given in the Exhibition room was as follows [blank].

Saturday — July 11th.

Hughes I breakfasted with. He paid me for Mr. Fryers pictures &c.

They had a musical party last night. Cumberland, Lawrence, Nield the singer &c. were there. — Lawrence has made an excellent drawing of certain characters who attend Mr. Blencowes concert. — Blencowe & his man, — Peter Denyss, & a Lady at the Harpischord.

Offleys I dined at. — Bob, Hamond, Outram there.

Sunday — 12th.

British Coffee House I dined at. C & J. Offley, Outram, Hamond & Bob there.

Monday 13th.

Malones I dined at. — Humphry there.

Lord Macartney is abt. 58 years of age. His Father was an Irish Country Gentleman who had abt. a £1000 a year. — Lord Macartney came to the Temple where He became acquainted with Mr. Burke. — Ld. M. has a most retentive memory, and knows more anecdote than any man. — He is particularly remarkable for knowing all that relates to families of any distinction throughout England. Their circumstances &c. — He has now abt. £4000 a year and some ready money. — Though He married a daugtr. of the late Lord Bute, He derived no political advantage from it. — He happened to be abroad at the time Charles Fox was first in Paris a very young man & prevented his falling into snares laid for him by Sharpers. He communicated such information on this subject to Lord Holland, the father of Charles, as engaged the friendship of that nobleman, who was the first cause of Lord M's promotion to political situations.

While Lord M. was on his Embassy to China, He kept a private journal in which he daily inserted the most minute circumstances that passed. His conversations &c &c.

Edmund Burkes Father was an Attorney in the County of Carlow abt. 30 miles from Dublin. — He came to the Temple when a young man but never took a degree. — While there He passed much of his time with a Mr. Dodwell, and a Mr. [blank] both men of talents and acquirements and much given to argument, in which Burke became a competitor. His studies have always been of a desultory kind like the manner of Johnson, reading accidentally, and variously, rather than systematically, and taking all opportunities of acquiring information by conversing with all men on all subjects.

Burke married a daughter of Dr. Nugent, an Irishman, a Physician & Roman Catholic. This accts. for his exertions in favor of those of that persuasion. Dr. Nugent resided in London.

Burke has associated in a domestic way very much with Irish people and has a strong prejudice in their favor.

His manner in conversation were it not for the great superiority of his talents & Knowledge, would be disagreeable. He seldom appears to pay any attention to what is said by the person or persons with whom He is conversing, but disregarding their remarks urges on whatever rises in his mind with an ardour peculiar to himself.

He was born January 1st. 1730.

Mr. Malone does not think His retirement is at all owing to a desire of pursuing private studies with a view to complete works intended for the press as has been supposed, on the contrary He does not think He has ever written but "on the spur of some particular occasion".

Mrs. Burke has very moderate abilities. Richd. Burke the son had a ‚portion of talent. To both Mr. Burke has accustomed himself to refer more than could be expected from his disposition & superior acquirements. To his Son, He yielded as if he had been the inferior, and wd. justify the observations by eloquently explaining & defending the force of them.

Boswell, recd. £1550 for his Quarto edition of the Life of Johnson from the Booksellers, which sum is to be made up £2000 on acct. of the Octavo edition.

The Honble. Andrew Erskine, with whom Burke [Boswell] had corresponded at an early period of life, was Brother to the late Earl of Kelly. He went into the Army but had no high preferment, and finally having retired to Scotland upon a small annual income of £100 or so, abt. a year since put an end to his life by drowning himself. — Their correspondence was published in a small pamphlet in 1763, the year in which Boswell became acquainted with Dr. Johnson.

The Duchess of Leinster, sister to the Duke of Richmond is abt. 65 years of age. Mr. Ogilvie to whom she is now married, is a Scotchman, and was placed as an Usher for £12 a year at a very small school in Ireland. After the death of the Duke the Duchess requiring a Tutor for her young Children, Ogilvie had the luck to be recommended; and being domesticated in the family, the Duchess conceived a passion for him which ended in marriage. They have three children, daughters. The Duchess has about £4000 a year jointure, and by savings it is supposed Mr. Ogilvie has abt. £20,000, which will be divided among them. — Charles Lock was married to the eldest a few days ago.

Fires we had at Mr. Malones today, the weather bleak & cold. — We staid till eleven oClock.

Tuesday July 14th.

Sir Francis Bourgeois called on me this evening. He said David Boswell had expressed a wish to succeed his Brother as Secretary for Foreign correspondence to the Academy. — Sir Francis said, J. Taylor had expressed a similar wish, and that Caleb Whitefoord also desires the situation, and said, Sir Joshua Reynolds had pointed it out to him previous to Boswells appointment. — I told Sir Francis it wd. be very disagreeable to entangle ones self among various candidates whom we might *individually* respect, and as it had not on former occasions been thought necessary to fill these vacancies till it could be done unanimously I thought it wd. be imprudent to stir in it. — In this he fully concurred.

Poggi called and talked abt. the disposal of Sir Joshuas drawings. — Humphry called. Marchant called.

Wednesday July 15th.

Mr. Grozier, an Engraver, called on me to state that General Stuart, Brother to Lord Bute, was collecting specimens of drawings by modern British Artists, and desired me to allow him to shew some of mine to the General — which I agreed to.

Westhall, I called on. General Stuart purchased a few sketches by him, but on the whole gave him a good deal of trouble, and did not purchase drawings which He desired might be made.

Dance I called on — Tomorrow morning he sets off for Ireland with Mr. & Mrs. Cockerell.

Caleb Whiteford spoke, mentioned to Dance on Sunday last the intention of his nephew Smith to become a Candidate to be an Associate. — Smith spoke to Humphry on the same day to the same purpose.

Thursday July 16th.

Gilpin I drank tea with at White Horse cellar Coffee House previous to my going to the Council. I told him the disposition the members of it were in with regard to him. — He is sensible of the honor, but, I suppose on arising from apprehensions of what others may think, He seems to wish the Compliment should appear in the newspapers. — I told him if the Council be unanimous that his name be put down it may be declared by whoever thinks proper in any way. The Council I went to.

Present

Mr. West

Tyler   Bacon

Bourgeois — Smirke

Farington.

Sir Wm. Chambers has written a letter to West, recommending that on acct. of the low state of the Academy funds at this time the execution of the Medal be postponed.

The Madrass statue of Lord Cornwallis was taken into consideration. I proposed that Members of the Academy alone should not be allowed to be Candidates, but that it shd. be open to all Sculptors to offer models. — Bacon opposed it. He said it is not probable that Artists of the first reputation will be Competitors with men little known therefore the Academy wd. probably be deprived of the chance of employing men of the first reputation, another & stronger objection was that an ingenious young man might probably produce a Captivating sketch in Clay who wd. by no means be equal to finish the statue in marble. He knew striking instances to justify such a probability. — He said more on the subject.

Gilpins name being put down was discussed. Bacon particularly, & West & Richards objected to anything like a Vote as being a bad precedent

though individually Bacon & West said they should give him a preference
to all others. — The subject was postponed, and it was agreed to hold an
adjourned meeting on Saturday next.

Friday — July 17th.

Offleys I dined at. — Mrs. Offley, — Mrs. Ball, — Outram, Bob, & C. J. &
W. Offley.

H. Hamond returned to Lynn.

Saturday — 18th.

Council at Academy in the evening.

Present
Mr. West
Bacon — Bourgeois —
Smirke — Farington

Ld. Cornwallis statue is to be carried into execution in the same manner as
that of Lord Rodney. I gave up my proposal of a general call on Sculptors
as I think while we are using the money of others in trust we must go upon a
certainty and can leave nothing to speculation. — The Academical
Sculptors are directed to be called upon to meet the Council at the
Academy on Friday next.

The Commemoration Medal is to be carried into execution immediately, and the Secretary is to signify to Mr^S. Burch, — Pingo & Milton,
that on Friday next they may send specimens of their ability & express if
they are willing to undertake it as Candidates.

Gilpins name was put down by me after the following motion had been
made by Sir Francis Bourgeois & carried unanimously. — Viz: "Resolved
unanimously that Mr. Farington be permitted to set down Mr. Gilpins
name in the list of Candidates for the ensuing election of Associates of the
Royal Academy".

The above Minute was entered in the Council Book by Mr. Richards.

Candidates for Associate, — the list was taken down this evening the
time for admission expiring. — As no election of Associates took place last
year, it was agreed to join the list of last year to the list of this year, agree-
able/to/a/precedent. The list of 1782 was carried on to the list of 1783.

The Council present were of opinion it would not be prudent to fill all
the 5 vacancies at once. — But this must be determined at a general
meeting. In 1781 there were *two* vacancies and 21 Candidates when only
one vacancy was filled up. — In 1782 there was only one Vacancy & 22
Candidates, and it was resolved not to fill it up.

Sunday — July 19th.

Offleys I dined at. Mrs. Offley, — Mrs. Ball, Outram, Minet, — Bob, — J,
C & Wm. Offley there.

Monday — 20th.

Weather very warm & fine. — Glass 74. Only Summer like day for many weeks.

C. Offley dined with me. — John & Outram left London.

Tuesday — July 21st.

The weather changed this evening. — It rained.

Wednesday — 22d.

Hardmans, 3 last cases I sent of today.

Baker, I went to at one oClock and met Henry Webber, who received from us the balance due to him and gave us a receipt in full as Executors for his Brothers will, — He being sole Heir at Law.

C. Offley dined with me.

Thursday — 23d.

Hodges left London with his family to settle at Dartmouth, in Devonshire.

Poggi I called upon.

Offley I dined with. — Mrs. Offley, — Mrs. Ball, — Bob & William Offley there.

Friday 24th.

Council at the Academy.

Present
Mr. West
Bourgeois — Bacon
Tyler — Smirke
Farington.

Messrs. Wilton & Banks attended in consequence of having been summoned as Sculptors to consider the business of a Statue of Lord Cornwallis. — Nollekens did not attend.

Much conversation took place on the subject but the principal point of debate was whether the statue should be in a modern dress or as has been generally the custom in the habit of a Roman. Mr. Bacon & Banks thought the latter: Mr. West defended the propriety of representing Ld. Cornwallis in the dress of the time, the unpicturesque appearance of which startled the Sculptors, who said, *Particularly Bacon* as the *chief speaker*, that in 20 years when the fashion had varied it would appear disgusting. That there was an ideal grandeur from association in the appearance of the ancient dress over the modern, and that it wd. greatly add to the effect. — Mr. West said He considered a Statue of an Individual should be an *Historical record*, and that the Ideal could not with propriety be admitted and that the prejudice in favor of representing Moderns in Ancient dresses was an absurdity. — That Sir Joshua Reynolds in his opinion had judged ill in accustoming himself to dress his woemen in fancied drapery and wd. have rendered them more interesting to posterity had He followed their fancies and described them in the fashion of their day with all the taste he was master of.

To obviate the main objection that of the effect of a modern dress, I proposed to take the advantage of Lord Cornwallis's rank in life, and add his robe of Peerage which might be so managed as to conceal or break the lines of our formal dress. This was directly admitted by Smirke, and made an impression on the others, but it was observed that Lord Cornwallis at Madrass was only in a military capacity. — I replied that He went to India in a civil capacity & his assuming the Command of an Army in the field was accidentally owing to war breaking out. That in short we were not limited to represent Ld. Cornwallis as a particular but a general character that if the statue shd. be dug up 1000 years hence the dress might explain that He was a Commander Noble & a Senator of Britain: That in *Bass relief* on the pedestal particular allusions to his services on the Madrass station might be executed. — Mr. West firmly supported what I said as did the rest of the Council, and Mr. Banks said that He was convinced by the reasons given, in which Mr. Bacon concurred. — It was then moved that Lord Cornwallis be represented in a modern dress with his robe of Peerage, and that the Sculptors deliver their models on Monday Novr. 2d., — which passed unanimously.

It being past eleven o'clock we agreed that a Council be held on Friday next to consider the commemoration medal.

Saturday July 25th.

C. Offley — William & Minet dined with me.

Bob went to Manchester in the evening.

Smirke I called on. Grozier has been with him as He says for General Stuart. — Smirke has not delivered to him any specimen of drawing.

The French Emigrant Corps has lost 600 men on the Coast of Brittany in the second engagement.

Sunday — July 26th.

Barroneaus, I went to at 2 oClock with C & Wm. Offley. — Captn. Darby dined there.

Monday — 27th.

Returned to town this morning with C & W Offley.

Offleys I dined at, Mrs. Offley & Mrs. Ball there.

Tuesday 28th.

Humphry I breakfasted with.

LORD CORNWALLIS

11. John Bacon the Elder R.A.
*Charles, first Marquess Corn-
wallis.* Fort St. George Museum,
Madras.

12. Henry Singleton R.A. *The Royal Academicians in General Assembly, 1795.* The Royal Academy of Arts, London.

C. Offley dined with me. — Old Morland wrote me a letter of thanks as one of the Council for voting him 10 guineas.

Wednesday 29th.

Shakespeare Gallery I called at. — J. Boydell approved the selection of views which I shewed him for Vol: 2 of the Thames, and thinks that as there are 4 large Plates in this Volume they ought to be considered as equal to 10 small Plates, so that including them 34 Plates will be sufficient for Volume 2d.

Offleys I dined at. — Weather today particularly oppressive.

Thursday July 30th.

Cade, who came Purser in one of the ships from China a few days since, called on me. — The Fleet of Indiamen were 23 in Number, and came from St. Helena with Convoy. — Some disturbances have happened in China, and many Piracies from among the people are on the Coast. — He says the China merchants at Canton, talk of the bad management of Government &c in a manner very different from their former custom. — The Markets in China were very bad indeed last season.

Mrs. Wheatly I lent 5 drawings to. — 2 of Webbers, 3 of mine, which she proposes to copy as lessons.

Friday — 31st.

Offley I dined with. Mrs. Offley, Mrs. Ball, & Wm. there.
Council at Academy I went to.

Present
Messrs West

Bourgeois	Smirke
Bacon	Farington

Commemoration Medal was the subject on which we met. — Burch, — Pingo, — and Wilton sent specimens. — It was the general opinion that in Burchs Hanoverian medal more knowledge of the Art is expressed than in any of the others produced. — The doubt was whether Burch is *now* capable of executing with the same degree of ability. That medal was executed in 1785. — The specimens of modelling which Burch sent to the last Exhibition were very inferior to his former productions.

It was at last moved and carried unanimously that Mr. Smirkes model be delivered to Mr. Burch and He be requested to make a model an *Accurate Copy* of it the same size of the Hanoverian medal, and that He deliver His model to the President to be considered by the Council. — Bacon in reply to an observation of mine said it had been an affectation in Burch to make His legs & feet small, with a view to encrease the effect of the body of the figure.

We conversed on the propriety of the Council taking into consideration the state of the living & Plaister Academys.

I proposed that Mr. Richards be allowed for his additional lights &c on acct. of extra duty — also that Mrs. Hadriel shd. have some addition to Her salary. — It was agreed to postpone the further consideration of these points till the finances of the Academy are settled.

The Council broke up at ¼ past 12. — We have never had supper there since that on new years eve last.

AUGUST 1795

Saturday August. 1st.

Charles Offley called. This afternoon He set of for Hastings.

Sunday 2d.

Nollekens I met this morning. — I spoke to him abt. the statue of Lord. Cornwallis. — He said Bacon would talk more than anybody else, and He would lay 100 guineas would have the commission. — I said I was convinced to the contrary if a majority of the Academy were not really convinced of his design being the best. — Nollekens said He had nothing at all to do at present.

Humphry I called on. — He is in good spirits abt. his situation and success in crayon painting.

Monday — August 3d.

Lindoe told me today that the Brewery business has been for several years very unprofitable. That a few Houses only, such as Thrales, Whitbreads, &c got anything by it. The high price of Barley leaves no room for profits to small houses which in proportion are at greater expences.

Spain, news of that country having made a peace with France was brought today.

Tuesday — 4th.

Lawrence I called on. Mr. Angerstein paid Comyns 15 guineas for cleaning the Landscape Cuyp, — and 5 guineas for a half length Vernet. Lawrence paid him 5 guineas for cleaning Vanderguchts Rembrant.

Boydell told me his uncle, Thomas Boydell died last Saturday. —Fuseli called on. — General Stuart saw but did not buy any of his sketches. Fuseli asked 10 guineas each for those the General selected.

I desired Fuseli to review Reptons publication. — Bromleys 2d. Vol: He has looked over. It is equally indifferent with the first. — He does not mean to take any notice of it but let it pass witht. reviewing.

Wednesday, August 5th.

Steers I breakfasted with in the Temple.

Mrs. Offley I called on, and in the afternoon dined with. Mrs. Ball there.

Wheatley I called on in the evening. — He is so far recovered of the last fit of the gout as to walk abt. and only one hand tied up. He proposes attending the Academy as Visitor tomorrow. A sister of Perry, Editor of the Morning Chronicle, supped there. — John Serres, has quitted his House suddenly and it is said has eluded his Creditors.

G. Dance I recd. a letter from at Dublin Castle.

Thursday — 6th.

Fuseli dined with me today and staid with me till Eleven oClock.

Mr. Lock & Mr. Ogilvie each settled an annuity on Charles Lock & Miss Ogilvie to enable them to marry, & the Duke of Manchester is to give Charles a situation under him in the Customs.

Fuseli said the adopting of modern dress for Lord Cornwallis statue is against a principle maintained by Sir Joshua Reynolds, that all dresses subject to change as being temporary fashions shd. be rejected in such cases.

Fuseli spoke highly of Lawrences portraits which were in the Exhibition last spring. — He thinks them superior in merit to Hoppner. In this He agrees with William Lock, Junr. of whose taste & judgement Fuseli has a high opinion, and considers him as much more sound in both respects than His Father.

Friday August. 7th.

Steers I breakfasted with. Called on Lysons & went with him to Nando's Coffee House to Lawrence, who proposed to me to set to him next Thursday that He might finish my Portrait. — While walking with him I told him that Lady Louisa Gordons picture was removed from the place it was intended to be hung in, as it was the opinion of West & others of the Council that it would be seen to more advantage in the place it was afterwards fixed in. — He asked me why I mentioned the subject, I replied because I was informed some of his friends had remarked on the picture being ill hung. — He said He had been surprised to see the picture in that situation but now He was acquainted with the motive He must consider it as a mark of attention to him. — I said He would find in the Catalogue that a Lady of Quality was inserted in the first edition of them to shew where the picture was first placed. N.B. I found myself mistaken in this. Richard had the Catalogue corrected in time. — Steers, called on me & sat while was painting on his picture of Kew Bridge.

Saturday 8th.

Lysons breakfasted with me. I went with him to Lawrence where He had appointed to meet Perry & Grey, Editors of the Morning Chronicle, who have become proprietors of the Polygraphic scheme. They are to agree, if they can with Lysons for the patterns of his Roman floor in order to make painted carpets of the same pattern. — Lawrence I explained the mistake to which I made yesterday, not then knowing that Richards had in time directed the error in the Catalogue to be corrected.

Mr. Drew the Solicitor I met and conversed with him on the subject of Christie not having yet settled for the sale of Sir Joshuas pictures. He has threatened Christie to advertise to the purchasers not to pay any money to him &c &c. — Christie said He wd. give securities for the money & pay the difference in the present price of the Stocks, but cd. not settle the acct. in money, blamed the nobility &c. who did not pay, particularly Lord Kinnaird.

Steers, called on me & I gave some finishing touches to the picture of Kew Bridge while He sat by.

Smirke called & approved of the pictures for Mr. Daulby & Steers.

Sunday August. 9th.

Paines, I went to, to dinner. — Only the family and Miss Hone. Horace Hone & Mrs. Hone are at Buxton where He has much to do.

Mary Paine is very desirous of practising in Oil. I told Paine I should on my return from the Country be glad if she wd. pass a morning in my painting room & I wd. shew her the process of a picture from the commencement.

Fuseli, I met when I returned to town & went home with him. He says George Steevens agreed with him that Wests Idea of dressing the statues in modern dresses is absurd & will totally prevent the artist from expressing the extent of his ability.

Monday — August. 10th.

Mr. Daulbys pictures I sent. — Harry wrote to me that Marianne [Farington] was brought to Bed of a daughter on Thursday last, — August 6th.

Tuesday — 11th.

Steers, I breakfasted with and carried him his picture of Kew Bridge.

Smirke I called on & told him Fuselis objections to the Statue of Lord Cornwallis being dresst in a modern manner. I proposed calling on Bacon to know if He *remained* convinced of the propriety and advantage of adopting it. Smirke thought it wd. be very well if I called.

The weather yesterday & today thick & very sultry.

Wednesday August 12th.

Glass in my painting room 76 today.

Mr. Drew, I breakfasted with this morning in New St., Spring gardens. — He has been again with Christie who by threatening has promised to settle in part in a few days. — I afterwards called on Christie to correct an error in my acct. Christie at all times sacrifices everything to answer the questions of the moment.

Yenn, I met. He told me He was with the King when Hoppner was introduced on the 5th. of May to know the Kings pleasure abt. the picture to be painted of the Princess of Wales. The King did not recollect Hoppner till His Name was mentioned by a Page. — Yenn condemns the behaviour of Hoppner as very improper. — When the King said He did not approve of red & yellow trees and that artists shd. look at nature, Hoppner said He had studied landscape as much as anybody. When the King directed his discourse to any other person present Hoppner replied as if He had been the person spoken to. He looked white & was much agitated. — After the King left the room, Hoppner spoke very passionately before Chamberlain, Brawn, and Yenn. He said He did not come there to solicit employment and that He knew He was the best Painter in England.

Chamberlain having expressed an assent to something which the King said to him, Hoppner afterwards told Yenn He was a Sycophant, and that if He called at His House He wd. kick him out. Yenn very properly gave Chamberlain a caution not to go there.

The King since said to Yenn that He perceived He had made Hoppner very angry by his remarks on the pictures exhibited and added He shd. not paint the Princess of Wales for him but Gainsborough Dupont shd. do it. — Yenn says Dupont has obtained the Kings favor by his respectful behaviour.

Thursday — Augst. 13th.

James Stone left my service. — Lawrence I sat to this day from 10 till past 4 in the afternoon. He finished the face down to the bottom of the nose.

One of the sons of Dr. Moore, who is situated in the Secretary of State's Office, lately privately married the divorced Lady Eglingtown (formerly Miss Twisden). — She has two natural children. She had before marriage £600 a yr. from Lord Eglingtown, & £400 a year from the Duke of Hamilton. — Young Moore after his marriage waited upon the Duke and gave up that settlement. — Dr. Moore & his family are much chagrined at the match. — Dr. Moore has five sons, viz. Col. Moore, — Captn. Moore, *Navy*, — Mr. Moore, a surgeon, — Mr. Moore in the Secretary Office and the youngest a Student in the Temple.

Hamilton dined with us at Lawrences. — We talked abt. filling the vacancies of Associates in the Academy. Hamilton was for filling three which we agreed to. Gilpin is their first man, — & Hamilton thinks Downman & Shee ought to come before Soane. — Lawrence is for Soane.

Mrs. Hamilton drank tea with us. — Much lightning this eving and sultry weather & rain.

Staid till past eleven oClock.

Ralph West told Lawrence that the Prince of Wales had offered his Father a commission for him which was not accepted, as Mr. West would not make the necessary annual allowance in addition to pay to enable Ralph to live with other officers in a suitable manner.

Friday — Augst. 14th.

Smirkes, eldest son called on me having copied my drawing of Ouse Bridge. He had done it so well that I asked him why He did not devote his attention to Art as a profession having so good a capacity for it. He said He shd. like it as an amusement, but for constant employ a more active business. — He was 17 years old last February and I told him it was time for him to determine on some way of life. He said He had left it to his Father whose opinion He should follow.

Will brought George to town and carried him to school.

Saturday 15th.

Lawrence I breakfasted with. — and sat for my portrait from ten till four when He finished the face completely. — I dined with him and Mr. & Mrs. Hamilton came in the evening.

Sunday — 16th.

Lawrence I went to at 10. — He sketched in the attitude of my figure.

D. Lysons I went to at Putney. He was not well & looked very ill owing to a cramp or collicke pain in the stomach. — Mr. Rutter came to Putney in his Uncles coach according to appointment with Lysons. — I returned with him & made a sketch of the view looking towards London from an upper window of the House. — Mr. Rutter Senr., — went out to dinner, — but I dined there with a Mr. Tasker — Mr. Farquhar., — Mr. Rutter, nephew of Mr. Rutter Senr. & a young german.

Mr. Rutter, Junr. expressed to me a wish of his and his uncles to be included in the list of subscribers to any work which may be coming out on the subject of the Thames. — He said His Uncle wished I wd. assist them in naming the place. — It is a beautiful situation, — dined at 4.

At 7 I returned from Putney to town.

Monday — Augst. 17th.

Yenn I called on at the Queens palace at ½ past two. — We walked through some of the rooms. Some of the Pictures of Cannaletti are excellent. A full feeling of Art is expressed in them. The Skies are *lowered* to the tone of the buildings. The lights broad and the shadows projected by objects in the masses of light *moderated* so as not to *disturb the breadth.* — The same caution prevails everywhere. These pictures were painted in 1742 & 44.

The Landscape by Rubens is admirable. — The Sunny light over the country is finely managed.

I went with Yenn to Kensington and dined with him. — Willis, Mrs. & Miss Willis, — a Lady, her guest, & Mr. Watson, who has a place under the Chancellor, dined there. — Willis proposed to me to become a Member of the Trent Club, held once a fortnight during the winter, at the Crown & Anchor. — It consists of 30 members. Hoppner, — Sharp, the Hatter, — & Dr. Gillies, are members. — I told him that I had no objection but that which I always had felt to the necessary risk of a balot, — He said it was *His & Their* custom to *sound the Members* before any one was proposed to prevent disappointment. I said I shd. commit myself to his discretion.

returned to town at Ten. Lawrence, — Humphry & Marchant had called on me.

Tuesday Augst. 18th.

Lawrence, I breakfasted with, — and sat to him till 12. He finished the Hair.

Hamilton & Lawrence dined with me. They concur in thinking Gilpin Downman, Soane, & Shee, are the 4 from whom 3 associates shd. be taken.

Harris called this evening. — Mr. Evans died in Dublin on Wednesday last. A paralytic stroke carried him of. Aged 67. He left £500 a year to each of his two nieces besides £2500, settled on them when they married.

Lawrence, I assisted this morning to make out a list of names of distinguished persons whose portraits He means to draw & form a collection Lord Orfords is the first He has made, with this view.

Gilpin & Sir George Beaumont called.

Wednesday — Augst. 19th.

Sir George Beaumont called on me, having come to town for a few days. He has begun pictures since He went into the country, but not satisfied himself and only finished a small one. — He cannot be satisfied if transparence & elegance of execution are not conspicuous.

He is going to the new forest with S. Gilpin to visit the Revd. Mr. Gilpin whose writings He commends much. — Lambeth I went to at one oCloc (after calling on Squire), and touched the buildings not before sufficiently made out, in my view of London from the top of Lambeth Steeple. — This day I concluded the preparatory drawings for the second Volume of the Thames.

Smirke I called on in the morning & talked with him on the subject of son studying our art. He seems much inclined to encourage him to pursue it.

Thursday Augst. 20th.

Mr. Drew I called on. Christie has only paid to Coutts & Co. 2 drafts at distant dates for £1000 each. I wrote to Mr. Malone today to Cheltenham that I had paid £381:18:6 to Coutts in Christies name.

Sir George Beaumont I called on & went with him to Gilpins, and from thence to the Queens House, and saw the pictures. — Tomorrow He is to go with Gilpin to the Revd. Mr. Gilpins. — Humphry I dined with. — He proposes to vote for Gilpin, Downman and Soane.

Friday Augst. 21st.

Lawrence I went to this morning. He finished the *Hand*.

J. Boydell I called on. — Lawrence I dined with. — In the evening called on Drew & talked to him abt. Christie.

Marchant called on me in the evening.

Saturday 22d.

Left London this morning at Six oClock in the Swaffham Coach. — Six Passengers. Got to Swaffham at 10 at night, — & slept at the Crown.

Sunday 23d.

Massingham I went to this morning, found Susan & Horace Hamond at home.

Monday 24th.

Mr. & Mrs. Henley & Miss Holingsworth of Lynn came from Sandringham to dinner, — also Revd. Davy from Ingoldisthorpe. — He staid all night.

Tuesday 25th.

H. Hamond went to Lynn to dinner. Davy dined & staid all night.

Wednesday 26th.

Davy returned to Ingolsthorpe. — High House we dined at. Mrs. Bouchere & Her sister and niece dined there, also Revd. Mr. Framingham. Mrs. Thom was too ill to come.

Thursday Augst. 27th.

H. Hamond went to Horace Dowsings at Barham near Walsingham.

Mr. Daulby wrote to me expressing himself pleased with the pictures.

Friday 28th.

H. Hammond returned. H. Dowsing & Killet dined with us. — Dowsing staid all night.

Saturday 29th.

Mr. & Mrs. Hamond, Richard, & Sarah & Susan Hamond dined with us, also Dowsing.

The weather this week has been beautiful, no rain.

Sunday 30th.

Killet dined with us, and in the morning we walked over Mr. Mordaunts pleasure ground. — Mr. Mordaunts Son is a promising young man 19 years old and of Christ Church.

Monday 31st.

Dr. Heath, a Physician 28 years old, settled at Fakenham, & Killet dined with us. — Another Physician, of the same age, Dr. Edmonds, is also settled at Fakenham. — Heath is employed by Marquis Townshend. — Edmonds is acquainted with Mr. Coke. — Edmonds told Dowsing He made £400 the first year He was at Fakenham. — He comes from Wendover.

SEPTEMBER 1795

Tuesday, Septr. 1st.

H. Hamond went to Lynn. — Miss Carr niece of Mr. Carr, dined with us. — I recd. a letter & draft from Mr. Daulby who is again confined by the gout.

Mr. Everitt came from Lynn with H. Hamond. — He told me the opposition to the Eau Brink Canal Bill had cost the town of Lynn £8000. The Corporation had subscribed £3000, and *private* subscriptions made up the remainder. — He subscribed £600 and bore his own expences while attending in London as a Deputy from Lynn to the amount of £200. — They employed 5 Council at 10 gnas. a day each, and two Solicitors at 5 guineas each. — Having obtained certain clauses they gave up the opposition to the Bill.

The Canal at the entrance from the River is to be 800 feet wide; The estimate of expence is £50,000, but Mr. Everitt says it will never be completed for less than £250,000, — and He does not think subscriptions sufficient to carry it into execution will ever be obtained. — No person in Lynn will subscribe. — One of the clauses limits that no tonnage shall be demanded till the whole plan is executed.

Wednesday — Septr. 2d.

H. Hamond & Mr. Everitt went from Massingham this morning early to Norwich, thence to Ipswich & Harwich, from whence they are to sail to London in Mr. Everitts cutter.

Richd. Hamond & Charles Randal called.

Miss Carr dined with us.

Rev. Mr. Barnard, Mrs. Barnard (a daughter of Sir Mordaunt Martin), came to tea from Lytcham, and invited us to dine on Wednesday next.

Thursday — Septr. 3d.

Killet came in the evening. — I have been painting two days on the view of Bridgnorth Bridge. — The weather continues remarkably fine.

Friday 4th.

Rain this afternoon. — Employed painting.

Saturday 5th.

H. Dowsing went to Barsham. — Employed painting. In the evening fine effects of Clouds till twilight. Made several Studies.

Sunday 6th.

Killett performed morning service at Massingham and dined with us at 4.
   Weather very fine & hot Glass 75 in the Hall.

Monday 7th.

Mr. Carr called this morning.
   In the evening walked out and made studies of effects of evening skies & twilight breadths.

Tuesday 8th.

Mr. Hamond sent to invite us to dinner tomorrow.
   Lord Inchiquin, a letter from I recd. — Complains of Christies conduct.
   In the evening walked to Massingham & made studies.

Wednesday 9th.

Revd. Mr. Barnards at Litcham we dined at. — He married abt. 2 years ago, the eldest daugtr. of Sir Mordaunt Martin. — He is 30 years old and younger Brother to Mr. Barnard who married a daugtr of Lord Willoughby de Broke. — I met him at Keswick in 1783. He is 37 years old. — They are Clergymen and the sons of a Clergyman who resided at Horseheath near Cambridge.
   Mrs. Langford and Her 2 daughters came to tea.
   Mr. Errinton, who was shot by Miss Broderick, resided at Essex near Purfleet where Mr. Barnard had a House for a short time. — The air was so bad, affected by the damps of the low country near him, as to cause a bilious complaint which in 4 months obliged him to leave that situation. — Dr. Reynolds told him the air would kill him if he remained there.
   Mr. Errinton was little esteemed. When He married He agreed to allow Miss Broderick ten pounds a month, but never paid her anything. — The pistol she fired with her left hand, the ball lodged in his lungs. — Miss Broderick bought a pair of pistols of Wagdon, the Gunsmith, 6 months ago before & under pretence of firing from her window to prevent boys from robbing her garden, by alarming them. — She desired Wagdon to shew her how to load them. — It appears that she from that time daily fired at a mark.

Thursday Septr. 10th.

Mrs. Richd. Hamond & Mrs. S. Bagge came from Lynn & dined with us.

Mr. Hamond has said to Mr. T. Bagge that he had accomplished his wish, having provided a fortune for Richard. — He has had thought of purchasing Narborough, but thinks it too dear at £35000.

In the evening, I made studies at little Massingham.

Friday Septr. 11th.

Mr. Carrs, we walked to this evening. — His nephew a young man of 17 is lately returned from France. — He was 3 years & a ½ at Rouen for education, and was not permitted to return before. — He suffered no particular inconvenience.

Saturday 12th.

Rode out this morning for the first time. Stadler sent me a proof print of Greenwich. Boydell does not choose to have him make up more than 400 of each plate for the 2d. Vol:

Troco, the game of, I played at this evening at Mr. Carrs. — A Ring of [blank] diameter, is fixed in the ground on a Swivel, so as to turn round when struck. — Four Bowls are played with, each Bowl 10 Inches diameter. These Bowls are pushed through the ring by an Iron ring fixed to the end of a Staff. The Ring [blank] diameter, the staff long. — Thus made

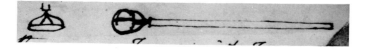

Eleven is the game. Two against Two, partners. If you pass your own or by driving it against any other force *that* through the ring you count one.

Sunday 13th.

Mr. Carr I rode out with this morning. — Kellett dined with us, and after Church drank tea. I walked with Susan to Little Massingham.

Monday 14th.

Rougham I rode to before dinner. — Mrs. Bligh called in the evening.

Tuesday 15th Septr.

Rode to Weasenham. — Mrs. Sparrow came. She & her husband are of the same age. 60. — Kellett drank tea.

Wednesday — 16th.

Mr. & Mrs. Mordaunt *called* on us.

High House dined at. Mr. Fountaine, Mr. A, & Miss Fountaine, —
Miss Ryley, — & Mr. & Mrs. Bailey dined there, — and young Randall.

Charles Fox & Mr. Coke were this day shooting at Castle acre. — Fox
killed 12 brace of partridges — is vehement in pursuit of game.

Thursday — 17th.

I returned from High House this morning. — Susan went with Mrs.
Hamond to Swaffham to see Mrs. Barrett but returned to Massingham in
the evening.

Mr. Carrs, I dined at. Miss Carr & Miss Pigg & the youngest Peckover
there.

Friday — 18th.

Miss Carr drank tea with us.

Saturday 19th.

Mr. Mordaunts I called at with Susan this morning. — Mrs. Mordaunt,
only at home. — Young Mordaunt is 19 years of age & is 6 feet, one Inch &
half high.

Sunday 20th.

Swaffham I went to at 8 this morning. — Bailey examined the root of a
large tooth on the surface of which a fungus flesh was growing. He
separated the flesh and then punched out the fangs of the tooth at two
separate efforts with great dexterity.

Mrs. Barret is declining fast. She may, Bailey says, live a week or a
fortnight, but it is probable she may die in a few Hours. — Mr. & Mrs.
Hamond & Sarah, returned from Stradset where they had passed the
night. — I went with Mrs. Hamond in the Chaise to High-House.

Mrs. Bewly I called on. She is near 70 years of age.

Sarah Hamond, is 15 years old, — Jane Bagge, 18 last July.

Mr. Hamond told me Mr. Case put the estates which He afterwards left
him by will, into his possession during his life, and Mr. Hamond paid him
as general tenant £1100 a year.

Mr. Lemon dined with us at High House. — In the evening I returned
to Massingham.

Miss Fountaine, on the subject of her complaint Bailey is to meet Dr.
Marshall of Lynn tomorrow morning at Narford. — Bailey is convinced
that Her cough &c are symptomatic only, & that an injury of the spinal
bones as described by Pott, is the cause. — She has another expressive
symptom, viz: a weakness & uncertainty in walking. — She is abt. 22 years
old.

Monday 21st.

Kellet dined with us.

Tuesday 22nd.

no company.

Wednesday 23d.

Mrs. R. Hamond and Mrs. S. Bagge dined with us & returned to Lynn in the evening. Mr. and Mrs. Bligh called.

Thursday 24th.

High House we dined at. Mr. Everitt, — Mr. & Mrs. Sharpin from Swaffham, dined there. returned to Massingham in the evening.

Arnold, the watchmaker, made a watch for Mr. Everitt which only varied from the regulator in four years two minutes, [32] seconds. — Mr. Everitt has been offered 300 guineas for it.

Rain, a slight mizzling for half an hour today.

Friday — Septr. 25th.

no company. — Studying effects.

Saturday — 26th.

no company — Studying effects.
    Rain a little.

Sunday 27th.

H. Hamond returned from London. — Kellett dined with us.

J. Boydell, a letter from yesterday proposing to come to Massingham Sunday next. I answered him by desire of H. Hamond that He cannot receive him in less than three weeks.

at Church — Mr. Kellett preached.

Monday — 28th.

No company.

Tuesday 29th.

Lynn, went to this morning with Susan & Horace. — dined at Mrs. R. Hamonds. — Went to tea at Mr. T. Bagges. Lord Walpole, Col. Astley there. — Went from there to the Ball, at the Town Hall, given by the new mayor, Mr. Everard. — Benj. Young, — Audley, — Mrs. Hogg, — Col. Walpole &c who I knew there. — Staid till one oClock. Went to Mrs. R. Hamonds with Mrs. S. Bagge.

Wednesday — 30th.

Mr. Lane, the Collector of Lynn, I had conversation with today. — Mr. S.

Bagge introduced us to each other. He is anxious for a son of his who is become deaf owing to a gathering behind one of his ears when He was 7 years old. — He has an inclination to drawing. — The Boy is now between 14 & 15 years old. I saw his drawing from Prints of Le Bruns passions. — Mr. Loyd, Master of the grammar school, has undertaken to give him some instruction in mathematicks, and I agreed with his father that it would be well for him to obtain as much as He could acquire in a year and a half of mathematical & classical knowledge. — I promised to send him some studies to copy when I got to town.

Mr. Everards I dined at. — The Company. Lord Walpole, Col. Walpole, Sir Martin Folkes, Col. Astley, Mr. Foster, Mr. Preston, Recorder, Mr. Wm, Bagge, Mr. Thos. Bagge, Mr. Hogg, Mr. Elsden, Mr. T. Elsden, H. Hamond, Major Everard, Revd. Mr. Everard, Mr. Scarlet Everard.

Mr. S. Bagges I supped at — Coln. Astley there, Susan & Mrs. Richd. Hamond & Mrs. Bagge.

OCTOBER 1795

Thursday — Octr. 1st.

Lynn I left and went to High House to dinner with Susan & H. Hamond. — Revd. Mr. Brett & Revd. Mr. Crowe there. In the evening returned to Massingham.

Friday Octr. 2d.

Mrs Barrett died this afternoon at 3 oClock. — aged 56.

General meeting at the Academy to determine the number of vacancies to be filled. — 3 out of 5 was the number fixed upon. — 9 for 3, 4 for 4, 2 for 1, 1 for 5.

Saturday 3rd.

at Home.

Much rain this evening. Council met at the academy on the Privy Purses letter.

Sunday 4th.

Much rain. The first we have had in any quantity since I left London.

Monday 5th.

Kellett dined with us.

Council adjourned at the academy from Saturday last to this evening on the subject of the Privy Seals letter upon retrenchments in the Academy expenses.

Tuesday 6th.

Dowsing came to Massingham. — H. Hamond went to Lytcham.

Smirke, a letter from relating what passed at the general meeting of the Academy, & the Council of Saturday last.

Wednesday 7th.

Smirke & G. Dance I wrote to on the subject of the Privy Purse letter & Sr.

Wm. Chambers conduct, — and on the subject of the approaching election.

Mr. Barnard, from Lytcham dined with us.

Thursday — Octr. 8th.

at home.

Friday 9th.

Mr. Barnard left us this morning.

Dance, I had a letter from with particulars of what passed at the Academy.

Saturday 10th.

Kellett dined with us.

Lady Folkes called on Susan.

Sunday — 11th.

Dance, I wrote to on the business of the Academy. — at Church. — Mr. Kellett preached.

Monday, 12th.

Council at the Academy.

Dowsing, reads to me, being confined by lameness. He has read Soame Jenyns., on revealed religion, and is now reading Paleys moral Philosophy. I have lately made extracts from various Books. I have been chiefly employed lately in finishing drawings for second Vol: of Rivers.

Tuesday, 13th.

H. Hamond at Lynn. — We passing our time in drawing — Dowsing reading Paley.

Wednesday 14.

Today as yesterday.

Mr. Carr supped with us. — He was at Petersburgh a few years since. There is a large & excellent Inn kept by a Scotchman [Joseph Fawell]. The Servants Calmuk Tartars who are chiefly preferred by the Russians as making better servants than their own people. The balance of trade is always considerably in favor of Russia against England owing to our importing such large quantities of Raw materials, — Iron, Hemp, &c &c. — The Empress was then making great exertions to establish manufactories in Her Dominions. — French is little spoken at Petersburgh. German much and many speak English.

Dance I had a letter from. On Monday night the Council confirmed the minutes demanding clearer accts. from Sir Wm. Chambers. — Dance proposed and carried a resolution that the Council do form itself into a permanent Committee of all its members to consider the papers presented by the Privy Purse.

Thursday — 15th.

J. Boydell, called this morning. He has been at Mr. Bartons, at Rougham, a few days.

Mr. Coke has bought Weasenham estate for £25,000.

Smirke, I had a letter from. — The Council have replied to Mr. Mathias, Deputy Privy Purse, acknowledging the rect. of his letter, and expressing surprise and concern at having a charge of such a kind brought against the members, — are certain it must have originated in misinformation, and declare their zeal at all times to promote the honor & interests of the Academy, and also to comply with his majestys most gracious commands. — A copy of this letter was inclosed to Sir Wm. Chambers, with a request that a new statement of his accounts might be made out conformable to a Plan proposed to him. — A permanent committee of the whole council is voted, to consider the papers recd. from Gabriel Mathias, — but no copies are to be made, from fear of the business being mentioned abroad to the disgrace of the Academy. — Loutherburgh & Zoffany have not yet attended the meetings and are ignorant of the Business. — The Members present were, Bacon, — Bourgeois, — Smirke, — Dance, West.

Friday — 16th.

Mr. Carr, called & invited me to meet Boydell to dinner tomorrow. — He told me Mr. Coke has 60,000 acres of land in the County of Norfolk, & mostly good land.

Saturday 17th.

Mr. Carr I dined with, — Boydell & His Son, — Mr. Stanforth, farmer from Little Massingham, — and young Barton there.

The Rougham Estate, which now produces £2400 a year was bought by a Mr. North, in the reign of Queen Ann for £8000.

Sunday — Octr. 18th.

At Church — Mr. Dowsing preached.

Mr. Henry Styleman called at noon.

J. Boydell & his son dined with us. — H. Hamond at Sandringham. — Dowsing at Rudham.

Northcote has painted a series of subjects the Progress of virtue & vice, — 10 pictures for which He asked Boydell 1000 guineas. — Boydell declined them as He said, on acct. of the times. — He recommended to Northcote to join with some engraver and share profit & loss with him as the only way of proceeding now. — Northcote talked of exhibiting them.

Monday — 19th.

To Houghton, I went this forenoon with Boydell & Dowsing. — I do not think the park has suffered in appearance from the cutting down of many trees. — We walked over the House. The pictures now there are

In the dining parlour
Theodore & Honoria from
Drydens Fables — by Fuseli.
Gypsy telling fortunes —
    Opie.
Birds — Reinagle.

Yellow drawing room
Chimney piece ⎫
Ariadne   ⎬ Cipriani
Birds — Reinagle
Bull, young girl —
Garrard & Opie.

Salon
Chimney piece — Empress
    of Russia —
AEdipus — Cipriani
Castor and Pollux — do.
Philoctetes in ⎱
Lemnos   ⎰ — do. |

Tapestry dressing room
Portraits of foreign
    figures

Blue Bedchamber
Lady — Sir Peter Lely

Cabinet
Chimney piece
Tydeus — Fuseli

Marble dining room
Two figures in plaister —
Locatelli, Mercury
            &
    a Boxer

Carlo Marat room
Chimney piece.
Rape of Orynthia — Cipriani
Birds — Reinagle
    do. — do.

State Bed Chamber
Puck &c. — Fuseli

I think the picture of the rape of Orynthia the best I have seen by Cipriani. — Opies Gipseys, is more neatly painted than in his present manner, but it has not so much force, and the shadows are purply cold. — The Theodore by Fuseli is not so well executed as the pictures He now paints. — I think the 2 figures by Locatelli are very indifferent.

Kings Head, Mrs. Kendals, we dined at, Mr. Mitchell with us. — It is 21 years since I met J. Boydell at Houghton. — Mrs. Kendal will be 50 years old in november. — Mitchell is 64.

Houghton has suffered, it is supposed from the Steps having been taken down in the front. In the Hall on each side the wall has cracked, in consequence of the building settling.

Tuesday October 20th.

H. Hamond went to London.

Wednesday 21st.

Susan & Dowsing went to Hillington to call on Lady Folkes. — I rode to High House to take leave. Mr. Hamond out, Mrs. H. gone to Swaffham. Killet dined with us.

Thursday 22d.

Wet weather — at home.

Friday 23d.

at home.

Saturday 24th.

H. Dowsing went to Barsham.

Mrs. & Miss Hamond called on us this forenoon & staid to dine & drink tea with us. — Mr. Hamond came from the meeting of justices at Hillington & also dined here.

Mr. Carr, called this morning to invite us to meet Mr. & Mrs. Campbell at dinner.

Sunday 25th.

Mr. Henley sent his chaise for us this morning and we went to Sandringham. Mr. Clarke of Chard was there.

Mr. Jenkins, of Rome, was born at Sidbury near Sidmouth in Devonshire. — His Brother was vicar of Sidbury & Rector of Upottery — Jenkins was apprentice to a Mr. Hake, a clothier, at Honiton, and absconded from his apprenticeship from dislike to the business. He has purchased property in the neighberoud of Sidmouth. The Sons of his Brother are supposed to be intended for his Heirs.

Madam Mara was born at Glastonbury or Wells, and was first taken notice of for her singing in the street at Wells, by the Bishop or Dean.

Judge Gould, Sir James Eyre, and Judge Burland, were all at Wells School at the same time, though there is some difference in their ages. — They are all Somersetshire men.

Lord Paulet, is a plain, good kind of man, much respected in Somersetshire. Hinton St. George is abt. 7 miles from Chard. — He has at least £12,000 a year. He married a daugr. of Sir George Pocock with whom He had £20,000.

Monday — Octr. 26th.

at Sandringham. — fine weather. The trees in the Park very little tinged with autumnal colours.

Tuesday — 27.

Sandringham we left at noon: Mrs. Henley brought us to Lynn, to Mrs. Richd. Hamonds. — at Dinner there, — Mr. Wm. Bagge & Mr. Lane, the collector.

Mr. Coke purchased the Warham estate for £57,750. — Sir Martin Folkes estate at *Hillington* is abt. £600 a year.

Lady Ann Townshend was married yesterday at Rainham to Mr. Hudson of Yorkshire. His estate is abt. £2300 a year.

At supper there were Mr. Everard, Miss Everard, Miss Sally Everard, Mr. Scarlett Everard, — Mr. T. Bagge, Miss Bagge, & Miss Jane Bagge, — & Mr. Thos. Bagge Junr.

Wednesday Octr. 28th.

Mr. Holland I met this morning. — He was obliged to leave France lately in consequence of not having been settled there before a certain period. — He superintended the farms of Monsr. Du Guerchy son to the Ambassador of that name. — The Marquis retains his property of 5 or 6000 a year. He was in prison sometime during Robespierres tyranny, but was released immediately after the death of that monster. — Mr. Holland says the People of France ardently wish for peace, and He is convinced, are satisfied, that the present government cannot last. They detest the Austrians &c but are much better inclined to the English than the English are to them.

The requisition of men was made in an absolute manner & no respect paid to rank, but as the bodies raised in each district had a power after they were raised to choose their own officers they frequently paid attention to quality or what had been esteemed so. — Many still gave the Marquiss his title when adressing him; and it was only here and there that a hot headed fellow expressed that violence which we in England have supposed to be general. — The great majority were calm but not satisfied.

Paris, when He had passed through it was very quiet; but everything of luxury, or appearance of trade, had vanished. Instead of streets crowded with carriages, and the palaces surrounded by coaches & gaiety, a stillness such as prevails in Lynn was observable. A few people were lounging in Coffee Houses; but no bustle.

Mr. Everards, time keeper watch, lost in 4 years 4 months, only 2 minutes, 32 seconds.

Mr. Lane, I called on, and shewed his son & Mr. Smith how to work with French chalk and white chalk. — I told Mr. Lane He shd. give all encouragement to his son by shewing his drawings to friends, & warm his mind towards the profession by putting books on painting and the lives of the painters into his hands. — The Boy was 15 years old in August. I told Mr. Lane that it would be well to give him the advantage of all the classical

& other improvement He could obtain in Lynn for a year & a half or two years to come, as He wd. hardly acquire it in another place. — That He might proceed in copying proper things in the mean time.

Mr. Thos. Bagges we dined at. — Col. & Mrs. Astley, Mr. R. Hamond & Mrs. Susan Bagge, — H. Hamond, — W. Bagge & Mr. Lane there.

at Eight went to the Assembly. Lady Folkes, & Miss, — Mr. & Mrs. Styleman, 2 Miss Martins &c &c. there and the Corps of Officers belonging to the East York Militia quartered here, — commanded by Col. Maister. — Left the Assembly at one oClock.

Mr. Lane told me today that since his son was deprived of his hearing He had never dreamed.

Thursday Octr. 29th.

Mr. Holland called on me this morning. He resided in France at Nanges, [Nangis] a town about the size of Swaffham. Many English prisoners were distributed in the Town and neighberoud; soldiers & sailors, and were quite at large, only obliged at stated times to attend roll call. Many of them were employed in such ways as they were able. Two young men Sons to Gloucester farmers worked under him in the farming business & they were all regularly paid. — There were also portuguese sailors. — The English sailors; and Horse soldiers; and Soldiers belonging to Marching Regiments behaved very well; but some of the guards, who were prisoners here behaved as ill: pilfering &c. &c. — This acct. corresponds with the complaint made of their conduct in Flanders when I was there.

The French are much improved in the practise of farming, since Mr. Holland first went into that country.

The change in the manners of the French since the revolution is very striking. That complaisance which was so general & habitual to them is no longer seen except in elderly people: but the young men, especially those who have been with the armies, are sour and rude in the adress: and the quaker like Thee & Thou is a common mode among them. The habitual gaiety for which they are distinguished has vanished with their former civility.

J. Boydell & his son came to Lynn, and dined at Mrs. R. Hamonds with us.

At three oClock I went in the Stage to Brandon, where Boydell joined me.

Friday — Octr. 30.

At ½ past 7 left Brandon, in the Swaffham Coach. — breakfasted at Newmarket, dined at Littleborough and got to Charlotte St. at a ½ past 10.

a Comb of wheat at Lynn is 4 bushells, Winchester measure. Eight bushells is a quarter.

Saturday 31st.

Dance I dined with. Tyler there — West has had a long conversation with the King on the subject of the Academy. He represented to His Majesty that the Annual dinner was of importance to the members as it gave them an opportunity of obliging persons of rank from whom they recd. favors, & that the dinner was very much an object with people of fashion. The King said He believed it must be continued. — West, further stated to the King that the accts. of the Academy were now regulated by Mr. Dance & Mr. Tyler and He understood it would appear that the income of the Academy, as it now averages, is adequate to the expences. — That till lately the Academy had never been in possession of a book of the Accounts; and that it was not till a book was delivered that the Council knew the extent of the obligation to His Majesty, who, it appeared, had paid £4791.8s.3¾d for the use of the Academy. — That Sir Wms. manner of stating the accts. was such as was not to be easily understood. —¿On all this the King expressed surprise; but observed that He had taken notice that in Sir Williams manner of keeping accounts there was always something obscure.

Smirke came to tea and we talked over the ensuing election of associates. — Gilpin certain, — and Shee, Downman & Soane, & Dupont considered likely to be supported. — It was thought on the whole best to vote for Gilpin, Shee & Soane. — The last year had the election taken place we shd. have supported Downman, Dupont & Soane, but in the last Exhibition the merit of Shee was allowed to be greater than that of the other two painters, which it was judged necessary to make the change as now proposed.

NOVEMBER 1795

Sunday Novr. 1st.

Hamilton called on me this morning. He told me Malton had promises of their votes from 17 Academicians, & appeared certain to carry the election against Soane if opposed to him. — I expressed the mortification I felt on the occasion, and my surprise that the Academicians could be induced to give Malton a preference to several who were on the list. Smirke came to us & we conversed on the means to be employed to prevent Malton succeeding. I suggested that the most becoming way would be for an Academician to call the attention of the members to the regulations of the Society by which Malton is excluded from being a Candidate as He is *only a draughtsman of buildings,* but no Architect. That Dance & Wyatt wd. certainly declare their opinion that Malton is not properly an Architect: which would put him out of the question — Smirke & Hamilton fully agreed that this would be the best way of proceeding and agreed to call on me in the evening, while, in the mean time I undertook to see Dance and send to Tyler.

Dance called on me, and on my mentioning the objection to Malton becoming a Candidate said the same had occurred to him & He proposed to make it.

Garvey called while Dance was here. He unites in the objection to Malton. He said He thought the votes wd. be indiscriminately given & the election uncertain, but thought there is still time to do something for the Candidates we approve.

Tyler & Dance drank tea with me. It was determined that Wyatt wd. be the proper person to move that Malton is not eligible as an Architect. — If He shd. not move it Tyler will.

Caleb Whiteford called on me this evening while they were with me. He brought a letter from J. Boydell recommending Charles Smith, Calebs nephew, to be an Associate. I told Whitefoord that I did not know how the votes were likely to go, that I hoped Gilpin is certain, and as to the others I should vote according to circumstances at the time. That there were 2 vacancies still open for the next year, and Mr. Smith [might] succeed then if He failed now. Dance & Tyler did not see Whitefoord.

Smirke called and we agreed to proceed as before mentioned. — Stothard told Smirke He wd. vote any way that was proposed to him.

I was at home all day.

Dance described Dublin to be one great stink. The Liffey runs through it. This river is about 70 feet broad, and before it reaches the city is a clear stream but it is so corrupted by filth of various sorts in its passage through the Metropolis as to become almost of the colour of pease porridge. — Dublin wants features to give it a stately appearance when viewed from a distance. No churches &c. of size to strike the eye. The Inns are dirty & disagreeable. In the Coffee Houses the difference of the manners of the poeple from those of England is strongly marked. Boisterous, noisy & un-ceremonious — The new custom house designed by Gandon is from its extent and quantity [blank]

Monday — Novr. 2d.

Dance called on me at 9 this morning and we went together to Wyatt, & stated the probability of Malton being elected, and his having no pretension to present himself to the Academy as an Architect. Wyatt agreed to support an opposition to his being considered a Candidate according to the prescribed rules of the Academy.

Dance called on Cosway & Bacon, both of whom promised to vote for Soane. He afterwards called on Copley who was doubtful, and upon Hoppner who promised him, as did Northcote.

I called with Dance on Wheatley, who promised for Soane & Downman.

Hamilton & Lawrence called on me. They are for Soane & Downman.

I called on Westall, who said He had promised Malton a vote, but would vote for Soane, if He did not oppose Malton, also for Downman.

Tylers I dined at. Dance & Smirke there. Between 6 & 7 Tyler & Smirke went to the Academy, and I & Dance went to Jacks Coffee House to take Wyatt to the Academy. He had dined there on arbitration business with Soane &c.

At the Academy present.

   Mr. West.

Wilton	— Dance	— Bartolozzi	— Tyler	— Catton
Zoffany	— Burch	— Cosway	— Barry	— Nollekens
Copley	— Bacon	— Loutherburgh	— Garvey	— Wyatt
Banks	— Farington	— Opie	— Northcote	— Russell
Hamilton	— Fuseli	— Yenn	— Wheatley	— Humphry
Smirke	— Bourgeois	— Stothard	— Lawrence	— Westall
Hoppner	— Richards	— Chambers	— Rigaud	— 2 Sandbys
				absent.

After the Minutes were read, Tyler rose & desired Richards to read the regulations for the election of Associates, which being done, Tyler said, in his opinion Mr. Malton did not stand qualified to be considered an Architect. — Wyatt supported Tyler and was violently opposed by Barry, & Fuseli said a little. Dance supported Tyler & Wyatt, and after much altercation Bacon proposed a motion which was seconded by Russell, "That the opinion of the Academy shd. be taken by Balot, whether Mr. Malton was eligible or not". — Barry resisted this and Copley moved the previous question, but the whole was got rid of by Bacon withdrawing his motion, as it was said the decision might affect Maltons welfare.

The balot for Associates then took place.

Candidates.

Painters	— Painters	— Sculptor
Thomas Walmsley	— Saml. Woodforde	— Charles Rossi
George Anthony Keenan	— Henry Spicer	—
Francis Towne	— Paul Barbier	—
John Downman	— Mather Brown	— Architects
Martin Shee	— R. Clevely	— John Soane
John Graham	— Charles Smith	— George Byfield
Daniel Brown	— Ant. Hickel	— Thomas Malton
Gainsborough Dupont	— Rich. Mart. Paye	—
Henry Bone	— J. T. Serres	— 28
John Landon	— Thomas Daniell	—
H Singleton	— T. Bonmaison	—
John Laporte	— Sawrey Gilpin	—

First Balot.

Gilpin 25 — Rossi 2 — Malton 2 — Daniell 1 — Bone 1 — Graham 1 — Smith 1.

Rossi & Malton having equal numbers Mr. West gave the casting vote for Rossi.

Gilpin — 27 ⎫
Rossi — 4 ⎭ 31

Second Balot.

Soane 14 — Smith 6 — Malton 4 — Dupont 3 — Rossi 3 — Downman 1 — Shee 1 — Woodforde 1

Soane — 17 ⎫
Smith — 12 ⎭ 29

Third Balot.

Downman 12, — Smith 6 — Dupont 5, — Shee 2, — Clevely 2, Malton 2, — Daniel. 1 — Rossi — 3.

Downman 23 ⎫
Smith — 7 ⎭ 30

Banks produced 2 Models for a Statue of Lord Cornwallis; one with his Robe on, the other with it laying behind him. No other candidate appeared. — To be decided which of the two shall be adopted on Decr. 10th. General Meeting.

Dance, Banks, & myself went to Soanes at 11 oClock when the meeting broke up but the family were in bed. — Banks went home with me for a little time. I asked him which of his models He preferred, He said *that with the robe on*. He says the blocks of marble which they work are brought from Leghorn. — He thinks for the execution of the model he shall require two years.

Gainsborough Dupont called on me this morning. I gave him no hopes of succeeding but told him it appeared to be very uncertain who wd. be chosen excepting Gilpin. He was very moderate in his expressions as to his claim and hopes.

Tuesday — Novr. 3d.

Downman I called on this morning and communicated to him that He was last night elected an Associate.

Mr. Abbot, the Exhibitor in Landscape, is a young man, nephew to Counsellor White of Exeter, and is likely to inherit an independent fortune from his uncle. — He had instructions from Towne. — He has lately made some beautiful studies on the Sea coast.

Dance called to inform me that Soane had been with him. Banks, by note, communicated to Soane his election.

Soane wrote to me this morning acknowledging his obligation to me for endeavouring to secure his election.

Tyler, I called on. Bartolozzi, Catton & Russell voted for Soane.

Wednesday 4th.

Soane called on me this morning to express his acknowledgements. He desires to invite many of the Academicians to dinner. I advised him not to invite a large body together but to take them at separate times. — recommended to him to let his dispute with Yenn pass of his mind. He said now the election was over, & it could not be supposed He had a particular interest in it, He wished to be on good terms with Yenn.

Lysons called on me, — and I went with him to the temple to look at his studies made in Gloucestershire.

Offleys I dined at. — Mr. Sealy there.

Thursday — Novr. 5th.

Dance called and we settled the names for Soanes first dinner.

Offleys I dined at. no Company.

Friday — 6th.

D. Bell, called on me this morning.

Mr. Steevens I met at the Shakespeare gallery. — He is not at liberty to communicate what He knows on the subject, but He is satisfied Sheridan has taken himself in, in the matter of Irelands pretended discovered play of Shakespeare. — not meaning that Sheridan believes it to be genuine.

Royal Academy Club I dined at, the first day of the season. — Westall told me some curious circumstances of Irelands manoeuvres, — O C P for Oliver Cromwell, — Of the Plays &c being claimed by him as belonging to him by descent — Globe Play House — Blackfryars.

Sir Francis Bourgeois told me Desenfans will soon have a finer collection of pictures than any he ever possessed.

Westall told me John Carr has called on him & says the Bank to which Hodges belongs is likely to answer well. Hodges is the acting partner, and rides four miles every day from his residence to the Banking House at Dartmouth.

Saturday 7th.

Caleb Whiteforde, at the Shakespeare gallery spoke to J. Boydell & me, abt. the last election at the Academy. — He said He concluded because I did not refuse to vote for Smith, He was to reckon on my vote for him. — I replyed that He came upon me unexpectedly, & that when I had read Mr. Boydells letter, I felt a desire to be as civil to him as I could; that I had not given him any reason to expect my vote; that I did not then know how I sld. vote, excepting for Gilpin. — and that I could not in truth say I would not vote for Mr. Smith, as, had He come against a candidate who was supposed to have much interest (*meaning Malton*) I should have voted for Smith. Some warm conversation took place which ended in an amicable manner. — He said He did not understand that Humphry voted for Smith. I declared that Humphry said He meant to vote for him & as far as I cd. recollect, mentioned to me that He had voted for him. — I told Whiteforde that if Smith looked towards the Academy it wd. be prudent if He wd. exhibit more, for *that* is the true way to make an impression on the minds of the members. — In the course of this conversation He said that had I told him when He called on me that I cd. not vote for Smith, He should have advised him to wave his expectations till another opportunity offered. I told him mine was a single vote and how cd. He rest so much upon it. He replyed that it was reckoned that I had many friends in the Academy with whom I had influence. — I mentioned that Dance had used his influence for Soane as it was very natural He should. — Whiteforde thought the election of Soane very proper. — On the whole in this matter I soon recollected myself, and endeavoured to be as candid and open as the occasion required. — Perhaps I was too open.

Humphry I called on, & He dined with me. — He affirmed the truth of what I said of his having voted for Smith. — He voted for him on the 2d. balot against Downman.

Murphy, was mentioned to me by Humphry as a proper person to succeed Boswell, as secretary for foreign correspondence. — Humphry has proposed it to Murphy who expressed the satisfaction He shd. have in obtaining such an appointment. — At the Club, on Friday, Humphry mentioned it to West, who was rather cold upon it; and said the King did not much approve these appointments, and thought the Academicians had better keep to themselves.

Sunday — 8th.

at Church. — Mr. Mathews preached.

Dance I called on. — John Hardman, first said He could not give any portion with his daughter to Mr. Smith, as his money was locked up: but has now agreed to give £200 a year for five years, and to consider her as a child at his death. — Smith has £500 a year and his mother will do something, so that they will have an income of £800.

Tresham has told Dance that Barry has recommended to Malton to bring an action against Dance & Tyler for declaring him not to be an architect.

Offleys I dined at. — Minet there. — Dr. & Mrs. Huet to tea & evening.

Minet told me that Mr. Angerstein is a natural son of Mr. Thomson a Russia merchant.

Thelussons father was a Clerk in the House of Barroneaus father who had another partner.

Monday Novr. 9th.

Sir George Beaumont came to town today and called upon me, and I dined with him & Hearne at Woods Coffee House.

Sir George passed three days with the Revd. Mr. Gilpin at Boldre in the new forest in August along with Sawrey Gilpin.

The whole profits arising from the sale of his publications of Tours down the Wye &c &c He has given to support a charity school which He established in the neighberoud. — This, He considers as a conscientious justification for having devoted part of his time to such amusements. — It appears that the lower orders of people in his neighberoud are much more civilized since He lived among them. — The profits of his publications amounted to more than £2000. In his drawings He aims to produce striking general effects, but has no power of imitating particular objects, and was surprised to see Sir George make a sketch of part of the Isle of Wight with accuracy, as it appeared to him a matter of great difficulty.

The new forest affords very little for the lover of Landscape scenery. — Sir George & Hearne agreed in this.

Tuesday Novr. 10.

G. Dance I dined with. Jack Hardman — Smith, & Soane there.

Harry is elected Borough rieve of Manchester. — Miers & [blank] Con-
tables.

Wednesday 11th.

Batty directed me to apply Goulards preparation for an inflammation in
my eye.

Sir George Beaumont called on me. — The motion for first reading the
Bill to prevent seditious proceedings passed the House of Commons last
night by a majority of 214 to 43. — The House broke up at 10 o'Clock. A
all of the House moved and carried by Fox. — Sir George thinks the
bill a strong measure but believes it to be necessary.

The personal deportment of Pitt is dry & rejecting, and this manner
seems to grow upon him.

Sir George acknowledges that attendance on the debates becomes
tedious, with little entertainment; as after a while you are prepared to
expect much of what each of the speakers will say.

C. Offley & John dined with me. Charles had been to the Shakespeare
Tavern to meet the Whig Club on the subject of the Sedition Bill. About
100 Members attended. The Duke of Bedford attended and was voted into
the Chair. Fox, Sheridan, Grey, Erskine, Mingay, Duke of Norfolk, Lord
Lansdowne, &c &c were there. — Certain resolutions were passed. The
Duke of Norfolk proposed to remark on the evil tendency of Thelwals
mode of proceeding. This was overruled by Lord Lansdowne & Erskine as
being improper to interfere in what related to other meetings. — A general
meeting of the people of Westminster is to be held in Palace yard.

Thursday 12th.

J. Boydell called. — There seem to be doubts in the minds of friends of
government of the safety of that part of the Sedition Bill which relates to
private houses.

Dance, drank tea with me. He had dined with Mr. Powis at the Chap-
lains table. — Bond, the Bow St. Magistrate, was there: He [said] that
government has used such precautions He has no fear from the attempts of
any designing persons to resist the Sedition Bill.

Boyle the publisher of Reymsdycks lectures called on me today. — The
Lectures were in the hands of Sir Joshua Reynolds who marked with red
Ink particular passages. — Since that West has had them, and encouraged
Boyle to publish them.

Friday Novr. 13th.

Sir George Beaumont, and we went to Daniell & saw two pictures by
Wilson belonging to Captn. Cowper. — Sir George was going out of Town
to Dunmow yesterday, but on seeing the multitude assembled at Copenhagen House returned to town.

Marchant came in the evening. — He says the last election of the Academy does not seem to be satisfactory. Copley told him before the election that He wd. oppose the election of an Architect. He thought them useless members, and that there ought not be more than two in the Society. — Copleys Son has lately obtained an appointment of £100 a year & rooms for *three years* at Cambridge. He is gone to America and returns next Summer. — It is understood that Copley would go to America but He told Marchant Mrs. Copley will not.

Saturday 14th.

Daniell called to see my pictures by Wilson.

C. Offley called & bought the picture by Wilson of the tomb of Horatii & Curatii.

Lindoe, called. — Mr. Barclay his uncle has proposed to him to sell & make over for an annuity, the business which He does for the Thrales brewery house; He will then be at liberty to pursue his studies in painting uninterruptedly.

Soanes I dined at. His first dinner to the Members of the Academy on his election. — West, — Tyler, Dance, Banks, Humphry, Hoppner & Wilton there. — Mrs. Soane & Miss Archibald, daughter of Major Archibald of the Marines there.

Banks informed us that Durno died at Rome 5 or 6 weeks ago of a malignant fever after three weeks illness. Durno was the Son of Mr. Durno who possessed the Sun Brewhouse at Kensington Gravel pits. He was pupil to the Chevalier Casali; studied for sometime at the Duke of Richmonds gallery in the year 1764. Afterwards was occasionally employed by Mr. West; and was with Mortimer & Wheatley employed at Lord Melbournes at Brocket Hall, in the year 1771. — Went to Italy in [1774]. He was about 50 years old.

Banks told us that He (Banks) was born at a house on Kennington Common. His Father was afterwards Gardener to the Duke of Beaufort at Badminton. — Linley, the musician, (father to Mrs. Sheridan) was the son of a Carpenter who worked at Badminton for the Duke. — Linley learned music under Mr. Chilcot, a musician of some eminence at Bath.

Notwithstanding the critical state of political questions on the *Sedition Bill,* We had no conversation on Political subjects.

Mr. West told us that a great change had taken place in the deportment of the Duke of York since He returned from Germany. — Before He went there His hauteur was excessive. His behaviour to the Duchess inattentive. — He is now the reverse: To the Duchess invariably attentive; and to others gracious & accessible. — West observed that adversity (his disappointments on publick service abroad) has probably worked this change and He believes the Duke to possess a good understanding; superior to that of the Prince.

13. James Gillray. *Copenhagen House.* 16 November 1795, hand-coloured etching. The British Museum, London.

14. James Gillray. *The Westminster Mountebank or Palace Yard Pranks.* 20 November 1795, hand-coloured etching. The British Museum, London.

Wilton promised me tonight that He wd. communicate to me such anecdotes as He knew of the artists of his time, particularly while He was in
Italy, whither He went in 1747.

Mrs. Soane told me that having only two Sons of her own & no girls, she
wd. willingly have taken a little girl of Mrs. Playfairs to educate; that she
had hinted as far as she could such a proposal, but Mrs. Playfair expressed
herself in such a way that she cd. not proceed.

We staid at Soanes till past Eleven.

Hoppner has been at Mr. Lascelles at Harewood House in Yorkshire.
Lord Harewood left Mr. Lascelles £30,000 a year and £200,000 in money.
— Hoppner says they are very good people. — He went with young Mr.
Lascelles, who has a taste for the arts, & has practised a little, several
excursions to see remarkable places.

Bolton Bridge, is a very picturesque spot.

Hoppner afterwards went to Durham & to Sir Henry Vanes where he
painted a whole length of Sir Henry, & a Horse, in a fortnight. — Durham
He was so charmed with that He resolved at the time to carry Mrs.
Hoppner there & reside a while & make sketches.

Hoppner speaks very well of Shee, who He says is a young man of good
understanding and gentlemanlike spirit; — and He thinks will advance in
the profession.

Sunday Novr. 15th.

Having had a cold in my eyes I did not go to Church today. I walked in
Hyde park with C & Wm. Offley and dined in Ormond St. — The day a
little frosty but very fine weather.

The Counting House has been removed from Ormond Street to the
City, and I could not forbear in conversation expressing an opinion
against the removal.

Mrs. Hewit & Miss Bulmer came to tea.

Monday 16th.

The Whig Club having given notice that the sense of the inhabitants of
Westminster would be taken at a publick meeting to be held this day in
Westminster Hall, at 10 oClock I went to the Shakespeare gallery and was
informed that Josiah Boydell & Nicol, who had undertaken with many
other respectable inhabitants to act as special constables to prevent riots,
were gone to Westminster Hall. I immediately proceeded thither and
found many persons assembled in the Hall & in New Palace Yard. On one
side of the Hall an Hustings was erected for the speakers. — a little after
Eleven General Tarlton came on the Hustings and having requested the
attention of the people, stated, that the Lord Chancellor had informed
His, the General's, friends that as the Courts of Law were then sitting, no
meeting could be held in Westminster Hall without great interruption of
publick business. That on that account the Hustings would be removed to

New Palace Yard, and the opinion of the people taken in that place. He concluded by exhorting them to observe a peaceable conduct, and retired with much applause. — I met Thackeray of St. James's St. who also attended as a special constable. Also Boydell & Nicol each of them having a small staff of Authority in his pocket. — In going out of the Hall, I met Banks, & Smirke & His Son, who I joined, telling them as they were Crops (Hair cut short) and Democrats, I should be safe under their protection. The Hustings was now raised immediately before the Kings Arms Tavern, in Palace Yard. In direction of which business Obrien was very active. At a window of the Tavern appeared the Duke of Bedford, Fox, Lord Lauderdale, Lord Derby, Grey, Whitbread, Sturt, &c. &c. — We took our station immediately opposite the Hustings. — A little after 12 the Hustings being prepared. The Duke of Bedford &c. came upon it. Much hallooing & clapping on their appearance. The Duke was dressed in a Blue Coat & Buff waistcoat with a round Hat. His Hair cropped and without powder. — Fox also cropped, and without powder, His Hair grisly grey. — Fox first came forward to speak, Sheridan on his right hand and Tierney on his left. The Duke of Bedford immediately behind him. — The Hustings was much crowded. Lord Hood was there, as was Lord Belgrave, and many friends of government. — After much acclamation Fox adressed the multitude stating the loss of the liberties of the people, if the Bill passed, and calling upon them to come forward and support a Petition to the House of Commons against it. He did not speak more than a quarter of an Hour, and paused for claps at set periods, which He recd. abundantly. — The Duke of Bedford next came forward and adressed the people much to the same effect. He spoke rather longer than Fox and was much applauded. He hinted that if Petitions failed the people must have recourse to other means. In the beginning of his Speech He spoke fluently but as He proceeded was occasionally a little at a loss and had recourse to his Handkerchief, to cover his hesitation. His voice is good and his delivery distinct. — Next Grey came forward and read the resolutions and made a short speech with volubility and a strong clear voice. — Lord Hood at this time stood on the left hand of Grey, and Sheridan on his right hand. Lord Hood then adressed the people in a low tone of voice. He observed that the present meeting could not be considered as consisting of the inhabitants of Westminster, and that it could only be had at meetings of parishioners, and He protested against it. — I could hear little of what He did say. He spoke for a short time only; and was followed instantly by Sheridan who had expressed great watchfulness and animation in his looks while Lord Hood was speaking. — He remarked that the noble Lord was only for taking the sense of the people of Westminster by a *Scrutiny*. He ridiculed, and was playful in this way on different passages of his speech, and entertained and extracted applause by many pointed hits against ministers & measures. He said the people of Westminster would suffer more by the bill than any other description of people would do, as the Magistrates who must be called on to attend all publick meetings, and judge of the propriety of what might be said, were in this district particularly appointed by Ministers and would be removeable at pleasure, therefore might always be expected to act always with a particular view to the ministers intentions. — Fox came forward again, and after speaking a little called upon the people to signify by holding up hands their assent or dissent to the petition, which He read and after each article appealed to them when a very general shew of hands of those who were stationed in the front and for some way on each side of the Hustings appeared. — Having quitted my first station on acct. of the pressure of the crowd & the heat, I now viewed the general appearance of the multitude from the terrace pavement before the Houses. — I expected more people would have assembled on this occasion. At least a third of the Palace Yard was empty or thinly scattered. — and where it was much crowded but at some distance from the Hustings, the people seemed to be merely Spectators, and took no interest in what was passing by clapping or hissing. — Indeed there was only one attempt at hissing, when Lord Hood first came forward, and Sheridan &c made strong motions to prevent it and succeeded. — Several of Pitts friends, members of Parliament, were in groups, conversing, where there was no crowding. — Canning, Lord Gower, Smith of the Treasury, — &c &c.

Lord Lauderdale after the petition had been approved, for I did not mark any dissentients, spoke a little, and Lord Mountmorris closed the list of speakers, a little before 2 oClock. I passed through the Alley of the Kings Arms and seeing some tables carried followed them. They were placed at the end of palace yard, and large rolls of parchment, with the petition drawn out on each, were laid down and many Ink stands placed. Obrien was at one table. The people were now called on to sign, but they gazed at the parchments as if they had nothing to do with them. A few low fellows in shabby dresses began to put their names down, while the officiating persons were calling upon others after the manner in which the populace at a fair are encouraged to purchase wares. — without the least disturbance or injury offered that I perceived, the people began to quit the place in droves, apparently having come there as Spectators. I saw, except in two or three single instances, no agitation or heard any expressions of discontent. One man hoisted up a Halfpenny loaf upon a stick but for a minute only.

I met Coxe, the Attorney, — and soon after Lawrence & Hamilton, who came too late for the exhibition. — We went together to Comyns the picture cleaner, Lawrence having been told by Sir George Beaumont that an extraordinary picture of Hogarth is there. It proved to be the whole length of Captain Coram, belonging to the Foundling Hospital. While we were at Comyns a great noise in the street caused us to go to the window, from whence we saw Fox in the middle of the street with Sheridan on one hand, and Tierney on the other: The Duke of Bedford & Grey close behind; rolling along, I may say, among a crowd of low people and black-guards, who filled the street, & huzza'd manfully. — The whole scene was such as when a drunken fellow is supported along, in the midst of an en-couraging mob.

From Comyns, where we found Garvey & Marchant, we went to the Shakespeare Gallery. Lord Pomfret was there conversing with J. Boydell Nicol, Downman &c. I came home to dinner pretty well tired, with the exer-tion of the day: but well satisfied from what I observed of the appearance of the people, that their minds are not in a state to create an alarm for the publick peace, and that the Bill may be passed with safety.

I communicated to a friend or two as my opinion, that it might have been more prudent to have proposed the Bill for a few years only, and not to extend it to the life of the King, and a Sessions beyond. — I do not think they concurred with me, but thought it wd. be renewing the difficulty each time it might be proposed if made *annual* or for a few years.

Bell, — Tyler — & Dr. Breedon called today.

Tuesday Novr. 17.

Westall I called on who lent me some Academy figures for Young Lane to draw from. — He told me West had in concert with Trumbull obtained some valuable pictures at low prices from France. — Trumbull went to France as an American, and carrying gold with him exchanged it for Assignats with which He purchased the pictures at comparatively very low prices, owing to the depreciation of the Assignats. — This cargo of pictures was in danger of being lost owing to a barge in which the Cases were striking against a pier of London Bridge.

Lindoe came today and recommenced his studies. He brought some drawings which shewed he is much improved since he first came here to study.

Wednesday 18th.

Offleys I dined at. — Mr. Wombwell a mercht., Brother to the late Sir George Wombwell, and Alderman Carlton of Dublin there.

Mr. Wombwell said the Porter Brewing business had been a losing trade for some years. That for several years together the House of Calvert had cleared £25,000 a year, but when it was considered that they employed a capital of £200,000, it proved that they only made twelve and a half per cent for their money. — He said that no article could with more justice be taxed than porter it bearing the same price now when Hops are at £4 that it did when the same quantity was sold for 30 shillings. But the apprehension of Government abt. proposing a Tax on this article was on acct. of its particularly affecting the populace of the Metropolis, as it is computed 5,8ths. of the consumption is within the Bills of mortality. So it is likely to remain untouched till some favourable period of ministerial popularity, or national success. — It is calculated that a halfpenny laid on each pot would produce upwards of £600,000 a year.

Mr. Wombwell resided 14 years in Spain. The people of Catalonia, of which Barcelona is the chief Town, are industrious and in a considerable degree flourishing: quite the reverse is the case in many other provinces. In Catalonia, English & American wheat is preferred as it makes white & delicate bread; but in other parts where the people are little employed & consequently poor much Sicilian Wheat is used which makes a hard & dry, flinty, kind of bread but goes farther.

Alderman Carlton said Ireland is very quiet at present, and is making rapid advances in commerce. The Lord Lieutenant is popular.

Minet was married last Friday to Miss Barker, daughter to Mrs. Barker who keeps Wills Coffee House, Cornhill, where He lodged. She has 6 or £700 to her fortune. — She is abt. 29 years old. He near 30.

Thursday Novr. 19th.

Offleys I dined at, no company. Charles Offley desired me to paint a picture for him as a companion to the Tomb of Horatii by Wilson: to be finished by March 25th. next.

Friday Novr. 20th.

Academy Club I dined at. — Nineteen Members present. A Social day, and much merriment from Nollekens conversation, at our end of the table. Bourgeois told me that the eldest Miss Boswell who died lately fell a sacrifice to her grief for the loss of Her Father. — The eldest Son is now abroad on his travels, He is at present at Leipsick.

Richards & Nollekens related to me some remarkable instances of the avaritious & narrow mind of Newton our former Secretary. — When He was in possession of £150,000 having attended a general meeting at the Royal Academy, He called on Richards afterwards for his allowance of five shillings; and the day following, He called again upon him to exchange one of the shillings which He said was a bad one.

Nollekens was pupil to Scheemaker. Banks was under Scheemaker, but had been before apprentice to [William Barlow] a carver in wood.

Notwithstanding the critical situation of publick affairs, and the question which agitates the publick mind, politicks were never touched upon as a topick of conversation.

Came home in Cosways Coach with Tyler & Downman.

Saturday 21st.

I have been employed the whole of this week in arranging my Letters, & papers of all kinds, which have been scattered abt. for years, and consequently they have been useless to me, as I knew not in what place to find any letter or paper which I may have had occasion to refer to. This task of assorting and methodizing them I have from time to time proposed but never had resolution to persevere in the undertaking before. — On reviewing the letters I have recd., commencing in my early youth, the retrospect of my life has been presented to me in a stronger point of view than I ever before felt it. — — From the impression made on my mind I shall think it a duty to recommend to others to preserve much of their correspondence with relations & friends; by which they will be reminded, at advanced periods of life, of many duties; and of former obligations; which may recal attention to some, & renew affection for others.

Mr. Pepyss I called on to ask his opinion abt. a Summons I have recd. to attend at Clerkenwell; He could give me no answer, but told me He would enquire what I had best do.

C. Offley passed the morning in looking over my portfolios, Sketches & Books. — I afterwards dined in Ormond St. — Minet, & Mr. Bush, the Attorney there. — Mr. Bush had been this morning to Hackney, where the Freeholders of Middlesex had been called upon to assemble for the purpose of considering the Bills on Sedition. — The Dukes of Bedford & Norfolk & many others were there. Skinner spoke & was applauded more than any other. — There might be 3000 people & upwards. The Petition against the Bills was carried almost unanimously.

We had much political conversation. Bush & C. Offley strongly opposing their opinions against the Bills.

C. Offley lent me two letters his late Uncle Mr. Nutthall the Solicitor to the Treasury and who was Deputy Ranger of Enfield Chase, by Mr. Pitt in the year 1763 before he was created the Earl of Chatham. — The following are copies.

Hayes, July 3rd. 176.

Dear Nutthall,
I returned from Stow on Thursday, and hope I am in time to catch you before any of your jaunts begin. The business I have to trouble you with is the sale of my House at Bath, which I wish to finish without loss of time. as the matter lies in a narrow compass I shall be obliged to you if you will despatch the necessary writings, and fix a time for the execution of them. I am sorry you have had any trouble about the respectable black personage*, who was sent back to your House. His merits are certainly not inconsiderable but He seems more fitted for the rougher sports of a chace than for the gentle occupations of a nursery. Lady Chatham desires Her Compliments and I am always, Dear Nuthall
Your faithful humble servan
W. Pitt.

*Supposed to be a black dog.

Sunday morning.

Dear Nuthall

A man who is mistaken in his reckoning only one half can not be said to be quite out. two hundred instead of one is a small difference, besides ploughing of fallows, dunging &c. but be the worth of the thing as it may, circumstanced as I am, I must agree to Ashby's terms: I therefore desire you will finally settle the matter with him, the sooner the better, and fix him by articles, lest his Improvements *in buckeram* shou'd grow upon us. if you can come down to Hayes Tuesday or Wednesday we may conclude, sign & seal. I know you too well to reccomend dispatch to your natural Celerity in Execution: I have some of that temper, and shall be doubly obliged to you, if you will give wings to that Snail-paced Thing call'd Business. At all Events, Dinner, and a sincere welcome waits you at Hayes. I am always, Dear Nuthall, most faithfully, yrs. W. Pitt.

Sunday — Novr. 22d. — 1795.

At Church. — A prayer of thanksgiving for the Kings escape when assaulted on his way to the Parliament House, was read after the Litany. The congregation listened with profound attention. — Mr. Mathews preached 15 minutes. His text "Felix troubled".

Sir George Beaumont called on me at noon. We talked of the agitation of the publick mind on the Sedition Bill. He said He had just seen Mr. Price of Foxley, who had been with Fox, who means to exert himself tomorrow night in the House of Commons on the Bill brought down from the Lords. — I told Sir George there appeared to those I conversed with something very objectionable the continuing the Sedition Bill during the Kings life. That extending it so far removed from Ministers the difficulty of again contending the question; but I thought as far as it immediately related to the King it was ill judged. It seemed to be putting the Kings life at issue with the constitution, in the opinion of those who are alarmed at any thing which seems like an attack on the latter. — Sir George thought it likely, from the opposition made to the Bill, that it would be more limited in its duration, than as first proposed.

at home alone this eving.

Monday Novr. 23d.

Smirke applied to me today for an account of Rossi who thinks Soane may probably have it in his power to give him some employ. Rossi at present receives wages employed or not from some persons by engagement, and as He is *unemployed,* feels for them, and wishes to relieve them. — I told Smirke we cd. apply to Soane through Dance, as well as personally.

Stadler was with me in the evening, and gave me a brief acct. of his progress through life as an artist. — Also some acct. of Schutz & Manskerch who are employed under him.

The Tower & Park guns were fired today on acct. of taking the Cape of Good Hope.

Tuesday 24th.

Mr. Hamond of High-House called this morning. He has been in town since Saturday and came on acct. of Philip having a return of a complaint in his head. Dr. Higgins has been again consulted, and recommends that He should be taken into the Country and be unrestrained by any tasks &c.

Mr. Hamond has called on Mr. Wm. Barrett since he came to town. Mr. Barrett says Oken was sold by his Son to Mansell for much less than its value. Mr. Barrett wd. have been glad to have purchased it from his son had he known his intention to dispose of it.

Sir George Beaumont called on me. The House of Commons sat till 2 o'Clock this morning. On the subject of Reeves's pamphlet, and on the Sedition Bill, the altercation was more violent & disagreeable than any He remembers. Wyndham is so warm, that He did & frequently does commit himself by unguarded expressions, & Fox went such lengths as to be content [constrained?] to explain his meaning. Sheridan joked Lord Belgrave on his Greek. — Wilberforce made an excellent reply to Grey, pointing out how clearly his expressions made it appear, that personality to the Minister, & not the good of his Country, swayed him. Sir George seems not to wish to be in another parliament.

1794
Dinners. —

Dec. 26. —
Mr. & Mrs. Hamilton
Mr. & Mrs. Wheatley. —
Batty — Tyler, —
Lawrence. —
in all 10. —
Total expence £2-9-10½
wine included
3 port ⎱
4 sherry ⎰ 17s.

Decr. 28th.
Messrs. Daniels,
Smirke, Batty,
Marchant, —
in all 8 —
Total expence £1-8-2½
wine included
3 port ⎱
1 sherry ⎰ 15s.
1 lisbon ⎰

1795.
January 3rd.
Mrs. Offley, —
Mr. & Mrs. Salusbury
John & Wm. Offley
and Carey
In all 9
Total expence £1-10-7
wine included
5 Port 0-11-0
1 lisbon
½ Bottle of 0- 2-4
Dutchmans 0-13-4

January 4th —
Mr. Baker
Hearne —
Edwards —
Humphry.
Total expence   £0. 18. 6½
wine included
wine
5 Port   0-11-0
pint white   0- 1-2
                0–12–2

Above   £ s. d.
4 dinners   6-7-2½

Jany. 12th.
G. Dance
Baker
Hearne
Charles West
in all 7 —
Total expence — £2-14-4½
wine included
4 port   s.d.
1 white   8-8

Jany 27th. —
Mr. & Mrs.
Molyneux
Mr. Carey
in all 5
Total expence £0-11-0
wine included
2 Port 0-3-6

June 21st
Baker
Hearne
Marchi
in all 4
Total expence £0-10-0
wine included
3 Port

June 26th.
Mr. Berwick
G. Dance —
Lysons —
Smirke —
Total expence £1-5-9
wine included
3 port —   0-6-6
pint white — 0-1-3
              0-7-9

July 25th.
C. Offley
Wm. Offley
Minet
Bob —
Total expence £0-18-10
wine included
Port
3 bottles   0-6-6

Wednesday, November 25th.

G. Dance I called on this morning. George Webb [Dance] has informed him by the last Ships from India, that He is happily settled at [blank] somewhere in the neígberoud of Benares, with a Mr. Russell a gentleman much respected. George flatters himself that in abt. 12 years he shall be provided with a sufficiency to return to England and pass his life comfortably.

Smith has been very zealous at the meeting in Surrey to oppose the Sedition bills; by this conduct he causes great uneasiness to his friends; and his political feelings seemed to have smothered those tender affections which in his present situation might be supposed to exclude all others.

I asked Dance what he could learn in the City among his numerous friends of the opinion prevailing there of the Sedition Bills. He declared that every respectable man with whom He is acquainted is decided in favor of the Bill. There are some persons of respectability who He is informed oppose the Bill; but these may justly be considered party Men, avowed Foxites on all occasions.

Lysons dined with me. He says many of the Lawyers consider the Bills as unnecessary and blame ministers for not having put the existing laws in execution on such occasions as seemed to demand them.

Lysons was much with General O'Hara at Cheltenham, and heard him describe his condition while in France. At Lyons they obliged him to remain near a guillotine while abt. 40 persons were executed, most of them Woemen; & some girls, not more than 15 years of age. — When His Conductors brought him to Paris, they carried him through many streets, to expose him to the publick; who expressed an abhorrence of him, by opprobrious language. — He was confined in the Luxembourgh prison, with abt. 3000 more persons. In a small room the General, his two Servants & Surgeon; a Drummer taken prisoner with him; a Spanish officer & servant, a German officer, and two others, were inclosed. The hardships they suffered during the tyranny of Robespierre, were very great. All weapons, even knives & forks, were taken from them; and the meat, which was brought for their subsistence, was already cut. It consisted of the offals of the market; like Dogs meat; and they were led out at stated hours, to feed together in droves; like cattle; the meat being deposited in troughs. — While the reign of Robespierres tyranny lasted, a certain number of persons were taken from this and other prisons daily; and executed; to keep up the publick apprehension. It was additionally shocking to see the careless manner in which the selection of those doomed for execution was made. If one of the name called was not found, one of a name, similar in sound, was taken, to make up the number; and bid to *march* with the rest. The General said it was astonishing with what fortitude, almost amounting to indifference, this terrible fate was borne; by the woemen, as well as the men. They spoke of it as some thing not to be avoided, and that must be submitted to.

A Lady, [Françoise-Thérèse, wife of Prince Joseph of Monaco] young, and handsome, and who appeared only to have been accused on acct. of her possessing a considerable fortune, was reported by the Publick Accuser [Fouquier-Tinville] and of course condemned. At this critical moment she pleaded pregnancy, and was remanded to prison; where she made up dispatches for some of her friends, and cutting off Her hair, which was remarkably fine, divided it into parts, and sent it with the dispatches. After this she wrote to the Publick Accuser declaring that she was not pregnant, & upbraided him with his wickedness in the strongest terms; and defied him. — Stung, and enraged by these reproaches, the Publick accuser ordered her to immediate execution; and also directed that nine other woemen, who were really pregnant, and in prison, should be executed with her, which was accordingly done. — This monster after the death of Robespierre, was himself tried and executed.

After the death of Robespierre, General O'Hara was allowed the indulgence of walking in Paris, but a person, as his guard, was appointed always to attend him.

Articles of accusation were preferred against the General and He was threatened to be tried before the Publick Tribunal; not as a Soldier, but for having proclaimed Louis 17th. at Toulon, and other crimes. The General brought a copy of the accusations to England. The death of Robespierre put a stop to this intention.

It was computed that 500,000 persons had been destroyed in France, by the Guillotine, shooting, drowning &c; exclusive of what had fallen in a military capacity. — At Nantes 3000 persons were put to death; and the execution of the Guilotine being too slow, they were actually cut down in ranks by chain shot. — It was common for the men and woemen to be tied naked together and then to be thrown in the River of that place.

The General had no opinion of any attempt on the French coasts being likely to produce a material effect. He foretold that the Quiberon scheme wd. not answer.

Lysons said an Officer who had been on board a Ship with Count d'Artois, related to them, that the Count seemed not to expect much from these attempts, and in conversation remarked upon the impolicy of many passages in his Brother, (the present Kings) proclamation to the poeple of France.

General O'Hara appears to be not more than 54 or 5 years of age.

The Play of Vortigern is certainly to be brought forward after Christmas. It seems there are some passages, or scenes, of an obscene kind, which it has been necessary to alter, for representation. Sheridan was too idle to undertake the task; others were proposed to do it; at last it was left to Ireland to cook it up in such a way as He could. Lysons hears the Play was not divided into Acts, & scenes, regularly, this has been part of the necessary task also. — He is told that it is a flat business; and that Ritson, who has read the whole, or parts, does not think it original.

Carter, the gothic draughtsman, has been at Durham lately and is much disatisfied with alterations making by Wyatt in the Cathedral; who, instead of restoring, which is all that Carter thinks ought to be done, is introducing parts quite out of character.

Humphrey called in the evening. He is strenuous for the election of Murphy to succeed Boswell.

Thursday Novr. 26th.

Hughes breakfasted with me this morning. — He was at Court yesterday, and met Wilberforce there who had addresses to present to the King. Wilberforce said He had some reason to expect a meeting would be held in Yorkshire in a few day[s] which He shd. be obliged to attend. He spoke this to Hughes privately, as it is not a matter quite determined.

Hughes is in a state of much apprehension from supposing the populace of London are corrupted by the principles propagated by Thelwall &c. — I told Him the English were not a people who wd. soon be moved to violent acts, they had too general a sense of the advantages they derive to put everything to the risk.

General Goldsworthy told Hughes that the King was much agitated on acct. of the attack made on *him* when going to the Parliament House: Not from any personal apprehension; but to find such a disposition prevailing. — The Queen, & Princesses, have been very uneasy.

Hughes dined lately at the Equerries table at Windsor. A report had prevailed that a mob meant to attack some Mills at Stoke near Windsor. It appeared from what he heard to Hughes that troops were so situated as to act quickly, and the communications of the Military well arranged. — General Goldsworthy told him that General Gwynn had the command of the troops about London, and He was assured, if necessary, would act effectually. Gwynn had desired field pieces, which had been granted him.

Mr. Fryer does not like the subject of London Bridge as a companion to the other picture. I told Hughes I wd. paint another in the room of it as soon as I had leisure. — Hughes desired to have the smallest of the pictures which I had in the last Exhibition.

Dr. Munro & Steers called on me. Dr, Munro wishes to obtain admission to the Royal Academy for Girtin, a young man of 20 years of age, as a student. I told him I wd. undertake to obtain it if He is sufficiently advanced in drawing the human figure. — The Dr. looked over my drawings in the Anti-room, and desired to have the Asphaltum outlined & washed drawing of Wenlock Abbey.

Mr. Wilton I dined with at His appartments in the Royal Academy. His Housekeeper only there. His eldest Son, the Clergyman, has now 5 children, and is lately appointed Minister of the English Church, a

Haddington, in Scotland; which produces him above a Hundred a year. —
living is cheap & the gentlemen of the neighberoud hospitable.

Mr. Wilton this afternoon began to give me particulars of his own professional life, and of other distinguished artists his contemporaries. — He
produced books containing a diary of his expences when on his travels,
and many particulars relative to himself, and others, of purchases, &
expences: but lamented not having extended his Diary to accts. of a
different kind, so as to have made up a progressive relation of everything
worth recording of himself and those with whom He has lived. He felt this
neglect forcibly while he lately read Boswells life of Johnson, which He
thinks one of the most fascinating relations He has ever met with.

Mr. Lawrence, a minister of St. Clements Danes, came in, and we talked
a little of the politicks of the day. He persuades himself that Pitt is very unpopular, — and thinks that when a peace takes place, the new principles
will be more prevailing and great efforts will be made by the poeple to
effect alterations in the state.

Though in his 74th. year, Mr. Wilton has generally good health. He is
subject to Rheumatic complaints, and feels a material difference in his
powers of moving according to the state of the weather. This day was cold
& frosty, and He had taken a long walk in the town; but when the weather
is damp or foggy He is little disposed to move. — He told me He called on
Sir William Chambers, about a fortnight since; who was then so feeble, as
to be obliged to be carried from one room to another. Sir William is more
than a year younger than Mr. Wilton.

Friday Novr. 27th.

Coombes called on me at nine this morning to breakfast. — He wanted my
opinion whether a Botanical acct. of the plants which grew on the sides of
the Thames throughout its progress should be added to it. It will take a
sheet and half additional, at most. I said I was not prepared to give an
opinion, but wd. consider & proposed to ask Mr. Steevens what He
thought of it, as I considered him a friend to the work: to this Coombes
agreed.

Cosway has but little business at present. — In his youth while under
Shipley at the drawing School, Having gained a premium from the Society
established for the encouragement of arts manufactures and commerce,
that Society voted him £100 to be paid to Pine for instructions in his art. —
Cosways Bill to the Prince of Wales was about £1500, — of which Cosway
had paid for various articles £200. — Coombes does not think Cosway
possesses more than the House He lives in, and £500 bank stock, except He
has money out on Bond. — He has certainly much money owing to him for
business done.

Mrs. Cosway is endeavouring to establish at Knightsbridge a House for the accomodation of Nuns who have been driven from abroad, to be supported by subscription and carried on under certain regulations.

Coombes does not think anything is to be apprehended from the State of the popular mind. He thinks the great majority is not affected by bad principles, but that a certain active set of men who are seen every where make a deceptious appearance.

I asked him about His History of the present reign. He spoke with great confidence abt. it, and said He felt the undertaking as something congenial to His mind. — At present he has a difficulty on one point viz: whether the influence which Lord Bute had over the King's mind at one period had arisen out of habit, and in fact had become disagreeable to the King, or whether it was the effect of inclination on the King's part. — Coombes thought He might, from Lord Harcourt, ascertain the fact; but it must be done with delicacy.

Coombes says he is 52 years old, and Cosway many years older. — Coombes when a Boy learnt accounts at a School in Windmill Street, where Cosway occasionally came, and at that time drew heads for 5 shillings each.

Soanes I dined at, Miss Archibald, — Wheatley, — Fuseli, Dance, Lawrence, Smirke, Hamilton & Tyler there.

Soane is very subject to complaints in his bowels and was but indifferent today having been very ill two days ago & not yet recovered. In conversation with Mrs. Soane as well as from himself I learnt that over exertion in his business frequently produces it. They have been married upwards of Eleven years and Mrs. Soane said He had seldom been free from some complaint of the kind for two months together.

We had a good deal of political conversation on the subject of Grants speech in the House of Commons on Wednesday last, which seems to have made a great impression. He stated the question of the Sedition Bills in a new manner, & supported the necessity for them with great weight of argument, which Fox laboured hard to answer. He is one of the Welch judges.

Fuseli was in Italy 8 years, which He said was much too long. A great deal of his time he passed among books, instead of applying to the *practise* of his art which He at that time thought was attainable, in a sufficient degree, at will. In Rome he said there is a want of sufficient stimulus to urge an Artist on, which causes most of them to idle away a great portion of their time in the most indolent manner. — Ramsay, the painter, said "Rome was a noble Theatre for an Artist; but it was dull playing to an empty pit". — After Fuseli determined to go to Italy in consequence of the advice of Sir Joshua Reynolds, to enable him to support the expence of it, Coutts, and some others ordered pictures from him here, which was a genteel way of supplying him with a few hundred pounds.

Young William Lock was mentioned by Fuseli, who said, His drawings, for invention, taste & spirit; and for the execution which is neither too much or too little; is unrivalled by any man of this day. — Lawrence told me afterwards that the dry manner of behaviour which appears in William Lock, and seems to be affected, is not so, but constitutional; He is frequently to his own family the same as to strangers; and has even confessed to woemen that He cd. not conquer it.

We left Soanes abt. Eleven o'clock. — Smirke and Fuseli came home with me & sat till near one oclock. — Fuseli remarked on the admirable choice of words, and the arrangement of his sentences, when Lawrence spoke on the political subject this evening. Also of the Acumen contained in his remarks. But both of them took notice that His manner is not pleasing in this respect, that He only directs his conversation to select persons, and does not shew sufficient attention to the rest of the company. — Fuseli being in spirits had after tea paid much attention to Miss Archibald & we laughed much on our return at his sudden & extravagant admiration of her, as she is a very plain woman.

Saturday — Novr. 28.

This day I was not well & staid at home; it was owing to my having, partly from necessity, eaten, two days following of dishes which do not agree with me. My Health depends much upon my diet. If I eat plain food, I am seldom unwell; but made dishes and sauces never fail to disorder me.

Lysons called on me after having breakfasted with Dance, where I was to have met him. He told me Charles Greville came to Sir Joseph Bankes', on Thursday morning and spoke of the admirable speech made in the house the night before by Grant. After He had concluded there was a buz of approbation which prevented Fox, who rose to answer, from being heard for near ten minutes. Fox laboured very hard to do away the effect of Grants speech but with no success. — The division on the motion made by Curwen, and seconded by Genl. Macleod, "that the Sedition Bill be deferred to that day week", was, for the motion 70; against it 269. — The Question for the Speaker leaving the Chair was then put, Ayes 273 — Noes 72.

Lysons got £1000 in the new Loan which Messrs. Boyd, Robarts, Solomons &c have taken; He afterwards sold it for 10, ½ pr. cent profit.

Batty called on me and prescribed a medicine.

Charles & John Offley drank tea with me. Mrs. Offley is very indifferent. Dr. Reynolds attends her. From the symptoms it is suspected she has water in her chest. Dr. Reynolds has not decided it, but Lewis the Apothecary, has mentioned to her his apprehension for which Dr. Reynolds has blamed him.

Sunday Novr. 29th.

Willis, called on me to inform me that I am elected a Member of the

Council of Trent Society, and that Hoppner would introduce me at the next meeting as He could not attend.

Sir George Beaumont & Hearne dined with me. — Lord Mornington told Sir George that Pitt said after Grant had spoken on Wednesday last, "Let the debate rest here on our part", — Grant made a speech on the Slave trade which raised his character very high, and had it been made at an earlier stage of that business would probably have put a stop to the mode of proceeding on it. — He is said to have but little professional business. — Lord Mornington said the Speech of Wednesday last ought to be printed, and circulated.

Monday 30th.

Clerkenwell Sessions House I went to this morning in consequence of having recd. a Subpoena to serve on the Grand Jury. — In the Supoena my name was written *Thomas* Farington, 59 Charlotte St., — As I conceived this a sufficient excuse I spoke to Mr. Blamire one of the Justices before the Court assembled. He said He could not say anything to it till the Court assembled, which it did a little after 10 oclock. When the names were called over, on Thomas Farington being called, I addressed the Justices & represented the circumstances, one of them asked me why I came, I said out of respect to the Court, another said I did right. They directed me to wait, as they did another or two who had apologies to make till all the names were called over. — It appeared there were rather more than 23, the number required present; on which after they were sworn in, I was told I might go and Mr. Blamire said to me "You need not have come", — Such as did not appear or send an apology, were fined £5 each. — If the party fined has anything to offer why the penalty should not be paid, He must plead it before the Justices in the course of the present sitting; otherways it becomes an Exchequer business; and is troublesome, & nearly as expensive as paying the fine, to get it taken off: so one of the clerks told me.

I dined at home and was alone this evening.

DECEMBER 1795

Tuesday Decr. 1st.

Flaxman, the Sculptor, called on me this morning, to desire I would, as one of the Council, attend along with Smirke, at the Custom House, to enable him to get his plaister studies passed duty free. — I told him I would attend any time on having two or three days notice. — He entered into conversation on the subject of having studies of artists admitted into this country duty free, and observed how advantageous it would be to extend the privilege further, so as to enable artists to bring into this country, duty free, such purchases as they might make of the works of others as should be declared to be for their own use, by which means it could not be doubted that many fine things wd. be introduced into England; and the object of duty is such a trifle as not to be worth consideration. — He said having considered the subject He shd. be very willing to attend the Council of the Academy and communicate what he had to say on it. I told him I wd. at the next Council, mention the matter. — He shewed me a printed Copy brought by him from Rome of Wests letter to the Commissioners of the Treasury, in consequence of a petition to them from English Artists at Rome. This letter wrote as from *himself, President of the Royal Academy*, and proposes his opinion on the subject, without referring to the Council of the Academy, so as to make it an Academical act. On this impropriety, and on the *incorrectness* of Wests letter, Flaxman remarked.

Flaxman, this morning, spoke to Mr. Rose of the Treasury, on the above subject; and found him well disposed to consider it.

Harris called on me, to determine who shd. teach his sister, Miss Arbouin, His niece, Miss Phillips, to draw. I recommended Mrs. Wheatley as being very ingenious; and they wd. also have the advantage of Wheatley looking over their studies. Harris highly approved of this proposal.

Wheatley I went to & mentioned what had passed between me & Harris, which He approved of, and said the terms shd. be such as Craig was accustomed to make. — He shewed me a large drawing He had made for Mr. Chamberlain, 3 feet 1 Inch by 2 feet 2 Inches ½ for which He is to

419

have 30 guineas. — Doctor Monro paid him 5 guineas each for the upright drawings. They are 14 Inches high, by 10 wide.

Dr. Monros I dined at. — Mrs. Monro is daugt. of the Rev. Dr. Woodcock of Bath. They have 4 children the eldest a Boy 6 years old. — Captain Hardy of the Navy & Mrs. Hardy, sister to Mrs. Monro, were there. Also, Henderson, Steers & Hearne. — Dr. Monro's collection of drawings by modern artists is larger than any I have before seen.

Captain Hardy is just returned from America. He speaks of the poeple of New York, as very sociable & hospitable, and well disposed towards the English. They are very well pleased with the Commercial treaty. He gave much the same character of the other parts of America where He had been. He never was at Philadelphia.

When Dr. Priestley arrived at New-York, He was taken notice of by some people who have formed themselves into Clubs, & Societies; but not by the people at large; who consider him a seditious character, like Muir, Palmer &c. — When He went to Philadelphia He expected to be recd. with particular honor by the President &c., but was disappointed; no notice was taken of him in the way He expected. The Government of America has many difficulties to contend with, from an ill disposition which prevails among a certain description of disaffected people in many parts of that country, and who are hostile to Government, and disatisfied with the laws. It was therefore not to be wondered at, that a man of Priestleys restless disposition & principles, should have been neglected.

Captn. Hardy described the disappointments of Emigrants who had left England & settled in America; they found the Country not sufficiently settled to insure them a protection such as they expected; and such as had carried money, had felt that their speculations had been unprofitable.

He said that the Americans will make as much of the French necessities as they can; but they look upon the proceedings in that country with the same horror as we do in England.

After Tea, I looked over a Portfolio of *outlines* of Shipping & boats, made at Dover by Henderson. Very ingenious & careful. We staid till past Eleven oclock.

Dr. Monro was at Harrow School, when Dr. Saml. Parr, the Grecian, was tutor there. After the death or resignation of Dr. Sumner, a majority of the Boys pleaded for Dr. Parr to be master; but the Governors appointed another. On which Dr. Parr retired from Harrow; and established a School at Stanmore, where about 40 of the Boys quitted Harrow and became his Scholars. — Dr. Monro was of the number. He described the singularities of Parr. Sometimes for a fortnight together He would lay late in bed & pay little regard to the School which of course became relaxed in discipline; He wd. then suddenly change his habit, rise at 6 in a morning, and with great severity force on his instruction. — These irregularities caused his School to decline. From thence He went to

Colchester; and from thence to Norwich. — Lord Dartmouth gave him a living in Warwickshire, where being settled, He took in a certain number of Boys at £100 a year each. — This Plan He continues. Dr. Munro says, that in his conversation he is sententious, like Johnson; and expresses himself in a very powerful manner on all subjects that He speaks upon. — He is a man of uncouth appearance; and is remarkable for looking much older than He is in reality. He cannot now be more than 46 years old, yet appears at least 60.

Captain Hardy told us, He brought over in the Thisbe frigate, among the passengers, Mr. Spiller, the celebrated pedestrian, who has been roving in the interior of America several years; this man was a quarter master in the army commanded by General Burgoyne at Saratoga. Sir Joseph Banks is his patron and encourager. Captain Hardy described him to be an excentric man, about 50 years of age; and without teeth; which according to his own account, He lost while travelling in the Woods of America, where, for many days together, He had no other food than a certain root, which had a mercurial effect on his gums. — He is much exhausted by the hardships He has undergone — and is imprudent in conduct, being often intoxicated.

Steers reprobated to me the conduct of Mr. Pitt in granting the loan to Boyd &c in the manner He has done it. All competition was given up, as Morgan &c declined making any offer after Mr. Pitt told them that whatever they should offer, Boyd &c should have the loan if they would give half per cent more. — As it is, Steers says he had £5000 of the loan, by which, He shall make £300.

Wednesday Decr. 2d.

Craig I wrote to, desiring to know his terms for teaching drawing. He informed me that whether He instructs at home, or abroad, He has half a guinea a lesson.

I dined, and remained, at home, this evening.

Thursday 3d.

Flaxman called on me. He has been with West, and stated to him the conversation He had with me on the subject of admitting the purchased studies of Artists duty free. West made no reply to him. — Flaxman says the duty at present is 27 and ½ per ct. on Sculpture &c, and that on an average Sculptural works of art purchased in Rome for £100 wd. when delivered from the Custom House, in London, stand the purchaser in £260. — A Book of prints not having a *title page* is considered at the Customs House as a collection of single prints, and each print pays 6d. duty. The expences in short are so great that artists forebear to purchase, or leave many works of taste behind them, as was the case with Flaxman who when He left Rome gave away many things which, but on acct. of the expences, He would have brought to England. Thus, for a Sum, arising from duties, so trifling as scarcely to be worth mentioning, were it allowed artists are prevented from importing such works as would be of great valu here to the profession, and of exercising their taste in selecting and pur chasing works of art which wd. add much to the national stock of Virtu. — Flaxman has talked on the subject with Lord Spencer when a Helvoetsluys; with Lord Mansfield &c. — Wheatley I called on, & proposed to him, that Mrs. Wheatley should give lessons of two Hours to Miss Arbouin & Miss Philips, and have for both 15s each lesson. Thi proposal was very agreeable to him & Mrs. Wheatley, who had proposed before to give lessons to both, an Hour, for ½ a guinea. — I wrote to Harri stating the agreement I had made.

C Offley called on me. He was yesterday at Grocers Hall at a meeting called of Merchants & Bankers, called together to support by address to the House of Commons the Sedition Bills. Foreseeing that an effort wd probably be made by the opposers of the Bill to get possession of the Hall and outvote the supporters or breed confusion, a great number of the Supporters had previously obtained entrance into the Hall; so that, when the doors were opened, and the opposers rushed in, though the meeting was proposedly stated to be of supporters only, they found a great part o the Hall occupied. Mr. Bosanquet was called to the Chair, & read the declaration: much tumult ensued — a show of hands was called when there appeared about two thirds for the declaration, and the remainder agains it. The object of this meeting was to refute the assertion that a meeting lately held at the Pauls Head, Tavern, Saml. Ferrand Waddington in the Chair, was properly a meeting of the merchants & Bankers of the City o London, — and to counteract a petition to the House of Commons agains the Bills which was voted at that meeting.

Offleys I dined at. — Mr. Crosbie, of Liverpool, who married a sister o Mr. Hesketh, Offleys partner at Oporto, was there; and Mr. Waters, who is engaged in a Post House.

Mr. Crosbie, said, Liverpool is now calculated to contain 60,000 inhabitants. Dr. Priestley, and, at another period, The Revd. Mr. Enfield with others, formed schemes for ascertaining the number of inhabitants contained in the three Towns, Birmingham, Manchester and Liverpool. — Mr. Crosbie was informed that it appeared that Manchester, including Salford, contained a greater number than either Birmingham o Liverpool. The powder tax produced at Liverpool about £3000.

Mr. Crosbie said that at the last election for Liverpool a certain number of gentlemen subscribed to defray the expences of Genl. Tarleton election, & that it cost them £5300, — Those gentlemen now differ so much, in politicks, from the General, that He has no reason to expect their future support. His own family are decidedly against him.

Mr. Crosbie mentioned that Miss Atherton, is to be married soon; but He forgot the name of the gentleman who has succeeded in his offer.

A son of Mr. Crosbie, 17 years of age, was taken in a vessell and carried into Brest, about a year ago. He was placed in Quimper prison, where the prisoners were hardly treated & in consequence his health suffered. An offer was made to the prisoners to remove 200 of them to another part of the Country, which he accepted. On their way there they suffered many hardships. In one situation where they were very ill used, General Hoche, happened to be, and He happening to speak French well, had leave to wait upon the General, who shook him by the hand, bad him sit down, & after hearing his complaints promised to relieve them; at parting, the General again shook him by the hand, and said He hoped to see him in England. — General Hoche is a young man, about 26 years old. He was dressed in Blue & richly laced.

By some address, assisted by two Americans, Young Crosbie passed as an American; and got to Paris; where He found the two Americans according to direction, who were much alarmed from an apprehension of their scheme being discovered: but Crosbie reminded them that they must now carry him through. This they did, & obtained a Passport for him as being an American. He walked abt. Paris; went to the Theatres, 13 of these being open. — went to the National Assembly, and was surprised at the tumultuous behaviour of the people in the galleries. — The Country everywhere, seemed quiet. He went from Paris, to Lyons; & from thence to Marseilles; where He took shipping for Leghorn. At Lyons He was struck with the appearance of many fine parts of that City being in ruins. Yet after all the calamities that City has suffered, the poeple seemed as in Paris quiet & Theatres were open. On the whole during the intercourse which He had with the people of France, a favorable impression was made on his mind. He thought them very agreeable. — He said while they were in prison the French woemen would come to them and dance with them.

Mr. Crosbie said it appeared that in Lancashire only 18,000 men had been raised for the publick service in 10 months. — The assessment of Seamen in Liverpool was 1660.

Morgan, & Co. — who were candidates for the new Loan, had placed 500,000, ready for that purpose. The conduct of Mr. Pitt appears to have been detrimental to the publick interest, by the partiality he has shown to Boyd, Benfield &c. — In the present Loan which already bears 6½ pr. cent premium, Benfields name was down for 5 millions. — It is understood that part of this sum others will share. The profit now is 300,000; and by the Imperial Loan Boyd, Benfield &c gained as much, it is said. — It is reckoned that 3 per ct. premium on a Loan is a good profit, which [makes] the present advantage of 6½ seem enormous.

Paine called on me today, to desire Mary Paine, may call on me when I begin to paint.

Friday Decr. 4th.

This day I completed the last outline for the 2d. Vol: of the River
Thames.

Mr. West wrote to me, requesting me to take the Chair at the Academy
Club, as He is prevented from attending by indisposition.

Young Ned Wakefield, — Lindoe informed me, was Secretary to the
meeting at the Pauls Head Tavern, assembled for the purpose of opposing
the Sedition Bills. He is abt. 23 or 4 years of age, and, it seems, has been in
the habit of attending disputing Clubs.

Academy Club I went to, and took the Chair. — nineteen members
present.

Lawrence told me that a young man his pupil, had painted a Copy of his
portrait of me which with 3 or 4 Hours sitting He cd. finish sufficiently,
and if I had any friend I wished to give it to it is at my service. I thanked him
and readily accepted it.

Lawrence said a Mr. Elliot with whom He is acquainted had been with
Mr. Burke, at Beaconsfield, last week, and found him in good health &
spirits, — and quite disregarding the attempts of Lord Lauderdale &c &c
to make a bustle about his pension.

Wyatt spoke favorably of the Duke of Northumberland as a prudent
man, but not defficient in proper spirit. In this respect shewing more
propriety than his father who was ostentatious in the greatest degree; but
was desirous to produce his effect at the smallest expence at which it could
be obtained. — The present Duke & Duchess were recd. by the King &
Queen with great partiality before the Regency business, the Duchess
being a particular favorite of the Queen. — Being invited to entertainments given at Windsor, the Duchess declined going on acct. of a young
Child she was nursing; on which the Queen had appartments fitted up for
the Duke & Duchess; the Children & attendants. notwithstanding this
attention, during the King's illness, the Duke took part with the Prince of
Wales, — which mark of ingratitude He is supposed now to be fully
sensible of; and it is privately thought, reflecting upon it has affected his
spirits, and added to his gouty complaints. — On the whole Wyatt does not
think his temper is good; but He is a man to be depended upon by those
who have business to do with him; is generally prudent in his conduct; and
appears to be much attached to the Duchess. — Wyatt thinks He has a
rooted dislike to Mr. Pitt. — The Duchess is an excellent woman.

I asked Wyatt what He thought of Young Sir Watkin Williams Wynne.
— He gave him an excellent Character, as being unaffected; of a good
disposition; & free from pride: & prudent in his conduct. — Lady Wynne,
his mother, is a woman of excellent sense; much cultivated. She is a
superior Latin Scholar. But she has something of the Grenville
disposition: proud, & satirical. — Sir Watkin is much attached to his

mother. — The estate is £33,000 a year, charged with a considerable debt; and with fortunes for 6 younger children: — Sir Watkin is very desirous of obtaining knowledge, perhaps more than his capacity will bear.

Hoppner gave me a very favourable acct. of the Council of Trent Society. It is limited to 30 members. At elections, one black ball excludes. — Several of the members of it are also members of the Eumelian Society, and of the Athenian Club; but they say this Society is more agreeable than either of the other Societies.

Marchant spoke very warmly in praise of a Bust of Mr. Udney, executed in marble by Flaxman; which He thinks worthy of a place among the works of the Greeks.

West was prevented attending the Club by a gouty complaint: and Tyler by a rheumatic cold.

Bourgeois, said that Monsr. Calonne, with several Frenchmen of distinction dined at Mr. Desenfans on Sunday last. I asked him what seemed to be their opinion of the government of France. He said they appeared to consider all chance of a restoration of monarchy as over: and that the Government of that country is now so shaped as to be likely to be the basis of something lasting. — Calonne much disapproved the edict of the present King, and said the confidence of the present rulers, and the disposition of the poeple, was fully shown, when the Government published and circulated through France, that edict, which it had been supposed by the framers of it, could only be introduced by stealth. — Calonne is incog., to avoid the Bills which He drew in favor of the Princes of France; & it is said Monsr. (Artois) does not land at Portsmouth, as He wd. be liable to an arrest on account of them. — Bourgeois said that the remaining hope of the Emigrants, He thinks, is, that when France is settled & peace is made, some favorable decree will be passed for their readmittance.

Wyatt is Architect to Westminster Abbey; of course has a good deal to do with the Dean & Chapter. Dr. Horsley, Bishop of Rochester, the Dean, appears to him in manners & other respects, very unfit to have been raised to the rank in which He is placed. Coarse & turbulent, He has little of the disposition which is required in the dignified characters of our Church.

Nollekens mentioned that the Duchess of Rutland is in great trouble on acct. of her eldest daugr., a fine young lady of 18, having fixed her affections on a person who is in a very disproportionate situation. — The young Lady is now placed with her grandmother, the Dowager Duchess of Beaufort.

Wheatley I called on after the Club to inform him, Miss Arbouin & Miss Phillips, will attend Mrs. Wheatley tomorrow at 12 oClock, of which Mr. Harris had acquainted me.

The reason why Willis will not attend the Council of Trent Society for some meetings to come is, that George Smith, who is a member, and was in the Chair, by rotation, at the last meeting, proposed a toast of a political

nature, which was objected to & not drank; but as waiters were present,
Willis on acct. of his situation, thinks it prudent to absent himself from the
Club for a time. Thus that indiscreet, intemperate young man creates
difficulties in Society. — I mentioned the circumstance to Dance, who
thinks the disposition of Smith makes it doubtful how far He will succeed
in his profession & in life.

Saturday Decr. 5th.

At home alone to day & the evening.

Sunday 6th.

At Church. Mr. Mathews preached on the patience of Job.

Lawrence I called upon. — He has nearly finished the whole length of
the Duke of Leeds; which is an excellent likeness, but the sky & distance
too much of a colour with the back ground. This He saw & proposes to
alter the distance. — Lawrence says the Duke of Leeds is an excellent
mimic.

Lawrence complained to me how much He suffers occasionally from the
weather, or some causes, by which His spirits are affected, so as to raise the
most melancholly ideas in his mind. This appears singular when his youth
& apparent health are considered. — He has derived great benefit from
taking Dr. Reynolds's Rhubarb & Ginger pills, at dinner time; which He
does regularly; and suffers when He omits them. — He has made an
excellent drawing, a portrait of Godwin the political writer; which He
means to be one of his collection. I think it the most chaste drawing I have
seen by him. — He has reason to expect Burke will sit to him.

We talked over the ensuing election of Academy Officers, & determined
to vote for the following. Council, — Lawrence, Hoppner, Westall,
Stothard, — Visitors, — Lawrence, Hoppner, Westall, Stothard, Burch.

Offleys I dined at, — Mrs. Offley much recovered, & at dinner. Mine
there.

Sir Joseph Banks's I went to in the evening with Dance who called upon
me. — The Duke of Leeds, — Lord Mountmorris, — Sir George Shuck-
borough, — Sir John Mordaunt, Major Reynell, — Mr. Dalrymple, —
Dr. Garthshore, — Saml. Lysons, — Danl. Lysons — Mr. Earle, — Sir
George Baker — Mr. Metcalfe — &c &c &c.

Sir John Mordaunt said Sir Wm. Hamilton is coming to England &
proposes to dispose of his collection of Virtu.

Mr. Dalrymple is of opinion that the Cape of Good Hope is very tenable
from the nature of the Country:- That the batteries which command the
bay, are wisely placed at some distance from the water; and of course
cannot be attacked with so much advantage as is usually given to shipping
by erecting the batteries on the edge of the water. — He seems to make
light of the value of possessing the spice Islands; and Trincomalee, would

·nly be a place for Ships to idle at instead of keeping the Sea or pursuing
he objects of their destinations. — Batavia, also, when its unhealthy
ituation is considered, cannot He thinks be looked upon as a desirable
·ossession.

Sir Joseph Banks, Major Reynell, and Dance, talked of a bridge lately
)uilt by Mr. Burdon at Sunderland; the length of which is 236 feet, — from
he spring of the arch 36 feet, — & the abutments 60 feet. So that from the
·evel of the water to the under part of the bridge is about 90 feet.

Major Reynell stated, that Smeaton who built the Edystone Light
House in 1759, — told him, that while He was laying the foundation of that
building, in rough weather, the weight of the Sea was such that the strokes
of the waves made the rock shake under him. — Smeaton had measured
with accuracy the height to which the Spray of the Sea rises in stormy
weather; and found it 160 feet, forming a white cloud; by beating against
the side of the rock & side of the Light House. The height of the rock in the
highest part, at high water mark, is 15 feet. — The height of the whole to
the top of the Lanthern is 90 feet. — Dance said the construction of it is
most admirable.

Speaking of Dances profiles, Sir Joseph proposed to him to publish
them in numbers. Came home a little before Eleven.

Monday Decr. 7th. 1795.

Smirke wrote to me this morning on the subject of Banks's model of Lord
Cornwallis.

The London Corresponding Society having signified an intention to
meet in Marybone fields today, at one oClock, I went into the New road
where great numbers of people were passing to and from those fields. — In
the second field from the road, on the right hand of the Jews Harp, Three
Slips of Hustings were erected in different parts of the field; and before
each, a crowd of poeple were assembled as at fairs, when a quack Doctor
exhorts the mob. — On one of these, Citizen Jones, was the principal
Orator; attended by a second, who relieved him by reading the petition &
Declarations. — Citizen Jones is a tallish, slender man; His complexion
pale, & face thin. He was without powder, His hair dark. He is afflicted
with a paralytic affection, which causes, excepting when He is exerting himself, an almost constant convulsive twitching of his head, Shoulders, &
Arms. — He was dressed in a green Coat, & had halfboots on; & on the
whole presented a figure such as is usually called shabby, genteel. — He
seems to be about 3 or 4 & thirty years old. — He has an excellent voice;
sharp; clear; & distinct; and his harangues at different periods were well
calculated for catching his auditory; and many passages ingenious enough.
— He said, that insulted, as the Society had been, and their petitions disregarded, it was rather a deviation from that spirit which freemen should
exhibit, again to think of adressing, or petitioning; but to prevent the mis-
representations of their enemies, the Society had resolved to propose to

the poeple a petition to the King. In this part of his harangue He hinted s&
much as to signify that the Society had views in which the King &
parliament are not objects of great consideration. — He spoke with great
inveteracy against Pitt, and of his being brought to publick execution. —
Of 28000 fencibles being armed to overawe the poeple, which, said He
may be done, if the poeple assemble without arms to resist them. — H&
mentioned Wyndham having said that if the Law wd. not do a power
stronger than the Law, must be used, — & played upon it to shew the views
of Ministers. — The tenor of his speech went to this — That if the Bills
pass, and attempts are made to carry them into effect, the poeple will then
be at issue with the King & Parliament, & the event must depend upon the
vigour of the parties. — At present we write, said He, our sentiments in
black; we may soon be obliged to express them in *red*. On another
Hustings, Astley [Ashley], Secretary to The Bill of Rights [London
Corresponding Society]; [P.T. Lemaitre] one of the persons taken up on
suspicion of having contrived an instrument to kill the King, it was called
the Pop gun plot; — another or two were stationed. — Astley is a tall
black, man; his dress dirty. — [Lemaitre] is a little man, pitted with the
small pox; & hooked nose; & drawling voice. The others who spoke are
common men, who spoke ungramatically. — Their arguments common
placed & abuse of Pitt gross enough.

On the third Hustings, Thelwall, — Brown of Sheffield, — Friend, who
was expelled from Cambridge; — and 4 or 5 others were stationed.

Brown is a middlesized man, stout in figure, & wears spectacles. In his
appearance a substantial, respectable looking man, about 40 years of age
— He was dressed in Blue. He addressed the people often, and delivered
himself intelligibly, and with attempt at candour; exhorting them not to
give their approbation to anything they did not fully understand and
approve.

Friend, — he spells his name *Frend*, — is a gentlemanlike looking Man
of good stature and bulk; apparently about 34 or 5 years of age: Dark hair
witht. powder. — He stated to the poeple that the Bill of rights, limited
even the power of parliaments, any act of which, inconsistent with the
principles of the constitution, would be waste paper, and should be
disregarded; and that Juries, before whom persons may be brought, under
the provisions of the proposed Bills, were bound as Englishmen to shew
their contempt of the bills, by acquitting the accused persons; unless they
had been guilty of some offence which is at present considered criminal. —
This was the principal point of his speech. — He was dressed in blue with a
white waistcoat; and seemed in appearance ill suited to those about him, —
Brown excepted.

Thelwall is a little, and very mean looking Man; of a sickly, sallow
complexion, & black, lank Hair. — He was covered with a large, thick,
loose great coat. When passive His countenance is simple, & common

nough; but the nature of his disposition, while Brown, & others were peaking, was strongly expressed by his gestures, & emotions. On the ontrary Friend, & Brown, were temperate in their manner. — Thelwall, ook up the argument of Brown, relative to Juries; & the power of Parliaments. Juries, said He, emanate from the Constitution; & are unconroulable by any act of parliament which can be proposed to interfere with heir judgement. They are not to be governed by such; but rigidly adhering o the Bill of rights; and the principles of the Constitution; are to guard the ubjects from the attacks of any new created power.

Brown said He was not much given to prophecy; but He would now enture to declare that He foresaw if English Juries defended the Constitutional rights of Englishmen, by exculpatory verdicts, the time vould soon come — when a limitation of their power would be proposed; nd decissions left to the Judges only; men paid by the Crown.

A thin, pale man, Richter, then addressed the poeple. He said He was ot a member of the London Corresponding Society, but came forward as Citizen to support their objects. He spoke of equality, and ridiculed the dea, & impossibility of equal property; it is equal rights; and equal protection from the laws; equal suffrage &c that were the reasonable & proper objects of the Society. — He proposed that thanks should be voted o such members of the House of Commons as have stood forward to lefend the liberties of the poeple. — He first proposed thanks to Mr. Sturt. — Then to Mr. Erskine. To the Duke of Bedford. — Then to Mr. Fox; & ere he entered into a warm eulogium of the speeches He has made on hese Bills, in the House of Commons; and of his definitions, and ussertions, relative to the Constitution. Mr. Fox had declared in the House, that should the Bills pass, it would no longer be a question of norality; or of duty; but of prudence; what the conduct of the people hould be. — He added much more to shew that Fox justified a poeple who vould resist the execution of laws of such a nature, if attempted to be carried into execution. — Thanks were also voted to Sheridan, — Grey — Whitbread.

Of all the Orators, Jones, appeared to me to have most genius: but he abours under a constitutional disadvantage, which seems to oblige him often to pause. Thelwall is a ready speaker; but does not, from what I heard, display so much imagination as Jones; & He has an acrimony in his ook & manner, which I did not observe in the latter, who never seemed out of temper.

I saw Lord Mulgrave, Coll. Phipps, Sir George Beaumont, &c together n the throng, — Also Smirke, & Stothard. — Many respectable poeple were in various parts of the field: but they all appeared, like my self, spectators of the proceedings of the day. — No tumult took place; nor was any offence given to such as did not hold up hands; or join in the plaudits. I was in every part, & where the crowd was greatest; yet never held up my

hand or expressed approbation. Indeed both Jones, to his auditors, — &
Brown &c to theirs, recommended strongly to give no offence to such as
might differ in opinion. — On the whole the number of poeple who at any
one time were in the field was not so great as I expected; a Crowd only
being near each of the Hustings. — A little before 4 oClock I left the field,
though the Orators had not then descended. — The day was gloomy &
unpleasant.

Jones said, if the King refused the Royal Assent to the Bills, it would
then be the King & the Poeple, against the Parliaments, but should the
assent be given then what wd. be the question, "The poeple, against both
King and Parliament". — He spoke lightly, & with ridicule of the attack
made upon the King; joking upon a pebble being flirted at the glass; and of
a little mud clogging the wheels of government. From no one of the
Orators did I hear a word of respect for the King: and I am convinced that
if vigorous means are not used in time, much mischief will come from the
attempts of these poeple. — From what I could collect they are resolutely
determined to assemble as before after the Bills are passed. — Then will
they be really at issue with government.

One of the Orators, in a course of misrepresentation of the Bills told the
poeple that, if they pass, from that time, no man could invite a dozen
friends to his house, on any occasion, without being obliged to invite a
magistrate to be with them.

Tuesday Decr. 8th.

Council of Trent Society I was at, and introduced by Willis; He having
proposed me. The Society is limited to 30 Members. The present Members
are —

Lord Molesworth —	Mr. Sharpe, —	Dr. Greive,
Revd. Dr. Pearce —	Mr. Willis —	Dr. Heming
Master of the Temple.		
Revd. Dr. Layard —	Mr. Hale —	Mr. Heaviside,
Mr. Nichol. Senr. —	Mr. Rogers — author of the pleasures of memory	Mr. Boylestone ⎱ merchant ⎰
Mr. Nichol. Junr. —	Mr. Hoppner —	Dr. Thomson master of a school at ⎫ Kensington ⎭
Captn. Budworth —	Mr. Carbonel ⎱ wine merchant ⎰ —	Mr. Thomson
Jos. Farington —	Mr. Carbonel, Junr.	Serjeant Marshall
Mr. Smirke —	Revd. Mr. Penneck	
Mr. Batty —	Mr. Delafield elected March 1 96.	

Mr. Norman ⎫ General Grave
Timber merchant ⎰ French emigrant
　　　　　　　　elected March 1st. 96

A Candidate is proposed at one meeting, and balotted for at the next. *Two Black Balls* exclude. Two guineas is subscribed by each member annually. — The first meeting this Season was Tuesday Novr. 10th. The Club is on Tuesdays, once a fortnight.
　　Mr. Sharpe was in the Chair.
　　The first Toast is, *The King & Constitution*. The Second, *The Queen & Royal Family*. The Third, *The Council of Trent, Esto perpetua.* after which the Bottles are passed but no toasts given. Dinner on the Table at ½ past 4, — & Tea & Coffee brought about ½ past 7. — Each stranger pays 8.6.
　　The members present to day were,

Mr. Sharpe	—	Serjeant Marshall	—	Dr. Greive	
Mr. Hoppner	—	Mr. Nicol Senr.	—	Mr. Nicol Junr.	
Mr. Rogers	—	Dr. Hemming	—	Mr. Willis	
Captn. Budworth	—	Dr. Thomson	—	& J. Farington	

　　Captn. Budworth & myself were this day introduced as new members. — After dinner Smirke & Batty, both proposed by Mr. Rogers, were balotted for & elected. ＼
　　I talked with Mr. Sharpe about Mr. Grant whom He knows. He described Him to be a very sensible man, whose studies have not been confined to the techical part of his profession, but of a more general nature; so that He has not advanced to publicity in his profession, proportionate to what his abilities might claim. He is a Scotchman; & was sometime Clerk to a merchant; which situation He quitted feeling himself qualified for greater undertakings. He is abt. 42 or 3, years of age.
　　Mr. Wilkes was spoken of by several present who have been acquainted. His wit in conversation is allowed to be superior to that of those who are now most remarkable for it. Jekyll, is overcome by him. They have contested, but Wilkes has always been victorious. — I'll file a Bill against you, said Jekyll. — You would file a guinea, replys Wilkes, if you could get one.
　　The depravity, as it may justly be said, of Wilkes, is remarkable. He speaks witht. reserve of the various profligate acts of his life; both moral & political; — and laughingly tells of his acts, & practices, to distress administration, under colour of defending the rights of the poeple.
　　One of the gentlemen mentioned having been in company with Wilkes, & Courtney, when the latter was silenced by the superior wit of the former. Wit flows from Wilkes witht. preparation or effort.
　　Dryden, was spoken of. Willis thinks his merits greatly over rated; in which opinion Sharpe partly concurred. — Willis thinks Thomson, also

has a higher reputation than He is entitled to; and that He is a Poet of words, rather than of thoughts. — Pope, He considers as superior to Dryden; and is satisfied this is *felt* by the world, if not acknowledged; Few read Dryden; but everybody Pope.

Mr. Nichols Senr. who was a member of two Parliaments, gave his opinion of Burke. — It is, that Burke thinks a few great Whig families in this Country ought to controul it. — He does not believe Burke ever studied *the constitution*. That is, the constitutional powers of magistrates; and the duties of subjects. — Speaking of the Oratory of Burke, He said eloquent, and ingenious as His speeches often were, Burke did not obtain the great end of a publick Speaker, in bringing His auditors over to his opinion.

Johnson, was mentioned; some observed who takes down a Rambler when he can procure a Spectator? To Hoppner, I gave my opinion, in favour of Johnson. In his works every sentence contains a Kernel. — He agreed with me.

Hoppner & Sharpe spoke with raptures of the works of Wilson. Hoppner thinks He was superior in mind to all his predecessors.

In consequence of the behaviour of George Smith in proposing the improper toast which He did at the last meeting, — Willis, Hale, Dr Pearce, Dr. Layard, & Serjeant Marshall withdrew their names from the Club; this being represented by Mr. Rogers to Smith, He very properly withdrew his, that the Society might not suffer from his conduct: on which Willis, Marshall & Hale have returned to it. The Toast was, "Success to Rebellion, in the cause of Freedom".

Mr. Sharpe has long been intimate with Romney, — who is now abt. 6 years of age & still persists in his practise of Portrait painting; though Sharpe believes him to be worth £50,000; — Romney did, for many years wish for independance; that He might be able to exercise the powers of his mind in his profession. He still looks forward to a time when He shall have that indulgence: But he is chained down by a spirit of avarice, which will prevent his ever arriving at that wished for period. He has only one Child, Son who is well provided for in the Church, by Lord Thurlow.

Sheridan was mentioned; and described as not excelling in conversation.

Came home at 10 oClock.

Wednesday Decr. 9th.

Mr. Malone I called on. — Christie has not settled the account of Lord Inchiquin's sale of Sir Joshuas pictures. He has given some drafts of Morlands house, dated for January next. Mr. Metcalfe enquired there Christie had cash there for the sums to be paid. They answered no, but the had no doubt He would; that He was an honest man &c &c.

Mr. Malone told me that Brown one of the Orators in Marybone field as formerly a Player, and that He had sometime recd. a letter from him on the subject of Shakespeare. This man was active in the seditious movements in Scotland.

Sheridan has spoken whimsically of the Speech of Fox when He went such lengths in debate, and said "if the bills passed it wd. not be a question of morality; or of duty; but of prudence, for the poeple". Sheridan said, "We were going on swimmingly, and should have produced great effect, but for Fox's *dagger scene*".

Flaxman called on me to inform me that, on Friday next, we may go to the Customs House, to pass his plaisters.

He informed me that Durno who died lately at Rome was of a gross habit of body, and had but indifferent health for sometime before He died. A putrid fever carried him off. His funeral was very respectably attended. Prince Augustus, & many English Gentlemen, were there.

Durno had been long connected with an Italian family; and it is supposed a girl of the family, abt. 16 years of age is his daughter. His expences on acct. of this connexion were considerable, and caused him to be frequently low spirited. So situated was He with that family that from an apprehension of personal injury if He had proposed to leave Rome; or from some other motive; He had given up all expectation of returning to England. He was, in addition to this aware, that his manner of painting was not likely to be popular in England. — He was abt. 50 years of age. — He had engaged himself, in some degree, in picture dealing.

More, the Landscape painter, was concerned with an Italian in picture dealing; and had a concern in the picture of Parmegiano, bought by the Marquiss of Abercorn, for 1500 Gs. — Some other profitable engagements of this sort He got money by; & was very well employed in his professional capacity; yet He left no more than abt. 14000 Crowns (abt. 3500,) and some pictures. — A connexion with an Italian woman had been expensive to him. — More, like others who have engaged in picture dealing, attempted to impose on ignorant persons, pictures which were not genuine. One which He called Michl. Angelo, He induced Prince Augustus to recommend to the King: but Flaxman & others convinced the Prince that it was not a work of that master.

When Prince Augustus first visited Rome He came from the German courts; and etiquette was carried so far that no Englishman sat down in a room while the Prince was standing. — On his second visit, when He came from England, this ceremony was waved; and the intercourse with him was as easy as with any other gentleman. — Flaxman described his disposition as being amiable. He has constantly recd. great marks of attention from the Pope; who has permitted him to make excavations, in search of antiquities. In consequence some fine things have been discovered. One in particular. He has purchased for the Prince of Wales & drawn upon him for £1300.

Flaxman was 7 years in Italy. He is 40 years of age. He thinks painters usually stay too long in Italy; where indolence generally becomes a habit.

Offleys I dined at. Mr. Boaden, a Lisbon merchant; Mr. Grellet, a Spanish mercht.; and Mr. Knowsley of Cottingham near Hull; a wine mercht., were there.

Mr. Knowsley condemned Mark Sykes, the High-Sheriff, for not calling a meeting of the County when required. — A meeting, however was held at York, which Mr. K. attended. Sir Thos. Gascoigne was called to the Chair, by the opposers of the Sedition Bills; but 2,3ds. of the people assembled were a majority in favor of Bacon Frank. It was then proposed to adjourn to the Courtyd. as there was not sufficient room in the Town Hall. This was opposed by Sir Thos. Gascoignes party. However the majority adjourned, while the minority remained and passed resolutions against the Bills. — Mr. K, said every art had been used to induce poeple to assemble to oppose the Bills and that the Rev. Mr. Wyvil had in a very improper manner exerted himself. Yet of 1500 persons assembled nearly 2 thirds were for the Bills.

Owing to the Kings message last night to the house of Commons, declaring the French Government sufficiently formed to treat with — the Scrip bore 10 & 12 pr. ct. premium.

William, came this evening from Deptford, where He Had been sent by Captain Barlow, to assist in fitting out the Phoebe frigate of 36 Guns, to which Captn. Barlow is appointed. — William was in the Aquilon frigate, with Capt. Barlow, during the action on 23d. of last June, when Lord Bridport took the Alexander; the Formidable; and the Tigre; French men of war. The French fleet, excepting the Alexander, sailed better than our fleet. The Alexander had been taken by the French from us. Had the French not attempted to cover & get of the Alexander, there would have been little probability of Lord Bridport bringing them to action. — The Aquilon, being the repeating frigate, William had a good opportunity of seeing the engagement. The French ships which were taken fought with much obstinacy: but it was observed throughout the action, that firing from those ships was much slower than that from the Royal George, Ld. Bridports ship; and the other English Ships. — About an Hour after the action was over, William was ordered to go on board the Formidable. The Frenchmen on their approaching in the boats called out from the Ports &c Vive George, and very eagerly pressed to get into the boats in order to quit their own Ships. The English sailors were surprised to find the Formidable in so dirty a state that she appeared as if Her decks had not been washed for a fortnight. — He went into the Cockpit where the Surgeon was dressing the wounded men of which there were a great number. The accomodations here were better than He had observed in an English Ship. There were cradles for the men to be laid in & other conveniences. The Surgeon seemed to be a humane man & to be much affected with the Scenes.

Thursday, Decr. 10th.

Marchi called on me. Lady Inchiquin does not come to Town till after Christmas.

Will, called. His business at the India House is referred to the Committee of Shipping to make a report on his petition. Captn. Cotton & Captn. Money, are of the Committee.

Dance drank tea with me and we went together to the Academy, to the General Meeting.

Members present.

Mr. West

Wilton	—	T. Sandby	—	Dance	—	Smirke	—	Hoppner
Westall	—	Lawrence	—	Stothard	—	Bourgeois	—	Yenn
Fuseli	—	Hamilton	—	Russell	—	Northcote	—	Opie
Farington	—	Banks	—	Wyatt	—	Rigaud	—	Garvey
Bacon	—	Copley	—	Nollekens	—	Barry	—	Cosway
Burch	—	Richards.					

The premiums of the year were adjudged.

The Silver Medal for the best drawing of an Academy figure was given to John Thomas Barber.

The Silver medal for the best model of an Academy figure was given to Edmund Coffin.

No Candidate appeared for the medal offered for an Architectural drawing.

The Balot for President then took place.

West 19 — Catton 1 — Westall 1 — Copley 1 — Burch 1.

Then the Balot for 4 new Council

	Rigaud 6	—	Fuseli 4	—	Wilton 3
Stothard 15	Wyatt 5	—	Barry 3	—	Garvey 2
Hoppner 14	Nollekens 5	—	Catton 3	—	Russell 2
Lawrence 12	Cosway 4	—	Opie 3	—	Banks 1
Westall 11	Hamilton 1	—	Hodges 1	—	P. Sandby 1
	Wheatley 1	—	Yenn 1		

elected { Stothard 15 / Hoppner 14 / Lawrence 12 / Westall 11

The Balot for 5 Visitors then took place.

elected { Burch 18 / Stothard 15 / Hoppner 14 / Westall 13 / Lawrence 11

	Bourgeois 7	—	Copley 2	—	Dance 1
	Cosway 6	—	Garvey 2	—	Farington 1
	Nollekens 6	—	Russell 3	—	P. Sandby 1
	Opie 7	—	Zoffany 2		
	Catton 2	—	Chambers 1		

Burch had solicited Votes, saying He was umemployed.

The members than proceeded to take into consideration the two models presented by Banks for a Statue of Ld. Cornwallis. After much conversation it was determined, that, Mr. Banks be appointed to execute the Statue; That the model which represents Ld. Cornwallis in his robe of peerage be adopted; & that He do proceed with the work under the inspection of the Council.

The difficulty on the above occasion rose out of the obligation the Academy is under to exercise its judgement critically for the benefit of the undertaking; and it was concluded that, in such cases, the Council for the time being were most proper to suggest to the Artist employed any remarks on his performance which might be approved of. — Mr. Banks concurred fully in this opinion.

The meeting broke up between 11 & 12.

Before the balots, Sir F. Bourgeois expressed to me a wish to be appointed one of the Visitors. He said He had not served that office. I told him that it had always been usual to select such members for that purpose as were known to be particularly intelligent in Academical Studies; and of course many of the members had never been appointed, or ever expected to be so. That I considered myself as holding a trust; & on looking over the list of Academicians shd. certainly vote for the persons I thought best qualified. — He said Loutherburgh, & Wheatley, had served the office, who only introduced figures in the way He used them. I replied that Wheatley had been early bred to Academical studies; and well understood the department; and that He ranked among the Historical painters, as His works shewed. Our conversation concluded; and I am well convinced not to his satisfaction.

Friday — Decr. 11th.

Flaxman & Smirke called on me this morning at Eleven, & we went together to the Custom House to inspect his cases imported from Italy. — The lids were taken of, and several small plaisters which He had purchased, and for which He is to pay duties, we looked at. The only work by himself is "The Torso restored in the marriage of Hercules & Hebe". Having examined the parts of this model so as to assure ourselves that we might declare as much as the regulation requires, we left the Custom House; and repaired to a Coffee House, where we wrote the following letter to Mr. West, to be delivered to him by Mr. Flaxman.

Decr. 11th. 1795

Sir,

At the request of Mr. Flaxman we have inspected the cases no. 1 & 2

marked   and imported from Italy, by the Salerno, Captn. Francis

Ruston. They contain the model of a groupe in plaister, which we believe to be Mr. Flaxmans performance & property.

We are, Sir,
Your most Hble. Servts
Jos: Farington — Robt. Smirke

Smith, the booksellers in Portsmouth St. Lincolns Inn fields I went to and bought several of the publications issued by the London Corresponding Society &c. — Smith was taken up about a week since for publishing a Sixpenny pamphlet entitled, "A Summary of the Duties of Citizenship". —As I did not see the Pamphlet in the windows, I asked him if such a one had been published. He said there had; but without his knowledge; that He was not at home when a quantity of them were brought to his house; but about 30 of them had certainly been sold there. That he was taken up, and only bailed yesterday; and expected to be brought to trial. — The Author He told me is a young man of the name of Iliff; son to a Clergyman who resides near Guildhall. I asked him why He did not give Iliff up to justice; He replyed, that Iliff had absconded.

He then produced one of the pamphlets, & said He did not think it prudent to dare justice by *openly* vending them; and depended for acquittal on extenuating circumstances. After this conversation He had no objection to selling me one of them. — He is a thin, black complexioned man; and from the appearance of all abt. him, in but moderate circumstances. His deportment was very quiet; and He seems to be one of those who are principally instigated by the expectation of a little gain to sell such publications. He appeared to be very sensible of the bad tendency of the pamphlet; and said His attorney had assured him it was full of chargeable passages.

Tyler I called on. He has been confined by a severe attack of Rheumatism in his back, and still remains indifferent.

Saturday Decr. 12th.

Sir George Beaumont called on me. — A nephew of More, the Landscape painter, who died last year in Rome, has been in Italy to look after the effects of his Uncle. He has assured Sir George that More was poisoned by a woman who lived with him sometime. — She died in a few months after him.

Sir George is full convinced that nothing is to be apprehended from the attempts of Thelwal &c since I saw how the meeting in Marybone fields was made up on Monday last.

Flaxman & Smirke dined with me. — Flaxman waited on West yesterday with the letter which Smirke & I signed. West gave him a letter to Mr. Long of the Treasury: — West brought on a conversation on the subject of obtaining permission from the Treasury for Artists to import to

England such works as they may have purchased for their studies duty free; and said He had with difficulty obtained the indulgence already granted, — and did not seem pleased that anything more shd. be done in this business. Flaxman replied that He had engaged himself to his Brother Artists in Rome to obtain farther indulgence and wd. proceed in it, if it should not be taken up by the Academy.

This morning waited on Mr. Long with Wests letter; and then entered on the subject of further indulgence explaining the advantages to Artists & this Country which wd. be gained by the introduction of good art, & how trifling an object the duty wd. be to the Treasury. Mr. Long expressed himself in the most liberal manner, stating that He had not understood the nature of the business before, or every indulgence shd. have been granted. That Mr. Tresham had observed that too great an indulgence wd. be a means of introducing much bad art into the Country; but He felt that no danger cd. be apprehended of any abuse, if it be left to the Royal Academy to vouch for what may be imported. Flaxman told him the matter wd. be regularly proposed by the Academy to the Treasury.

Flaxman went from Florence, to Carrara, to purchase marble for the monument of the late Lord Mansfield which He is to execute. The Town of Carrara contains about 9000 inhabitants and the poeple are chiefly employed in working in the Quarries in that neighberoud. Some of these Quarries are very large, equal in space, to Grosvenor Square. These are the only quarries from which we can import White, Statuary marble. The Greek quarries, now in the hands of the Turks, not being allowed to be worked, by that ignorant & superstitious poeple. — From Carrara, marble is exported to every part of Europe; but, before the Revolution, the French were their best customers. Two dealers in marble, one in Paris; & one at Lyons; had contracted each for 1200 palms a month, a palm is 6 Inches. — The Revolution has put a stop to this trade; and impoverished the town of Carrara. The dealer who resided in Lyons, now lives on Charity in Carrara. Flaxman expended for the marble intended for Lord Mansfields monument 600 pounds, including all the charges of bringing it to England.

Several years ago, a person [Alexander Baillie] who [had] been benefitted by a decission of Lord Mansfields, bequeathed £1500, to erect a monument to his Lordships memory, whenever He might die. The interest accummulating on this sum now makes up with the principal £2500, — which is to defray all expences.

In selecting blocks of marble, to avoid those black veins which would disfigure a statue; it is necessary to remark when the course of one vein is determined, where an opposite vein or black crust, appears; for the phlogiston, which causes the veins, usually branches of, and the intermediate space is generally found to be pure.

The French Academy in Rome, established by Louis 14th., was a noble foundation. It was under the management of a Directeur. Four painters;

Four Sculptors; & four Architects; were provided for in every respect while pursuing their studies. — The time allowed for the students to remain in Rome on the foundation was Four Years for each painter; & Sculptor; and Three years for each Architect. — While Flaxman was in Rome, there were several very ingenious men who pursued their studies with great industry. In the architectural branch they particularly excelled.

This excellent institution was broken up about two years since. A Democratic spirit had for some time prevailed in the Academy; as well as in France. This disposition was encouraged by Monsr. Bassville a Frenchman who acted as a sort of Consul, — and elated with the great success of the French Arms on the borders of Italy; the members of the Academy began to foment democratic principles among the Romans; and even to threaten the officers of Government. A Plan was formed by them to raise an insurrection, of which Bassville was to be the principal mover. Signals were agreed upon, and everything according to their scheme prepared: But the design being discovered, Bassville was put to death, and the Students either fled from, or were ordered to quit Rome. Under these aggravating circumstances, the Pope conducted himself with great moderation; and even gave money to some of the offenders to enable them to defray their expences to France. The Palace, in which the Academy was established is now converted by the Pope to another purpose. — The first act of the members of the Academy was, to take down the Arms of Louis 14 the founder, which the Pope permitted; but wd. not suffer them to place any other Arms over the gateway in their room. It was on this acct. they threatened one of the principal officers that the armies of France should advance against Rome & that the streets should run with blood.

The annual expence of the establishment was reckoned about £3000.

Flaxman said the French Artists held the character of Wilson, as an Artist, very high.

Flaxman while he remained in Rome modelled, and executed in marble, a Groupe about the size of the Laocoon. Lord Bristol, (Bishop of Derry,) employed him to do it, and engaged to give him £600 for it. The expence of the marble, and workmans wages, cost Flaxman abt. £550; so that He had not more than £50 for his design & about Two years labour. But this He does not regret as it gave him an opportunity to exert his powers. — Lord Bristol behaved to him as He has done to most Artists, by delaying payments, & acting in other respects in his usual capricious manner. — The Subject of the Groupe is [*The Fury of Athamas*]. Lord Bristol proposed having it conveyed to Ireland

Jenkins, the Ciceroni, Banker & dealer in works of art, obtained from the late Mr. Weddel of Yorkshire, £2000, and an Annuity of £100 for his life, for a statue of Venus.

Extract of a letter from Rome to Howard, — "I suppose you have heard of Poor Durno's death. His funeral was conducted with great solemnity.

Prince Augustus, (much to his honor), and all the English nobility here, attended: the service was read by Grignion".

Lysons called on me this morning and brought with him Fissinger, a german Engraver. — Speaking of the bombardment of Manheim, Ridinger said, the people of the town having little advantage from Commerce; & consequently not being wealthy; it is not likely that the Town will soon be restored.

Sunday Decr. 13th.

At Church: The Revd. Gerrard Andrewes, one of the evening preachers at the Magdalen, preached a Sermon for the benefit of the Female Charity Children, — His text 1st. Verse 15th. Chap. St. Luke, "There was a certain rich man who had a steward" &c &c.

His discourse was well written and strongly pointed; and I think well calculated to have a strong effect on the Congregation.

He dwelt on our responsibility for whatever we possess of faculties; riches; or authority; — remarked on the attempts made to weaken the veneration due to the Christian religion; and observed that the art of engraving by multiplying frivolous designs, of scriptural, and other subjects, did much mischief; for which such as were possessed of that elegant talent were responsible to God. — He concluded by shewing that both policy in this life; & duty to God; should dispose us to support the education of Female Children for whom their parents could do little; by which means, we should protect them from vicious habits; impress on their minds proper notions of religion & morality; and rescue them from the temptations of depraved men.

Mr. Baker called while I was at Church.

Dance I called on. Beechy was there, having sat for his profile, and Tyler, who is recovered.

It being mentioned that one of the principal piers, which supports the dome of St. Peters, has shrunk, as it is supposed, owing to Bernini having cut a stair case in it; Dance said that one of the piers which supports the Dome of St Pauls has also shrunk; and it has been found necessary with bolts & other applications to strengthen it.

Sir Joseph Banks I went to in the evening.

Lysons produced his book of the Roman Villa, at Woodchester.

I mentioned to Sir Joseph having heard that the King proposed to give the assent to the Sedition Bills in person. He said, the King had been advised not to go to the House on that occasion: but He Had determined to go; and Sir Joseph thought He judged right.

The Company tonight were —

Duke of Leeds — Sir John Sinclair — Dr. Russell
Lord Morton — Major Reynell — Dr. Garthshore

Lord Palmerston   — Mr. Dalrymple   — Mr. Keate
Lord Mountmorres — Mr. Marsden   — G. Dance
Mr. Abernethy   — S. Lysons   — Mr. Home
Arthur Young — &c &c &c.

Dance was yesterday with Lord Eardley, who he describes to be a good humoured man, that has many laughable oddities.

In St. James's St. He proposed to Dance to go into a Silversmiths Shop. I want, said He, to make a present to the wife of the Mayor of Coventry. He chose a Silver *Tea* pot: what motto shall I put upon it? I have it, Amo te. Dance laughed, and the motto was ordered to be engraved.

Monday Decr. 14th.

Taylor I called on this morning to dissuade him from publickly noticing a paragraph published Novr. 4th in the Telegraph; calumniating him in a very gross manner under the appelation of the "reptile Occulist". — In consequence of applications, & threats, Taylor obliged the author of the paragraph to come forward; it proved to be Mr. Merry, author of the poems signed Della Crusca; Who wrote a letter to Taylor styling him his dear friend and apologising for mistate, & drunkenness, which occasioned his writing the paragraph. — I found Taylor instigated by Beechy, & others, had delivered a statement of the affair, & a Copy of Merrys letter to the printer of the True Briton, which were printed this morning.

Taylor shewed me particulars of a transaction with Dr. Wolcot. In a conversation with Heriot, proprietor of the True Briton, Taylor had jokingly proposed to *buy* of the Doctor, and induce him to write in favor of government. This was followed by serious proposals; and it was ultimately agreed *with the Doctor*, that He should receive £300 a year. Sometime elapsed but the Doctor did not produce any work, & it being mentioned to him, He seemed to think He should receive £300 a yr. to *suppress* what He might have intended against government. He was assured to the contrary. In short the Dr. required the payment of half a year salary, witht. having done anything & probably wd. have recd. it; but found himself likely to be in a situation where persons could expose him if He did not act according to his agreement and thus circumstanced He declared of from the engagement He had made.

Several booksellers united together at present allow the Doctor for the privilege of publishing his works £250 a year.

Taylor has had several conversations with Opie on the subject of Mrs. Opie having left him. She went off with an Irishman, a major Edwards, a married man of 53 years of age, who she had frequently been in company with at Mr. Hickeys. — Opie went into Cornwall to examine the Parish Register for the date of his birth; but his name had not been entered. He could only prove his age, by that of another person who was known to be older than him. The object of this examination was, to prove that being *under age* when He was married to Mrs. Opie, the marriage is not valid in law: but Taylor observed to him that if He produced such proof He wd. render himself liable to be indited for perjury; as, at the time of his marriage to procure a license, He had sworn that He was of age. — At present Opie seems to be pretty well reconciled to his situation, having been assured that Mrs. Opie will not put him to any expence by contracting debts. — He does not think of applying for a divorce.

Dr. Monro called on me to invite me to meet Hamilton at dinner on Thursday next. Wheatley is again confined by the gout. The Dr. desired me to finish for him the stained drawing of the inside of Buildwas Abbey. — He proposes to sell part of his collection of drawings next Spring, as He thinks He has too many of Laportes &c. — He considers Hearne as superior to everybody in drawing, & that Laporte has not enough of the great principles of the art.

Smirke called on me. A Mr. Walker who has a place in one of the publick Offices & resides at Hackney has placed his only son under Smirke for 3 years. The terms are 100 guineas down, and 100 guineas a year board etc. included: The young man is between 15 & 16 yrs. of age.

Flaxman I went to with Smirke to see his model for Lord Mansfields monument. He has since He returned to England executed a small basso relievo monument to the memory of Collins, the poet, to be erected at Chichester: and is now executing one with a whole length figure of the late Sir Robt. Ladbroke. Flaxman shewed us a very fine cast of the Apollo of Belevidere. There is great reason to believe that the marble figure in the Belvidere is a Copy from an original which was executed in Bronze. The manner in which the ringlets of the Hair are formed has given rise to this opinion; and Flaxman offered a further remark in confirmation of the supposition. He desired us to compare the folds in the front of the drapery, with the opposite folds, which ought to, but do not, correspond. From which He inferred, that in the *Original* it was formed of a material (*bronze*) which would admit of *indents*, but marble, from its weight, requiring support throughout, an imitation throughout of the fluctuating lines of the drapery could not be ventured. The consequence is the front of the drapery is probably an exact imitation of the Original; while the back is carelessly folded without any relation to the front of it. — Speaking of the apparent projection of the left shoulder, Flaxman said, He had copied the figure, & could assure us that from the nape of the neck it was 4 fingers too broad for just proportion, & so far from being an advantage in his opinion, He was convinced that Had the right shoulder been *fuller*, & the left of due proportion, the figure wd. have been more perfect & more striking. — He accounts for the disproportion by supposing that the Artist who made the Copy not having the best access to the figure might have been mistaken in his measurements; and having projected his left arm too far, to soften the general appearance of disproportion & bulk reduced the size of the right shoulder. — Thus does He on the whole differ from certain Criticks who have ascribed the evident [disproportion] to intention, and have descanted on the advantage which the figure acquires from the disproportion.

The number of *Antique* Copies, found in Italy, of the Venus of Medicis, is very considerable. Many years ago upwards of 100 had been discovered.

The only son of Hayley, the Poet is now studying under Flaxman. — He is about 15 years old, — From a circumstance in his conversation He seems well prepared by a classical education.

Thelwall, the political lecturer I went to hear this evening at His room in Beaufort Buildings. The admittance was one shilling each. The doors opened at 7 & the lecture began at 8. — I judge there could not be fewer than 800 persons crouded together. — He spoke in a bold & decided manner; but the matter had little originality or entertainment in it. His argument was loose, and information common. — Of the Constitution he said it consisted chiefly in principles and maxims. That Montesqieu had justly described the poeple of England as being free because they thought themselves so. — That *freeman* in England was formerly a real distinction between one class of subjects and another; the latter being villains or slaves: & that virtually such as did not possess a right of *suffrage* were of the *latter description.* — Equal representation was the object He contended for — equal rights; equal protection from the laws &c. Equalization of property He described as a wild & wicked idea, impossible to be realized. — Popular commotion is to be dreaded from the consequences which follow: but if necessity urges it, nothing is to be feared but the distresses attending a struggle; for in the hearts of Englishmen principles & maxims are established which will restore order; and storm will be succeeded by a calm, when truth & justice will prevail. — The Jacobin Society in Paris, was, at its first establishment, excellent for principles & in practise. Bad men afterwards obtaining sway in it, most cruel & wicked abuses of its power were occasioned by them; but happily they had perished from the causes they had created; and France is still bound to look back to the *institution* who secured for Frenchmen the liberty they enjoy; and whatever they have of good; though the present laws are not, as far as relates to the poeple at large, what they ought to be.

He was abundant of metaphorical flourishes; which, though they were sometimes well expressed, had little variety.

He spoke an Hour & half; and concluded by saying that the Sedition Bills wd. not pass so soon as was expected; therefore He should give his concluding lecture on Wednesday evening.

Many Ladies were in the room: many Gentlemen: and the generality seemed poeple of the middle rank. — The Plaudits came from a third or 4th. of the whole, the great majority appearing to be merely visitors out of curiosity.

Thelwall addressed the Ladies as *Female Citizens.* — He wd. n
pronounce the Aristocratic word *Lady.*

I met C & J. Offley & Minet in the room & with them to the Bedfo
Coffee House. — Lord Mulgrave & Sir G. Beaumont called. I was ou

Tuesday Decr. 15th.

This day I staid at home.

T. Sandby I recd. a letter from on the subject of his not having recd. h
salary from the Academy for the last year on account of his not havi
delivered his lectures. I am to lay his letter before the Council.

Wilton this day sent me a continuation of his professional life; wi
some account of Cipriani.

Stadler drank tea with me. Fissinger, is a native of Suabia. He paints
miniature, and draws heads with a pen extremely well. His princip
employment is engraving. He engraved a Head of Miraubeau, whi
though done from an indifferent drawing, He told Stadler is like. He was
Paris during the revolution, but was ordered away with other foreigne
sometime since. Stadler says he is a classical scholar; and a sensible ma
rather partial to democratic principles.

A German who left Paris about 10 days ago told Stadler that the poe
seemed to despise the new established Government, which could
nothing to relieve them. In the interior of the country their decrees are lit
attended to.

The Paris papers brought over state that on the 10th. inst. 5050 Livres
Assignats were given for a Louis d'or.

Humphrey called.

Wednesday Decr. 16th.

Flaxman called on me at 12 & we went together to the Treasury to speak
Mr. Long on the subject of farther indulgence to Artists returning fro
abroad that they may import works of art purchased by them as studi
duty free. — Mr. Long was not at the Treasury.

I asked Flaxman what impression Rome made on his mind when h
first saw that City. He said He was disappointed. On entering the stree
He found them narrow & dark; and when He came among the ruins
ancient buildings He found them on a smaller scale, and less striking, th
he had been accustomed to suppose them after having seen the prints
Piranesi.

Flaxman observed to me that there are many antique figures of Venus
the same attitude as that of the Venus of Medici; which figure may
supposed to represent a girl of 16 or 17 years of age; whilst others, standi
in the same attitude, represent woemen of 20 years, and upwards: t
general character of the figures also varying; and some of them appe

from the quality of the workmanship to be of a much earlier date, than the Venus of Medici, & before the art had been carried to so great perfection. From all which, Flaxman infers, that an early & popular idea of the Venus, in this attitude, prevailed; and being often attempted to be executed by artists of different ages, the multiplicity is accounted for. The Venus of Medici derives its reputation from its superior excellence, not from its originality; but many of the other antiques are fine figures, and are as much original.

Flaxman assured me that one of the Popes Secretaries told him that on an average 1500 persons are murdered annually in the Papal dominions. From the reports which were made, it appeared that in 20 years of the present Popes reign 30,000 persons had been murdered. — Whereas in Tuscany, the adjoining state, not one, or but one, person had been murdered in the same length of time. — These murders are almost confined to the lowest orders of the poeple, & is regarded with great indifference. — The principal cause why regulations are not made which wd. prevent such crimes, is, the independant state of the Roman Princes; These great feudal chiefs value themselves on their power of protection, and as each Pope usually rises from a low rank, and his power passing at his death, to a new man, the series of exertion is interrupted; and each Pope must be content singly to do what He can, but so circumstanced it would perhaps be impossible for him to overcome the habits of a poeple, with so many protecting Lords at their backs, ready to defy the power of the Pope.

The day before Flaxman left Rome, He was at a dinner given by Prince Augustus to the English Artists. The entertainment was very splendid.

The English Artists in Rome are well recd. by the English Nobility &c. and by many foreigners, if their merit is considerable and their manners proper.

Flaxman thinks the allowance of £100 a year from the Academy to the travelling student is ample. — His expences, Mrs. Flaxman being with him, amounted [to] no more than £120 a yr. They were oeconomists; but were comfortable.

Shakespeare gallery we went to. — Steevens, Coombes & Lodge there. — Boydell does not approve of the proposed addition of a list of the botanical plants which grow upon the sides of the Thames: and on referring it to Steevens, He does not think a work like ours requires it.

The ninth number of Shakespeare was published this day, which completes half the work.

Nicol spoke highly of a botanical work executing by Baur, a German. It is to consist of 40 specimens of different sorts of *Heaths* from samples in Kew Gardens. There are to be 80 Coloured plates at half a guinea each. — Only 100 sets are to be completed, & the etched outlines are all to be coloured by Baur himself.

Offleys I dined at. — Smirke & Michl. Bush there.

Bush is acquainted with Alderman Skinner, and related his progress in life. He was apprentice to an Undertaker; and marrying early became a Coffin maker; which trade He worked at. He then kept an open Brokers Shop; and by degrees became an Auctioneer. He is supposed to be an excellent judge of the value of estates. — Throughout life He has preserved a character of great liberality; and is not supposed to be nearly so rich as has been imagined. — He is near 60 years of age.

Bush stated that the Room in Beaufort Buildings in which Thelwall lectures, was taken for him by a set of gentlemen who became responsible for the rent, £120 a year, which they raised by subscription.

Wm. Augustus Miles, author of the celebrated letter to the Prince of Wales, is natural son to a Nobleman. He has passed through a variety of situations in life; and was once in the West Indies.

Thursday Decr. 17th.

Bread, to reduce the consumption of it, a resolution was yesterday adopted by the Houses of Lords & Commons, to be signed by the Members, that they will use only in their families bread in which flour of an inferior quality is mixed with that of which bread was usually made. — Lord Mansfield stated that the crop of Wheat on an average through out the Kingdom had failed one third. — The lower orders of the poeple have persisted in using only the best kind of bread, from believing it contains the most nourishment; but Lord Hawkesbury observed, that in Scotland their bread was made of Oats, at Newcastle of Rye, and in Cornwall of Barley; and yet those poeple were as robust as any in the Southern parts of the Kingdom.

Bush mentioned yesterday that He had been told by a Dealer in Corn, that *He* apprehended February as likely to be the month of greatest scarcity.

The quartern loaf is this day, Thirteen pence, halfpenny.

Shakespeare Gallery I went to, and met there Westall & Ireland.

Kemble told Boaden that He had read the play of Vortigern, and that it was wretched stuff. Ireland sd. another of the players had told him, that the Play would be damned the first night.

Contrary to expectation the King did not go to the house of Lords today to pass the Sedition Bills in person.

I walked home with Westall & saw one of his large drawings made for Lord Berwick. The size of each drawing is abt. 28 Inches by 21. Westall complained of the length of time they take him; at least 7 weeks each. Lord Berwick gave him an unlimited commission as to size &c only desiring to have the best drawings he can make at this period of his life. Westall proposes to charge 300 Guineas for the two drawings.

Westall told me that at Lord Grosvenors table lately the Democratic disposition of the members of the Royal Academy was mentioned. — He thinks it wd. be prudent for the Council to pass a resolution "that it is not necessary for a President to deliver a discourse". — If such a motion failed in its effect to follow it up with another, "that no discourse shd. be delivered by the President which had not been approved by the Council".

Owen the bookseller told me today that Sheridans lenity in proposing not to prosecute Him, & the Printer, on acct. of Reeves pamphlet, was owing to Sheridan knowing, that if prosecutions were ordered against them He shd. have no evidence against Reeves.

Dr. Monros I dined at. — Dr. Paul & His Son, — Mr. Chas. Monro, Henderson, Hearne & Hamilton dined there.

The conversation chiefly political and Hearne described the inconsistencies of Fox with great effect; and shewed him to be a political character in no respect to be depended on.

Hamilton told me Malton proposes to paint views of London; in order to qualify himself for the Academy as a painter.

Hamilton & myself staid to supper, and till ½ past 12 oClock.

Friday — Decr. 19th [18th].

Flaxman called on me this morning & we went together to the Treasury, but Mr. Long was in a Committee at the house of Commons. — We returned through the parks; and Flaxman spoke of Wests last discourse at the Royal Academy which He considered both for matter and delivery a disgrace to the profession: and thought some means shd. be used to prevent him from delivering another discourse.

Flaxman has understood that it is necessary for a Candidate for Associate to canvass the members; but I told him I considered it unbecoming the members to encourage such a custom, and am well convinced an Artist of distinguished merit will succeed witht. it.

Carey called on me. Major Le Merchant has obtained from the Duke of York, by means of General Harcourt a Cornetcy in the 16th. dragoons for Carey, without purchase. Being one of the additional, beyond the peace establishment of the regt., He will be reduced at the peace: but will then have half pay abt. £40 a year. He means to pursue his studies. — His full pay is now £140 a yr. and He is not obliged at present to join the regt.

Careys Brother, who is in the guards, is advanced to the rank of Lieutenant with *Captain's rank;* He was 18 years old yesterday. — His pay is abt. £140 a year, & his expenses altogether abt. £250 or 60 a yr.

Carey mentioned to me a young man of the name of [blank] who has been under West: but who seems to have a good taste for landscape. He has lately been in Wales, & has painted a view of Snowdon which Carey thinks very ingenious.

Royal Academy Club I went to. — Eighteen members present.

West & Bourgeois being at the Club sooner than others: West asked us if we had heard of an application made by an Academician for his Son to succeed to the place held by Boswell in the Academy. I told him I had not; neither had Bourgeois: who guessed it must be Copley. While we were talking, Copley & others came in so no more was said on the subject.

West told us that Burch had this day been with him; and described his situation to be very distressed. He lately removed to Kentish Town, where He has a house at a very low rent; yet He cannot subsist upon his income which is little more than what He receives from the Academy as Librarian; and his being occasionally visitor. — I said Banks had stated at the Academy on the 10th. of Decr. that Burch was in good circumstances and the members were deceived by a misrepresentation.

Nollekens related to me what He knows of the transaction between Mr. Weddel & Jenkins, relative to the Statue of Venus. — Nollekens says, the Trunk of the figure, and one of the thighs, & part of the leg, is antique. The Head, Arms, and the other thigh & leg are modern. This figure was in the possession of the Dowager Princess Barberini, an expensive woman, who had the care of her Sons property while a minor. When she occasionally wanted money she was accustomed to apply to her Custodini (Keeper of the Rooms) to offer such articles for sale as wd. produce the sum required; and He accordingly applied to Artists, or Dealers, or Gentlemen travelling & made bargains with them. This Venus He sold to an Italian Sculptor for a Small Sum: but the Head which had been put on not suiting the figure well, Jenkins looked among collections for one which would match better; and finding a Head of Agrippina with a Veil falling from the Hair, He had the Veil chizzel'd away and the Head trimmed and set on the body of the figure. — He then exposed it advantageously and finally sold it to Mr. Weddel; but Nollekens never could learn on what conditions. — The late Lord Rockingham was desirous of knowing what Mr. Weddel gave for the Statue, and employed Lady Rockingham who was Sister to Mrs. Weddel, to find out from Her sister what was the price given; but Mrs. Weddel pleaded ignorance. — Nollekens says, that what is antique is good; and the statue may be worth 150 or 200 pounds. — The figure of Minerva in the possession of Mr. Weddel, was found in a vineyard near Rome and bought by Nollekens for 60 Crowns. It is a draped figure, and, when found, wanted a head. Jenkins having met with a Head which matched the statue offered Nollekens 125 pounds for the figure. — They at last agreed to make it a joint concern, with an allowance to Nollekens as the figure was the most valuable part. — It was then offered & sold to Mr. Weddel for £600. — Nollekens says it is a very fine figure and worth £1000, and Mr. Townley would give that Sum for it.

Nollekens was at Wilton (Lord Pembrokes) abt. 6 weeks ago. The Collection of marble statues & busts; with the exception of three busts, and one draped figure of an Empress, (as it appears to be), which have merit, is so bad that He would not pay the carriage of them to London to possess them.

West spoke of a sleeping fawn in the Barberini Collection, as a work of art in sculpture which had made a lasting impression on his mind. Copley, — Nollekens, & Zoffany joined him with expressions of admiration. Nollekens has a Cast of the Head, which Sir Joshua Reynolds always contemplated with admiration whenever He called upon Nollekens.

Copley gave his opinion that Michael Angelo, when He added parts to antique statues to restore them, had not succeeded. There appeared to him to be something of extravagance, and want of simplicity in these attempts. — In his original figures there is also a tendency to extravagance though the parts of his figures are treated in a learned manner and are finely executed. — The others present did [not] incline to concur to the full length of Copleys Criticisms.

West related a strong instance of the vanity of Pompeio Battoni. West visited him in Rome, and saw him painting. He had wrought up part of his picture to receive the finishing touches, and proceeded to give them while West was present; which, when He had done; all the while uttering tones of delight, He fell back into a chair & cried out, Viva Battoni.

Nollekens described a Head of an infant Hercules now in the possession of Mr. Townley as being an exquisite piece of art. Jenkins purchased it from the Princess Barberini.

Zoffany related to me many particulars of his professional life. He was born at Frankfort on the Maine, March 13th, 1734.

Saturday Decr. 19th.

Dance I called on. Mr. Rogers was sitting for a profile. Lysons there.

C & J Offley dined with me. — C Offley had been to the Whig Club, Mr. Erskine in the Chair, who in an opening speech, reprobated the Sedition Bills and proposed a Committee of members of the Club, to determine on a petition to the legislature against the Bills; and by this example, it wd. be seen whether the poeple at large are for the Bills or not. — Fox & Duke of Bedford also spoke.

Flaxmans I drank tea at. Smirke, & young Hayley, there. — We looked over the etched imitations of Flaxmans designs from the Iliad, — the Odyssy, — & Dantes Inferno, — & OEschylus. These designs he made at Rome, as evening studies.

Flaxman shewed us three drawings from pictures painted by Lucas Signorelli, which He found in a Church at Orvietto, 10 miles from the Lake Bolsano, and about 80 miles from Rome. The subject of the picture is the last judgment. Signorelli was the predecessor of Michael Angelo, and the manner of the latter which is generally considered as singular, & purely original, so closely resembles that of Signorelli, that several of the figures in the last judgment of Angelo seem to be copies from the work of th other. — That Michl. Angelo carried his Art much further than Signorel did is undoubted; but his claim to bold and uncommon conceptions; an to a mode of thinking altogether peculiar, is very much weakened, by thes proofs of the ability of Signorelli. Michl. Angelo evidently adopted th thoughts of the former, and imitated him in the contrivance of his figures — To Dolabella [Donatello] too, He owed much.

Flaxmans designs for the Iliad; Odyssey; & Oeschylus; are strictl formed on the Greek model. Whatever is introduced is Greek; each circum stance being copied from some authority. As such they are valuable t refer to by those [who] have occasion to study the costume. Many of th figures are elegant, and in a pure taste; appropriate to sculptural art.

Smirke observed that in several of the figures there is a *forced simplicity* very proper to such subjects, when treated after the manner of antiqu designs; which observation is just, for where the Heathen Mytholog becomes mixed with the actions of mortals, it requires that whateve approaches to common appearances, and common life, should be strictl avoided.

Hayley objects to his Son studying at the Royal Academy from an appre hension that His morals may be corrupted by the example of young me who attend there: but, Flaxman says He is so convinced of the necessity fo it; that if He is to have the care of Young Hayleys education, it will only b on the condition that He studies at the Academy.

We supped & staid till 12 oClock.

Sunday, Decr. 20th.

At Church. Mr. Mathew preached. Text from Genesis 19 Chap. Verse 14 — He observed that the present condition of many parts of the world may be considered as the effect of the displeasure of the Almighty; whic towards this nation is at present suspended; and thus circumstanced, H pressed the necessity there is for us to secure mercy & pardon for our Sins by fulfilling our religious, & moral duties; and by resisting the attacks c wicked men, who are endeavouring to sap the foundation of our religion & to eradicate our moral principles.

William came up from Deptford & dined.

Bakers I dined at. — Hearne, — Marchant, — and Harrison, th Architect, there.

Harrison has been employed at Lancaster in building some additions t the Castle for the reception of Felons, & for other purposes. — In thes additions He has not used any wood: the whole being formed of Stone; & Iron He occasionally used. — The roofs of the Upper Apartments ar composed of stone only, and the manner in which they are laid H described thus.

The building 21 feet long by 14 feet ½ wide.

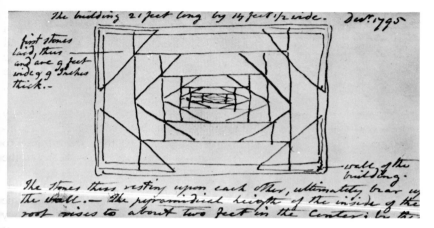

The stones thus resting upon each other, ultimately bear upon the wall. — The pyramidical heigth of the inside of the roof rises to about two feet in the Center; by the gradual addition of the thickness of the stones which form the roof. — If the building were required to be higher, the weight of the additional wall pressing upon the first stones diagonally laid, would give it sufficient strength to bear a floor upon the roof of the first room, so that apartments thus constructed of stone only might be raised above each other.

The length of the Bridge at Lancaster, built by Harrison, is, to the extremity of the walls, about 205 yards. — There are 5 Arches, each Arch is abt. 68 feet wide; & the piers are abt. 11 feet wide. — The Bridge cost about £15,000.

The estimate of the expence of the New Canal from Kendal, which is to be carried over the River Lune by means of an Aqueduct of 5 Arches is £550,000.

Harrison is a plain man in person & manners, with an embarassed delivery in conversation, but very clear & ready in explaining with his pencil. — He was born at Richmond in Yorkshire. His Father was a Carpenter. When a Young Man his talents were so conspicuous, that Sir Thomas Dundass was induced to send him to Italy, where He remained 6 or 7 years. When Marchant went to Rome in 1773 He found Harrison there, who while pursuing His studies in that City, was distinguished for his abilities & industry. Having offered himself for the Architectural premium given at St. Lukes Academy, the medal was adjudged to another of inferior merit, owing to a jealousy which was entertained by the Italians of his rising abilities. This being represented to Pope Ganganelli He directed that a Medal shd. be given to him as a testimony of the opinion held of his skill.

Hearne related that the late Mr. Willet of Merly in Dorsetshire at early period of his life, formed a connexion with a young woman w whom He cohabited many years. On Her death bed she solicited him marry her, which He did while she was in that situation. After Her de He employed the late Mr. Penny to paint a picture representing ceremony as it took place. — He also engaged John Hunter to open body, had her heart taken out, and preserved it in a glass case which sto in his bed room.

Mr. Willet left his great fortune, said to be £10,000 a year to Mr. Ad who has taken the name of Willet. — To Sir Ralph Payne (now Lc Lavingdon) who was his relation in an equal degree, He left only £15 and to the Brothers, and Sisters of Ld. Lavingdon, only £1000 each.

Monday Decr. 21st.

Flaxman called on me this morning, & we went together to the Treasu where we waited till 12 oClock when Mr. Long came, but being obliged go to the House of Commons on the Loan Committee He desired us come to the Treasury tomorrow at Eleven oClock.

Flaxman concurs with Copley in thinking that Michl. Angelo when has attempted to restore antique statues, Has not adapted His addition the true character of the original parts. — He instanced one in particula a deity to which M. Angelo had added a Head in which too much passio expressed; for the ancients properly considered that Deities of ev degree were supposed to possess power which rendered exertion necessary; and accordingly have uniformly represented them as sublim calm and composed.

I remained at home this evening alone. — Mrs. Hughes wrote to me desire Mr. Bunbury may see my drawings & Webbers Portfolio.

Tuesday, Decr. 22d.

Flaxman called on me, and we went together to the Treasury, but w again disappointed, Mr. Long being at the Loan Committee.

Flaxman has seen Mr. Knights collection of small Bronzes; amo which there are 5 or 6 good ones, among many very indifferent. He s that modern Artists, Banks, He particularly named, could execute much better than what makes up such a collection as this, that it exci impatience to hear so much said abt. it. — Of Mr. Townleys collection spoke with warm praises, as ranking next after 2 or 3 which are to be fou in Rome.

Flaxman described Hayley to be a man of great liberality of dispositi His fortune is but small. He proposes that His Son shall be a Sculptor profession.

Downman called on me.

The Trent Club I went to.

Dr. Thomson in the Chair.

Mr. Nichols   — Serjeant Marshall — Dr. Heming
Mr. Nichols Junr.   — Willis   — Hoppner
Mr. Rogers   — Captn. Budworth — Mr. Carbonel Senr.
                                                       Mr. Carbonel Junr.

Mr. Norman, recommended by Mr. Nichols was elected. — A resolution passed, "*that no person shall be admitted a Candidate who has not been previously introduced to dine at the club*".

Mr. Nichols senr. told me He thought our ministry had miscalculated in their opinion of French finance. In his opinion the depreciation of Assignats, when they fell below a certain point, became an advantage to the government of that country. That after the depreciation had become so great that a Louis d'or sold for 5050 assignats, the proposal of the government to receive in payment of the forced loan assignats at half that depreciation, would be chearfully accepted by the poeple who in this instance wd. consider themselves to be gainers; thus might the national debt be liquidated. — He does not believe that so much specie has been exported from France as is generally considered to have been the Case. To England, for instance, had so much been imported as has been supposed, it would certainly have lowered the value of gold & Silver, which has not been the case.

Budworth told me He was the Author of a pamphlet entitled, "a Fortnights ramble to the Lakes in Cumberland & Westmorland". He wrote it in 1792.

Willis said the late Mr. Wedgwood of Etruria, in Staffordshire, who died last year, had accummulated by his Pottery manufacture £400,000. He had three Sons, and three daughters; to each of whom He left £75,000: and to his widow £100,000. Susan returned from Norfolk this evening. — She left the Revd. Mr. Coxe at Wolterton. — He is collecting materials for a History of the administration of Sir Robt. Walpole. — Among the papers of Horace, late Lord Walpole, He found one in which it was stated that at the conclusion of the peace of Aix La Chapelle, Lord Walpole, (then Horace Walpole), reccomended this country to subscribe £50,000 for 12 years to restore the *Barrier* towns. — The motion was not agreed to.

Coxe is a very singular man in his manners. — He told Susan his principal characteristics are *Shyness* & *Vanity*.

Wednesday Decr. 23d 1795.

The Shakespeare Gallery I went to. G. Steevens & Nicol there. — We talked of Irelands Shakesperian discoveries, which both of them ridiculed. — I told Steevens it had by some been supposed that the whole was a fabrication of fun made up by him. He said He had heard the same, but were He

disposed to play such a trick it wd. not be in conjunction with S.
Ireland.

Ireland the Editor of Hogarth moralised came in. He told me tha
S Ireland now disclaims any knowledge of the person who gave the Shakes
perian Manuscripts to his Son: but that, with them, He settled at the same
time £280 a year on him. — He now avows having found a Bible found
filled with marginal notes by Shakespeare.

The deed of gift of this collection of materials which S *Ireland* says was
delivered to an Ancestor of his of the same name, Ireland laughs at, from
knowing that *S Ireland* cannot trace back to a great grandfather. —
Humphry I dined with. — Fuseli, — Westall, — Flaxman, Davis there. —
Green, & Harrison, the architect, came in afterwards.

Much conversation on the works of some of the old masters. — Fuseli
spoke lightly of the last supper at Milan, by Leonardo de Vinci. — Among
the Apostles some of the characters are expressive, but not elevated. The
Saviour is a common placed conception of the character. The picture has
been painted upon (restored) but this, Fuseli said, made no difference as to
the original characters, as they were not affected by it. — Flaxman did not
seem fully to concur in these criticisms.

Thursday — Decr. 24th.

at home all day.

Mrs. Hussell informed Susan that the Duke of Portland is so much in
debt, that even common household Bills are not paid; and in the neighboroud of Bulstrode the poeple complain very much. — Since the death of
the Duchess, the Duke has indulged an ostentatious taste in his dinners. As
a Cabinet minister, the dinners He gives in rotation are more expensive
than those of any other of the ministry. — In short his situation is such in
regard to finances that He may be considered as looking up to Office for
the sake of the emoluments.

Christmas Day — Decr. 25th.

At Church, Mr. Mathews preached. — Malachi, Chap. [3] Verse [10] In
recommendation of the Sacrament. — The Sacrament well attended.

Henley, Susan wrote to this day; to remind him of the legacies due by his
mothers will. They were due Novr. 10th. and He has hitherto taken no
notice of them.

Stadler came in the evening.

At Berlin, & throughout Saxony, the best German is spoken; at Vienna
very bad; In Bavaria worse still. In Suabia as bad. In the Palatinate rather
better. At Frankfort pretty good; but not with such correctness of
pronunciation, as the Saxons. On the Rhine, from Mentz [Mainz] down to
Cologne, the poeple speak a very bad language, Stadler could not understand them. — The language spoken in Hamburgh is in Germany called

Plat-deutsch, or flat Dutch. Stadler does not understand it when spoken. The Plat-deutsch is the nearest to the *ancient German* of any language now used. It is not considered as vulgar; but as a language distinct from the German: but Authors do not write in it. The Hanoverians also speak Plat-deutsch. In both these Countries High German is only learnt in Schools. Authors throughout Germany write only in High German: all other dialects are considered as provincial. — The Bohemian; The Hungarian; The Polish; and the Russian languages have some affinity: but are quite distinct from the German. The Swedes, and Danes can understand each other. The Dutch has most affinity to the Hamburgh: but is a more complete language having been more cultivated.

Saturday Decr. 26th. 1795.

Alderman Boydell I dined with. Mrs. Loyd & Richards there; & Stadler to tea.

The Alderman shewed me his manuscript notes of the early part of his life; of which I took a Copy.

An opposition was made on St. Thomas's day, at the election of a Common Council, to turn out several of the late Common Council on account of their having voted for the adress in favor of the Sedition Bills. — This attempt of Democratic opposition had little success. Only Eight changes took place in the whole Common Council; & the whole of this number is not of that description.

The Alderman says, poeple of property are in general in favor of Government; as are also respectable people of a lower class.

Sunday 27th.

At Church Mr. Mathews preached. — Hebrews 13th. — verse 16th.

On Charity: reccomending it; and that a mild and soothing deportment is due from the rich towards the poor.

Kershaw called on me. — He complained much of Macklin having extended the quantity of his numbers of the publication of the Bible: which will increase the whole expence from abt. £40-to £60. — He wrote from Manchester to Macklin, and also remarked on the very bad prints lately delivered. Some, with the name of Bartolozzi, are very indifferent: and the Vignettes since Macklin ceased to employ Landseer, are poorly executed.

Captn. Dewhurst, at 80 years of age, broke his leg last summer in his hay field; but is now well recovered, — and continues painting with his usual ardour. He desired Kershaw wd. request me to procure him some foreign brushes & pitch pencils.

Baker I met. Landseer is again employed by Macklin.

Byrne has commenced a second volume of Antiquities from drawings by Hearne.

Macklins Bible, — and Bowyers Hist: of England, — now sell at auctions, at not more than two thirds the original price of the numbers already published.

Monday Decr. 28th.

Byrne I called on this morning. — He shewed me three etchings intended for a continuation of the antiquities of Great Britain. — Mr. Peachy & Mr. Jo: Windham, called on him sometime since to ask him if He proposed to continue that work; if not, they proposed, as He understood, that the work shd. be continued by some other means. — He then determined to carry it on. — He intends to print the 2d. Vol: on larger paper than the first Vol: & will publish each number at 15s. — the nos. of the first Vol: were published at 12s. — Byrne promised me a set of etchings. Only 12 sets will be taken of.

Byrnes eldest daugr. proceeds in drawing flowers &c and now instructs some young Ladies. — She is abt. 22 years old. — The second daugr. Mary, has made an excellent copy from Sir Joshuas picture of Sir Geo. Beaumont, — and has begun a copy from Sir Joshuas picture of Lady Beverly. She has also painted a very good miniature a portrait of Her mother in law. — The third daugr. is very ingenious in etching. — Mary Byrne will be glad to paint miniatures from the life at 5 guineas each.

Underwood has called on Byrne to make a apology for former misbehaviour, but this was followed by a proposal to go shares with him in the 2d. Vol: of Antiquities.

Humphry drank tea with us.

Smart says He has not brought over near the Sum of £20,000, — which was his object.

Humphry believes Zoffany has received from India in all £26,000. — One of his children born & left in India, a Son, is taken care of by Col. Martin.

Tyler called today. — Dance & He cannot complete the report on Sir William Chambers' accts. before new years eve, so they must pass over to the new Council.

Soane told Tyler that at the last Architects Club, Yenn said to him that the Academy had, or would have a letter from the King on the subject of the Academy accounts & finances. — Soane was surprised that such a matter shd. be mentioned to him *by Yenn,* as they have been at variance sometime.

Thomas Sandby has applied to Lord Amherst to assist him on obtaining the office of drawing master to the Academy at Woolwich, for young Tom Sandby, in the room of his father, Paul Sandby who wishes to relinquish it to his Son. — Lord Amherst told Tyler he has no interest with Lord Cornwallis and, that he thought it wd. be imprudent in Paul to substitute

Sons name who might possibly die before him & he would then be
⟩rived of all advantages from that appointment.

Tuesday Decr. 29th.

ᴀkespeare Gallery I went to, — met Mr. Lodge of the Heralds Office
·re. He gave me his opinion of Irelands Shakesperian manuscripts which
re published last Thursday. He saw the manuscripts 6 months ago in
ɴpany with Mr. Pye, the poet Laureat, and to him then declared his
ɪnion. He thinks them such gross forgeries that there is sufficient in
·ry page to detect them. There is both internal an[d] external evidence
ᴀinst them. Speaking of the orthography, He said it is rather an
ɪtation of that of Henry 7th. than of Elizabeth; and that were He to copy
‹ whole agreeable to the orthography of the latter reign it would be a
ffficient exposure of the forgery. — But in imitating the orthography, as
ɔommon in forgeries, they have overdone it: and have added more letters
words than were ever known at any period to have been used. — *Nor*
d *or* for instance are spelt *nore* & *ore* and this by various supposed
rsons. — The Earl of Southampton is addressed my Lord, — which is
ɪte modern; it would have been Right Honourable. He is also styled
ʋr grace, which would never have been used to a lower rank than a
ʋke. — Lord Southampton in turn writes to Shakespeare, *Dear*
illiam., and the letters conclude after the modern manner; one of them
th *yours.* — The word *composition* was never used in those [times] in the
ɴse in which it is now frequently accepted viz. to signify a *work* of *author-*
ip. — The word *Compliment* was never, in those days, introduced to
press reciprocal civilities. — Lord Southampton gives Shakespeare
000, a sum perhaps equal to £15000 at this time; and Shakespeare with
ʋal gallantry returns one half of it. These acts of bounty and dis-
ᴛerestedness are performed in those days of feudal dignity, between an
ᴀrl, and a young player. — *Anna* is modern. There is no instance of the
ɔrd being spelt but as Ann*e* till modern times; when sentimental love
⟩etry became fashionable.

G. Steevens came in. He brought in his pocket a manuscript play written
ʋ Middleton, to prove the difference of orthography when compared
ɪth Irelands imitations. — I went over to Edwards', the Bookseller, to see
elands publication. Three or four gentlemen were there who scouted the
ɔnsense of the matter, & the form of the forgeries: In this Edwards joined,
ᴀying that what Ireland has published will cut of all hopes of his
ᴀcceeding in the imposition.

Edwards said Ireland had been very active in procuring names to his sub-
·ription list which amounted to 126. The Duke of Leeds told Edwards
ᴀat Ireland called upon him, and the Duke supposing that four guineas
he subscription) was his object, offered ɪhe money; but Ireland declined it

saying it was the name of His Grace he wanted. Of course He got both name and money; but the Duke seems to think with other people.

Soanes I dined at. The Company Mr. & Mrs. Soane.

Tyler — Edwards — Bourgeois — Copley — Westall
Bigg — Garvey — Beechy — Rooker — Downman

Bigg related to me many particulars of his own, & George Casters, professional lives.

The evening being very wet I did not leave Soanes till near twelve oClock.

William came up from Gravesend.

Wednesday Decr. 30th.

William returned early this morning.

Burch called on me. — He said that in the last 4 years He has only had one commission; and that, but to the amount of 20 guineas. — That He had removed to a small House in Paynes place, Kentish Town, No. 1., and with all economy could scarcely support his expences. — That He proposes to publish by subscription, at 3 guineas each, a set of impressions from his works, but that the expences attending this publication are such as He cannot support without assistance. He therefore as an Academician proposes to apply to the Council for relief. That a fund was set apart, in consequence of a proposal made some years ago by Meyer, for the purpose of relieving members of the Academy if any should require assistance; and that the fund had now encreased to upwards of £4000, — 3 pr. cent. — That the sum of £100 would enable him to carry his scheme of publication into execution; and He trusted the Council would comply with his request.

I replied that I should at all times earnestly wish to unite in endeavouring to assist the members of the Society if any should stand in need of assistance so far as we were enabled to render it; and I had no doubt of others being of the same mind.

He said Bacon He trusted to as a friend and had no doubt of others. — Russell He said, had told him, that Copley, while engaged on the picture of Lord Chatham, had such support from the Academy. I told him that if that had been the case, I had never heard of it. — Kershaw, — Baker, — Hearne and Byrne — dined with me.

Craig told Kershaw that in the past 3 years, He had got by his professional practise upwards of £1900. — That his annual expences are about £500 a year.

Hearne this day finished a drawing of Lantony Abbey, for Byrnes 2d. Vol: of Antiquities. He said He had been *16 days* employed upon it, — The days have been short & the weather dark, which has made some difference. Size of the drawing —; [blank] inches by [blank] inches.

Thursday Decr. 31st.

mirke called on me this morning, and we talked of Burchs request to the cademy, which He is very willing to comply with.

He told me Bowyer is desirous of having a partner in his undertaking of ιe History of England who might have a third share or 4th. share, rovided he could advance 2 or 3000 pounds. — The Executors of Bond lopkins have given Bowyer full time for payment of money advanced by ιat Gentleman on acct. of the work; but the expences are very heavy. He ιas upwards of 800 subscribers: but on delivery of a number He requently receives very little money, & it wd. be dangerous to press his ιbscribers.

Smirkes 2d. Son, aged 15, is now head Boy at a School in Bedfordshire, ιhere there are 150 Boys. He reads Latin, Greek & French well. He shews ι inclination to drawing. I gave it as my opinion that Smirke wd. be able ɔ educate this Son as well as the eldest in some branch of art, with more ɔnvenience to himself than in any other profession. This He concurred in; ιd mentioned Architecture. I said I would apply to Dance for His ·pinion.

Council at Academy. — Present
West
Bacon — Smirke — Bourgeois — Farington.

Sir William Chambers has addressed two more letters to Richards, in ιhich He dwells upon the retrenchments proposed by him through Lord ʿardigan, as they evidently are. The last of these letters comprehends his ιhole view in a concise proposal. He writes "That the members are not to eceive any pay for attendance at General Meetings", — and as He seems ɔ mean it, "not for attending Councils". He then requires from Richards ιn acct. of what they have been doing at General meetings, and at Councils ately; and, as the sense of his letter appears to be, this is to be delivered to ιim regularly as the "Agent of His Majesty". — Thus would He supersede ιll the standing regulations and engross a controuling power which would ender the Members of the Academy mere Cyphers. He mentions in the etter that He had sent *Rose* with the accts. to be audited, and reccomends ɔ the Council to invite him to Supper.

Every person present felt proper indignation at such a continuation of ιnsult. Bacon proposed not to invite *Rose* when so dictated to which I, and ιhe others agreed to. Richards was directed to take no other notice of his letter, than in conversation with Sir William to say that He had shewn it to ιhe Council; and that a Committee is proceeding in regulating the accts. — Richards was directed neither to give Sir William a Copy of what has been ιransacted at General meetings; and at Councils, lately, nor, should He ʿequire it, allow him to see the Journal Books: it being strictly out of order.

I read the letter from Mathias to Sir William; in which the proposals for regulations were inclosed. The gross manner in which the members of the Academy are treated in these papers; particularly in the *proposals,* goes beyond what could be imagined. The whole is evidently drawn up by Sir William himself.

He proposes that instead of 50,000 catalogues, there should be half a dozen lists hung up in different parts of the room.

That only the two upper rooms should be made use of for Exhibition. That fewer works shd. be received; and then the Exhibition wd. be better.

That the Hangers shall have 5s. each a day board wages. — The Carpenters kept to meat hours.

That there shall be no Annual dinner, by which £170 a year will saved.

That there shall be no Jubilee medals or Jubilee dinners, with singers & musicians, who only spoil conversation.

That the Members shall have no pay for attending General meetings; where they assemble only to debate & throw the Academy into a flame &c &c.

That the Whim of a Jubilee medal, shall at least be postponed.

I read a paper delivered to me by Tyler stating that the Academy may be carried on, on the present Plan for the following expences.

Council, General meetings, salaries to Officers.	486-0-0
Visitors and expences of models.	187-0-0
Servants, Coals, Oil & Candles	217-0-0
Taxes	80-0-0
Incidents	60-0-0
carried over }	1030-0-0
Medals.	30-0-0
Pension at Rome.	100-0-0
Expences of Exhibition	750-0-0
Charity	150-0-0
	2060-0-0
The expence of Books, & Casts is now trifling, and cannot exceed	40-0-0
	2100-0-0

Therefore suppose the Exhibition to produce the sum of £2100 we do not break into our capital or even upon the dividends of our funds, which would be left to accummulate.

But as the dividend on the solid fund is annually £294 it will always supply any deficiency.

Thus does it appear how grossly and falsely, Sir William has misrepresented the situation of the academy affairs to the King.

I said, that when Mr. Dance & Tyler had made out a fair statement, of
he accts., and the whole of our situation is known to the King, I had no
doubt of every impression of an unfavourable nature being removed from
his Majestys mind: but that should it unfortunately prove otherways, and
f the influence of Sir Wm., or of any other person, were to supersede the
Council of the Academy; our meetings would then be a farce, and the
Society would be contemptible. — In this Bacon fully concurred and
spoke of quitting it as would He conceived be a general opinion. West also
spoke out, and said, that, if, after any body of men had exerted themselves,
to support the institution for 27 years, in so disinterested a manner that
their conduct is without parallel in the history of the Arts, they were now
to be treated in the way which Sir William proposed, it could no longer be
considered as honourable to be of such an association. — Smirke &
Bourgeois & Richards all concurred in the same feelings. West said if a
dozen Members whom He could name were to retreat from the Academy
the Exhibitions must fall.

A letter from Burch was now read and Bacon stated that He believed
Burch to be a distressed man; that 7 years ago B. had applied to him for a
Sum of money; and had repeated applications to him at different periods.
That he had never lent any money to Burch as the Sums applied for were
always more than He chose to lose; and He did not believe, had He lent the
money, that He should ever be repaid. — West related what passed when
Burch first applied to be Librarian, & said the King & the Duke of York,
then gave him commissions: The King having been informed of Burchs
poverty & want of employ. This was when Serres was nominated
Librarian.

These, & other circumstances related induced the Council to pass an
unanimous vote that, "Mr. Burch having represented his distressed
situation & requested assistance from the Academy £100 be voted to him".

I read a letter which I had received from Thomas Sandby, stating, that
after having been four months employed in preparing a fresh set of
drawings intended to be exhibited at his proposed lectures last spring, ill
health, partly occasioned by over application had rendered him incapable
of delivering his lectures. — This apology was unanimously considered to
be sufficient, and his salary was directed to be paid. — The Bye law on this
subject, made in 1784, states, that five pounds shall be paid for each lecture
given; and, that in case of the Professor not delivering his lectures, His
Salary shall be paid, provided it shall appear that such professor be
incapacitated by ill health.

Mr. Wilton having mentioned to me that the Students in the Plaister
Academy continue to behave very rudely; and that they have a practise of
throwing the bread, allowed them by the Academy for rubbing out, at each
other, so as to waste so much that the Bill for bread sometimes amounts to
Sixteen Shillings a week; and this relation of Mr. Wilton, being

corroborated by Mr. Richards, I moved that "In future no bread be allowed the students". This was unanimously agreed to. — Mr. West said independent of every other consideration it would be productive of much good to the Students to deprive them of the use of bread; as they would be induced to pay more attention to their outlines; and would learn to draw more correct, when they had not the perpetual resource of rubbing out.

The Annual Accounts were audited. It appeared that the Stock of the Academy now is general fund, including Marybone Bonds⎱— £9800

Charity fund⎰—   4000
                                                ——————

                                        • 13800

Richards, stated, that He had been unhandsomely treated by Copley who had repeatedly demanded payment for two or three days attendance to hang the pictures when He was in the Council. Richards shewed the rough drafts of the minutes to prove no entry had been made allowing such a claim by the Council. — We recommended to Richards that in case Copley applied again, He should refer him to the Council.

Sir William Chambers in his letter sent this evening by *Rose*, to Richards, reccomends that *Rose* be invited to supper. The Council were of opinion that the gross behaviour of Sir William to the Council & Academy in general, did not entitle him to any attention from them, therefore Mr. Rose was not invited.

The Three New Associates were then admitted.

Mr. Gilpin, — Mr. Soane, and Mr. Downman, and their Diplomas delivered to each, in the order in which, as to priority, they were elected. At Supper there sat down

Mr. West

Wilton, — Richards, — Gilpin, — Downman, — Stothard, Farington, — Westall, — Soane, — Hoppner, — Smirke, — Bourgeois.

The Associates had been invited to Supper.

The evening passed pleasantly. At 12 oClock the New Year was drank in.

Some talk about Irelands manuscripts. All concurred in believing them to be forgeries.

Animal Magnetism, & Dr. De Maineduc's practises were pleasantly described by Hoppner & Downman.

Gilpin related to me some particulars of Marlow; and of Scott, his master.

We remained at the Academy till past two o Clock. — Expence to the Academicians, Twelve shillings each.

JANUARY 1796

Edwards, Marchant & Humphrey dined with me.

Edwards told me that he had compiled much of what related to modern artists: but did not propose publishing his anecdotes & opinions during his life. That they would facilitate the labours of such as may hereafter take up the subject. He has classed Gainsborough, Barrett & Wilson, as three original men. He has also written of Mortimer &c.

Linley, the Musician, who died lately, was 64 years old. He fell a sacrifice to irregular pleasures. His constitution was undermined by the effects.

Revd. Mr. Este, called on me this morning. He spoke highly of the conversation powers of George Steevens.

Saturday 2d.

Mr. Malone I called on this morning, and found young James Boswell t breakfast with him.

He began a conversation on the subject of Irelands manuscripts; on which He is preparing some remarks which will fully prove the manuscripts to be forgeries. I told him that having seen his advertisement, I called to mention to him some observations which I had heard on the manuscripts by Mr. Lodge &c.: but before I stated them to him, He repeated most of them as having occurred to him. — He shewed me a racing of the handwriting, & signature, of Queen Elizabeth; and the same of Lord Southampton; In both instances but particularly in the writing of Lord Southampton, the forgeries were grossly manifested.

Ireland once called on Mr. Malone to whom He was a stranger, to request He might see a cast from the Head of Shakespeare at Stratford upon Avon. Mr. Malone not being very well pleased with such an intrusion of a stranger, declined shewing it at that time. — Some time before the manuscripts now so much spoken of were announced to the publick, Mr. Byng an ignorant man in such matters, but ardent, and violently prejudiced in favor of their authenticity by Ireland, told Malone of this extraordinary treasure, and expressed a strong desire for him to see them. Malone recolecting what had passed between him & Ireland on the subject of the cast of

463

Shakespeares head, & doubting the originality of the manuscripts, resolved not to go to Irelands to see them: but said, if the letters were original they might be proved such beyond doubt, by comparing the hand writing with letters known to be original. Mr. Byng desired Malone to come to his House on a certain day to see the letters; when He might compare the handwriting. He went, but no manuscripts were brought; and the excuse afterwards made was, that Dr. Joseph Wharton was that day examining them. Malone in consequence of what then passed wrote to Mr. Byng a private note for the purpose of seeing them in the way proposed by Mr. St. John; which note Mr. Byng very improperly shewed to Ireland; who from hearing it read, (He did not obtain Mr. Malones note) wrote down a Copy of it, suppressing all the circumstances which caused Malone to write the note, shewed it to many persons as a proof that Malone desired to obtain a sight of the manuscripts in a clandestine manner. This transaction caused Malone to call St. John to account, and explain it.

Malone spoke of Steevens as having been formerly much acquainted with him: but the intimacy has ceased.

He has a difficulty to find an engraver to imitate the handwriting for the publication. I told him I thought it might easily be etched.

Westall I called on. Ireland He knew more than thirteen years ago. The Children were then called Irwin. Ireland had an Uncle, who was a Brick-layer, on whom He had a little dependance. He was, Westall understood originally intended to be an Architect; but became a Spittal-fields, weaver. In this business he failed. — It was Mrs. Freeman with whom Ireland lived in Arundel street.

A friend of Westall, observed to Irelands daughter, that unless Her father could prove his pedigree clearly as being descended from William Ireland the friend of Shakespeare, He could not maintain his claim to the deeds &c. The girl faulteringly said that it was pretty nearly proved; not more than 30 years wanting proof.

Westall describes Young Ireland to be a lad of no parts. Two yrs. ago He was in some part of the country hunting with a party, & was invited by a gentleman to dinner, where the Company got drunk. In this state, young Ireland, speaking of himself, said he was bred an Attorney; but that he did other things besides writing law deeds: that he had been employed in writing a Copy of all Shakespeares plays. The gentleman observed that must be a great waste of time, when He might purchase an edition for very little money.

Burch, called on me to thank me for my vote at the Academy, in his favor.

Sunday January 3d.

At Church, Mr. Mathews preached.
Kershaw called on me.

Malone, I called on; and proposed to him to have his facsimiles of the Hand writings of Queen Elizabeth & Lord Southampton, etched with a black lead pencil on a soft etching ground, which I think will produce a more perfect imitation than can be obtained by the Engraver. — I offered to assist him; & with the further assistance of Stadler, I told him I thought we should be able to complete the plates. — He asked me to breakfast with him tomorrow morning, and to go with him to the British museum, to trace the Hand writings of Queen Eliz: & Lord Southampton, which I engaged to do.

He told me He had written to Mr. Windham to request him to write to Lord Cornwallis, Governor of the Tower, for leave to inspect papers there; as probably some letters of Lord Southampton, written when He was Master of the Horse, will be found there.

Baker called on me, and brought with him Munden, who is desirous of having a small drawing of mine, which He saw at Hearnes, "a view of St. Pauls from the River". I could not find the drawing.

Monday 4th.

Malone, I breakfasted with. Young James Boswell there. He is still at Westminster School and not quite 18 years old. He is to be bred to the English Bar. His eldest Brother is now at Leipsig. James has £150 a year settled on him, as an Annuity by his father. His sisters have £100 a year annuity: And they inherit shares of £500 which their father had bequeathed to the eldest sister who died lately. She died of a rapid consumption not being seriously ill more than Six weeks, and attributed her illness to a pressure while assisting to lift her father during his illness. — Lord Auchinleck, Boswells father, married a second wife, who is now about 64 or 5 years of age. She has an annuity of £400 out of the Boswell estate. When this falls in, Young Boswell, now at Leipsig, will possess £2000 a year. He is studying the rudiments of law in that University; after which He is to go to Edinburgh, being intended for the Scotch Bar.

The late James Boswell had about £900 a year clear income. Out of this He maintained one Son at Eaton, and another at Westminster. His intemperance for some months before He died I imputed to a species of insanity. Malone told me Boswell had an aunt who was confused.

The British Museum I went to with Malone, and traced the parts of two letters of Queen Elizabeth with Her signatures; also parts of two letters of Lord Southampton with his signatures. One of the letters of Queen Eliz: was written to King James 1st. then King of Scotland; the other to Sir [blank].

One of the letters of Lord Southampton was written to the then Lord Keeper Williams in the reign of James 1st. the other being, as appears, only the concluding part of a letter, the persons name to whom it was adressed is not on any part of it.

While we were at the Museum the Revd. Mr. Ayscough, and Mr. Planta, came to us. The former read a difficult hand with fluency.

Wilton wrote to me inclosing an acct. of the establishment of the Duke of Richmonds gallery.

Malone I dined with. Humphry there.

Mr. Wyndham, the Secretary at War, is about 48 years old. He was educated at University College, Oxford. Sir William Scott, told Malone that Wyndham was then considered as possessing great abilities. — During Lord Townshends Vice royalty in Ireland, Wyndham visited him. He was then 22 or 3 years of age. Mr. Jephson was then in Dublin; and Wyndham would quit, at that age, the splendour and gaieties of the Castle, for a private dinner and conversation at Jephsons. Wyndham in private society is temperate in his manner of conversing.

Courtney, is son to a merchant at Belfast. He had a commission in the Army; and during Lord Townshends administration there, a Court martial having sat on some occasion, attended with circumstances that the celebrated Dr. Lucas misrepresented in order to make the Government unpopular, Courtney replied to him in a pamphlet and defended the proceedings at the Court martial with so much success, that Lord Townshend enquired for the Author. Courtney was introduced to his Lordship, who liked his conversation, and they became fast friends. — When Ld. Townshend returned to England & was appointed Master General of the Ordonnance, He made Courtney Secretary to the Board; and afterwards Surveyor of the Ordonnance. A seat in Parliament accidentally happening to become vacant, Lord Townshend, who had the nomination, fixed upon Courtney intending him only to remain a short time in that situation to fill up the gap. Before the time elapsed [Courtenay] spoke in the House with such effect that Lord North told Lord Townshend that Courtney must remain. Courtney therefore considers himself bound to *that* party. — Lord Townshend indeed acted very handsomely by continuing Courtney in his seat at the last election though they differed in their politicks. It is not expected that Lord Townshend will again bring him in.

Malone joined us in the opinion that Courtney had cheapened his value in the House of Commons by his habit of joking & his ridicule.

Among Sir Joshua Reynolds papers, Malone found characters drawn of three or four persons but without names. One of them only was that of [blank] and Barry is the man evidently intended.

We talked about Sir Joshuas will, and Malone defended the right He had to dispose of a property which He had accummulated by his labors as He thought fit. — Sir Joshua had done a great deal for his relatives. By his interest with the late Duke of Rutland He had obtained an Irish Deanery for Lady Inchiquins eldest Brother; and He procured a good living in the West of England for her younger Brother. Yet Dean Palmer, who owed everything to His Uncle refused to attend at his funeral. Sir

Joshua had served the Dean, though he was not partial to him, — The Dean is an ordinary & conceited man.

Malone thinks Boswells description of Goldsmith a caricature. Goldsmith was introduced into company rather late in life, and acquired reputation suddenly by his writings. Before Ladies He was desirous of shewing off as a Man of Gallantry: but in the Society of Men his manners were natural.

Mr. Byng who supports the authenticity of Irelands manuscripts, is Brother to Lord Torrington. He is abt. 50 years of age. He was formerly in the Guards, and married a daur. of the late Commodore Forrest. Byng is ardent and ignorant of what is required to judge of the authenticity of ancient manuscripts.

When Lord Torringtons affairs became desperate Byng sold his Commission to relieve his Brother, — The Duke of Portland has obtained for him the place of [Commissioner of Stamps] which enables him to live comfortably. He has 5 or 6 Children; the eldest will succeed to the family title.

We talked of the singularities of George Steevens. He is so much offended with Mr. Cracherode for declaring in favor of Irelands manuscripts, that Mr. C. has told Malone Steevens will scarcely speak to him.

In conversation Steevens is limited to certain subjects. On Scholastic, or Shakespearian topicks, He speaks much: but on political, Historical, or general topicks, He has little to say; and is apt to be impatient at the Literary Club, till He turn the conversation from such subjects.

Malone spoke of the powers of the mind. Were Johnson, said He, to have treated such a subject as Irelands Manuscripts, He would have preceded the investigation by a general review of forgeries and their effects; and in the course of his examination disputations would have risen on passages, which would have elucidated and strengthened them. I, said Malone, think only of facts, and confine my mind to them.

Dr. Brocklesby, has, with but moderate pretensions, contrived throughout his life to be acquainted with distinguished men. Early in life he was well known to the Honble. Chas. Townshend, afterwards Chancellor of the Exchequer. — On some occasion the Dr. wrote to Mr. Townshend when the latter was in office, and expressed with surprise how much his professional practise had encreased. This letter with others, as was usual, was tied up by Mr. Townshends Clerk, a dry man of business, who for the convenience of Mr. T. wrote on the back of each letter when folded the principal subject of it. On that of the Doctor, under the date, He added, "Dr. Brocklesby astonished at his own success".

We staid till ½ past 10 o'Clock.

Tuesday, Jany. 5th.

J Boydell called. The plate of Major Pierson is delivered finished, this day, by Heath. It has been upwards of 9 years in hand, and will require 4 months for printing.

Coombes told Boydell this morning that He had delivered the last sheet of the 2d. Vol: of the Thames to Bulmer completed.

Wilton I dined with. Bourgeois, Edwards, Mrs. [blank] the Housekeeper and Miss [blank].

Bourgeois mentioned having been present at dinner at Charles Townleys, when Sir Joshua Reynolds & Northcote had a warm contest upon the merits of Nicolo Poussin. Northcote spoke of the powers of Poussin with contempt. The next day Bourgeois called on Sir Joshua, who remarked to him the extraordinary declarations of Northcote & said it shewed a narrow mind as to his art.

Mr. Wilton said Roubilliac the statuary, agreed to execute the monument of the Duke of Argyle in Westminster Abbey for £1200. He was paid £200 more, yet lost by the engagement £300 besides His labour.

Dick came to town today. The India Ships for the season were taken up; on account of not being ready, Dick could not profit of Mr. John Roberts nomination, and the ship is stationed for China direct.

Wednesday, Jany. 6th.

Offleys I called at.

View of London from Lambeth Steeple I delivered to Stadler today.

Blamire, the stationer, who lost his eldest son a youth of sixteen, about two months ago, has been so afflicted by it, as to have been confined to his room 7 weeks by a nervous disorder, & on Christmas Eve he had a paralytic stroke, which affected one leg and arm, and his mouth. He is now better, and Dr. Carmichael Smyth thinks He may recover.

Thursday, Jany. 7th.

Malone sent to me. I called on him, & traced from Irelands book part of Queen Elizabeths letter, part of Lord Southamptons, and Shakespeares note of hand. The grossness of the forgeries is evident.

Offleys I dined at with Dick.

Friday 8th.

Shakespeare Gallery I went to. G. Steevens there. He was full of Irelands Shakespearian forgeries — neither Payne, or Edwards, have sold one copy. — He has found the word *derange* in Irelands Book. This is a modern derivation from the French. Were it used at that period it would be called *dis*eranged.

Ireland outmaneuvred Sheridan by giving out that He wd. offer the play to Harris at Covent Garden. This caused Sheridan to engage that it shd. be played at Drury Lane. Sheridan has since scouted the play. Richardson who has £12000 engaged in shares at that theatre, to avoid

Law suits agrees to let the play be brought forward. Royal Academy Club I went to. — 17 members present.

Richards called on Sir William Chambers since the Council met on New Years Eve, but Sir Willm. did not pay him the money to settle the quarterly accounts with as usual; and said He did not know whether the accounts would be allowed. He asked for the proceedings of the General meetings & Councils. Richards told him He had not brought them. Sir Wm. said Copies of the proceedings would do. Richards replied that He had sufficient to do already, and the additional trouble wd. be considerable, and waved saying more on the subject. Sir William said He had been accused of charging interest for monies advanced to the Academy, while He had their money in his hands. Richards avoided the subject.

Hamilton gave me some acct. of Zucchi, & of himself.

Nollekens spoke to me of the Torso discovered by Wilson, now in the possession of the Duke of Richmond, He having bought it at Mr. Locks sale. Wilton added Arms, Legs & a head to it, which Nollekens advised the Duke to have disjoyned from it as these additions are very badly executed.

Saturday, January 9th.

At home all day.

Sunday, 10th.

Kershaw & Bowden called. I was out. Not at Church today. Damp weather.

Offleys I dined at, Dick there.

Monday, 11th.

Dance I called on. He & Tyler have proceeded in clearing Sir William Chambers Academy accounts. Yesterday they wrote to him requiring the Bills of 1794 and the Bills of 1769.

Tuesday 12th.

Malone I called on, and returned him the tracings of the Shakesperian handwritings, as my etching from them would not answer. He sent to Young Longmeat who undertook to do them. Malone wishes me to obtain, through Westall, particulars of the Christening &c [of] young Ireland, from Mr. William Aytoun his Godfather.

Dances I dined at. The Company were

Captn. Grey — Wm. Dance — Daniel Junr — Shields —
Do. Coggan — Humphry — Devis — Dick.
Do. Dance — Daniel — Isaacs —

The Company too unsuitably mixed & too numerous for conversation. At the time Shields, Wm. & George Dance played & sung some glees &c. Staid till ½ past 10.

William Dance said that in the years 1763, 64 & 65, He went to a day school in Exeter Court, Strand, along with Sheridan, & His elder Brother Charles Sheridan, and two Sisters. Mr. Sheridan, their Father then lived in Bow Street, Covent Garden. It was said that when Boys they talked of being Members of the House of Commons, and made speeches. Richard Sheridan is about 45 years of age. In April 1773 He married Miss Linley. After the marriage she twice sung in publick, once at [Oxford] and at Worcester Musick Meeting: but her name was never inserted in the Bills after marriage.

Humphry told me that the late Mr. Linley left a fortune of £25000, which is to be equally divided among his children. Two sons and two daughrs. Out of it His widow has £300 a year for her life. Young Sheridan will lose his share of the above property owing to his mother having died before her father, — Her name only being in the will.

William came from Hoddesdon.

Wednesday Jany. 13th.

Westall called on me. I proposed to him the questions stated by Mr. Malone relative to the christening of Irelands children. He said He wd. write to Mr. Aytoun for information.

Mrs. Freeman who lives with Ireland and is the mother of the Children, had, it is said a fortune of £12000, and is of a good family. Her Brother is now living in London in great circumstances, but disowns Her: Westall does not know her maiden name. Ireland behaves very ill to her. — The Children for many years bore the name of Irwin; and it was at the birth day of one of them, when many persons were invited, & Westall one of the party, that it was signified by Mrs. Freeman that the young poeple were to be addressed by the name of Ireland. They had passed as her neices. She still retains the name of Ireland.

Mr. Aytoun told Westall that Irelands effects will not pay to his creditors under his bankruptcy 20 shillings in the pound. He now owes Coxe, his printer, £800, for work done & money lent.

Bowden was with Westall today. He proposes to publish his remarks on Irelands manuscripts tomorrow.

Westall told me that He has an intention of publishing a poem of upwards of 900 lines; The subject a Walk.

C Offley called on me. He has purchased coloured prints after Westall to the amount of £25 today.

Thursday 14th.

Malone sent to request me to go to the Prerogative Office, Doctors Commons, to trace the name of Hemynge annexed to his will. On inspecting the will we found it to be only a Copy, the original not being in the Office. From thence we went to Aldermanbury to find out the Parish

Clerk in order to see the Old Registers, as it is possible the name of Hemynge or Cundall may be in one of them. The Clerk was out.

Malone went to School with the present Lord Mountmorris. He was then a very parsimonious Boy, and saved every half crown that was given him. His estate at the time was about £1800 a year; charged with several thousand pounds for his Brother & Sister: yet by the most rigid oeconomy, living upon a few hundreds a year, Lord Mountmorris not only paid off those charges, but from the increased value of estates, and by good management, His Lordship has now an estate of near £4000 a year, but his habit of saving is now so confirmed that he continues to live upon the same scale as formerly. — His sister married the late Marquiss of Antrim.

I asked Malone if he knows anything of Mr. Riston who is said to be writing upon the Shakesperian manuscripts. Riston He said had attacked Steevens, Johnson, Dr. Wharton & himself, on the subject of Shakespere. He is a Northumberland man, and was bred an Attorney; has abilities and much acrimony.

Mr. Malone left me to go to Mr. Albany Wallis, in Norfolk street, and in the evening He wrote to me that his visit had been crowned with success beyond his expectations; Mr. Wallis having lent him an original signature of Shakespeare that has never been seen, and which proves that He wrote his name Shaks*pere*. — Mr. Wallis had also lent him a signature of *John Hemynge* which turns out a small fair hand. — On His way home Malone called on a friend who told him that Ireland says He cares not what Mr. Malone may write for as soon as He shall have published, Ireland will produce irresistible proof of the authenticity of all this *trumpery*.

Poggi called on me this evening. He is to go to Lord Howe next Sunday evening previous to completing his letter press account of the action of the 1st. of June.

Smirke called. Poggi said that should the French press forward into Italy nothing could stop them, unless the mass of the poeple could be induced to consider it a religious war. He said He thought the poeple of Rome had less religion than those of any other part of Italy; and that the Italians in general, had less religion than the French poeple had before the revolution.

Friday Jany. 15th.

Malone I called on this morning, & traced the names of Shakespeare & Hemynge from deeds signed by them which are now in the care of Mr. Albany Wallis, who lent them to Malone for three days. I also traced several other names. Shaks*pere*, the Poet writes it.

Offley I dined at. A large party there,

Mrs. Gale — Harris — 3 misses Arbouin — Mr. Philips Senr.
Mrs. Richardson — Mrs. Harris — 2 Mr. Arbouins — Mrs. Philips,
                                                                Harris sister
Mr. Carlton —   Miss Philips —

A considerable addition to the Company came to tea & a dance. I left them before supper.

Harris told me that Mr. Philips senr. who is to marry his neice resided in Jamaica & has a large fortune — His only child, a daughter, married at 14 a Lieut Cameron, now Coll. Cameron. She is dead and has left several children. Mr. Philips had the misfortune to kill an antagonist in a Duel many years ago.

Bob came to town from Oxford. The friends of Sir William Scott have been very active to secure his election to represent that City in case of vacancy. Sir Wm. was Tutor at University College. Addington, the Speaker, was of Brazen-nose: His interest will be strongly supported by that & other colleges.

Dick left London to go to Parrs-wood. A Committee of East India Directors, this day agreed to grant Wills petition for £80 a year as being a Captain in their employ under particular circumstances.

Saturday 16th.

Craig I called on this morning. He shewed me several drawings by Lord Morton. Mr. Fawkes of Yorkshire has exchanged the pictures which Hodges painted for him, and for which he paid £420 guineas, for a set of Books.

Shakespere Gallery I went to: Steevens there. He had got Boaden pamphlet on Irelands manuscripts which was published this day. It seems a superficial attempt. Steevens mentioned many more errors which He had discovered in Irelands publication.

John Ireland came and shewed me many words absurdly spelt in Irelands publication.

J Taylor joined us. He had a whimsical conversation on politicks a few nights ago with Tom Kershaw, at Mr. Ratcliffs of Russell street.

Steevens speaking of Sir Joshua Reynolds' habit of taking Snuff in great quantities, said, He not only carried a double Box, with two sorts of Snuf in it, but regaled himself out of every Box that appeared at the table when He sat; and, did His neighbour happen to have one, He absolutely fed upon him. When I expected to meet Sir Joshua in company added He always carried an additional allowance.

Sunday Jany. 17th.

At Church, Mr. Mathews preached.

Sir Alexander Hamilton I called on.

Malone I called on.

Lysons dined with me. He has been told Mrs. Freeman wrote a play which was rejected. — He has made further discoveries at Woodchester and has engaged several men who are now employed in clearing the ground.

Sir Joseph Banks's, we went to, much company there.

Lord Mountmorris —	Mr. Dalrymple —	Willis —
Drs. Garthshore —	Major Reynell —	Heaviside —
Blane —	Mr. Cavendish —	Marsden —
Burney —	Mr. Salisbury Brereton —	Greathead —
Greive —	C. Townley —	Keate —
	Craven Ord —	&c. &c.

Much conversation about Irelands manuscripts. Craven Ord is a believer in their Authenticity; so is Dr. Greive, to whom Ireland has shewn an Edition of Spencer with marginal notes by Shakespere. Willis told me He is also a believer.

Sir Joseph Banks said the *internal evidence* is sufficient for him. He is convinced they are forgeries.

Lysons told me that Mr. Byng says Young Ireland frequently tells him He is going to dine with the gentleman who gave him the Manuscripts. Old Ireland still says *He* does not know who the gentleman is.

Monday 18th.

Flaxman called on me, and I took him to Dance & introduced him.

Sir Wm. Chambers has returned a mild answer to the letter which Dance & Tyler wrote him.

Dance & Tyler are of opinion that under the present circumstances of the Academy £100 cannot be granted to Burch, unless the payment be postponed till after the Exhibition.

Burch called on me, & shewed me a Certificate of his age. He was christened at St. Botolph, Aldgate, October 30th, 1730. He shewed me a small Gem he is executing. The execution appears to me to be feeble as if his eyes failed him. West has mentioned to him that there is some difficulty about the Academy accts. & finances which I corroborated to prove that we cannot at present command money.

Tyler called.

Bacon called on me this morning abt. Mr. Humberstone Mackenzies subscription to Webbers South Sea etchings. He spoke of Henry Webber who was his pupil, and said He never seemed to have the feeling of honor or principle, or even anxious to preserve the appearance of it. I gave him, Bacon, my opinion of him & related some circumstances of his conduct.

Dance I went with to the Freemasons Tavern to celebrate the Queens Birthday. He called on Smirke this morning who has applied to him at the instance of Bowyer who wants to raise 5 or £600 on the credit of His History of England, to bear the expence of carrying it on. I told him I thought that if the whole work were given as a security it would certainly be a good one. He said he would apply to moneyed acquaintances of His.

Dance talked with Smirke about His Second Son and thinks He may be safely ventured in the Architectural line. Since the conversation this morning Dance has seen Soane who will admit the Young man into his office free of expence.

Queens Birth day dinner; there were present.

Mr. West

Dance } Stewards — Wilton — Richards — Burch — Banks — Bourgeois
Cosway } Stewards — Smirke — Hamilton — Zoffany — Tyler — Hoppner.

Associates

Downman — Soane — Beechy — Tresham —
Marchant — Bigg —

Mr. Wadd — Heriot — J Taylor — Cockerell — P Coxe — Daniell —
Devis — Molini — &c &c—

Hoppner & Stothard were nominated Stewards elect.

A Party supped.

West

Downman		Tresham
P Coxe		Hamilton
Bigg		Cosway
Philips		Farington
Soane		Hoppner
		Tyler

Dance

We staid till 2 oClock. West, Dance & myself in Cosways Coach. We remained in it some time at Wests door who told us that He had lately seen the King at Windsor and had much conversation with His majesty on the subject of the Royal Academy. West mentioned Burchs petition; The King started at it, & observed that Burch had already the place of Librarian which was considered as a situation of relief; and that the giving £100 to him must depend upon the state of the Academy finances, which would appear when Dance & Tyler make their report. West said a great deal to shew there is a design somewhere to overset the Academy, and that the Exchequer wishes to possess the Building — *My private opinion is that West talked on this head much at random.*

I mentioned to Smirke what Dance had said of Soanes offer, which Smirke felt the value of.

Hoppner told me that He is now painting a half length of the Prince of Wales for the Queen. — Tyrwhitt is now the Princes favourite companion.

Tuesday, Jany. 19th.

Shakespeare Gallery I went to. Steevens there. He has learnt through

Humphry, that I Have traced the Handwritings of Queen Elizabeth & Lord Southampton for Malone. He says there is a genuine letter of Queen Elizabeth in the Heralds Office. We made out a list of such as are Believers & Disbelievers of Irelands Manuscripts.

Disbelievers

Dr. Farmer	Bishop of Dromore	D. Lysons
The Chief Baron	Isaac Reed	S. Lysons
Mr. Malone	Fuseli	Ant. Storer
Lodge	Courtney	Sir Wm. Scott
Steevens	Porson	Sir Wm. Musgrave
Ritson	Grey	Roger Wilbraham
Henley	Ld. Lauderdale	Holte White
Lord Orford	Sir Jos. Banks	Barnard
O. S. Brereton	Duke of Leeds	Rev. Mr. Langham.
Geo. Hardinge	Humphry	
Mr. Cracherode	Cosway	
Mr. West	Farington	
Hoppner	Hamilton	
Dance	Mr. Rogers	
Westall		

Believers

Craven Ord — Master Pepyss —
Honble. John Byng — Sir Isaack Heard —
Mr. Chalmers — Dr. Greive —
Revd. Dr. Parr — Mr. Bindley —
Caldecot — Caleb Whiteford —
Albany Wallis — Mr. Champion —
Mr. Townshend Heralds Office

Steevens told me that he usually rises at 6 oClock or sooner and immediately after dressing drinks 2 or 3 dishes of Chocolate, in a short time; after which He walks to London though at this time of the year it is dark at that hour. His first place of stopping is at Isaac Reids in Staples Inn where He generally arrives before 8 oClock. From thence He frequently goes to Sir Joseph Banks's, whose Breakfast Hour is 10 oClock, where various persons assemble. He passes the morning in visits, and returns to Hampstead about half past three, when He dresses and dines about ½ past 4. He usually, when alone, drinks about a pint of wine; and in about an hour and half or two hours after sitting down to dinner, drinks two or three dishes of very strong Coffee. He takes no other refreshment throughout the evening, and devotes the whole time till eleven oClock, when He goes to bed, to reading &c. At Dinner he eats of only one plain dish; mutton or beef; and a bit of pudding. He neither eats soup or fish.

The Trent Club I went to.
Serjeant Marshall in the Chair.

Mr. Heaviside	Dr. Thomson —	Revd. Mr. Penneck —
Nichol Senr.	Rev. Mr. Wrangham	Mr. Boylstone.
Captn. Budworth	Mr. Nichol Junr.	Mr. Rogers.
& a Stranger —	and Mr. Stodart —	
Dr. Heming and a	Hoppner.	
Stranger		

Dr. Heming told me that 12 of the *Licentiate Physicians* have united to try the question again with the *Fellows* of the College of Physicians, "whether the Licentiates can be prevented by a Bye law from enjoying all the privileges of Fellows". The question He said had been formerly lost by the Licentiates owing to their not having proposed their claim properly. Dr. Garthshore & Dr. Letsom are two of the twelve. Dr. Sanger is the person fixed upon to make the claim and He is to be supported. At present graduates of the Universities of Oxford & Cambridge only are admitted to be fellows. The examination in all that relates to Physick is the same whether the Candidate comes from Oxford, Cambridge or Edinburgh &c. but in addition some questions in Greek on the works of Hippocrates are put to the Graduates of the English Universities only and on this distinction their adoption to Fellowships is founded.

The Revd. Mr. Penneck told me He was Chaplain to the late Earl of Orford thirty seven years. Mrs. Turk, who lived with Lord Orford, was daughter to His Lordships House keeper in Green street, Grosvenor sq: She had several Children but they all died.

Mr. Rogers mentioned that His acquaintance the Revd. Mr. Wesson saw Irelands manuscripts and observed to Ireland that one of the letters was dated three years after the death of a person (Lord Leicester as I understood) alluded to in it as being then living. Soon after the manuscript being again seen it appeared that the date had either been expunged or was torn of.

Mr. Langham saw Captain Watson who was wounded in the late duel yesterday in bed at Cobham. He is a young man of about 22 years of age. Major Sweetman was considerably older. They had never seen each other before they met in the Opera House. The Major was an Irishman — so is Captain Watson. They stood about 6 yards from each other at the Majors request, as He said He was near sighted. Captain Watson told Mr. Langham that when they raised their pistols, He expected certain death. They fired nearly together. The Captains Ball hit the Major on the right breast and carried a splinter of a rib into his body. He never spoke, and died before He could be taken to the Inn. The Majors Ball hit Captain Watson in the upper part of the thigh, and passing through the bone, came out on the opposite side, and fell on the ground flattened. There are hopes of his recovery but the thigh is prodigiously swelled, and frequent bleedings have reduced him to a very low state. — Major Sweetman was in liquor when the quarrel commenced at the Opera House. The cause of the Quarrel was very differently stated to me by Mr. Heaviside, (who said He recd. his information from the second of Major Sweetman,) from the account I recd. from Mr. Langham. From the latter description it appeared that Major Sweetman was to blame; from the former that Captain Watson behaved very ill.

Mr. Stodart who was introduced today by Mr. Nichols Junr. was described by Mr. Langham and Mr. Rogers to be a very extraordinary Young Man; as a second *Crichton*; He is about 22 years of age, and was a Student of Christ Church, Oxford. He was reccomended by the present Bishop of Durham to be Tutor to his nephew Sir Thos. Clarges. In a conversation with the Bishop, He said that He thought himself bound to inform His Lordship that He has doubts of *Christianity*; the Bishop reccomended to him to read certain Authors on the subject; Stodart replied He had read them & doubted still. The Bishop said you will proceed to act as Tutor to my nephew. Stodart added, I am also a *Republican*. Proceed and do your duty as a Tutor. — This seems very extraordinary.

Mr. Nichols Senr. invited a small party of us to dine with him on Friday next He, Hoppner & myself walked towards home together. Mr. Nichols spoke of his Father, who was educated at Oxford, and was at 22 years of age appointed Professor of Anatomy, though then unqualified not having studied that Branch. By severe study in twelve months He obtained sufficient information to venture to give a Publick Lecture, as well as private lectures, and succeeded, and gained about 150 guineas which He always said was the only money He ever recd. with pleasure. He afterwards became an eminent Anatomist and resided in London, in Lincolns Innfields. — Dunning told Mr. Nichols that he once asked his father whether in case of illness He should apply to a Young Physician, or an Old one. — The difference replied Mr. Nichols is this, "The former will kill you; the other will let you die".

Wednesday, Jany. 20th.

Malone I called on this morning. He has completed his remarks of Irelands Manuscripts, and is proceeding to write them out fair for the press. I told him what Mr. Wesson had said about cancelling the date to one of the letters. He knows Wesson and will write to him. I mentioned that Humphry had told of my having traced the Handwriting, & that Steevens had attacked me on it. I gave him Steevens' list of persons who are for & against the authenticity of the Manuscripts.

Westall I called on. He has not recd. an answer from Mr. Aytoun.

Mrs. Roberts called on me today, and described the melancholy state of Her Husbands health, who has had an Ulcer in the bladder near two years.

Thursday 21st.

Harry called this morning having come to town yesterday as a Delegate.

Malone I dined with. The Revd. Mr. Courtney, Son to Mr. Courtney, Member of parliament dined there.

Impressions of the two plates of Queen Eliz: & of Lord Southamptons handwritings, were brought to us finished.

Mr. Concannen, who keeps the fashionable gaming house in Grafton Street, is an Irishman, and is nephew to a person who kept a great Snuff Shop in Dublin. This young man came to England, and married the daugr. of a person reputed to have a great fortune, while to the young Lady he passed for a Man in an affluent situation. The deception was mutual, neither side had a fortune. Thus circumstanced the Young Couple went to Paris, where agreeable to the mode which prevailed before the revolution, they took an Hotel, saw much Company, who were entertained at Petits Soupers, and gaming went forward, by which Mr. & Mrs. Concannen were maintained. In London they have established a similar plan. Mr. Concannens wine & entertainments are the best & most expensive, yet his profits are such that He is supposed to be worth £25000.

Malone observed how difficult it would be to establish a Plan for collecting select Society in the way Sir Joshua Reynolds carried his on. Malone only knows three persons who could undertake it.: & each is unfit in many respects. Sir Joseph Banks, as President of the Royal Society & possessing a large fortune, might undertake it: but His knowledge and attention is very much confined to one study, Botany, and his manners are rather coarse and heavy. — Mr. Burke, as He now possesses an income of 4 or £5000 a year has fortune and fame sufficient, but his talents are of a kind which render him unfit. By his eloquence and habitual exertions in company, He would keep his guests too much under. — Mr. Windham is also well qualified being a Classical man with reputation sufficient, but He is too fastidious to admit that varied intercourse which gives such Associations peculiar value. — Sir Joshua Reynolds on the contrary relished all the varieties of Character & knowledge, and assuming little himself, each person was encouraged to conversation.

Malone thinks Sir Joshua was a rare instance of a man relishing pleasure, yet suffering little from disappointments, or what others would have thought mortifications. He certainly had not very strong feelings. — I asked Malone what He thought of Sir Joshuas state of mind when his death was approaching. He said He saw him in his bedchamber about three weeks before his death and then He spoke chearfully. He does not think Sir Joshua felt more than that sort of depression which was the effect of his disorder. To Burke a little time before his death Sir Joshua said he had lived a happy life.

Malone thinks Sharpe a Pedant. Staid at Malones till Eleven oClock.

Friday, Jany. 22nd.

Mr. Wilton called on me. Sir Wm. Chambers is now so debilitated as to be obliged to be carried up stairs & down.

The Weather is uncommonly fine and has been so some weeks. Wind South west, and as pleasant as May. The Glass continuing from 55 to 58 on my Stair case.

Smirke I called on. He has spoken to Dance about raising 5 or £6000 for Bowyer, who, as a bonus, would give his pictures, 60 in number, painted for the History of England, besides paying 5 per ct., to such person as would supply him with the Sums He wants, which He wd. repay in four years. I told Smirke the offer was too great, and, in my opinion would rather deter than encourage any person from lending him the money, as it would be concluded that only a man in desperate circumstances, would propose such an offer. Smirke agreed with me. I told him I thought He had better only offer the work itself as a security, which would create no suspicion.

Mr. Nichols, I dined at in Charlotte St., Bedford Square.

Mr. Boylstone — Willis — Hoppner — Stodart — Mitchell —
— Rogers — Dr. Thomson — & Mr. Nichols Junr.

The weather speaking of, Mr. Rogers said He had been told by an observer, that the average height of the Thermometer in the open air, in January 1795 was 24; The average height hitherto in this month 47.

Mr. Rogers told me that the cause of the Bank Directors limiting the Discounts is to prevent the exportation of gold, which, in consequence of the payment of the Emperors loan, and other exports has raised the price of gold so high that a guinea in weight is now worth 24 shillings which induces the Jews to melt them down.

Mr. Rogers is much acquainted with Horne Tooke whose political principles He says have been much mistaken; that he is a friend to the Monarchical part of the Constitution, but an enemy to the Aristocratic power, which has grown to so great a height in this country, as to controul both King & poeple.

Mr. Nichols who was in parliament during Lord Norths Administration & after the Coalition, said that Monarchy is so pressed by the aristocratic power that no will is left to the King. Crewes Bill to prevent placemen &c including Custom House Officers from having votes for representatives, only strengthened the Aristocracy by still more limiting the influence of the Crown. This Aristocratic power will encrease, till the poeple no longer bearing it, will overthrow that and monarchy together.

Mr. Nichols mentioned that the cause of Burkes implacability to Hastings was, the latter having prevented Will Burke, in conjunction with The Nabob of Arcot, from oppressing the Rajah of Tanjore or as Mr.

Nichols expressed it, "having prevented Will Burke from being in effect Rajah of Tanjore".

Mr. Stodart told me He had been at the Lakes in Cumberland last Summer. He preferred Keswick &c to any other Lake, and was delighted with Mismery whither He went in consequence of Sir Geo: Beaumont having reccomended it. Mr. Stodart draws as He says a little, which caused the Boatmen to mention me to him.

The Duke of Clarence sat to Hoppner today for a three quarter portrait, for the Queen. Hoppner remarked on the difference of his disposition from that of the Prince of Wales. The Duke has a pleasure in mortifying those He is with; the Prince the contrary. — The Prince has little opinion of the Duke.

Willis was at Court on the Queens Birth day. In the evening at the Ball, the King talked to Mr. Pitt the whole evening, and Willis understood it was chiefly about Corn. The Prince of Wales never spoke to Pitt.

Nollekens I called on, and saw his groupe of the late Mrs. Howard of Corby Castle &c. She died in Childbed of her first Child, which died before her. She was one of the daugrs. of the late Lord Archer, and had a fortune of £50,000.

Nollekens also shewed me his Bust of Miss Le Clerc, natural daugr. of the Duke of Richmond. She is abt. 20 years old, is tall & handsome. She lives at the Dukes, & the Duchess is very fond of her. She has been introduced at Court. The Duke comes with her sometimes to Nollekens & seems very fond of her.

Saturday, Jany 23rd.

Sir A Hamilton I called on, to speak to him abt. Dicks compensation.
C Offley dined with us.

Sunday 24th.

At Church. A Stranger preached.

Soane called on me. He is much pleased with the Royal Academy Club; but thinks the Architects Club will not last long: The members consisting only of persons who are too much in a state of rivalship and frequently crossing each other.

Mr. Berwick called on me. His partner, the Lord Mayor Curtis, gives a Grand Ball tomorrow night, which it is supposed will cost him near £2000. It was intended as an honor to the Branches of the Royal Family. The Prince of Wales was invited, but declined going. The Duke & Duchess of York accepted the invitation: but yesterday the Duke sent word that the Duchess could not bear late hours, therefore He declined going. This disrespect is felt by the Lord Mayor. The Duke of Clarence, & the Stadholder & family are expected.

Mr. Berwick told me the profits of their Banking House this year will be very great. He verily believes that on the whole His income this year, including profits on the Loan, will be £25,000. He proposes building a house at the back of the Isle of Wight to retire to occasionally. He desired me to purchase any good pictures at Auctions, which may not exceed £100 a piece. He is willing to purchase to the amount of £1000.

Mr. Berwick was the first who proposed establishing the Banking House. Robarts, Ware, Hornyhold, & Curtis agreed to be partners. One day the last week they paid £750000.

C Offley called. I gave him his acct. & proposed to him to have a view of Fountains Abbey as a Companion to his Tomb of the Horattii by Wilson, which He agreed to.

Harry dined with us. In company with J. Thackeray & Richardson, and two Delegates from Bolton, yesterday at two oClock they waited upon Mr. Pitt, where Coll. Stanley met them. Mr. Pitt came to them *alone* in 5 minutes. He was dressed in a worn Blue Coat & Red waistcoat, a dirty pair of leather Breeches, and a pair of Old Boots. They sat down at a Table and entered on the subject of their Delegation. He proposed questions, and their answers and statements of objections, were so convincing that finally Mr. Pitt told them He would neither tax the manufacture in the town nor the raw material, *Cotton*. He expressed his sense of the great support Government has recd. from the County of Lancaster. At the motion of Coll. Stanley, Harry stated to Mr. Pitt, that after the meeting at Manchester, which had been held on the subject of taxing the raw material &c no advertisement had been published, as the Committee determined to keep the country free from alarm till the Delegation had seen Mr. Pitt, but the Jacobin party, with a view to make him unpopular, published the proceedings in a paper which they support, also in the Courier &c. Mr. Pitt was also informed of a Society having been established by the Jacobins, since the Sedition Bills passed, where the members, at their meetings, sit with a kind of muzzle over their mouths, and converse only by signs and writing. Pitt laughed at the ridiculous description.

Nanncy—B—& P Whittaker are gone to Liverpool to reside contrary to the advice of their friends. About 130 gs. was subscribed for them, besides some subscriptions which they did not mention. Dan is to board with them, and pay them 15 shillings a week: — they have together abt. £750 which Harry fears Dan will obtain from them.

Trade is at present very brisk in Manchester.

Monday Jany. 25th.

Sir A Hamilton I called [upon]. He undertakes to desire Mr. Roberts will not move upon a letter which Dick has written to him *urging as another claim to compensation, "that the new ship might have been ready last year"*. Sir A says this Plea cannot be supported, and Dick had best keep to the ground of having lost Mr. Roberts's nomination this year.

Hoppners I dined at. Mr. Wilton & Mr. & Mrs. Wheatley there.

The Powder Mills at Hounslow were blown up yesterday. The con cussion was so great as to break windows in the town of Hounslow Hoppner having been at Eaton, on his return rode to the spot where the Mills had stood, not a fragment of them remained. They were scattered over the country in small pieces. Three men were killed. Hoppner has placed his eldest son at Eaton.

Mrs. Wright, mother to Mrs. Hoppner, died at the age of 57. Her Father was a rigid Quaker but she became a Protestant. Mrs. Hoppner shewed me a letter from General Washington to Her Mother, written in December 1785 in which He expressed His esteem for her in strong terms. — Mrs Revely has committed indiscretions with a Mr. Jennings, an attorney Mrs. Jennings has proclaimed it. Revely has called on Banks for advice Mrs. Revely is still in his House but they do not speak.

Young Mr. Lascelles of Harewood House, is reckoned very like the Prince of Wales. The Prince is not pleased at it. He calls Lascelles *the Pretender*. Making a remark on a portrait painting of him by Hoppner H desired an alteration, at present, said He "*It is more like the Pretender*". At Brighton the Prince has been struck on the shoulder familiarly with a "H Lascelles how is it"? — To which He has returned a marked look of disapprobation.

Staid at Hoppners till 12 oClock.

Tuesday Jany. 26th.

Shakespeare Gallery I went to- Steevens &c there.

The Literary Club at Parslows in St. James's street find their own wine allowing a certain sum for each Bottle. The expence to each Member that attends is near a guinea each dinner. Dinner is not on the table till oClock, and the members generally begin to go away between 8 & nine, so that it is not a great temptation for a person to come down from Hampstead to the meeting.

Mr. Steevens is son to Admiral Steevens who commanded formerly in the East Indies. His Father & some other relatives died of Apoplectic disorders. Mr. Steevens by using great exercise seems desirous of keeping off such a complaint. Yesterday He had a Head ache & in consequence applied a blister to his back.

A Proof finished print of the death of Major Pierson was this day hung up at the Shakespeare Gallery.

Wednesday Jany. 27th.

Sir Alexander Hamilton sent me a letter He had recd. from Dick, desiring me to answer it. I called on him, He is entirely for resting Dicks claim for compensation on having lost Roberts' nomination by the delay in coming afloat with the new Ship. I wrote to Dick.

Smirke called to speak to me about Bowyers want of money.
Offleys I dined at. The Company.

| Mr. Ray | of Hull | Harry | C Offley |
| — Borne | | Bob | J & W Offley |

At the meeting at York to oppose the Sedition Bills there were 12 to one in favor of the Bills. The manufacturing part of the Country were entirely for supporting them.

Coll. Thornton appeared at York on this occasion. It is known that previous to this meeting, in consequence of his unbecoming behaviour, He had recd. an intimation from the Duke of York, which convinced him that He must resign his Commission in the York Militia. He took this publick opportunity of doing it, endeavouring to make it appear to be the effect of a resolution taken on general grounds. He made a speech to a Mob in the Guildhall, and terminated it by throwing His Regimental Coat, His Sword, His Cockade &c among the poeple. Thus terminated the Military career of a worthless man.

There are about 1600 voters at Hull, and it is a regular custom to pay a great majority of that number 3 guineas a man. This is done after the election to avoid the penalties of the Act. Harry told me that the Committee of Shipping had reccomended to the Court of Directors to restrict the Commanders from disposing of their Commands for more than £5000.

H. Hamond came to town to Offleys. Staid at Offleys till 12 oClock.

Thursday, Jany. 28th.

Bob went.

Sir Alexander Hamilton called on me. Captain Mackintosh has informed him that Mr. Dundass has written a strong letter to the Admiralty desiring the compensation to the India Commanders may be settled. Mr. Nepean, at the Admiralty, has said the business shall be forwarded to the Navy board, & Sir Andrew Hamond assured Mackintosh that from the Navy Board it should be immediately referred to the Court of Directors for them to report what captains are entitled to the Compensation; It is therefore probable the business will be settled in a few days. All this I wrote to Dick; and that He was this day summoned to attend at the Jerusalem Coffee House tomorrow at 2 oClock, to meet the East India Commanders on urgent affairs. (The resolution of the Committee of Shipping about the sale of commands.)

C Offley & Smirke called on me by appointment. At Smirkes desire, I stated to C Offley that Bowyer is in want of money to complete His History of England, owing to the expences being greater than He calculated upon and His returns slower, though He says He has upwards of 800 Subscribers. That Bowyer is desirous of raising £6000 to be paid by installments. Two Thousand in a short time Two Thousand towards the end of the year, and Two Thousand in abt. eighteen months. That Bowyer will give his work as a Security, will agree to pay 5 pr. cent, and to repay the whole in four years; and that as a Bonus to the person who advances the money, He will give the choice of Ten pictures to be selected from the Sixty pictures, painted or to be painted for his work; which pictures He has paid for at the rate of 120 guineas each picture. That it has occurred to Mr Smirke & myself that Mr. Barroneau who has some knowledge of what relates to publication and being a monied man, is a proper person to apply to. Offley thought the proposal tempting, and said He would willingly speak to Barroneau. That had He the money to command at present, He would advance it; and would offer to go half share with Barroneau if *H* would advance the money, to prove his opinion of the goodness of the proposal. Finally He proposed that Smirke & myself should meet Barroneau in Ormond Street, the beginning of next week to talk over the subject & in the mean time He would prepare Barroneau for it.

The late Mr. Offley, Barroneau &c did advance a considerable sum of money to enable William Rylands plates to be published, all which had been repaid by installments.

After Offley left us I spoke to Smirke on the necessity there is for him & myself taking care that, should money be advanced in consequence of any exertions of ours, the security be fully sufficient. That, in fact, Bowyer is a stranger both to him & myself, and his real situation must be examined. In all this Smirke fully concurred.

While we were together I took the opportunity to deliver to Smirke my sentiments on the duties of parents, in what relates to religion: That I esteemed it to be the sole bond on the mind of a female; and that by its influence the woemen of England are the most amiable and best principled in the world. I mentioned instances of the sad effects of the neglect of such duties; and how much any family obtained of the good opinion of Society, when it is known that a due sense and observance of religion, and its duties prevails in it. Smirke fully concurred with me.

Dr. Aikin, having heard that Hayley has placed his Son with Flaxman, has been with him. Smirke thinks with me that sculpture is not a branch to be reccomended to a young man, it is too uncertain. Banks has had great difficulties, — Nollekens has now nothing to do.

Flamstead House View from of London &c I finished this & delivered it to Stadler. This is the last for the second Vol: of the Thames.

Sir George Beaumont called on me. He came to town yesterday.

Harry came in the evening.

Bob went to Oxford this morning.

Friday Jany 29th.

Batty I called on this morning, when He examined the state of the skin &c about the place where the tumour had formed in my back.

Boydell I called on to desire him to procure me a copy of Reptons work
or Mr. Erskine of Mar; I followed Boydell to Cawthornes trial at the
orse Guards, whither He had gone at Coll. Cawthornes request,
xpecting to be called as a witness. The Court Martial was sitting. Lord
owis, the President. Lord Euston; Lord Grey; Lord George Cavendish;
1r. Stanley, son of Sir John Stanley, &c &c were on the Court Martial.
ieut. Coll. O'Kelly the Prosecutor was there, & Captn. Mason was on his
xamination. I saw Mr. Bradyll there, who is much changed in His
ppearance, his face spotted with inflammatory Humours.

Garvey I met, who told me Artaud, the student sent to Rome by the
cademy is a violent Democrat.

Sir George Beaumonts I dined at. Lady Beaumont and Miss Willes
here.

The Duke of Montrose out of kindness to Mr. Parker of Settle, who He
emembered at School at Eaton appointed one of his Sons a Page to the
ing. Parker is grown so large as to weigh 23 Stone.

Miss Emma Bowles 4th. daugr. of Mr. Bowles, is to be married to the 2d.
on of Mr. Brandling, Member for Newcastle; He is a clergyman, and has
n estate of [blank] a year independent of Church preferment & to the
mount of [blank].

Saturday Jany 30th.

Mr. Berwick I called on at the Banking House in Cornhill, at his request,
his morning, and went with him to see some pictures in the possession of
Mr. Bellamy of Charlotte Row near the Mansion House. There are many
small pictures by various Masters, but none of superior quality. Mr.
Bellamy shewed us a Madona by Carlo Marat, as He called it, which He
bought at a sale in Cornhill, a few days ago for 9 guineas, & for which, He
expects 50 Gs. I doubt the originality: but if it be a Carlo Marat, I would
not purchase, it is a tame, uninteresting picture.

Before we went to Mr. Bellamys I went with Mr. Berwick to the
Rainbow Coffee House and told him that as He expressed a desire to purchase some good pictures I had to mention to him, that an opportunity
offered and that He might purchase five pictures of the first quality of
those which belonged to Sir Joshua Reynolds, at a price very much lower
than Sir Joshua had fixed upon them.

	guineas	
Daniels Vision, Rembrandt for	210	Sir Joshua valued
Susannah & the Elders do. do.	160	them at guineas
or both together for	350	950.
Sampson & Dalilah, Vandyke	120	Sir Joshua gave 300.
Two of the designs for the		
ceiling at White Hall	110	
The Good Samaritan, Bassan.	50.	

Mr. Berwick said He wished particularly for pictures of Rembrandt an
desired to see them. I told him I could shew them to him at my Hou
whither they would be brought, but I could not answer for shewing him th
others as they belonged to other persons.

I gave Mr. Berwick my general opinion that it is most creditable & ce
tainly most prudent, to purchase only pictures of undoubted value, as the
may always be disposed of, and when purchased on reasonable terms th
proprietor is certain not to lose by them. He agreed to what I said,
proposed to call on me tomorrow for the chance of seeing the picture
which, He said, should He purchase, He must desire to leave with me fc
some time till He builds a House. I expressed how much I wished to hav
the benefit of seeing them as long as He chose I should have the care c
them.

Mr. Nichols called on me, and sat a considerable time, and we had muc
conversation on political subjects. Mr. Nichols thinks Mr. Pitt is superic
in debate to any Member of Parliament of this Day. The arrangement c
his matter is as regular as a studied composition; and he has the happy a
of introducing his answers to the principal points of argument of h
opponents, each in its proper place thereby giving them full effect. H
seems to have comprehended and to have matured the whole subject c
each debate, and to leave little to chance; and his speeches have an unifor
strength. Of perception He is as quick as Fox; of invention of momenta
argument not so fertile; but the equal vigour which He maintains throug!
out His speeches overmatches the occasional springs of exertion of h
opponent, who is always irregular and often weak. When Pitt first can
into Parliament His language was too verbose, and wanted strength; i
this respect He is greatly improved. In grammar He is perfectly correct. A
a Minister, Mr. Nichols thinks Pitt has not done anything which prov
him to possess foresight or resolution, in such a degree as to establish th
character of a great Politician. He is arrogant, but not resolute; rath
following circumstances; and acting upon them, than forming a Plan, an
maintaining it. He entered into offices of responsibility at too early an ag
by which His mind was confined to the detail of business, before He ha
sufficiently acquainted himself either with Politicks or Men, in the larg
view in which both ought to be studied.

Mr. Nichols has acted with Fox in parliament, and thinks him a real sup
porter of the power of a few great families, which for a considerable tim
have attempted to monopolize the power of the State. Whether it were th
Portlands & Cavendishes, or be the Bedfords &c. the labours of Fox ar
with the same view viz: to support an Oligarchy (the Aristocracy of
certain number of united families) and equally to controul the King an
the poeple. Fox is rash and would be a dangerous minister. The Portlands
Cavendishes, Bedfords, Fitzwilliams, &c. hold themselves distinct from
the nobility in general in a political respect. Having contributed to th

stablishment of the present family on the throne, they claim a sort of right
o extraordinary power under it. The present King has resisted with
agacity & success their united endeavours. Burke has made himself accept-
ble to this Oligarchy by flattering their pretensions — The encreased
ower of the Crown has been the constant cry of the Confederacy, but
verything obtained by their efforts has encreased the strength of this
Aristocracy and equally contributed to limit the freedom of the King and
Commons.

Wyndham is a man of parts, but not calculated to maintain an influence
n the House of Commons. His language has great strength, and is
ondensed; and in grammar He is remarkably correct: but in argument He
s so mathematical, & metaphysical, and his reasoning is of so unnatural a
pecies, that instead of convincing by the evident truth of what He
advances, He fills his hearers with astonishment at the strange analogies
which He adduces, and the odd mode by which He proceeds to draw his
conclusions.

Formerly, in Cornwall for instance, the Crown had considerable
nfluence in the election of members of parliament. The Falmouth, & other
amilies, were rather the agents of the Crown in nominating Candidates
han independent of it. Through them all officers of Customs &c &c were
bestowed, which created a great interest without expence to Individuals.
But it having been found that those who return members of parliament can
demand of government instead of soliciting , several families have exerted
their power to obtain an influence in the Cornish Boroughs and have
succeeded. In consequence Lord Falmouth whose family have returned 9
members, now only returns one for Truro, & at the next election will not be
able to nominate any. Sir Christopher Hawkins has succeeded both
against Lord Falmouth in one Borough and against Sir Francis Bassett at
St. Michaels.

Mr. Nichols is a friend to the shortening of the duration of parliaments,
for this reason. That were the term of each Parliament shorter, it would
prevent the attempts of the Oligarchy from succeeding in dividing the
House of Commons in to two parties whose chief object is to support the
views of their leaders. It always takes some time before this can be completely effected which short parliaments would not allow. At present,
when a question comes before parliament, which, for convenient reasons,
the leaders of the two parties concur in supporting or opposing, a few
solitary individuals whatever may be the justice of their cause, in vain
attempt to make any impression. — A strong instance occurred lately
when Mr. Barsham moved the enquiry into the conduct of Sir Charles
Grey & Sir John Jervis. The subject was bullied out of the house, and Mr.
Barsham & Mr. Thornton treated with contempt, in consequence of Pitt &
Dundass on one side concurring with Grey & His supporters on the other.
— It is certain that Sir Chas. Grey, & Sir John Jervis, both good officers,

had opressed the conquered French in the West India Islands, and ha
committed rapine, in the most scandalous degree, which alienated th
minds of the French inhabitants of the Islands from English dominion

Sunday Jany 31st.

Malone, I called on this morning. Harding, who paints Portraits, was wi
him. I read some pages of his Remarks on Irelands Manuscripts.

Mr. Berwick called on me at noon. I shewed him the pictures with whic
He was much delighted and immediately purchased them. Lysons calle
on me and saw the pictures and Mr. Berwick informed him of the pu
chase. Lysons has been with Lord Orford this morning who is desirous (
seeing the second Volume of the Rivers published.

Sir George Beaumont, Lord Mulgrave, & Coll. Phipps called on me.
shewed them Smirkes pictures which much pleased them. The *Falsta*
acting the King particularly. I also shewed them my Valencienn
drawings.

Harry came & dined with me.

FEBRUARY 1796

Monday February 1st.

Flaxman called on me to desire me to take notice, as one of the Council, of
drawing made by a young man aged 17 whose name is Picard, who
desires to be admitted a Student in the Plaister Academy.

Smirke called on me to inform me that He had related to Bowyer what
had passed with C. Offley relative to raising money for his use. Bowyer is
much gratified. Smirke thinks it might be prudent if three persons were
each to advance £2000 on Bowyers work, and each to have four pictures as
bonus. He gave me to understand that Bowyer to obtain the £6000 would
admit a person to a 4th. share of partnership in the work if it could be had
on no other terms. Smirke then talked to me of the offer of Soane to take
his Son. I said Dance had convinced me that it would be for the young
mans advantage, Smirke concurred in it, & I reccomended to him to
request Dance to inform Soane of his approbation.

Sir George Beaumonts I dined at with Susan. Miss Willis, Dr. Monro &
Hearne there.

We talked a good deal of the present state of the stage. Sir George thinks
Mrs. Siddons owes most of her fame to her figure, countenance & deportment. He does not believe Her to be a woman of superior understanding;
and Her delivery in Her speeches is often very incorrect.

Tresham has sent his poem "The Sea Sick Minstrel" to Sir George. Part
of it Sir George read after tea; and it was universally allowed to be an extraordinary instance of words without ideas.

Dr. Monro is a remarkably silent man in company. He told us that his
professional situation does not allow of his quitting London for several
days together. He has not been four days together absent from London in
he last four years.

Tuesday Feby. 2d.

Dick & Eliza came to town to day to dinner. Harry dined with us.

The weather has been a little frosty; and the glass down to 48. — A
general Cold, with pains in my back & limbs caused me to keep the House
today.

Wednesday 3d.

I staid at home today.

Thursday 4th.

Dance called on me. Soane is ready to take Smirkes Son. I staid at home today and Batty reccomended a continuance of James's powders.

Lysons called on me. He has seen the part of the Play of Vortigern appropriated to Mrs. Siddons, and says it is contemptible. Association Reeves is a believer.

Harry dined with us.

I began to paint to day.

Friday 5th.

Lord Inchiquin called on me today. Christie has not yet paid the whole of the money. I reccomended to his Lordship to make him pay interest, as He had acted so shamefully, both in his extravagant charges, & in detaining the money.

Poggi has expressed to Lord Inchiquin a hope that some additional allowance will be made him on acct. of the expence He was at in preparing Desks &c for depositing and selling the drawings. This being a voluntary & unrequired expence is not thought a reasonable ground why He should be paid more than his agreement. Lord Inchiquin thinks of taking the drawings out of his hands, and selling them at Hutchins'.

William came to town this morning. He & Horace Hamond dined with us.

Carey called on me. Gen. Harcourt has offered him a Lieutenancy in a Regt. of Light Horse, if He chooses to go to the East Indies.: this He has declined. I reccomended to him to apply to his drawing and painting as in any case it will be a source of amusement to him throughout his life; and will always be a reccomendation, and may be a real advantage. He said He had attended the Academy regularly and attended to his studies constantly.

Smirke called on me. He has been told that Soane does not give his Pupils such means of information in many necessary parts of professional knowledge as He ought to do, and that they generally leave him having much to learn. — I repeated Dances character of Soane, and said He had little to apprehend as Soane would not be likely to neglect the Son of a man who He wd. be constantly in the habit of meeting, as a Member of the same Society; A young man also reccomended by Soanes best friend Dance Smirke concurred with me.

Saturday Febry. 6th.

William went to Gravesend to his ship the Phebe.

Carey I called on. He has nearly finished three or four pictures. Majo.

e Merchant reccomends him to put some of them into the Exhibition,
hich He proposes to do *without a name,* as He now has a military appoint-
ent.

Dr. Reynolds at my request called on Eliza and reccomended Dr. Wards
rop to be taken by Mrs. Miers, as an antiscorbutic, for the humour in her
ace. He reccomended one drop to be taken at night and one in the
iorning in half a pint of Sarsaparilla tea for a month. Dr. Reynolds told
liza that Dr. Ward was a very able man whose medicines were in great
epute [at] the beginning of the present Kings reign: That the use of them
aving become very general they were now considered as quack medicines,
ut He had known instances of extraordinary cures having been wrought
y them. Two instances of Leprosy having been cured. *He* had taken
Vards medicines in the early part of his life for an erruption in his face: it
vas while He was studying Physick, at which time He fancied himself
fflicted by half the disorders He read of.

Will came to town & brought George; & carried him to School.

Sunday Febry 7th.

)ffleys I breakfasted at with Smirke. Mr. & Mrs. Barroneau there. Smirke
& myself conversed with Barroneau & C. Offley, on the subject of raising
noney for Bowyer. Barroneau said His money is all employed, and that
uch is the present value of money that 9½ pr cent may be made by
urchasing Navy Bills, which sell at 5½ per ct. discount & bear 4 per ct.
nterest, & will be paid of in a year. Of course no common temptations will
revail upon people to lend money. The only proposal made to Barroneau
vas, that of giving a certain number of pictures as a Bonus. The reserved
roposal of giving a 4th. share of partnership which will produce £4000
rofit according to Bowyers calculations, was mentioned to Offley, but
iot to Barroneau. Offley said Bowyer had better make out his proposals
in paper, & it then could be duly considered.

Alderman Boydell called on me about the Index for the 2d. Vol: of the
Thames. He was shewn into the Drawing Room and saw Smirkes
sketches.

Sir George Beaumont called. Coll. Phipps has a sort of nervous
affection in his right hand which has partly taken away the use of it.

Mr. Berwick, Lysons, & Smirke dined with me.

Monday Febry 8th.

Lord Inchiquins I dined at. Captain Welsh, an Irish gentleman dined
there. He told us that Counsellor Vanhomrig of Dublin, a young man of 28
years of age, was the person who proposed the Kings Health to be drank
when Erskine presided at the Crown & Anchor on Fox's Birth day. He
proposed it after 5 toasts had been given, the last of which was Mr.
Erskines Brother, the late Dean of Faculty. Erskine was much dis-

concerted & Grey called on Vanhomrig vehemently, to state if any dis
loyalty had been expressed. Vanhomrig said that at least a dozen person
on their going away came up to him and shook hands with him, which
showed how the meeting was mixed.

After Captn. Welsh went away Lord & Lady Inchiquin talked to me abt
selling Sir Joshuas own works this spring.

Tuesday Febry 9th.

Sir Alexander Hamiltons I dined at. Susan, Dick, Eliza and Capt
Mackintosh there.

Captn. Mackintosh went to China with Lord Macartney. He utterly
denied that the Embassy was disgracefully forced to quit the country. They
had completed the professed object of the Embassy, and it was intimated
that the winter which was approaching would not be favourable for travelling; this hint certainly caused them a more early departure, but another
motive was assigned by the Chinese, Lord Macartneys indifferent state of
health. They travelled upwards of 2000 miles to Canton. The whole
expence while they were on the Embassy was borne by the Emperor of
China. The politeness of manner on the part of the Chinese to them, was in
the most polished degree.

Glass 45 lower than it has been since Christmas. Ice abroad.

Wednesday Febry 10th.

Sir George Beaumont called on me & I went to dinner with him; Miss
Willes there.

Sir George has brought three pictures to town with him, one or two of
which he proposes to finish for the Exhibition.

Sir George is very strenuous for the necessity of painters occasionally
copying the works of former masters, as being a great source of
improvement.

The Criticism I made on his pictures was that the colour of his *lights* is
too much the same, which weakens the *points* of his pictures from a want
of contrast in the tones.

Sir George has lately seen a large picture of several whole length figures,
painted by Hudson. It is hung up at Goldsmiths Hall, and has great merit.

Mr. Knight told Sir George that He had seen Treshams poem at a
Booksellers, and said they were nonsense verses, mere rhimes without
sense. Chas. Greville told Sir George that some persons thought the poem
had great merit.

Thursday Febry 11th.

Greenwood, the Auctioneer, I called on this morning to ask him how He
wd. accommodate himself with a room if his own room were not large
enough to contain a collection to be shewn at once. He said He believed the
room in Spring gardens might be had.

Lady Inchiquin I called on to look over some pictures & determine which shd have frames. The frames offered to her will come to about £2.3- each. I told her what Greenwood said & promised to call on Malone to prepare him to speak to Mr. Metcalfe about agreeing with Greenwood for the sale of the Portraits &c. which must be done by the Executors, to avoid the disagreeable responsibility of it falling on Lord & Lady Inchiquin. The Executors order it as a duty.

The Duke of Gloucester told Lord Inchiquin on Monday last that He thought the portraits not claimed should be sold witht. ceremony, as they had not been taken away in so long a time.

Malone I called on, & stated what had passed with Lord & Lady Inchiquin. I told him I was ready to meet Greenwood at his House, & that He might prepare Metcalfe for the business. It seems something unpleasant has passed on this subject, Metcalfe & Mr. Burke, thinking it may affect the reputation of Sir Joshua, if all His works are brought forward for sale. I said discretion in the selection would of course be used.

Antiquarian Society I went to, for the first time this season. Sir Henry Englefield in the Chair.

Lysons I went to tea & staid till Eleven oClock. Dance & Smirke there, also D. Lysons & [blank] a Frenchman who teaches drawing.

We looked over Lysons prints & drawings of the foundation of the Roman Palace at Woodchester. Also his two fragments of small statues, and are of opinion, contrary to what He believed, that the *feet* do not belong to the other marble remains of the groupe of Cupid & Psyche. The former is of a superior style of sculpture, and the feet are too large to have belonged to the Cupid & Psyche.

Bowyer has made fresh offers. I met C. Offley today at Smirkes. Offley will carry the proposals to Barroneau on Saturday.

Friday Febry 12th.

Mr. Malone sent to desire me to meet Mr. Metcalfe at his House tomorrow at one oClock.

Dick brought intelligence from the City that a convention preparatory to a general peace is agreed upon between the Emperor & the French Republick. The stocks rose 2 & ½ per cent. upon it.

Saturday 13th.

Peace the report of, proves to be the effect of a forgery, probably to affect the funds. Mr. Pitt in answer to Grey disclaimed all knowledge of the trans- action & disbelieved it.

Greenwood I called on, and went with him to Mr. Malone where we met Mr. Metcalfe. The business of selling the collection of Sir Joshua Reynolds's own works was taken into consideration. Greenwood said his terms for selling pictures are, Seven and a half per cent on all sold, but nothing on pictures bought in. For the Seven and a half per cent Greenwood pays all expences, of Catalogues, advertisements &c &c. But in case a large part of the collection should be bought in, it be understood that some allowance should be made him for expences. Mr. Metcalfe desired him to state in a letter adressed to *him* these terms, also to state his terms for selling Prints & drawings. Greenwood said His terms for selling the latter are ten per cent, unless the whole should sell for more than £1000, in which case He only charged seven & half per cent for the whole. The great trouble of lotting prints & drawings, made the additional expence only reasonable.

I proposed to Greenwood to sell the pictures either in the week following Sunday April 10th. — or Sunday April 17th. to which He agreed.

Westall called on me this morning. General Stuart has again attempted to use him unhandsomely abt. a drawing ordered: but Westall has by a spirited conduct made him pay 40 guineas for it.

Lord Inchiquins I dined at. The Bishop of Waterford (late Dean Marl[ey]) Mr. & Mrs. Bellingham, Miss Forrest, Mr. Malone, & Major Darby there.

All went to the opera, except the Bishop, Malone & myself, we drank tea.

The Bishop of Waterford has about £3000 from his Bishoprick, and an estate of £2000 a year from his late Brother. He is a Bachellor, near 70 years of age, — He is a man of humour, and his forte in telling facetious stories, *with the licences*, well known.

Mr. Bellingham is Son to the late Mr. Bellingham of Castle Bellingham, in Ireland, & has an estate of perhaps £1200 a year. Mr. Bellingham was an officer in the same regiment with Lord Chatham who became so attached to him that eventually He was made a Commissioner of the Navy. He married Miss Cholmendely, daugr. of the Honble. & Rev. Mr. Cholmendely, who having been disgraced for cowardice in the Army became a Clergyman, and married a Sister of the celebrated actress Peggy Woffington. Mrs. Cholmendely herself was on the stage for a season, but did not succeed. Isaac Read told Malone this as a fact, though it is not generally known. She has borne the character of a wit, & having sufficient confidence, has been much in the world. The present Lord Loughborough when He first came from Scotland, was glad to have the countenance & introduction of Mrs. Cholmendely. She is now towards 70 years old.

Lady Inchiquin spoke to me about Poggi having a share with Greenwood in the profits of selling the *drawings only,* as some recompence for his disappointment.

Malone was at School with the late Mr. Fitzmaurice, Brother to Lord Lansdown, who He said was a light headed foolish Boy. Lord Lansdown had been at the same school and bore the character of a heavy headed but plodding Boy.

Sunday Feby 14th.

Byrne called. He is to give Hearne ten guineas for each of the drawings made for the Second Volume of the antiquities, of Great Britain. Munden, the player, has been introduced to Byrne by Baker, and has desired to have the refusal of such drawings as Byrne proposes to part with.

At Church.

Carey I called on & made remarks on three pictures which He is finishing.

Craig I called on to see a large drawing He has made for Mr. Fawkes, the same subject with one of those painted by Hodges. — Hodges charged 70 guineas each for the pictures He painted for Mr. Fawkes. They were abt. the size of half lengths. — Young Borron of Wassington was with Craig.

Monday Febry 15th.

Stadler called. He went to J. Boydell at the Shakespeare Gallery today, who told him He meant to have another Volume of the Rivers, but that the Prints must be executed on one Plate each, and printed in black or brown. Stadler told me He could not undertake to execute them for less than Six Guineas each plate.

Green called in the evening.

Humphry also came. He dined lately in company with Sheridan & J. Richardson. Speaking of Irelands Manuscript play of Vortigern, Richardson jokingly said to Sheridan, "perhaps you think it as good as Shakespeare". The fact is Sheridan does not think so highly of Shakespeare as poeple in general do.

Tuesday Febry 16th.

Shakespeare Gallery I went to. J. Boydell made calculations of savings for another Vol: of Rivers. He thinks it will be most prudent to give the River Forth for the next Vol: Steevens & Lysons there. — Lord Salisbury has refused to licence Irelands Play of Vortigern.

Nichol I spoke to for Copies of Lord Macartneys China Embassy. Three large paper; one small paper.

Trent Club I went to,

Dr. Greive in the Chair,

Mr. Nichols Senr. — Willis — Batty — Heaviside —

Do.   Junr. — Boylstone — Rogers — Carbonel Senr.

Dr. Thomson — Thomson — Hoppner — Budworth

Visitors

Mr. Adam, the American Minister to Holland. Monsr. De Grave. — Mr. Parker, an American & a mercht. proposed by Mr. Boylstone was voted a member. Monsr. De Grave was proposed, by Mr. Nichol for Willis.

Monsr. De Grave, was Minister in France till 1792. He had been governor of Lisle.

Hoppner spoke in raptures of the fine face and form of Lady Caroline Campbell, who is now sitting to him for a whole length. He says she has more of the *antique beauty* than any woman He ever saw; and Her neck is exquisitely formed.

Wednesday, February 17th.

Mr. Malones I dined at. Mr. Luttrell, Jephson, & Kemble there.

Mr. Luttrell is a natural Son of Lord Carhampton, by a Miss Otty, a Lady who had a handsome fortune in Jamaica. Till lately he went by the name of King. It is probable Lord Carhampton will leave him a considerable part of his estates, as his Lordship has no children by his wife, and is on bad terms with his Brothers.

Luttrell is now in the Temple. Miss Otty has since had several Children by a Mr. Nugent of the Guards. — Jephson is nephew to Jephson the Author. He is of the Temple.

Kemble mentioned that the Lord Chamberlain had expunged several passages in Irelands play of Vortigern. Kemble thinks contemptibly of it.

Thursday 18th.

Lord Inchiquins I dined at. Lord Fincastle, Sir William Scott, Mr. Becher, Mr. Metcalfe, Dr. Lawrence, Mr. Barnard, Son to the Bishop of Killalow, Mr. Gwatkin, Coll. Goat there.

After the Company went away, Lady Inchiquin talked to me abt. the sale of the Pictures, Prints & drawings. She thinks it reasonable that Marchi should have a share of the profits of selling the Prints.

Lord Inchiquin told me that Burke is carried away by his attachment to & confidence in French Emigres, which seem to subvert his judgment.

Sir William Scott said that in the year 1715 a majority of the poeple were in favour of the Stuart family. Lord Bolingbrokes letter to Sir Willm. Wyndham caused all hopes of restoration to expire.

Friday Febry 19th.

Carey I called on to select two of his pictures for Exhibition.

Mr. Metcalfe I called on in Hill street; and talked with him on the ensuing sale.

Lady Inchiquin I called on & told her Mr. Metcalfe would see Greenwood tomorrow morning, & that I had left a note for Greenwood desiring him to call on Mr. Metcalfe.

Academy Club I went to.

Hamilton told me of the death of Zucchi. He died in Rome December the 26th. after an illness of ten days. He was 71 years of age. He carried out of England about £9000. He has left his fortune to his relations. Angelica had saved in England about £14000. Her fortune being settled upon her,

Zucchi has not left her any part of his fortune. Hamilton says she is about 53 years old.

West, Cosway & Humphry spoke warmly in favour of the designs of Blake the Engraver, as works of extraordinary genius & imagination. Smirke differed in opinion, from what He had seen, so do I.

Coombes breakfasted with me this Morning.

Saturday Febry 20th.

Mr. Metcalfe I went to early this morning & met Greenwood who agreed to allow Poggi a 4th. of the profits on the sale of the drawings, and to allow Marchi something on the sale of the Prints. He also agreed that unless more than a 4th. of the pictures are bought in He will not charge anything for such as are bought in, & for all above a 4th. which may be bought in He will only charge 2,½ per cent.

Lady Inchiquin I called on, & told what had passed. She said it must be conditioned with Poggi that instead of a 4th. of the profits on the drawings He should have a percentage profit on the sale both of drawings & prints, which would make him more careful in assorting the latter as He wd. have an interest in the sale of them.

Sir George Beaumont called & afterwards Lady Beaumont, to Her I lent the Mecenas' Villa by Wilson for Sir George to have by him while He is painting a similar subject.

Lysons I dined with. Lawrence there.

The Duchess of Gordon has desired Lawrence to make some alterations in the picture of Lady Louisa Gordon. The Duchess told him the picture had been much complained of; by Lord Mulgrave, Sir George Beaumont, & by Hoppner. Other instances of Hoppners illiberality to Lawrence were mentioned.

Sunday Feby 21st.

Dance I called on to look at his designs for new Docks & Warehouses. Saml. Wyatt was there: He contends for the liberty of Wharfs for landing goods being allowed wherever a person possessing a certain portion of land on the Banks of the River, will build them. This would extend the general convenience & greatly add to the respectable appearance of the banks of the river.

Monday 22nd.

At home all day, having got cold.

Tuesday 23rd.

Westall called this morning to desire me to look at a drawing He has finished for Mr. Chamberlain, the subject "Reapers in a Storm". It is the same size as those He has made for Lord Berwick, but not having taken him so much time, He charges only 100 Guineas for it. He shewed me the manuscript of his Poem entitled a "Wintry Day" consisting of about 900 lines. He proposed publishing it this Spring but thinking that in the present times it might pass unnoticed, He has resolved to postpone the publication. Should this when published be well recd. He has many others in a state of forwardness which He would make a Volume of.

Wednesday Febry 24th.

Christies I went to. The pictures which belonged to More of Rome are on Sale. Garvey was there. He told me More valued the Claude (A Seaport) at 1000 guineas; and the Michl. Angelo, [*A dying Christ*] at as much. A large Landscape by More, with Diana hunting, is in the collection. More had for pictures of this size 150 Sequins (125 Guineas).

Col. Stanley was there. The Rev. Mr. Douglas introduced me to him at his desire, as He wished for my opinion of a landscape, called a Hobbema, I told him it was a poor picture and not a Hobbema. I gave him my opinion of 2 or 3 others.

Bryants Gallery I went to with Garvey. It is the suite of rooms below stairs belonging formerly to Cosway, & built by Astley. The Ice picture by Cuyp is excellent, and the Cuyp with the large Horses which belonged to West I think equally excellent.

Poggi called on me in the evening. Mr. Metcalfe has been with him, and spoke of the business of the sale. Poggi says Lady Inchiquin in their last conversation appeared to be disatisfied with him. He thinks it will be most prudent to bring the Prints & drawings as well as pictures, to sale and seems satisfied with the proposed mode of giving him a share of the profits.

Thursday Febry 25th.

Lord Inchiquins I called at this morning. The terms proposed & agreed to by Greenwood are that Poggi shall have a fourth of the profits on the sale of the prints & drawings. Lord & Lady Inchiquin complained of Lawrence putting of his setters.

C. Offley called on me & I sent to Smirke to meet him. Barroneau is willing to lend the whole £6000 to Bowyer on certain terms, and with proper securities. Smirke is to state this to Bowyer.

C Offley told me that *He* is to go half in the concern with Barroneau; I said that before the business is concluded it behoved him to see the exact situation of Bowyers affairs, viz: What monies he owes to the estate of Bond Hopkins, &c &c, and what monies He has recd. on acct. of the work.

Christies I went to.

Bryant told me He had bought the whole of Pradburns pictures abt. 10 in number. Pradburn gave 1000 guineas for the *Ice piece* by Cuyp.

Flaxman called on me this evening to shew me a letter of thanks He has recd. from British Artists in Rome in consequence of their having understood that permission is already granted for them to import their *purchased* studies duty free.

Copy of the letter.

Rome
English Coffee House
January, 24th. 1796.

Sir,

We have recd. the grateful and satisfactory information that the Right Honourable the Lords of His Majestys Treasury, in addition to the former indulgence, have been pleased to grant us, a full and free liberty to import with us into England, our Collection of Books, Prints, Casts from the Antique, and such Materials in art, as shall appear to the inspectors of the Academy, to be for our private use and study.

We are highly sensible that to your zealous interference, and solicitation with the Royal Academy, and every person who by his influence could forward and protect our cause; that we owe its full, its happy, and important termination. It is a most grateful sense of these personal and patriotic services that induces us to return you this testimony of our earnest, and united thanks. We have the Honor to be, Sir, Your most obedt. & obliged Servts.

Gavin Hamilton H.P.	William Artaud H.P.	Hugh Robinson H.P.
James Neway H.P.	Francis Sandys Ar.	Alex: Day, Miniat: P.
Christophr. Hewetson Sc.	Joseph Gandy Ar.	Wm. Theed H.P.
Charles Grignon H.P.	J. Deare Sc.	John Fearson H.P.
Guy Head H.P.	John Moir Ar.	
Robt. Fagan P.	Jn. James Rouby H.P.	
Thos. Pye H. P.	William Young Ottley H.P.	
Henry Thomson	G. A. Wallis Land: P.	
Richd. Westmacott Sc.		

Addressed to Mr. John Flaxman, No. 6 Buckingham St., Fitzroy Square, London.

H.P. History Painter, Sc. Sculptor. Ar. Architect. Land. — Landscape. Minit: Miniature.
These distinctions are added by me. N.B. There is another English Artist in Rome of the name of Tatem.

Flaxman read to me a letter addressed to the Royal Academy on the subject of admitting works of art into churches. He proposes publishing it in three newspapers.

Friday Febry 26th.

Lawrences I went to, to breakfast. S. Lysons there. We gave our opinions that nothing more shd. be done to it, and Lawrence came into our opinion, and varnished the picture.

Lawrence desired me to apologize for him to Lord & Lady Inchiquin for not putting his Lordships picture into the Exhibition. The *private reason* is, that He has undertaken to paint a picture containing two whole lengths, of Mrs. Charles Lock, (late Miss Ogilvie), & Her sister, Miss Ogilvie, daughtrs. to the Duchess of Leinster.

Burkes pamphlet to the Duke of Bedford I bought today. It was published on Wednesday morning & the *fourth Edition* is now selling.

Tyler called on me. He says there will not be money to pay Burch £100 and He considers it a bad precedent, as several others may make a similar claim. West has told Tyler that the King is against it. Speaking of the necessity for Oeconomy, He said that Dance & He concurred in thinking it will be proper to suspend sending a Student to Rome, to succeed Artaud, and that the gold medals should only be given once in 4 years instead of once in two years. I proposed to represent to his Majesty that £60 a year is too much for the trouble which a Treasurer has, & that it ought to be reduced to a smaller annuity.

Flaxman came to tea & informed me that He wrote to Mr. Long this morning, who has appointed him to call in Grosvenor place on Monday morning at half past nine o'Clock. Owing to a supposition that permission is granted for the introduction of works of art purchased as Studies, Flaxman has this day been informed by Howard that the Artists in Rome have adressed a letter to the Royal Academy and one to Marchant for the part He took at the commencement.

Saturday Febry 27th.

Cold weather with slight snow.

C Offley called on me with a draft of conditions on which He & Barroneau will advance Bowyer money.

Christies I went to. Remainder of Mores sale; and some Flemish pictures from Brussells belonging to Monsr. Lyss. Bryant & his connections laid out abt. £1200.

Baker was at the sale & dined with me afterwards.

Bryant is a Newcastle man; He was once upon the stage; and went abroad as a rider to some mercantile House. He met with Lord Shrewsburys sister in the Low countries, and afterwards married her.

Marchant came in the evening.

Sunday 28th.

C Offley dined with us. Smirke came in the evening, when Offley conversed with him on the subject of lending Bowyer money, Smirke had shewn Bowyer Offleys statement which I gave to Smirke this morning. Bowyer only excepted to paying interest on the Sum advanced thinking the *Bonus* of £4000 for £6000 for 4 years sufficient. I observed that Mr Barroneau had stated that He could now make 9½ per cent on Navy Bill which in four years would make a large Sum on £6000, and that the *overplus* could only be considered as a *Bonus* which would not, were interest not paid, amount to more than £1600, and that shd. a peace take place before the expiration of 4 years, the stocks wd. probably rise in such a proportion as to make a difference of more than £1600 on £6000, so that eventually Mr. Barroneau wd. be no gainer by the bargain. These remarks Offley & Smirke felt to be just, and judged that Barroneau when he spoke of interest saw the matter in the same light. Smirke said He wd. state to Bowyer what passed in our conversation.

Monday Feby 29th.

Flaxman breakfasted with me this morning and at ½ past 9 we were at Mr. Longs in Grosvenor place by appointment from Him to Flaxman. We stated the purpose of our visit, viz. to know if he thought an application from the Academy to the Lords of the Treasury through Him wd. be attended with effect, the object of the application to be the obtaining permission for British Artists, to import, *duty free,* such works of art as they may have purchased for their private studies and not for sale. Mr. Long said He had no doubt of obtaining the permission and wd. undertake the business if the Academy proposed it; the Council of the Academy becoming guardians of the publick interest to prevent any *trading* business from being carried on.

Lawrence I called on. He has seen the head of Grovatius by Vandyke and is anxious for me to give him another sitting. I advised him not to touch my portrait again the picture being completed. I also told him I wd. not change his Rembrandt for the Grovatius. Lysons was there.

Lord Inchiquins I dined at. Mr. Malone & Mr. Drew & Captn. Callogan there. After Tea Malone wrote an Advertisement in the name of the Creditors.

Malone shewed me an answer to Irelands attack on him for delay; this answer is to be inserted in the Gentlemans Magazine. Malone thinks Burkes Pamphlet to the Duke of Bedford admirable.

MARCH 1796

Tuesday March 1st.

Daniel called to see the Mecenas Villa.
Trent Club I dined at.

Captain Budworth in the Chair.

Messrs.	Nichol Senr.	N. Willis	Norman	Carbonel
	Carbonel Junr.	Thomson	Batty	Heaviside
	Boylestone	Hale	Delafield	Farington
	Penneck			

Visitors
Revd. Dr. Tayler — and two others

Mr. Nichols said the enemies of Burke wd. rejoice, & his friends might weep at his Pamphlet. I find that the opinion of it depends on the political feeling of the party who gives it.

St. Davids Day was kept at the Crown & Anchor today. Abt. 400 dined. The Prince of Wales & the Duke of Clarence were there.

Wednesday 2nd

Easterly winds continue. The Glass is abt. 40 and has been down to 37 on my staircase.

Flaxman called to make a small addition to the statement in favor of introducing works purchased by British Artists abroad for their private studies, duty free.

Freebairn called from Sir G. Beaumont, to see my picture of mecenas villa by Wilson. I was out.

Smirke called to shew me two letters from Bowyer. He agrees to the whole proposal of Barroneau, but shews the difficulty of getting security.

C Offley called & I sent him to Smirke who had called on him.

Thursday March 3rd

William came up from Portsmouth this morning; the Phebe, Captn.

502

Barlow, being ordered to sail to Falmouth to day. Mr. Hastings has granted to him by the Board of Controul £4000 a year for 28 years ½, commencing in June 1785.

Friday 4th.

Mr. Berwick & Lysons called on me a little after 9 this morning, desiring me to [go to] Vanderguchts to see the Escurial by Rubens, which is recomended by Lord Orford. I told Mr. Berwick of my having purchased the Wynants for which He settled with me. We went to Vanderguchts, but the Escurial had been sent to Christies preparatory to the Sale. — We went together to Bryants gallery & from there to Christies. Mr. Berwick did not find the Escurial to his taste. — Bryant I went to afterwards & spoke to him about the 2 Ruysdaels. He values them together at 140 guineas 80 & 60 gs. To professional men He makes an allowance.

Hearne I called on & took him to Bryants Gallery. He decided entirely in favor of the smaller Ruysdael, the other having been touched in & has less taste. He wd. rather have the smaller than 10 such as that cold Ruysdael purchased by Lord Suffolk at [the] de Lyss sale for 40gs. Hearne coinciding with me in opinion I purchased the smaller picture.

Bryant gave Hearne an introductory card for himself and friends. Mr. Campbell I talked with at the Gallery. Mr. Fawkes was there. He has given 300 Gs. for a Ruysdael at the European Museum, which for *that* picture is a monstrous price.

Academy Club I went to. West invited me to come to his House to see the pictures He has obtained from France, particularly His Berghem.

West speaking of Wilsons Niobe in the possession of Sr. George Beaumont says it is the finest landscape He has seen except one by Rubens, to which it wd. make a fit companion.

Saturday, March 5th.

At home.

Sunday 6th.

Wests I went to this morning, and met the 2 Bakers, Hearne & Rooker &c there.

Saw the Berghem, the 4 pictures by Teniers, one by Morilio, Dijanira by Pordenone, Angelica & Medora by Guercino, a Madona, Guido.

Bakers I dined at. Hearne & Edridge there.

I asked Hearne what He thought of the Berghem at *first sight.* He said it appeared to him to be a heavy picture. In this I concurred with. The composition is skilfully arranged, the forms elegant & the execution admirable, but it wants a general Hue, that *hue* which renders the pictures of Cuyp so exquisite.

Lysons called on me in the evening.

Monday 7th.

C Offley dined with me.
William came from Hoddesdon.

Tuesday 8th.

West sent to me at eleven this morning to inform me that Sir William Chambers died at ½ past nine o'Clock this morning.

Lysons I went to this evening. A party of near 60 ladies & gentlemen there. Mrs. Hughes, Mrs. Ambrose (late Miss Mahon) and a girl niece to Mrs. John Kemble sung, and a Mr. Wilson.

Lord & Lady Suffolk & their daughr., Sir Frederick & Lady Eden, Mrs. Hawker & Miss Shuttleworth, Miss [blank] & Miss Salusbury of Gravely, Mrs. Watts, Mrs. J. Kemble, 2 Miss Siddons, &c &c &c. there Mr. Peach, Lawrence, Siddons, Hughes, Greathead &c. I came away at ½ past 10.

Lawrence told me of the death of the Duke of Hamilton, at Bristol, of a deep consumption caused by drinking. (This report not true).

Jackson, the Bruiser, abt. 5 months ago was engaged by Lawrence to sit to him for a figure one morning. As He came after his appointment, He apologised by saying that [the] Duke [of] Hamilton had kept him up till 7 oClock that morning drinking. Lawrence asked him if the Duke was in spirits, no said the other. He was *downish*. The fact was the state of depravity to which He had reduced himself, preyed on his mind. For some time before the Duchess left him, He had alternately committed outrages to her, and then repented on his knees in tears.

Wednesday March 9th.

Northcote called on me this morning. He and the person who has pur chased his set of pictures describing the progress of Virtue & Vice in two females, are desirous that the 10 pictures shd. be exhibited at the Royal Academy provided that they can be so arranged up stairs or in the Council room, as to follow each other in succession. Northcote desired me to state his wish to the Council and Committee, which I undertook to do.

Edwards called on me to borrow a frame for a large landscape He ha painted.

Soane called on me to ask my opinion if, in consequence of Sir Wm Chambers vacancy, it wd. be proper for him to exert any interest to procure an election. I told him the vacancy could not be filled before February next, & I thought it wd. be useless to take any notice of the vacancy at present. That I thought He stood a good chance for one of the *earl vacancies* as the Architects had a right to expect their number of 5 to be filled, when proper persons were on the list.

Dance I called on. Tyler there. They were examining the Academy accts Tyler was with West 3 Hours last night, conversing on the state of the

Academy, and the vacancy made by Sir Wm. Chambers as Treasurer. West said He wd. this morning go to the King, and endeavour to induce his Majesty to nominate Tyler to be Treasurer, but He feared Yenn wd. be appointed, in which case He shd. request His Majesty not to nominate till the accts. &c had been made up by the Council & such regulations proposed as wd. make the business of the Academy go on with the Treasurer smoothly. That it wd. otherways be impossible for him to go on as President, having a Treasurer with such undefined powers.

Thursday March 10th.

Vanderguchts sale of pictures, I went to see at Christies.

Launch of the Henry Addington, East Indiaman I went to. The day very fine. Launched at 10 minutes past 2. After the launch went to Wills long room where a cold collation was set out. Including side tables about 130 persons sat down. Ld. Grey, Ld. Belgrave, Mr. & Mrs. Harrison, Eliza & Miss Hardman, Hale, Mr. & Mrs. Ackers, & Miss Brown, 3 Offleys, William & George, Liddel &c at one end of the table. Sir A. Hamilton, Dennis, Rolle & Coll. Rolle, Bombay Hornby & family, Lady Hamilton, Mr. Addington Junr. &c &c &c. at the other end. At three oClock or soon afterwards the company separated & returned to town. Coll. Rolle named the Ship.

Dances I went to to tea. Tyler & West there. Before West came I stated to them that I had been with Flaxman to Mr. Long abt. admitting purchases by Artists for studies, duty free. — West informed us He had not yet seen the King, since the death of Sir Wm. Chambers. That Mr. Brown, Mr. Collins, & Mr. Andre, an Attorney, are Executors to Sir Williams will, that they had called on him to speak abt. the funeral; that Sir Wm. had directed that no more than £100 should be expended, which seemed to shew that He desired no ostentation: of course nothing could be undertaken similar to the expence on acct. of Sir Joshua Reynolds funeral; which West understood from Mr. Metcalfe amounted to near £1000. — West proposed that the Council, as the Acting part of the Academy, shd. attend the funeral, which was approved by Mr. Brown &c. They mentioned Westminster Abbey as the place of interment.

West promised to see the King tomorrow morning, and wd. at least endeavour to prevent a nomination of Treasurer at present. We made extracts from the acct. books to shew West that Sir Williams accusations are totally unfounded, and that He might assert to the King that the Capital in the funds had been gradually increasing and had never been touched in any one year.

I represented that our business might be so managed as to render it unnecessary to produce the letters from the Privy Purse to the New Council, for if a report is made by Dance & Tyler, and a *general letter* only alluding to no *particulars*, presented to be officially sent to the Privy Purse by the

Secretary, it would prevent recurring to former letters, and all disagreeable consequences resulting therefrom. This was agreed to by West, Dance & Tyler, and I further stated that by adopting this mode of a *general letter* to the Privy *Purse*, we should avoid acknowledging his right to controul us in the disgraceful manner proposed by Sir William Chambers, which, if we entered into particulars of refutation, or offered reasons of justification for certain expences, we should in a great degree admit. — To all these remarks they gave their sanction.

West said he had traced that Sir William Chambers gave to the King before His Majesty last went to Weymouth, the papers of accusation & reform, which his Majesty gave to Mr. Mathias, Deputy Privy Purse to His Majesty, who copied them as ordered & sent them to the Academy: but afterwards told West He did not like them. West does not think Lord Cardigan, (the Privy Purse) ever saw them.

West has been informed that Yenn has been upon cool terms with Sir William Chambers during the last four months, in which time He has never even enquired at the House of Sir Wm. after his health.

West spoke of Sir Wm. Chambers as certainly having been the first mover to obtain the institution of the Royal Academy; and it was after Sir William had settled the mode of proceeding with his majesty, that a meeting was held at Mr. Wiltons, and it was agreed that Mr. Chambers, Frank Cotes, Moser, and West, shd. attend his majesty with a paper to solicit his majesty to establish an Academy under his own immediate patronage. The paper was presented by Cotes, and his majestys answer was gracious and approving.

We agreed to go through the common business of the Academy only on Saturday night and to adjourn the Council to Monday, when there would be sufficient time to go through the business of Dance & Tylers report, &c.

West stated that His Majesty does not approve the proposal to give Burch £100, as He already possesses the place of Librarian. Tyler & Dance are entirely against, and I said that if to give Burch £100, Ten or twelve of the poor annuitants must be deprived of their annual allowance I wd. vote against it.

I mentioned Northcotes proposal to exhibit his series of pictures which West thinks shd. by all means be accepted.

We suppd. at Dances & staid till past 12 oClock.

Friday, March 11th.

Shakespeare Gallery I went to. J. Boydell told me he has had conversation with Coombes abt. proceeding with the work of the Rivers, if it cd. be done at a smaller expence. Coombes said it wd. be impossible for him to write a He cd. wish unless *He saw* the countries and that He thought in three weeks He might at a moderate expence, go down to Scotland and pass over the ground.

Saturday March 12th.

Northcote I called on to look at his series of the good & the wanton girls.

Vanderguchts sale I went to. A damaged $^3/_4$ picture by Sir Joshua Reynolds of Vanderguchts 2 children was bought in yesterday for 60 guineas, a much higher price than I shd. have expected.

Walton I met at a sale & went with him to Lord Lansdownes to see the pictures. Some very fine by G. Poussin, one large by Teniers, &c &c. There are two large pictures by Vernet for which Lord Lansdowne paid him 1000 guineas. Walton sold the little Nicolo Poussin which He bought at Sir Joshuas sale for 200 gs. to Sir Thos. Beauchamp Proctor for 100 gs. profit.

Walton gives a high character of Lord Lansdowne. His Lordship lives in a *small* suit of Rooms in Lansdowne House, His Bed room being a sort of Library in which He has a tent bed. He is solicitous of the society of men of ability in any respect.

Dance I called on & went with him & Tyler to the Academy Council at 8.

Present — West

Dance, Tyler, Bacon, Hoppner, Lawrence, Westall, Stothard, Farington.

When the Minutes of the last Council were read & the resolution to *give Burch £100* Tyler rose and said that He shd. move that the resolution be postponed, as such is the present state of our finances, if the Vote be confirmed, the money cannot be paid. Bacon in reply said that He was for having the vote confirmed, that He was sorry the Charity fund had ever been confounded with the solid fund, & described the hardship of not being able to give a member of the Academy relief when it seemed necessary. West hinted that shd. the vote be confirmed it wd. not have his majestys sanction. Bacon adhered to his purpose, & I said to him, why should we vote the money till we can pay it. Bacon thought if we required the money we should sell out of the funds as much as may be wanted. Tyler objected to it as a dangerous precedent, which, if admitted would lay the Academy open to claims from others. A vote passed that the *resolution be suspended*. Bacon the only negative.

A Committee of arrangement was fixed. Lawrence proposed that He & Hoppner shd. draw lots which of the two shd. be excused. I advised them both to serve, as it would be [a] very disagreeable responsibility for either of them singly to take on himself, as there wd. be of course so many works in their branch of art to be disposed of. Hoppner, Lawrence & Westall were the committee appointed.

I stated to the Council the request of Northcote which was agreed to unanimously. — that his pictures shd. be arranged *as a Series* in the great room or in the Council room.

Mr. West notified the death of Sir Wm. Chambers, & the proposal that the Council of the Academy, with the Keeper & Secretary do attend the funeral, which was approved.

He notified the death of Zucchi.

He stated that a letter has been recd. from Thomas Sandby, stating that He returned from Bath to Windsor Lodge little benefitted & was unable to give his Lectures this spring. It was admitted to be a sufficient apology but the letter must be produced regularly and a vote passed on it for the sake of precedent.

It was proposed that no gold Medals be given this year. Dance & Lawrence thought they shd. only be given once in 5 years. I thought that time too long, as able young men might thereby be deprived of any advantage from being sent abroad by the Academy, as they wd. probably either go before that time elapsed or have given up the intention. Finally it was settled to postpone this year giving any gold medals.

I then stated that I had been with Flaxman to Mr. Long of the Treasury, when Flaxman read a paper containing a request from the Academy that Plaisters, Prints & Drawings purchased by British Artists shd. be imported duty free, and that Mr. Long had said that He wd. take charge of the request if the Council of the Academy directed it to him. — I made a motion that a letter be addressed to the Lords of the Treasury which was agreed to. The Council broke up at Eleven and adjourned to Monday.

West, Dance & Tyler I came with from the Academy, West said He saw the King yesterday morning who had said He wd. suspend the nomination of a Treasurer to the Academy till Dance & Tyler have made their report. That He wd. not make the Surveyor of the Board of Works, Treasurer to the Academy, as otherways it might come to be considered as annexed to that Office. That He *Himself* only knew who He meant shd. be Treasurer. That He was at a loss to know how the appointment should be given, when West said that He thought it might be through *him* as *President*.

Sunday March 13th.

Dance I called on, Tyler there. I stated the necessity there is for establishing a communication between the Academy & the King on a regular footing, by resolving that all business to be laid before the King should be formally stated by the Council and presented to His majesty by the President accompanied by the *Secretary* or *Treasurer*. This Dance & Tyler agreed to.

West & Tyler I met at Dances in the evening, and the report intended to be made to the Council tomorrow on Sir Wm. Chambers accts. was read to us. In conversation, Dance & Tyler, mentioned to West the necessity for a regular communication with the King. This I spoke upon fully. West made no reply.

West said Copley had been with the King & asked for the Office of Treasurer to the Academy. The King made no reply. Staid at Dances till past 12 oClock.

Monday 14th.

Lady Inchiquin I called on. She is undetermined abt. the sale this Spring. Greenwood came & said He cd. not obtain the room at Spring Gardens. I proposed to him Bryants room in Saville row, which He undertook to enquire about.

Council at Academy I went to.

Present — West.

Hoppner, Tyler, Dance, Lawrence, Stothard, Westall.

The report on the accts. of Sir Wm. Chambers was read by Tyler. Sir Wms. Book is merely a Cash acct. & so confused that Dance & Tyler have not yet been able to make their balance taken from the Bills agree with Sir Wms. acct. They must examine it by another process.

They proposed many regulations for the office of Treasurer, which were agreed to. If his majesty sanctions them, the Academy will be on a better footing than ever it has been hitherto.

Tyler concluded with proposing the regulation that all business to be communicated to his majesty shd. be presented by the President accompanied by the Secretary or Treasurer as the nature of the business shd. require. It was agreed to unanimously. The Council broke up at Eleven oClock. Lawrence, Westall, Hoppner & myself went to Holylands Coffee House & staid till past 12.

Tuesday, March 15th.

Dance I called on & talked with him abt. the Treasurer not having a permanent seat at the Council Board which [West?] on Sunday night expressed his opinion that the Treasurer shd. not have. Dance thinks it better that the Treasurer shd. continue to have that privilege.

Trent Club I went to and was in the *Chair*. Willis, Heaviside, Boylstone, Nichols Senr., Batty, Carbonel Senr., Lawrence, Marshall, Budworth, Grave, Dr. Thomson.

Visitors. Revd. Mr. Wrangham, and Capt, Willis' friend. Staid till 10 oClock.

Thames, for the second Vol: I this day coloured the last print.

Marchant called in the evening.

Lysons called in the evening.

Wednesday, 16th.

Flaxman, I called on this morning and stated to him what had passed at the Academy on the business of applying to the Lords of the Treasury.

General Paoli came to Flaxmans to sit for a Bust. He is 73 years of age, but looks remarkably well. He told Flaxman that he was weighed at one period in his life 300 Italian pounds: (an Italian pound is 12 English ounces) but that now He weighs 160 pounds less than He then did.

Steers called on me.

Poggi called on me. He understands there is a doubt whether the pictures, Drawings & Prints of Sir Joshua will be sold this Spring, and desires to be satisfied abt. it, and requested to me to obtain from Lady Inchiquin the determination. He complained of Lord Inchiquins behaviour to him. Of the trouble & expence He had been at on acct. of the drawings &c. He mentioned his bad success in business.

Wilson, Tyler, & Hoppner dined with me. Soane sent an excuse before dinner, Dance came in the evening having been detained at the House of Commons.

Hoppner & Tyler staid till one oClock.

Thursday March 17th.

Lord Inchiquins I went to this morning. Lord Eardley was there at Breakfast.

It was finally determined that the Pictures, Prints & drawings should be sold this Spring and Greenwood came and the advertisements were drawn out. Before the determination I mentioned that Poggi thought it required much more time to arrange the prints & drawings than is now left; but Lady Inchiquin said that if the sale did not take place this Spring Marchi must be kept on & the House cd. not be painted; and the publick wd. think it strange after an advertisement had been published, if the sale shd. be postponed.

Poggi I went to & told him the sale was to be this Spring. He desired me to express to Lady Inchiquin his wish to have the portrait of Sir Joshua which she had lent to him to be placed in his room.

Thames, the last print for the second Vol: I finished colouring today. The view from Flamstead House.

Lady Inchiquin has been lately employed in copying a Picture painted by Sir Joshua Reynolds. She told me that by Sir Joshuas *strict direction* in painting her heads she never used *any yellow*. She only used white, Light red, vermilion, Black and a little blue. On this preparation she glazed.

Friday March 18th.

Sir Wm. Chambers funeral I went to this morning as one of the Council of the Royal Academy. mourning Coaches were sent round to us and we assembled at his house in Norton St. at 10 o'Clock. The 3 Executors, Mr. Collins, Mr. Brown, & Mr. Andre were there. Sir Richd. Kaye, Rev. Mr. Penneck, Wyatt & Yenn as visitors. Mr. West, Bacon, Lawrence, Tyler, Hoppner, Stothard, Westall, Richards & Wilton were there from the Academy. Mr. Craig, Brettingham, Groves, from the board of Works. About Eleven the procession moved to Westminster Abbey. 19 Coaches in all. Mr. Chambers, Sir Wms. Son followed the Corpse from the west door as Chief mourner; after him Mr. Harward, Mr. Milbanke, Major Cotton, Sir Wms. Sons in law, and his nephew, Mr. George Chambers followed. Then the Executors, then the Academy & lastly the board of Works. The body was interred about one oClock in the Poets Corner, — There were no Pall bearers & the common funeral service only was read. — After the ceremony we separated at the West door. A considerable number of respectable tradesmen to the board of works attended and formed two lines to shew their respect to the memory of Sir William.

I went with Lawrence to the sale of Lord Butes, *High Cliff* collection of pictures, chiefly sea pieces & very bad, the collection having been gleaned by Genl. Stuart. Three Canalettis good pictures. We called at Bryants and at the European Museum, & from thence went to Lawrences, who has completed his whole length of the Duke of Leeds.

Royal Academy Club I went to. Twenty members present. Lawrence came home with me in the evening.

Yenn told me at Sir Wm. Chambers' house that the King had sent for him and nominated him to be Treasurer to the Royal Academy. He told me that sometime since Sir William Chambers had asked him to be of his Executors which He had declined on acct. of his business being too much.

Sir William has left Lady Chambers £800 a year & £2500 to dispose of. He has made up the fortunes of His five daughters £6000 each; £1500 to each of his grandchildren, *Mr. Chambers children 8 in number*, to accumulate till they came of age; £1100 a year to Mr. Chambers the residuary Legatee. The will is much approved of.

Mr. Collins, Mr. West introduced me to. Mr. West had before desired me to see a picture by Wilson painted for Mr. Collins, as He had promised Mr. C. that either He or I wd. clean it for him. Mr. Collins reminded me that we had formerly been together at Steevens, Sir Wms. pupil.

Wyatt told me at the Club that He had not yet recd. any notice from the King of his being appointed Surveyor General of the board of works; but He had been informed the warrant is making out. He has not been to the King since the death of Sir William, and has been told by a friend He judges right in not going. The King told him lately that He had judged well in bringing up one of his Sons to be an Architect. As He wd. have the reccomendation of his Fathers reputation. The Queen expressed a wish to see Wyatt on acct. of some alterations which She proposed. A friend of Wyatt told her Majesty that He had refrained from coming to the Queens Palace out of delicacy.

Saturday March 19th.

Ld. Butes, sale of his High Cliff pictures, I went to. Mrs. Soane gave 36 guineas for a Canaletti & 35 guineas for its companion.

Bryant I saw at the Sale and bought a little picture of Teniers of him, which He this morning bought for twelve guineas. It belonged to Parke the musician, who gave 15 guineas for it. Council, adjourned I attended.

West

Tyler, Stothard, Bacon & Lawrence there.

Read the report of Dance & Tyler again, and it was agreed that the Books containing the statements of accts. should be carried to the King tomorrow morning by Mr. West also the proposal of regulations for the office of Treasurer, &c &c to have his majestys opinion before the business is brought formally forward to a general meeting. It was doubted whether it wd. be delicate to propose to the King that the Treasurer shd. give security to the Academy; I, on reflection, contended for it, as I am convinced it will cause him to look towards the Academy with more respect than He might otherways do: Sir Wm. Chambers having always asserted that the Academy had nothing to do with money matters. It was finally agreed to submit the proposal to the King in a separate note. Left the Academy at Eleven oClock.

Sunday March 20th.

Sir George Beaumont I breakfasted with this morning. He having sent to me. I looked at two pictures He intends for exhibition, and gave him my opinion as to certain additions.

Bryants Gallery I went to, & found Baker there, & I went with him to see the Orleans Exhibition, (Slades) in Bond st. of which Du Cort has the management. I afterwards returned to Bryants Gallery, and saw him and paid him for the Teniers. Lord Carlisle has bought the large high finished picture by [Gossaert].

Sir George Beaumonts I dined at. Hoppner there.

Monday March 21st.

Sir Francis Bourgeois I called on, & saw his large picture of "The washing Horses in the Sea", intended for Exhibition. It is a whole length canvas. He wishes it to be *under the line* in the Exhibition room, & I told him I wd. speak to the Committee.

I sat a little time with Mr. Desenfans who is much afflicted by nervous complaints, and has been for 7 or 8 years past. His collection of pictures is now completely arranged in his house, is very fine. Sir Francis told me that it was intended for the King of Poland; but that He, Mr. D. has now resolved never to part with one of them.

Council adjourned, I went to. Present

West

Bacon, Tyler, Hoppner, Lawrence, Westall, Stothard.

West reported that yesterday morning at 8 oClock He attended the King at the Queens House with the Books, and the proposal for regulating the office of Treasurer. — That his Majesty was much struck with the judicious manner in which the accts. of the Academy have been drawn up by Dance & Tyler in the Book made up from the Bills and Sir Wms. accts. —. His Majesty said in Money matters he approved of Securities such as that expected from the Treasurer; & finally said He wd. take the Books & papers to Windsor and directed West to come to Him on Saturday next when He wd. give his answer on all the points.

I moved that the Cast of the Farnesian Hercules which is now in one of the ground rooms of the Academy shd. be brought up & placed in the Vestibule. This was agreed to and Bacon, Hoppner, Lawrence, Stothard & Westall went down stairs, to consider which part of the Vestibule it will be best to place the Statue in. It was judged best to place it on *Castors*, between the windows, from whence in the Summer Season it may be removed for the advantage of students to the fire place side.

Sir Francis Bourgeois told me this morning that Mr. Heriot had said to him that if the Catalogues of Exhibition were printed off an *Octavo size* a great saving wd. be made. This I proposed to the Council, and Richards was directed to obtain from Cooper the Printer, a Page set up to see what appearance it would make.

West in conversation said Desenfans has realised £1500 a year to his knowledge. That He has left his collection of pictures by will to Sir F. Bourgeois, as well as something handsome besides. He says Sir Francis is Son to a Swiss who came from near Yverdon in Switzerland, who married an English woman, and by her had two Children, Sir Francis & a daughter. His wife dying He quitted England, and left the two Children here unprovided for. — Desenfans was at this time a language master, & by some means became with others interested in the fate of these Children to whom He was in no way related. He declared His resolution to take care of the Boy, and the girl was sent to Switzerland to the friends of her father.

Desenfans knew nothing of pictures. He became a picture dealer in consequence of having lent some money to a Dutchman who had brought over some pictures, and eventually He purchased them and sold them for £100 profit. This success induced him to go on.

Tuesday March 22nd.

Flaxman called on me this morning, and gave me a Morning Chronicle of yesterday, in which a letter adressed to the President & Council of the Royal Academy, wrote by him, appeared. It is on the subject of admitting works of art into Churches.

Col. Cawthornes sentence was yesterday read at the Court Martial, Horse Guards. His conduct is declared to have been scandalous & infamous, unbecoming an Officer & a gentleman; & He is cashiered & rendered incapable of ever serving his majesty in any military capacity, and for the sake of example the sentence is directed to be read at the head of every regt. of militia in England.

Wednesday 23rd.

Mrs. Roberts called on me. I reccomended to her to apply to Mrs. Raws
torne for a reccomendation to Miss Atherton for assistance; and also to
apply to John Bissell her nephew.

C. Offley called on me. Barroneau's attorney says that the proposal o(
Bowyer would subject the party agreeing to it, to a charge of usury
Barroneau therefore is disposed to decline any further concern in the
business.

Sir Robert & Lady Salisbury called in Ormond street yesterday and C
Offley today returned the visit.

The wind has been easterly several days and has affected me.

Thursday 24th.

J. Boydell I called on at Guildhall where He was attending as a Com
missioner. Giffard was there. He was sworn in as a Commissioner since the
commencement of the present Lottery. Lord Belgrave procured the
appointment.

J. Boydell went with me to Alderman Boydells, where we gave direc
tions for the Prints belonging to the second Volume properly selected, so
as to have good impressions for the first subscribers. Alderman Boydel
said he thought the Volumes of the Thames should be raised in price to Six
guineas a Vol: or we should not be indemnified if we allowed to the trade.

Lieut. Col. O.Kellys sentence of Court Martial was read yesterday. The
charge found against him was for applying coals belonging to the regt. to
his own use. *He was judged* to pay £100 and to be dismissed his majesty;
service. N.B. This was mitigated by the King. "No fine to be paid, and to be
dismissed from the Lieut. Colonelcy of the Westminster Regt. only".

Friday March 25th.

Mr. Fryers I called at. He was but indifferent & I think much altered since
saw him last. Revd. Mr. Penneck & Mr. Fitzhugh there.

Saturday 26th.

Offleys I dined at. Mr. & Mrs. L. Salusbury, Outram, Smirke & Dick
there. Council at Academy I went to.

West

Bacon, Dance, Tyler, Hoppner, Stothard, there.

West said that his majesty having inspected the Books, and approved o(
the manner in which it is proposed they shall be kept, and approved also o
the regulations proposed for the Office of Treasurer, excepting the Article
of his giving security to the Academy which the King thought not usua
and not necessary.

The regulations were put & carried unanimously & a general meeting is
to be called to pass them.

West told us that He is now subject to so many interruptions in the day that of late He paints most by Candle light after tea till 12 o'Clock or later, and that the strong light from his lamp enables him to see better than by day light.

Council Broke up at Eleven, when I went with Hoppner to Georges Coffee House.

Hoppner is now very full of business, and shd. it continue must get £2000 a year.

Sunday March 27th.

Sir George Beaumont called on me & I went to dinner with him. No company.

Monday 28th.

Dr. Breedon came to breakfast with me. Sir Francis Sykes & Lord Eardley have compromised for the election at Walingford. Young Sykes goes out and Sir Francis & Ld. Eardley are to be the members.

David Hunter this afternoon communicated to Dick a resolution of Sir Alexander Hamilton that Dick should not dispose of the new Ship, Henry Addington, for more than £4,000 and not for more than 3 voyages. This iniquitous resolution Sir Alexander has made evidently that at the end of three voyages He may have the Ship to dispose of and put the money into his own pocket. A few days ago Dick said to Sir Alexander that He hoped Sir A. had no objection to His making his own terms in the sale of the Ship, to which Sir Alexander [said] "He had not". Yet in contradiction to that declaration He now comes forward with this fraudulent resolution. On Friday or Saturday last Hunter mentioned to Dick that Sir Alexander had said something to this effect. Sir Alexander was so conscious of the injustice of his conduct that He would not mention the matter to Dick but desired Hunter to do it. Hunter declined it unless he had documents under Sir Alexanders hand, which being sent to Him He this day shewed them to Dick.

In the meantime witht. communicating anything to Dick on the subject Sir Alexander had privately told Mr. Kirkpatrick, a relation of Admiral Paisleys, who was 3rd. mate of the Lascelles with Dick the last voyage, that He shd. command the Henry Addington. This, though Hamilton desired Him to be silent, Kirkpatrick out of respect mentioned to Dick.

This evening Dick went to Hamilton & had a conversation with him on the subject of what Hunter had communicated to him. Dick told me He found him unfeeling & determined though He had not the courage to look him in the face. Hamilton said that no person shd. have the Ship for more than 3 voyages, by which time a friend of his wd. be ready to take her. Dick represented that he did not believe that any person wd. give £4000 for the Ship for 3 voyages, if He was to be bound up not to receive anything at the expiration of that term; and he asked Sir A. who was to receive the £5000 to be allowed by the Company when the Ship is worn out. Sir A. seemed to make light of this as an allowance not likely to be made, but when Dick shewed him that there is no doubt about it, He replied, "then it will be so much the better for my friend". What said Dick, then is it to be that He who has paid money for the Ship is to have no return, and He who has not paid a Shilling is to have £5000. The Knight Here seemed to see that he had explained himself too far. Sir A. said that it was the determination of other Ships Husbands to get the *patronage* into their own hands. You have the whole patronage and have always had it said Dick. The fact is He meant by patronage the *disposal* of the Ship as suited his interest. Sir A. rested his pretence to limit the sale of the Ship on a security given to Captn. Wakefields relations to return £4000 of the £8000 which He recd. from Wakefield if Wakefield died during the voyage. But this was never mentioned when Dick purchased the Ship either by Wakefield or by Hamilton. Dick told Hamilton that He wd. certainly go the voyage.

Tuesday March 29th.

Westall called this evening to offer me a place in a Box on Saturday to see Irelands play of Vortigern.

Dick told Sir Alexander Hamilton He wd. go the voyage, who replied "then you remove a weight from my mind." In conversation He told Dick He had made money in the Ship & had no right to complain. As if Dick, having made money, justified the former in depriving him of his right.

Wednesday March 30th.

Dick called on Sir Alexander and told him that by his proposal He would take the money from him to give it to the company. The other could not or would not understand it. Dick often observes how stupid the other appears to be in comprehending matters of business.

David Hunter told Dick Sir Alexander had said to him "well all is up, the Ice is broken", or words to that effect. Outram I dined with at Freemasons Tavern. C & J Offley, L. Salusbury & Dick there.

Thursday 31st.

Malone called early this morning, & left for me his book on Irelands forged papers, which was published this morning.

Lady Inchiquin I called on. She had sent to me, and informed me the sale of the Prints and drawings is postponed to next year, as they cannot be got ready this Season. She has not yet informed Poggi or Greenwood as she says they will slacken their preparations.

APRIL 1796

Friday April 1st.

Bell called this morning & paid me for instructions given to Lindoe. He told me Mr. David Barclay had settled an annuity on Lindoe sufficient for his support, and He had now a maintenence for life should He not obtain a guinea by painting. I said Lindoe was a man of great good nature, and of late improved much; but I thought He had a constitutional indolence. Bell said my observation was right.

Academy Club I went to the last of this Season. Zoffany desired me to obtain good situations for 4 pictures which He had prepared for the exhibition, which He was to shew to the King before they were sent.

Humphry told me that Wyatt a nephew of James Wyatt He dined in company with yesterday, and heard him strongly support the authenticity of Irelands manuscripts and assert the futility of Malones book.

Saturday April 2nd.

Lysons called on me early on acct of obtaining time for a drawing He meant to exhibit.

Academy I went to to Breakfast to The Council there all attended. Agreed to a letter I had drawn up to be presented to the Lords of Treasury to abolish duties on works of art belonging to British artists. Smith the Printer attended. He said a saving of £70 or £80 might be made by printing names of Exhibitors with a smaller type. He reccomended to the Council to print the names of the Portraits and sell them separately. He said He wd. give 30 guineas this year for that privilege & 50 the next.

Proceeded to examine the pictures &c. The portraits of young Kearsly were much approved. Ibbetsons panel of 9 Landscapes, — Abbots.

Jean sent a whole length of the King in robes. Very indifferent, & objected on that account, as unworthy to be placed in the great room.

Dined at the Academy. Irelands play of Vortigern I went to with Westall, Hoppner & Lawrence. Lord Berwick, Mr Clarke his Tutor, Honble. Mr. Tufton, Revd. Dr. Grant, Dance, Porden, & Braine in our Box.

Prologue spoken at 35 minutes past 6: Play over at 10 — A Strong party was evidently made to support it, which clapped without opposition frequently through near 3 Acts, when some ridiculous passages caused a laugh, which infected the House during the remainder of the performance, mixed with groans. Kemble requested the audience to hear the play out abt. the end of the 4th. act and prevailed. The Epilogue was spoken by Mrs. Jordan who skipped over some lines which claimed the play as Shakespeares. Barrymore attempted to give the Play out for Monday next but was hooted off the stage. Kemble then came on & after some time was permitted to say that the "School for Scandal would be given", which the House approved by clapping.

Sturt, of Dorsetshire, was in a Stage Box drunk, & exposed himself indecently to support the Play, and when one of the stage attendants attempted to take up the green cloth, He Sturt seized him roughly by the head. He was slightly pelted with oranges.

Ireland, His wife, son, & a daughter, Pratt (Courtney Melmoth) & two others were in the Center Box, at the Head of the Pitt. Ireland occasionally clapped, but towards the end of the 4th. act He came into the front row, and for a little time leant his head on his arm, and then went out of the Box and behind the scenes.

After the play I went to the Hummums Coffee House with Hoppner, Lawrence & Westall. Speaking of the pictures we had reviewed today, Lawrence spoke very favourably of the Landscapes of Pether, & Westall partly joined him. Hoppner on the contrary said He detested them. I said they are certainly the works of an ingenious man, but that there is no true character of nature in them. I also said the drawings of Turner are very ingenious, but it is a manner'd harmony which He obtains.

Sunday April 3rd.

Malone I called on this morning. Harding at breakfast with him. He was at the Play last night in a private Box, and when it was over the Duke of Leeds took him, Sir George Beaumont & Kemble home to supper, where they staid till 3 o'Clock. — The Play house He said contained an audience that amounted to £800.

500 Copies of Malones Book are sold already. Steevens & Sir Wm. Musgrave wrote notes of approbation of it to Malone, which He read to us.

The scurrilous advertisements & hand bills published by Ireland against Malone makes him desirous that somebody should publish an acct. of Irelands progress through life that his character may be fully known.

Westall I called on. He shewed me some verses on Johnson & Mackpherson being buried near to each other. I told him I thought them too favourable to the latter.

Kirkpatrick called on Dick. He dined yesterday with Sir A. Hamilton. He thinks Sir A. bears Dick a grudge. Sir A. said Kirkpatrick must look to him for the Ship if he had it. Dick offered it to him for £8000.

Offleys I dined at. Susan, Eliza, Dick, Outram there.

Monday April 4th.

Flaxman called. He wishes to exhibit in consequence of Fuseli & Stodart having pressed him to do it. He desired my opinion of His putting his name down as a Candidate to be an Associate which Fuseli particularly urged him to do. I said that as there are 3 vacancies it is certainly a very good time. He wrote a note to the Council requesting to be admitted to exhibit & I undertook to deliver it.

Christies I went to. Met Cosway there. He wishes for a Charter to be obtained to incorporate the Royal Academy.

Academy I went to to Council. It was proposed to place Jeans picture of the King in the Council Room. I recommended to Westall to bring his two pictures of Cottage Children from bottom of the room and place them on each side the Duke of Leeds, the center picture, at upper end.

Yenns nomination to be Treasurer came; It was not read formally on acct. of restrictions laid on his office not having passed the General meeting.

Tuesday April 5th.

At Academy in the evening. Sir George Beaumont wrote to Hoppner by advice of Gilpin declining to exhibit his large picture this year.

General meeting was held, passed regulations for the office of Treasurer; referred the question of securing the Academy funds, for the opinion of Council.

Yenn told me that He had said to the King that if the Regulations proposed by Sir William Chambers were adopted the Academy would be ruined by the discontents arising. He talked of Soane I told him Dances opinion was in his favour. Went to Coffee House with Hoppner, Lawrence & Westall.

Wednesday April 6th.

At Christies. Got Willis to purchase two pictures of Canalettis for me.

Academy I went to in the evening. Hoppner, Lawrence & Westall have resolved to desire to withdraw one of his whole lengths & Hoppner will withdraw one. Beechy proposed to send 4, Hoppner 5. Hoppner wrote to me this evening desiring me to act for him tomorrow as one of the Committee of arrangement.

Thursday 7th.

Academy I went to, to breakfast. I proposed to remove Northcotes series of pictures from the door side of the room, to the lower end, as being a more conspicuous situation. Westall wrote to Beechy a letter requesting him to withdraw a whole length. Beechy wrote for answer that He shd. send 4 whole lengths & wd. rather the Committee shd. decide which shd. be returned as it would relieve him from making an excuse.

Friday 8th.

Academy I went to to breakfast at the request of Lawrence who is engaged like Hoppner in finishing his pictures. Beechy this morning wrote a letter very different from that of last night, insisting upon having his pictures & frames returned if they could not all be hung. In the evening a Council was held, when Beechys letter was read and an answer was agreed to which was written by Mr. Richards — as Secretary, signifying that the indulgence granted to Beechy enabled him to withhold those pictures which He had not sent; but such as were placed agreeable to the rules of the Academy cd not be removed. It was also expressed that he had not shewn due respect to the Society.

This evening the invitation list was made out. Omitted of last year Chevl. Pisani, Monsr. Calonne, Montagu, Sir Jas. Wright, Bishop of St. Davids, Sir Wm. Dolben, Sir G. Baker, Sir Wm. Young, Sir Alan Gardner, Sir N. Gresley, Honble. Mr. Nassau, Mr. Pierrepoint, C Pybus Esqr., Mr. Banbury, Mr. Bastard, Mr. D. Boswell, Dr. Herschill, D. Hailes Esqr., G. Hardinge Esqr., Dr. Reynolds, W. M. Godschall, Mr. T. Walpole

new invitations

proposed by		
proposed by Hoppner	Duke of Bedford, Edwd. Lascelles, Junr. Esq. Lord Paget.	
Westall	Ld. Berwick,	
Lawrence.	Mr. Wallace. Bishop of Landaff, Mr. Wm. Locke.	
Dance.	Mr. S. Lysons.	
Farington.	Lord Walpole, Mr. Price.	
Tyler.	Mr. Rose of the Treasury.	
Bacon.	Coll. Humberstone Mackenzie. Sir Robt. Lawley.	
West	Honble. Chas. Herbert, proposed for P Sandby.	
	Sir Philip Steevens	do. for Beechy.
Humphry	Bishop of Rochester	do. for Humphry
	Sir Watkins Wm. Wynne } Mr. Penn	do. for Wyatt
	Attorney General	
	Mr. Currie	do. for Bonomi.
	Stadholder. Honble. Chas. Fox.	

Total Invitations.

Prince of Wales.
Duke of York
— Clarence
Prince Ernest
Lord Chancellor
Archbishop Canterbury
— York
Dukes, Norfolk.
— Dorset.
— Leeds
— Bedford
— Buccleugh
Marquiss Townshend
— Salisbury
— Buckingham
— Abercorn

Earls Harcourt
— Suffolk
— Hardwicke
— Fife
— Carysfort
— Carlisle
— Inchiquin
— Lucan
— Morton
— Spencer
— Warwick
— Darnley
— Ashburnham
— Aylesford

Viscounts, St. Asaph
— Palmerston
— Belgrave

Bishops, London
— Rochester
— Salisbury
— Durham
— Norwich
— Lincoln
— Landaff

Lords. Thurlow
— Walpole
— Paget
— Mulgrave
— Yarborough
— Sheffield
— Lavingdon
— Amherst
— Clive
— Eliot
— Berwick
— Dundass
— Middleton
— Grenville

Sir Richd. Hoare
— G. Beaumont
— R. Ainslie
— R. Lawley
— W. W. Wynne
— P. Burrell
— A. Hume
— P. Stephens
— J. Sinclair
— J. Banks

The Margrave of Anspach
— J. Mitford
Honble. C Fox
— C Herbert
— Coll. Greville
— Chas. Greville

Ambassadors
Germany
Prussia
Denmark
Saxony
Portugal
Bavaria
Hanover
Spain
America
Sweden

Mr. Pitt
Ld. Mansfield
Mr. Dundass
— Wyndham
Lord Grenville
Marqs. Cornwallis
Lord Mayor
Alderman Clarke
— Boydell
Mr. C. Long M.P.
— Rose M.P.
— P. Knight M.P.
— P. Campbell M.P.
— Wallace M.P.
— Currie M.P.
— N. Dance M.P.
Wm. Smith M.P.
Coll. H. Mackenzie.
Mr. Malone
— G. Steevens
— Seward
— U. Price
— Seward
— T. Harris
— Wm. Lock, Junr.
— Penn
— Udney
— C. Townley
— Pye
— Hope
— Wm. Hope
— Lascelles Junr.
— S. Lysons.
— W. Hastings
— E. Burke.
— Burdon.

This day I met Lady Inchiquin at Squibbs room and assisted her in arranging the pictures painted by Sir Jos: Reynolds.

Saturday April 9th.

Met Lady Inchiquin at Squibbs this morning.

Academy, I went to, to breakfast. This morning Beechy wrote a very impertinent letter to Richards to be communicated to the Council, in answer to that sent to him, demanding his pictures & frames that he may have no farther trouble in the business. The Committee directed his frames to be taken down & placed ready in the Hall ready for delivery, but resolved to retain the pictures placed agreeable to the order of Council. — Tyler being in the room went down stairs & had some conversation with Steevens, a frame maker, who came from Beechy, whtht. the knowledge of the Committee. In the afternoon another letter came from Beechy in which He stated that as He understood that the Committee meant to retain *all his pictures* He consented that one of them shd. be placed in the Anti-room & shd. send them on Monday. It afterwards appeared that Tyler had proposed no such conditions but only said the pictures cd. not all be hung in the great room. On Sunday Tyler went to Beechy and denied having sent any proposal to him, so it seemed that Beechy having found that He had gone too far was glad to seize any pretence for sending his pictures.

Hoppners I went to early this morning. His whole length of Lady Charlotte Campbell in a bad state. I gave my opinion freely. Dinner at home, Lysons, Mr. Malone & Hughes dined with me.

Sunday April 10th.

Hoppner I called on early & went with him to Squibbs room to see the pictures painted by Sir Joshua on sale. I met Lawrence there. Went home with him & proposed alteration of sky &c in his picture of the Duke of Leeds which has twice been placed in the Exhibition room, and alterations have appeared necessary. I left him making the alterations I suggested. One of his sisters was married this morning.

White of Deptford called, also Kershaw & Byrne. Bourgeois is displeased that his whole length picture is placed on the line.

Monday 11th.

Academy I went to to breakfast. Lawrence wrote to Beechy from Committee denying having made proposal & desiring him to determine. He sent pictures but no answer. In the Exhibition room my picture of the Sun setting & moon rising appeared very dark. West suggested that making the moon a more spirited & silvery light wd. have great effect. This observation I found to be just. He reccomended to Lawrence to make the ground on which the figure of the Duke of Leeds stands lighter & warmer. Lawrence who had brought the picture this morning took it back and nade the alteration which did not answer. The effect of the picture was estroyed. Westall & I advised him to alter it which He did & made the round cooler and of a stronger tint which answered. West said there hould always be 3 points in a picture.

Fuseli called on me this eving. to propose invitation of G. Steevens. He vas invited on Friday last.

Tuesday 12th.

Academy to breakfast. Called at Hoppners, Lady C. Campbells picture much improved. Sir George Beaumont sat with him yesterday while He vent over the picture. Lawrence came to Academy to dinner, thinks Beechey's pictures better than they last night when brought in appeared to ne.

Tresham brought his picture of Virginia, which at his particular desire I hung in a very good place by removing several pictures.

Hoppner came to tea. Reinagle painted the background to Gilpins oxes.

Wilton told me Sir William Chambers was married at Rome 5 months before the Birth of Mrs. Milbanke his eldest Child. Young Chambers is a weak man, so are most of the daughters. Lady Chambers a Milliners girl, followed Sir Wm. to Paris.

Wednesday 13th.

Academy to breakfast. At 12 o'Clock went to Lady Inchiquins. Greenwood there. Lord Inchiquin proposes two Irish gentlemen to bid. Lady Inchiquin fixes the price of Lord Melbournes Children at 250 gs. and 150 gs. for Lady Ilchester & Children. Sir Joshua was to have had 300 for it. Greenwood had offered 30 guineas for the naked child. The Tygers, now Hardmans, was mentioned. Lady Inchiquin regretted it. I said I did not believe it to be Rubens & wd. not give 100 gs. for it.

Lawrence asked me if his pictures this year wd. restore his reputation. I told him the Duke of Leeds is his best whole length & Sergeant Shepherd His best half length, therefore if the world did him justice He must have his reward.

Yenn came to the Academy. We talked abt. his situation as Treasurer. He told me the King did not take the books made up by Dance & Tyler to Windsor, but put them into *his hands* to make his observations. The King passed a morning in considering them.

I told Yenn his situation wd. be agreeable if He acted in Unison with the body. He said I and others had done ourselves great honor in supplying the letters sent by Sir William Chambers, and He had informed the King of it. He desired me to take care of Merediths drawing.

Richards told us that some years ago G. Steevens was very troublesome by daily visiting his painting rooms at the Theatre & that He had spoken to

Mr. Harris in consequence who mentioned it to Steevens who never cam afterwards.

Mr. Garrick told Richards that Steevens once came to his house a Hampton when it was full of company. Garrick was obliged to procur him a bed in a neighbours house, where Steevens became acquainted wit a married lady who He seduced. Garrick disliked him extremely. Si Joshua Reynolds also complained to Richards of the daily interruptions c Steevens.

Mrs. Hussey wrote to Susan today that Miss Randall is gone off wit Captn. Stothard.

Thursday April 14th.

First days sale of Sir Joshuas works. Academy to Breakfast. Hoppne brought Lady Charlotte Campbell & Mrs. M.A. Taylors pictures, the former He thinks wants glazing & force. Westall thinks head of Lady Charlotte not well turned. Richards thinks arm of Mrs. Taylor appears too stumpy.

Lawrence brought picture of Duke of Leeds, having altered the ground on Wests Idea. It is too warm & sandy. Lawrence took it back the 4th time.

Stodart came, thinks Exhibition excellent. Spoke warmly of my little picture of the Mill, so had Hoppner in the morning.

Lawrence dined with us. Sheridan has got the property of the Linleys i his power to the great uneasiness of Mrs. Linley.

Wilton told me in his opinion there was no just ground of reproach against the late Sir Horace Mann. — From the day Wilton came to the Academy as Keeper He has had no *domestic* intercourse with Mr Richards or his family. Mrs. Richards never called on Mrs. Wilton as they supposed she naturally would have done.

Friday April 15th.

Academy to breakfast.

Lord Inchiquins I went to. He is mortified that many articles were yesterday bought in. Lady Inchiquin told me she cd. not bear to let them go at low prices. Cribb, the frame maker, bid for her and 2 Irish gentlemen.

Sir Joshuas sale I went to with Westall, and bid for one lot for Lady Inchiquin. Westall bought three pictures and Beechy two, the latter dear.

Mr. Hussey at the sale spoke to me about Miss Randall. Mr. Sandby wd. have again offered to her.

Dined at the Academy. Yenn had been there, wanted an invitation for Lord Melbourne, and a picture of Ferrières to be admitted.

Poggi called in the evening, & Marchant to thank me for invitation to Mr. Banks who is engaged.

Saturday April 16th.

Academy to breakfast. Called at Ld. Inchiquins and took prices of 6 lots which I engaged to bid for today. At sale much company: over at 5, — dined at Academy, Tyler & Dance there.

removed Banks' Bassrelief from the side to the center of life Academy.

Council in the evening to receive answers. By mistake Lord Leicester & Sir Joseph Banks had not been invited. Cards were sent.

Sir George Beaumont told me at the sale that Hoppner had spoken to him of my picture of the mill.

Hoppner desired me this evening to tell him what Westall & Lawrence had said of His pictures. I said they had spoken of them with high encomiums, but Westall thought the head of Lady Charlotte not well turned, and they objected to the present appearance of the arm of Mrs. Taylor.

Lord Fife at the sale today complained of the manner in which Lord & Lady Inchiquin [spoke] abt. a picture of Lady Fife.

Sunday April 17th.

Academy to breakfast. At one called on Lady Inchiquin. She out. Kirkley told me when Marchi gave acct. of the sale she broke out in passion, but Kirkley afterwards pacified her by shewing her what lots of sketches &c had sold greatly.

Sir George Beaumonts I dined at with Dick. G. Dance & Revd. Mr. Huddesford there.

Monday 18th.

Academy to breakfast. Called on Lady Inchiquin. Mrs. Hoppner had called on me before to desire me to speak to Lady I. abt. price of picture of Mrs. Musters, for which Lady I. has asked 80 gs. Hoppner has offered Kirkley 5 gs. for procuring it, so it will cost him 85 gs. On my mentioning price to Lady I. she said she wd. not sell it for less than 80.

Lady I. mentioned that Mr. Metcalf notwithstanding his intimacy with Sir Joshua & the high prices he has given for pictures has no picture by Sir Joshua. She expressed some resentment.

Lady I. told me price of the ½ length of a Grecian Lady should be 50 gs. I went to Squibbs room with Westall who agreed to purchase the picture.

Dined at Academy. Hoppner came. Lord Paget desires to dine at Academy. A card was made out by Hoppner, Westall & me & one to Mr. Lambton.

Northcote & Gaugain the engraver came to the Academy, & Richards having said to Northcote that His pictures were not all hung together, He became much alarmed. Richards desired me to go to them. They talked of having them out. I described the situation & said He wd. have reason to be satisfied with the manner in which they are placed. They went away apparently satisfied.

Tuesday April 19th.

Academy to breakfast. G. Smith, portrait painter, who had written to me making use of Mr. Harris' name called at Academy and earnestly requested that one of his pictures rejected, might be placed in the room of one which is hung. I desired him to send it, & had it placed witht. removing his other pictures.

Mackenzie came to me abt. his medals of Academicians. At one went home to paint on my Exhibition pictures. returned to Academy to dinner, but before called on Lysons, Mr. Cracherode there. Lysons told me of the unhandsome behaviour of Mr. Knight the Surgeon, in sending to Wood-chester an Alabaster figure to be put in the ground that it might be dug up as a discovery. The figure of course was found & sent up to Lysons who was subjected to the imposition some days. — Mr. Fryer died this morning in the 64th. year of his age.

Academy I dined at. West, Richards, Yenn, Dance, Tyler, Stothard, Hoppner & Westall there.

At Mr. Wests desire Mr. Udney was invited. Daniel wrote to me abt. varnishing his pictures. Marchant called on me in the evening to request a Ticket to the Academy dinner for Lord Lavington. Lord Lavington called with Ld. Carlisle on Marchant, and said in Sir Joshuas time He had been invited. After they went away Lord Lavington returned to Marchant & desired him to apply to Mr. West for a Ticket as He was not acquainted with Mr. West.

Wednesday April 20th.

At home painting. dined at Academy: Westall there. West came to tea. Bonomi through West requested a Ticket for Mr. Currie, which was made out & I got one for Lord Lavington.

I mentioned to West that last year He hesitated too long between the toasts which He said was owing to Ld. Mansfield engaging him too much in conversation.

Bacon & Hoppner came, 22 pictures are now out of the great room.

Thursday 21st.

At home painting this morning, & finished my Exhibition pictures.

Sent to Marchant & gave him the Ticket for Lord Lavington. Went to the Academy. West, Lawrence & Hoppner there, having put up their pictures. West advised them to wash over *parts* of their pictures with water colours. He uses India Ink, Brown, Pink or Terra Sienna, & Blue. He says it is reccomended by Leonardo.

Smirkes pictures much admired. Hamiltons archbishop of Canterbury

Stothards small study, but Lawrence thought He had better have kept to his own original ideas than follow Rubens.

West told me his large picture was like a Royal Sovereign coming in, Dukes & Lords fell back into their places. He painted it in less than 3 weeks, chiefly by Candle light, and shd. have completed it sooner had the Canvass been better primed. He worked by Candle light from 7 o'Clock till 12 or 1.

Hoppner came to tea, anxious about his pictures of Duke of Bedford & Lady Paget. I told him both well.

Came home in a Coach with West. He does not think Northcotes man to deliver acct. of his pictures can be allowed to stand in the academy passage. He thinks Northcotes pictures poorly executed when examined. Smirke will contribute to introduce a better taste for finishing &c. & make it necessary for artists to qualify themselves by severer study in drawing. His (Wests) sketches & small pictures have led the way to it.

Friday April 22nd.

Academy I went to at 9 with Mrs. Offley & Mrs. Salusbury, Susan & Eliza. Mrs. Posden & Miss Westall & her Cousin also went. I introduced them all to Mr. Wilton that they might see the Royal Family.

The King, Queen, Prince of Wales, Prince Ernest, Princess Royal, Elizabeth, Augusta, Mary & Sophia, attended by Lord Harcourt & [blank] came at 10 o'Clock & staid till 12. West, Wilton, Yenn & Richards told me they expressed great satisfaction & thought it one of the best Exhibitions for many years.

Wilton told me the King particularly dwelt on Westalls drawings & said He had never seen anything equal to them, and wanted to know who they were made for.

The King said as Portrait Painters Beechy, Lawrence, & Hoppner had the entire lead; but it seemed that He particularly noticed Beechys.

At ½ past one the Duke of Gloucester, Prince William & Princess Sophia of Gloucester came to Academy & staid an Hour or more.

Lady Inchiquin I called on to offer to shew her the Exhibition today; but she was going to a launch at Blackwall with Ld. Inchiquin.

Sir George & Lady Beaumont came to the Academy at two oClock & saw the exhibition. Also Mrs. West &c, & Mrs. Hoppner, & Mrs. Hamilton with Lawrence.

Sir George was delighted with Smirkes picture of the Conquest (Lady Pentweazle) and desired me to engage it for him. He as well as the rest thinks Lawrence much improved. He expressed great approbation of my pictures, as did Hoppner, particularly with the wood scene.

I returned home to dinner with Susan. Dick dined with China Hunt, & Eliza at Offleys with Sir Robt. & Lady Salusbury and the Barroneaus.

Mr. Fryer has left Mrs. Fryer £2000 a year & £20,000 to dispose of at her death. About £1500 each to Mrs. Dunnage & his two nephews, with remainder after Mrs. Fryers death. Abt. £5000 in different legacies. The houses in Queen Square & at Taplow to Mrs. Fryer and £1,000 to begin House-keeping with. He died worth £109,000.

Saturday April 23rd.

Smirke I called on and engaged picture of the Conquest for Sir George Beaumont to be a companion to that from Catherine & Petruchio which is exhibiting and which Sir George had ordered. — to have both for 45 guineas.

Offleys I called at to select pictures to be sold at Greenwoods.

Academy I went to at Eleven & met West & Lawrence who came to varnish a picture. West passed a little water colour over the arm of Miss Ogilvies picture & that in Lady Jane Longs picture. He also put a little water colour over a too warm tint in my wood scene & in two or 3 places of the Mill picture. I varnished Westalls Cottage Children.

West & I put names on plates. George Steevens came soon after one oclock while we were thus employed.

Northcote & Bourgeois came, the former much mortified on seeing the arrangement of his series of pictures, on acct. of Wests sketch of *Death on the White Horse* being placed in the center of them. I told him I thought his pictures were well hung & it had been the wish of the Committee to oblige him.

At 3 oClock I went home to dress and returned to the Academy at 4. The room now filled fast. Richold had laid plates for 140. The following persons came who had not sent answers.

Duke of Leeds — Marquiss Buckingham — Ld. Berwick, Ld. Ashburnham — Ld. Spencer — Ld. Clive, Bishop of Durham — Charles Fox — Sir Peter Burrell — Lord Darnley — Bishop of Salisbury, Sir W. W. Wynne.

The consequence was no places had been kept except for Duke of Leeds, Ld. Ashburnham, Lord Spencer, & Bishop of Salisbury. Of course the others were obliged to take such seats as were left. Marquiss Buckingham sat by the singers. C. Fox between Zoffany & Rooker in Nollekens place. Bishop of Durham got between Mr. Price & Mr. Knight.

A little before 5 a letter came to inform Mr. West that the Prince of Wales could not come being obliged to go to Windsor. Prince Ernest wrote to West in the morning apologising the same cause for his absence. At half past 5 dinner was served up.

After dinner G. Dance came to me to mention his concern that Mr. Fox was so improperly situated; on which I went to Downman & requested He wd. come & sit by me which wd. leave an opening for Mr. Fox between Mr. Price & Mr. Knight, witht. Downman being obliged to leave his place; an opening sufficient was made. I then spoke to Mr. Price & Mr. Knight who were very happy at my proposal. I then went to Mr. Fox & requested He wd. remove to a seat prepared for him. He very good humouredly said He was very well situated but on my repeating my wish went with me & took his seat between Mr. Price & Mr. Knight. I observed this attention to Mr. Fox was much approved of. Malone told me it was a good maneouvre.

I conversed much with Mr. Long for whom I had reserved a place on my left hand.

Speaking of the monuments voted to the memory of General Dundass, Captn. Faulkner, and the Captns. killed on the first of June; He said it was a business wh. must be moved by the Treasury to his Majesty; and that He had some time since prepared a paper for the purpose, which Mr. Pitt had frequently carried with him to the King, but other business more pressing prevented his mentioning it. Mr. Long said He had inserted the names of Bacon, Nollekens, & Flaxman, for his Majestys consideration thinking each might have one, & that they shd. give in designs. I mentioned Banks, but I clearly understood that his conduct with regard to politicks made him appear an improper person.

I told Mr. Long I thought these monuments should be referred to the Royal Academy to determine on the designs, both for the credit of His Majestys institution & to secure that the best designs shd. be selected, and asserted my firm belief that no party feeling would prevent the Academy from doing strict justice to the best designs. He approved of what I proposed. ·

I observed to Mr. Long that *we* could not but regret that Mr. Pitt did not seem to feel much for art, and that He had never visited us, which Lord North in his administration had done. I added that it had been said that Mr. Pitt possessed everything but taste. He replied that it was a re[a]son of a private nature which had prevented Mr. Pitt from attending our dinner, & that He cd. assure me Mr. Pitt had a great pleasure in considering works of art. We talked on the subject of allowing British Artists to import their works and *purchases made for study* duty free. He said He expected to have heard from the Academy upon it, & had prepared for it. I said that expecting the pleasure of seeing him at dinner, I had deferred waiting on him with the petition till I could when it wd. be convenient for him. We fixed that I shd. breakfast with him on Wednesday next.

The Stadholder sat today on Mr. Wests right hand, & the Lord Chancellor next to him. The Stadholder joined in the Choruses and seemed desirous of expressing his satisfaction.

Lord Suffolk proposed the health of the Stadholder and the House of Orange, which was drank with 3 cheers. He drank health of the Company and staid till past 9 oClock. The Chancellor went a little before. The Duke of Leeds then drew up to Wests right hand & Lord Morton to his left. Sir Abram Hume, Mr. Long, Soane &c. sat opposite to them. Soane introduced me to the Duke. He said the Clerks in the Secretary of States office where He had presided had made a present of the whole length, His Portrait, painted by Lawrence, to the Duchess. He thought Lawrences portrait of me very like. The Duke staid till past 10. West left Chair at ½ past 10. Dance took it & we broke up at Eleven. Lord Morton staid till near that time.

A warm conversation took place in another part of the room between Fuseli & Hoppner, in which witht. directly quarrelling they said many severe things on each others works. Lawrence, Wm. Locke, & Lysons made up that party.

Downman, Edwards, Opie &c. spoke very handsomely to me of my pictures. Edwards thought some of my foliage handled with too small a pencil.

Smirkes pictures, particularly Lady Pentweazle (the Conquest) were much admired. I think more pointedly than any others. G. Dance, Hoppner & Lysons went with me to Holylands Coffee House to tea. Hoppner told me "I saw Landscape with a new eye". Company at dinner &c. stated in April 27th.

Sunday April 24th.

Offley I called on and shewed him how to varnish pictures before they go to greenwoods.

J. Taylor I called on and took him to the Exhibition, where we staid half an hour. Humphry was there with an acquaintance. He was very full of Lawrences merit & said Vandyke never painted such a picture as the half length of Serjeant Shepherd. He admired the pictures of Du Cort.

Kensington I went to with Hoppner & Westall. We walked in the gardens and dined in the Coffee House at ½ past 3 and walked home before dark.

Smirke I called on. He had recd. a letter from Ld. Carlisle requesting to know if the picture of the Conquest is to be disposed of & the price.

Westall told me today that Boaden has informed him that Beechy is inveterate against me, and calls me "Warwick, the King maker". If not chosen Academician next year He is to exhibit no more and says West approves his determination, which I am sure is not true. Gilpin & Soane, Beechy & Tresham say are to be elected before them.

Hoppner told us today that He had never been paid for what he had painted for the Royal Brothers. He had applied to the Duke of York. Sir George Beaumont & Mr. Long called on me while I was out. Also Mr. Berwick & a person with him.

Monday, April 25th.

Exhibition opened.

Tyler I called on. Lord Walpole much pleased with his situation on Saturday by Tyler.

J. Taylor I called on & gave him list of names. Merry has written to him. I advised Taylor to take no further steps in that business. He has ceased to visit Mrs. Robinson, as Merry goes there.

Boydell I called on. He has seen Coll. Cawthorne frequently, and engaged Coombes to write a defence for him under a feigned name which Bulmer has printed. Coombes asked £100 for writing it.

Lord Delaval stands by Cawthorne, so does Lord Tyrconnel. His spirits have been much depressed, but he has now recovered them.

Perry requested information of Academy dinner from Boydell, who met J. Ireland at a Coffee House in the evening.

Mr. Pinckney, the American Ambassador, proposed to Boydell that the Academy shd. be drank. Boydell applied to the Lord Mayor who gave the toast.

Bulmer I called on. He has been with Coll. Cawthorne today. His spirits have been much depressed but are now quite recovered & He talks of going to the House & making his defence. Lord Tyrconnel & Mr. Dent are to support him. They assert there is not ground for expulsion. Coombes pamphlet has raised the spirits of Cawthorne.

Oracle today attacked the Academy about situation of C. Fox at the dinner. I called on Westall abt. it. He had before explained the matter to Boaden, & in the evening we drew up the following & sent it to Boaden, who printed it next morning.

We have authority to say, "That the situation of Mr. Fox at the dinner of the Royal Academy, noticed in Monday's Oracle, arose entirely from his having omitted to answer the card of invitation. The Marquiss of Buckingham, The Bishop of Durham, and several others of the nobility, were from the same cause, subjected to similar difficulty. Had the Academy been aware of their intentions to honor the meeting with their company, every possible attention would doubtless have been shown to men whose rank and talents are so eminently distinguished".

Opie was the person who gave Boaden the misrepresented account, and also an unfavourable criticism on Hoppners portrait of Lady Charlotte Campbell.

Boaden told Westall, Beechy was distracted abt. arrangements of his pictures, Westall referred to Boadens own observation, who said, they could not be better placed.

Tuesday, April 26th.

Richards I called on & gave him an adress which I had drawn up in the room of that which I lost at the Play of Vortigern. It is to the Lords of the Treasury in favour of British Artists. Richards copied it & a Card to Mr. Long and sent them to me in the evening.

The Exhibition yesterday was attended by 1512 persons who paid for catalogues. — It is universally declared by the newspapers to be the best of many years.

Wilton told me Tresham said I had placed Mr. Fox very unluckily by Mr. Knight who He much disliked. I replied I did not believe so, as I had been lately told by a person, (Marchant) who had visited Mr. Fox at St. Annes Hill, that Mr. Fox had spoken highly of Mr. Knight.

I dined at home having a troublesome cold. Marchant came in the evening. He told Lord Lavington that I procured the Ticket for His Lordship. — Freebairn called on Marchant today & spoke very favourably of *my* pictures; and expressed himself much gratified with the situation of his pictures. Marchant told him he believed I hung them, which I said was true.

Stothard had before spoken to Marchant in favor of my pictures.

Mr. Knight called on Marchant today and invited him to dinner on Monday next to meet Mr. Fox, Sir. Geo: Beaumont, Mr. Price &c.

Wednesday April 27th.

My cold being troublesome I sent an apology to Mr. Long this morning for not breakfasting with him, and staid at home all day.

Westall called in the afternoon. He was at the Exhibition yesterday 3 Hours with his sister &c. & suffered by it. His medical friend has told him that unless he takes great care He is in danger of going into a consumption. He spit blood on Thursday last, and again last night. He is forbid wine and exertion of every kind. I urged to him the utmost caution.

Boaden has told me that Fuseli has been abusing the pictures of Hoppner. "His cold flesh & hot backgrounds".

The Company at the dinner of the Royal Academy were as follows.

The Prince Stadholder.

The Lord Chancellor — Archbishop of York — Earl Mansfield
        Silverheim — Baron de Jacobi — Count de Wedel Jertzbergh
Count Bruhl — Baron Haslang — Thomas Pinckney Esqr

Duke of Leeds	Viscounts Belgrave	Bishops of
Marquiss Townshend	— St. Asaph	Durham
— Buckingham	— Palmerston	Salisbury
Earls Suffolk	Lords Walpole	Rochester
— Carlisle	— Mulgrave	Norwich
— Ashburnham	— Yarborough	R. Honble. C. Fox
— Harcourt	— Sheffield	— Wm. Wyndham
— Spencer	— Grey de Wilton	— C. Greville
— Hardwick	— Berwick	Honble. Coll. Greville
— Fife	— Lavington	— Chas. Herbert
— Carysfort	— Paget	The Lord Mayor.
— Inchiquin		
— Darnley		
— Morton		

                    Sir George Beaumont
                    — Henry Englefield
                    — Abraham Hume
                    — Robert Lawley
                    — W W Wynne
                    — Joseph Banks
                    — John Sinclair
                    — Philip Stephens

Alderman Boydell   Mr. Payne Knight MP
    — Clarke   Chas. Townley —
Coll. Humb[erstone]: Mackenzie   Edmd. Malone —
John Hope   Thomas Harris   —
Williams Hope   Edwd. Lascelles —
William Lock Junr.   John Penn   —
Robt. Udney   James Pye   —
William Seward   George Steevens,
[William] Harrison   Revd. Mr. Peters.

                    Chas. Long MP
                    Price Campbell MP
                    Uvedale Price
                    Saml. Lysons
                    Thomas Wallace MP
                    Currie MP
                    Nat. Dance MP
                    Josiah Boydell.

Captn. Wakefield called this evening. The Duke of Hamilton is at Bristol Hotwells accompanied by Mrs. Esten. He amuses himself at times with fighting cocks in a room. He is quite neglected.

Thursday April 28th.

Mr. Long sent me a note this morning. He will be glad to see me any morning except Friday on the Academy business.

Shakespeare Gallery I went to. Sir John Blaquière came there from the Exhibition which He spoke highly of.

Dr. Breedon, Shelley & Collins called on me in the eving. Dr. Breedon thinks the *2d. Vol: of Rivers* a great improvement in regard to the Prints.

Ralph Kirtley called in the evng. He told me the two ladies in the whole length I purchased are Lady Mills & Her sister Miss Moffatt and that they were painted abt. 20 years, Lady Mills was a daugtr. of Mr. Andrew Moffatt. She acted imprudently with a footman & was separated from Sir Thomas Mills her Husband. The other Sister afterwards married.

Kirtley told me Sir Joshua Reynolds was so assiduous, that for months together He did not go out between the Hours of 9 in the morning & 4 or 5 in the afternoon, unless to see a sale of pictures or some work of art mentioned to him.

Kirtley had been with Sir Joshua near 30 years compleat, when He died. When Kirtley first went into his service Sir Joshua had 20 guineas for a three quarter; but was so over run with business that in that year He first raised his price to 25 Gs. & before the end of the year to 35 Gs. which checked the crowd of sitters.

The Head of Mr. Bennet was painted near 30 years ago. Sir Joshuas price 25 gs. When Kirtley waited upon Mr. Bennet from the Executors to know if He wd. take his portrait Mrs. Bennet told him from Mr. Bennet & said "The Executors might put it on a Post".

Friday April 29th.

Alderman Boydells I went to this morning and selected some sets of 2nd. Vol: of Rivers. Richards told me the Alderman told him not to take in subscriptions for a continuation, on which I went to the Shakespeare Gallery & found that Subscriptions for a continuation had been taken in there, & J. Boydell told Mr. Burbidge immediately to inform Richards that Subscriptions for a continuation are to be taken in.

Tylers I dined at with Dick, Eliza, & Susan. Mr. & Mrs. Soane & G. Dance there.

Dance said He lately dined in company with John Wilkes & thinks He is decaying fast. Wilkes told him He has had a slow fever for twelve months past. He said Miss Wilkes intended to erect a temple to Fever. He then quoted a line from Horace & observed that the ancients erected Temples to Fever.

Exhibition I went to. Dick, Eliza & Susan there. Met Captn. Wakefield who has taken a House in Cliefden Mall, near Bristol for 12 months. The Miss Athertons were at the Exhibition but I did not see them. Rects. of the Exhibition this week

	Persons	£ s. d.
Monday April 25th.	1512	75.12.0.
Tuesday — 26th.	1568	78. 8.0.
Wednesday — 27th.	1600	80. 0.0.
Thursday — 28th.	1941	97. 1.0.
Friday — 29th.	1728	86. 8.0.
Saturday — 30th.		
	——————	——————
		£
	——————	——————

Mr. Walpole of New Burlington St. called while I was out.
Smirke I called upon. He is not satisfied with the manner in which Soane

conducts himself to his pupils. He seems to be proud & peevish, and not instructive. There are 5 or 6 pupils who appear to have little respect for him.

Observing on the pictures of Northcote of the "Good & Bad Girl" Smirke said that it seemd to him that the *cause* of the different dispositions of the two girls would be a proper subject for representation. That is by what faults in education the vicious girl became so. Northcote has only shewn the effects.

Lady Inchiquin & Lady Beaumont wrote to me each desiring to see the Exhibition tomorrow. I proposed to Lady Inchiquin tomorrow week as I had engaged myself previous to receiving her Ladyships note.

Mr. Long I *prepared* a petition for from the Royal Academy which He has undertaken to present to the Lords of the Treasury. The petition has been copied by Richards & is as follows,

"To the Right Honorable The Lords Commissioners of His Majestys Treasury". "The President & Council of the Royal Academy beg leave to state to Your Lordships that the Duties of Customs on Casts, Prints, & Drawings, operates as a prohibition to the introduction of Works of Art; which would add to the national stock, and continually contribute to improve the publick taste."

"It is found on enquiry, that these duties produce a very small sum at most to the Publick revenue, while the apprehension of expences of importation to England, discourages the British Students abroad, from exercising their judgements in selecting specimens of art, which would greatly assist them in their studies." "Therefore the President & Council of the Royal Academy humbly request the Lords Commissioners of His Majestys Treasury that Casts, Prints & Drawings, the property of British Artists, returning to England, may be imported Duty free, on affirmation being made by Deputies from the Council of the Royal Academy, that they have inspected the Articles, and believe them to be intended for the private use and Study of the Artists who may solicit the indulgence, and not for sale."

Royal Academy,

April 20th. 1796. John Richards R.A. Secty.

"The President & Council of the Royal Academy, request Mr. Long will accept their united Thanks, for his obliging offer to lay the inclosed petition before the Lords Commissioners of His Majestys Treasury".
                              Royal Academy John Richards R.A. Secy.
April 20th. 1796.

Marchant called in the evening. Mr. Clavering who has been in Spain with Lord Bute, told him that the picture of Lady Charlotte Campbell is not liked. He said Lady Charlotte is going into Scotland, and is over head

& ears in love with Her cousin Mr. Campbell, an Officer in Her Father the Dukes Regt. of Guards, and Heir to £12000 a year.

Northcote told Marchant yesterday that Gaugain, the Engraver is almost desperate abt. the arrangement of the Series of pictures in the Exhibition. Northcote will readily impute any want of approbation of the pictures, to their being arranged in a certain manner.

[*No entry for Saturday, April 30th.*]

MAY 1796

Mr. Berwick & S. Lysons called this morning. Mr. Berwick is much pleased with the Wynants, Ruysdael & Marietti [Marieschi] which I have bought for him.

Mrs. Wheatley called. Wheatley is again laid up with the gout, which now always affects his hands.

Academy I went to, and met Sir George & Lady Beaumont, who brought with them, The Marchioness of Abercorn, Lady George Seymour, Lady F. Hamilton, & two Sons of Lord Abercorn, & their Tutor, Lady & Miss Clarges, Miss Copley & Lord & Lady St. Asaph.

There were also Sir Francis Bourgeois & Mons: Calonne, whose hair was cropped. Mr. & Mrs. West, Mrs. Brouncker & an old Lady. Mr. & Mrs. Richards, & Mr. & Mrs. Howard, & 2 or 3 other Ladies.

Mr. Howard told me that He saw the Duke of Norfolk yesterday evening, who at ½ past 4 yesterday afternoon, had met in a field near Paddington, Lord Malden. Lord Maldens second gave the word to fire, when they were at 12 paces distance. Lord Malden fired first, and missed; the Duke then fired & missed; The seconds then interfered and Lord Malden consented to acknowledge that He had wrongfully, from misinformation accused the Duke of having broke his word, in regard to giving entertainments to the Electors of Leominster, which the Duke & He mutually agreed not to do at present. The seconds were, to the Duke Captain Wombwell, to Lord Malden, Captn. [Taylor].

Sir Francis Bourgeois told me that he met Lord Ossory this morning, when the Academy being mentioned, Lord Ossory said he had not been invited these two years, and did not know why He was ommitted. Sir Francis afterwards told Monsr. Calonne who was present, why Lord Ossory had not been invited, viz: "from his having spoken disrespectfully of the Exhibition after the dinner". Calonne said the Academy did right & He wished Sir Francis had told Ld. Ossory *why*.

Sir George Beaumont told me He had sent a draft for £50 to Smirke for the 2 pictures for which I had told Sir George He was to pay 45 gs. Sir George said he believed Mr. Long would engage with Smirke for the 7

537

stages of Man, from Shakespeare, which Smirke has proposed to paint on speculation.

Mr. Long sent me this evening an invitation to dine with him on Tuesday; This caused me to call on Lady Hamilton & postpone Sir Alexander & Her Ladyship dining with us to another day.

Westall I called on at Tea time. Braine there. A strong contest between the Telegraph & Oracle on the merits of Hoppner & Beechy.

Sir Joseph Banks' I went to in the evening. He is confined by the gout in his Knee. Lord Morton — Marsden — Dalrymple — Ingenhouz — Mr. Hope — Garthshore — Loyd — Sir J. Blagden — Williams Hope — Keate — Earle — Mr. Peachy — &c &c &c.

Monday May 2nd.

Rose this morning at ½ past 6. Dick, Eliza & Susan went to Gravesend. I called upon Lysons early who gave me Catalogues of the Royal Academy Exhibition for the years 1772, 75 & 76, which make my set compleat from the first year of Exhibitions 1760.

Steers I breakfasted with. He lamented that a picture painted for him by Du Cort is placed very high in the great room. He gave Du Cort 60 guineas for it. It is 3 feet 9 by [blank]

He gave him for another 20 inches by 15, 25 guineas. I told him the prices seemed high, He replied that it was owing to the finishing, which is *like that of Vander Heyde.*

I called with him on his nephew Mr. Warren at his Chambers, and afterwards went into the City.

I told Alderman Boydell that it has been strongly recommended to me to make the *River Severn* the next object. He was agreeable to it. He said we could not afford to publish the Thames for less than 12 guineas, if we made a proper allowance to the trade.

The Alderman thinks some of Northcotes pictures indecent which will prevent the sale.

Battersbee I called on in Bond St. He was not at home, neither was Mrs. Battersbee.

Shakespeare Gallery I went to & related to J. Boydell what the Alderman had said relative to price of the Thames, and of the Severn being the next river. He desired to consider these points & I am to meet him on Wednesday & to go with him to Lord Orfords to deliver the 2d. vol: of the Thames.

I dined at home alone. — Stadler came in the eving. He likes the Exhibition, & of my pictures, the largest, He spoke handsomely.

He gave me a direction for making soft ground which Byrne, on Sunday last, desired me to procure for Mr. Joseph Windham. — J. Satterthwaite I met today at Loyds Coffee House, to remind him of a set of the Lakes sent to him. He told me Joe Thackerays eldest son who died last week aged 2?

of a putrid fever, expired at 9 o'Clock in the morning; and the corpse was on account of its putrid state obliged to be buried at 4 o'Clock in the afternoon.

J. Wilson who is now confined in St. Pancras workhouse by illness applied to me for relief. I sent him by Betty half a guinea. He told her he had been to Mr. West who advised him to apply for the Academy charity, & that his petition is in the hands of Mr. *Charles* in the Strand.

Tuesday May 3rd.

Mr. Longs I dined at. Went at ½ past 5 Dinner abt. ½ past 6.

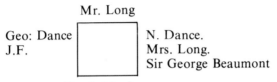

Mr. Long

Geo: Dance		N. Dance.
J.F.		Mrs. Long.
		Sir George Beaumont

Revd. Mr. Long.

Before dinner we talked about Mr. Cawthornes expulsion from the house of Commons yesterday — The Revd. Mr. Long said every means had been tried to enable him to vacate his seat to avoid expulsion, after the Chiltern hundreds had been refused him, it was attempted to procure an Army Agency for him. When summoned into the House on the order of the day being read, He came in attended by Lord Tyrconnel. He read his defence sufficiently audibly; but on the whole looked a little down in spirits. Sir George Beaumont said He did not think Cawthorne felt so much for himself as He felt for him. — While General Smith was speaking Sir George left the House, as did many members. Mr. Long did the same, and was of opinion that had not General Smith brought the subject forward probably no one else would. Mr. Pitts speech certainly determined the minds of many members who, before, were undetermined how to act.

Sir George Beaumont dined at Mr. P. Knights, Mr. Fox was there, He had been down to the House; but on seeing Cawthorne retired, not chusing to remain during so disagreeable a business. Sheridan was not there.

The Academy petition I delivered to Mr. Long before dinner, who said He had no doubt of succeeding in a day or two.

At, and after dinner, a good deal of conversation upon the distinctions between beautiful & picturesque, particularly between N. Dance & Sir George; and upon variety being the cause of beauty. A portion of it Dance admitted to be a necessary ingredient, but He wd. not join with Sir George in admitting Hogarths analysis in favor of this form. — On the whole, when explained, there seemed to be little real difference of opinion, but the conversation was long and not sufficiently close to come to decision. —

Mr. Long told me when on his way from Rome He accidentally purchased for 3 sequins a Galatea which the person who offered it to him called a Julio Romano. Mr. Long rolled it up and happened to mention it to Sir Joshua Reynolds, who seeing it, expressed a desire to have it. Mr. Long gave it him & Sir Joshua in return desired Mr. Long to chuse a picture from among his fancy three quarter pictures which Mr. L. did. Sir Joshua as he frequently did rubbed the picture almost to the outline & then worked upon it several days. It was sold at the sale by Christie. The picture never had any real value, but Sir Joshua was apt to be struck in this way with pictures of little merit.

We staid at Mr. Longs till near Eleven. Sir George brought me home. He expressed himself much pleased with the manner in which Mr. Fox conducted himself yesterday. He converses like a Man who wishes to learn from others what He cannot be supposed to know fully, & does not seize opportunities of pressing down others by his superior powers of speech. He expresses himself doubtingly, as if He desired to be determined by others. Sir George remarked how much in these respects Mr. Fox differs from Mr. Pitt. The latter when He cannot have the advantage of the argument seized an opportunity to raise a joke at the expence of his antagonist, being rather desirous of quitting the subject than to consent to be informed. From the difference which He feels in many respects, Sir George said that He courted opportunities to address Mr. Fox or Lord Grenville; but always felt a difficulty when He sees Mr. Pitt.

I mentioned Mr. Wyndham, as appearing to be a Man of extraordinary Hauteur. He replied than when you enter into conversation with him, there does not seem any difficulty. I said that is owing to his passions being engaged; but He had not the less Hauteur for it.

Wednesday May 5th [4th].

Lord Walpoles I went to this morning with Susan. Mrs. Hussey, & Ld. Frederick Cavendish there.

Shakespeare Gallery I went to. Coombes & J. Boydell there. Mrs. Cawthorne has been much affected by her Husbands situation.

I told Coombes that I was very sorry He had introduced the word *prettiness* into his acct. of Strawberry Hill. He asked why I did not object to it before; I said because when I saw it, it was too late, the sheet being printed.

Coombes said He had expected that Westall would have invited him to the Academy Dinner. — Lord Orfords I went to with J. Boydell, and carried him the second Vol: of the Rivers. We found him seated on a sofa bed in his drawing room. He looked over the Prints of the Rivers and expressed great satisfaction, and thought them much superior to those in the first Vol: He said He was afraid He shd. not have lived to have seen the Volume completed, & that He had been in a critical state, but was now out of present danger. He mentioned that He had been told there was a very strong likeness of me in the Exhibition.

A Mr. Bertram came in, and the conversation turned on Irelands forgeries. Ld. Orford expressed his surprise that any credit shd. ever have been given to them.

Stadler I called on. He is engaged on a plate for Bowyer, undertaken by Pollard after Loutherburghs Spanish Armada. He shewed me a drawing of a Castle situated 18 leagues from Vienna, in which Richd. 1st. was confined.

Westall I called on in the evening, Braine, & Porden were there. Westall dined at Mr. Knights on Monday. The company consisted of Mr. Fox, Price, Sir George Beaumont, N. Dance, Marchant & another. The conversation chiefly turned upon Poetry & Art. Fox spoke much, but in a doubting qualified manner, free from assertion. — To Westall it appeared that a sense of Fox's superiority of talents prevented each person from speaking so fully as He probably wd. otherways have done, so that the conversation was rather amusing than close & instructive.

Speaking of the works of Shakespeare Fox gave the preference to Lear, as being the strongest proof of his extraordinary powers, for the Fable of Lear is childish & poor as a girl could write; yet it is so treated by Shakespeare that its weakness in this respect is never felt. Knight thought Macbeth superior to Lear, in its machinery & poetical excellence.

The colour & form of rocks was spoken of, and the Chalk rock preferred to the Slate. Mr. Price said at Foxley He had the disadvantage of Slate rock.

The Isle of Wight was allowed to be, excepting one particular spot of a few acres, unpicturesque; & as affording little matter for the Painter.

Westall observed that Mrs. Siddons expressed the following passage improperly. "I have given Suck, and know how tender 'tis to love the babe that milks me. I would, while it was smiling in my face, Have pluckt my nipple from its boneless gums".

Mrs. Siddons "I have given suck &c" in a tender, soft manner, till she came to "Have pluckt my nipple" whereas in Westalls opinion the whole should have been expressed with indignation & spirit. N. Dance justified Mrs. Siddons by saying that Her object being to work upon the feelings of Macbeth artfully, tenderness in that instance was proper; in this opinion He was seconded by Price, Knight doubted, but Fox repeated to Westall several times "You are right".

Thursday May 5th.

Mrs. Hamond came to town.

Sir George Beaumont and N. Dance called to look at the Rembrants; Dance invited me to dinner to meet Sir George, Dr. Wharton, & G. Dance but I told them I had company at home: while they were with me Sir Alan

Gardner called, He knew Dance who invited him to dinner, but He was engaged. Sir Alan told me his eldest son, Capt. Gardner of the Heroine frigate is married to Miss Adderley, a Young Lady daugr. in Law to Lord Hobart. Sir Alan has had a very handsome letter from his Lordship on the subject, dated Madrass. Captain Gardner is 24 years old, The Young Lady 17. Sir Alan told me it had been intimated to him that He must go to Plymouth (on election business) before He goes to Sea. He said to be in Parliament is a Feather, but He is not anxious abt. it. He said He told Mr. Pitt when Ld. Spencer was appointed first Lord of the Admiralty that He had shewn great courage, being totally unprepared for the business as He knew nothing of naval matters. Lord Spencer did not give Sir Alan proper notice to quit the Admiralty. Sir Alan read a letter He had just received relating that the Dutch inhabitants in the country near Cape Town are hostile to the English; & those in the Town disaffected. The English soldiers were abt. 3000.

Lord Grey & Lord Curzon called upon Dick. I recd. them in my painting room and they talked of the report that Thackeray had not kept his manufacturing rooms clean.

Sir Alexander & Lady Hamilton, Mr. Liddel, & Marchant dined with us.

Mr. Jameson called on me with a note from Mr. Erskine on acct. of prints for Lieut. Drydale.

Friday May 6th.

Shakespeare Gallery I went to. Alderman Boydell came. On his proposing it, it was settled that the 2 Volumes of the Thames are to be sold to Subscribers, & to the Trade for Ten guineas, to non subscribers Twelve guineas. — Steevens was there. He thinks our regulation of taking places for the company at the Academy dinner a good one. He finds that Northcotes pictures do not please. They are ill-executed & some of them indecent.

The Bishop of London, was an Esquire Beadle at Cambridge. Steevens say He is a Prig.

Sir John Sinclair was consulting with J. Boydell abt. the intended publication of prints of farming animals.

Will & William came from Hoddesdon.

Lord Cholmondeleys cause against Lord Walpole was determined today in favor of the former.

Saturday May 7th.

Steers I breakfasted with. Susan & Eliza went with me.

Sir Alan Gardners I called at. Sir Roger Curtis came there. We talked of Dance making a profile drawing of Ld. Howe, Sir Alan having mentioned it to Lord Howe yesterday. I explained to Sir Roger the nature of Dances plan, & solicited him also to sit. He said Lord Howe felt modest about sitting; but he wd. today explain the matter [to] his Lordship.

Sir Alan told me He gave for His house, No. 25 Portland Place £14400, & had a lease for abt. 80 years. In this agreement all the furniture was included. The *House* only cost the Banker from whom He purchased it £3400.

Sir Alan told me The Queen was so much damaged on the *29th. of May* 1794 that She would have been cut off by the Montaigne, had not Admirals Graves & Bowyer bore down to his assistance. The exertions of Officers & Men to refit her were unequalled, & she was again quite fit for service on the 1st. of June.

Academy Council I went to.

West

Tyler   Hoppner   Dance

Yenn

West reported that His Majesty had signed the regulations of the office of Treasurer. Messrs. Drummonds were appointed Bankers to the Academy. West, Richards, Dance & Tyler were appointed a Committee to obtain Counsels opinion of the best mode of securing the stock property of the Academy.

I reported having been with Mr. Long, and having delivered the petition to the Lords Commissioners of the Treasury to obtain the indulgence for British Artists to import Works of Art for their private study duty free.

Yenn stated the receipts of the Exhibition amounted this night to £1002, which is £183 more than was recd. in the first & second week last year.

Hoppner I went with to the Coffee House. He is to go tomorrow with Uvedale Price to Horne Tookes at Wimbledon. Price is preparing to publish a second Edition of his Essay on the Picturesque, and wishes Tooke to point out any faults which may be in the *grammatical* part.

Banks talked the other night with Hoppner on the ensuing election of an Academician & said He should vote for Tresham.

Dick this night recd. information from Gravesend that the Henry Addington had sprung a leak; owing to a bolt having loosened.

Yenn invited Hoppner & me to dinner tomorrow — I was engaged.

Sunday May 8th.

Lysons I breakfasted with. Mr. Berwick there. At 10 we went to the Exhibition & met Mr. & Mrs. Masters of Cirencester, Major Masters & his 2 sisters. Mrs. Masters is sister to Ld. Sherborne, & to Mrs. Coke of Norfolk.

Mr. Lechmere, Mr. Berwicks Son in Law, was also there.

Humphrey came with Sir George & Lady Yonge & Miss Codrington, an Old Maid, natural daugr. to the late Sir Wm. Codrington.

When we came away, Mr. West had just come in with the Duke & Duchess of Leeds &c.

Offleys I dined at. Susan, Eliza & H. Hamond there. Dick went this morning to Gravesend & retd. in the evening. No damage done by the leak except to about 20 hundred weight of bread.

Mr. Berwick mentioned today that He had promised to Valentine Green to pay the expence of one of his plates for his History of Worcester; and had paid one half the expence £12:10:0 & that lately Green had dunned him for the remainder in a very unhandsome manner.

Lord Orford, Lysons told me, desired me to recommend somebody to clean some portraits, which, now the cause is determined in favor of Lord Cholmendeley He means to send to Houghton.

Monday 9th.

Mr. Bensley, the Actor, took leave of the Stage last Friday night; He came out in Pierre at Drury Lane, with same season as Powell, abt. 32 years ago. He went with Powell to Covent Garden, & continued there till his friend Mr. Colman sold the patent. Then He returned to Drury Lane. Before his appearance in London He had played in the Theatres of the elder Mr. Kemble and He had been a Lieutenant of Marines.

H. Hamond was with Lord Orford today, who told him He heard I had a very beautiful Landscape in the exhibition & wished He could have seen it. He proposed to Horace [Hamond] to go down to Strawberry Hill, as the air of that place wd. probably carry off his cold. Such is the attention of his Lordship, & his politeness at an advanced period of life.

H Hamond & Will dined with us.

Mr. Gilman breakfasted with us.

Westall I called on in the evening, He desiring to shew me a proposal for publishing a Print from his drawing of the *Harvest Storm* now exhibiting. Lady Oxford called on him today, wishing to purchase the two drawings He has made for Ld. Berwick. She ordered two, & bought one, He had in his possession.

Malton complained this eving. to Westall of the situation of his drawings, & thought *because He styles himself an Architect,* His views in London had been placed in the lower room intentionally. — Westall told him the fact, which is that the drawings were not discovered having been left in the lower room, the upper rooms were arranged. Westall is informed that Soane is not satisfied with the situation of his drawings. Lord Berwick has bought the Cuyp with the Large Horses from Bryant. West some years since gave 400 guineas for it: Lord Berwick pays Bryant 800 guineas.

Tuesday May 10th.

In the Herald this morning the following article appeared. [*No cutting has been inserted.*]

George Meredith called on me, & paid for himself & Brother their subscriptions for the publications of the Rivers.

Mackenzie called on me having procured a print of Zoffanys portraits of Royal Academicians. — Trent Club I dined at, on my way I met J. Taylor, & walked with him in the Temple. Opie means to proceed with a suit in Doctors Commons to obtain a separation from bed & board. Taylor advised him not to proceed to a divorce as it would only enable him again to do a foolish thing.

In the Chair

Heaviside

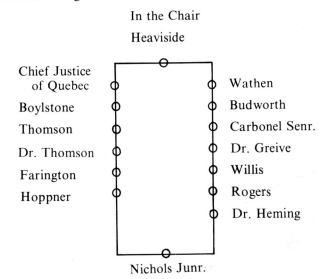

Chief Justice of Quebec — Wathen
Boylstone — Budworth
Thomson — Carbonel Senr.
Dr. Thomson — Dr. Greive
Farington — Willis
Hoppner — Rogers
Dr. Heming

Nichols Junr.

Hoppner told me He went with U. Price to Horne Tookes on Sunday last and staid there two Hours: Price had before sent his Essay on the picturesque to Tooke, who now said He had not observed any defects in the grammar &c that He recollected or if He had they wd. be found in the margin it being his custom thus to point out inaccuracies.

Speaking of Tooke, Hoppner said He is destitute of taste, having no feeling for poetry or painting; and that his conversation is generally of a mixed quality exhibiting a radical want of taste. Stories of a gross nature, told in a vulgar manner Tooke frequently introduces when the subject of conversation does not lead to it. Young Nichol remarked that Tooke did not seem satisfied if He had not the full lead at the table. Bryan Edwards was mentioned and his History of Jamaica spoken highly of by Hoppner as a work of great taste & interest; yet He observed that in society Edwards has too much of the manner & grossness of Tooke.

Tresham has informed Mrs. Hoppner that Beechy seems to think He has acted imprudently in his transaction with the Academy.

Tooke means to offer himself for Westminster at the ensuing election Instancing His grossness He said that when speaking of Pitt & Dundass Tooke wd. say "If I had one on each side, I shd. soon have a knife in their guts".

Wednesday May 11th.

I have been employed several days in rendering some of my various studies, into subjects fit for painting, and in drawing them upon canvas and paper. The slight sketches founded on my studies from nature I have pasted on brown paper and collected them together to refer to.

Shakespeare Gallery I went to. Coombes has given J. Boydell his opinion that the Forth & the Clyde might be included in one volume, which I think a good proposal, and it may be done if the Volume is made of the full size of the first Volume of the Thames. I asked Boydell if Coombes is not in the pay of Government, He said, He is, but He believes not by annuity, but is paid for what He produces.

I gave Boydell my opinion that The Severn should be the River next undertaken, and if the *Wye* could be connected with it, the advantage would be great. He thinks the Severn may be given alone, & should the work answer, the Wye & Avon may be included in one Volume afterwards.

Sir Edward Pellew came to the Gallery while I was there.

Burbridge told me the large prints in the 2d. Vol: seem to give much satisfaction.

Boydell said the print of Major Pearson goes off very well. 1200 have been printed to serve the subscribers, and the plate is now given to Heath to retouch who says He will make it better than ever. Boydell thinks they shall make £4000 by it.

Will this morning called & gave me various bills brought from Hoddesdon for Dick, Bob & myself. I talked with Dick in the evening on the *subject*.

Westall I drank tea with. Mrs. Porden there & Porden afterwards. A puffing advertisement appeared today in favor of Downman which was put among the *common puffing advertisements*. Westall is but indifferent and does not sleep at nights, though He takes paregoryck. I told him drinking much coffee might probably prevent him.

Thursday May 12th.

At home all the evening studying Compositions. Will dined with us.

Revd. Mr. Newel, a clergyman who resides near Oxford, called after dinner, and brought his son, a fine Boy of 14 years of age who on the recommendation of Captn. Douglas of the Queen, Dick takes out midshipman. This Boy is entirely protected & supported by Mr. Clarke.

Lysons I went to, to tea. The Bishop of Durham & the Revd. Mr. Coates there, & Danl. Lysons.

The Bishop mentioned the extraordinary likeness which Lawrence had made of me; & thought his exertions this year would re-establish his reputation. I told the Bishop my opinion is that Lawrence had better pictures in the Exhibition than He ever had before. He particularly mentioned the picture of Serjeant Shepherd, which, He said would be purchased as a work of Art. I apologized to the Bishop for the situation in which He was placed at the dinner, and said it was owing to no answer having been recd. He said He had concluded that if He did not send an answer He should be expected. He said He had a previous engagement which He had put off to come. He took notice of my having *good naturedly* as He said removed Mr. Fox from his first situation. The Bishop staid till about 10. He had dined at Merchant Taylors Hall & was in his gown. He mentioned Flaxman with admiration of his restoring the Torso, and observed that you forgave Wyatt his disappointing you when He appeared. He thought pews in Churches a bad custom; and prefers benches. In a Church under his direction, He has adopted benches, from designs of Wyatt. The Bishop is not in my [opinion] a refined man. His manner this evening was plain and easy; but his language & observations of a common sort. His application of words is not always proper. Looking at a drawing of a monument in Tewkesbury Church of ancient Gothic Architecture highly wrought, He said it was very *handsome*.

Mr. Daines Barrington, Lysons told me, never goes beyond the limits of the Temple; and proposes to pass the remainder of his life within this circumscribed place.

Poggi I found on my return home. He said He had been with General Paoli who is become very thin & much altered. Poggi thinks his mind is affected by circumstances which have happened in Corsica.

Friday May 13th.

Continued regulating compositions. Shakespeare Gallery I went to. J. Boydell told me He this morning shewed the 2d. Vol: of Thames to Sir George Beaumont, who said it was a pity they were coloured: He remarked that *smoke* might have been introduced into the view of London. I told Boydell that my object was to shew the *form* of the City & the particular circumstances, of course I should not sacrifice this necessary explanation to picturesque obscurities. — Mrs. Offley, Mrs. Hamond, C,J, & Wm. Offley & Outram, dined with us & H. Hamond.

Major General Dundass this day fixed to go with Dick to the Cape of Good Hope.

Saturday May 14th.

Continued regulating compositions. Shakespeare Gallery I called at, & selected Volumes for subscribers.

Antony Pasquin published his Critique on the exhibition.

Steers called on me & desired to know for a friend if I have sold the large *Bridge* scene (Offleys) in the Exhibition. I told him I had, to be a Companion to a Wilson. He paid me a Crown, a wager on the originality of a view of Tivoli by Wilson, which was sold at Christies. I decided that it *is original.*

Drew I met with Mr. Bastard. Drew told me that Mr. Bastard was a principal cause of the Tax Bill on Colateral succession being thrown out. Bastard asked Grey what the opposition meant to do, Grey replied nothing, as their attempts wd. be in vain. Bastard said He wd. divide the House upon it if there were only 3 voices with him; If so answered Grey, we will take it up. The consequence it came to a casting vote of the Speaker upon 54 & 54. The Speaker gave his Vote for the Bill; and Pitt then declared that as He found it unpopular among the Country Gentlemen, He wd. propose some other Tax in its place, & moved that the 2d. reading be put off for 3 months. Rolle was truly patriotick on this occasion, for though He does or will possess vast landed property and of course be considerably affected by the Bill, yet He said that as money must be raised He wd. not oppose it & voted *for* it.

Drew told me He had settled all the accts. of Sir Joshuas pictures delivered but one. — Byrne called & brought No 1 finished proofs of his 2d. Vol: of Antiquities. He only takes off 40 sets of Proofs.

Will dined with us.

Smirke I called on in the evening. A complaint in one of his eyes has rendered him incapable of working for 3 weeks past. He relapsed twice in consequence of exposing his eye. I reccomended to him to take this opportunity to turn his thoughts to consider compositions for small pictures, which would engage his attention usefully.

He desired me at the request of Anchor Smith the Engraver, to speak to Boydell about making him an additional allowance, for a plate, the subject Wat Tyler, from Northcote. Two hundred guineas Smith was to receive but that Sum is so little that he thinks Boydell ought not to consider a *verbal agreement* so disadvantageous to him as binding. Smirke reccomended to Smith not to enforce an additional payment if Boydell shd. refuse as the verbal agreement ought to be binding though Smith shd. suffer. — *Bartolozzi* reccomended Smith to apply to me to speak to Boydell — I said I would mention it.

Marchant called in the evening.

Sunday May 15th.

Holylands Coffee House I breakfasted at with H. Hamond, C Offley & Mr. Everitt. I took Hamond & Offley to the Exhibition. Hoppner came there & met Coll. Phipps, Lady Mulgrave & Her sister Miss Malyn, Lady Bathurst, & with Her, Mrs. Lyndhurst.

Hoppner told me He was informed that the Princess of Wales was in tears at the Queens Palace a few evenings since, & that she is very ill treated, neglected by the Prince: Lady Jersey rules his mind.

Lady Mulgrave is a pleasing, artless young woman. Lady Bathurst more dry & proud in manner. Hoppner thinks Coll. Phipps is attached to Lady Mulgraves sister.

Will dined with us. Byrne wrote in the evening to desire Dick wd. bring a box of China Colours for his daughtrs. particularly He mentioned the white.

Monday May 16th — Whitsun Monday.

Carey called on me, having come up from Wantage in Berkshire where his Troop has been quartered. He joined his regt. at Alnwick in Northumberland, when the regt. moved from thence to the South they only advanced one *stage* in a day. His pay as Cornet is £120 a year subsistence. The arrears make the annual amount abt. £145: but these are paid with great deductions, once in 5 years. The pay of Lieutt. of Dragoons is only abt. £20 a yr. more. I asked Carey what He supposed He must spend as a Cornet, He said near £300 a year. In their regt. the 16th. they have 2 Cornets & a Lieutt. who were advanced from the ranks on acct. of their merit. These Officers live upon their pay: but do not mess with the officers who have purchased on acct. of the expences. They are very useful in the regt. as they do that duty which the young men are apt to neglect.

I told Carey his pictures intended for exhibition were too cold, in colouring, therefore I only proposed to have one of them exhibited as He wd. judge of the defect from that. He was well satisfied with my reason. He thought Sir George Beaumonts Landscapes pretty; but not equal to that of last year. He said Lawrences portrait of me, & of Miss Ogilvie, superior to any of his other productions. *Painting* I began today, after having been sometime employed in regulating compositions from my studies, and in drawing them on Canvass.

Tuesday May 17th.

Dick & Eliza set off for Gravesend today at twelve oClock. I told him before He went the contents of my Will and of my having made him & Horace Hamond Executors. He much approved the purport of my will. I shewed him the annexed note relative to my Diaries and private papers.

Tyler called on me. I spoke to him of the necessity there appears to be for our encreasing the *Charity Fund* of the Royal Academy, as at present there is no adequate provision made for aged or necessitous members, and too little for the relatives.

We talked of filling up the vacancy of Sir William Chambers, and He fully agreed that Gilpin shd. be the man.

Thomas Sandby is in great tribulation on acct. of one of the piers of

Walton Bridge, now building, having shrunk; and by some it has been imputed to his neglect in not attending to the operations.

Shakespeare Gallery I went to, & spoke to J. Boydell about Anchor Smith. The answer He gave me was, that the plate had been many years in hand, and is not a good one, and is not likely to sell; that Smith had had several of the small Shakespeare plates to do at 80 guineas a plate which they cd. now have engraved for 40 gs. a plate; so that He has been much benefitted by his engagements with them. Finally Boydell said He wd. agree to give Smith £100 if ever they should sell £300 worth of the Wat Tyler, if He would give the same sum if they never should sell to the amount of £200.

Mr. Daulby had declined continuing his subscription to the Rivers till He sees how the next Vol: appears. Mr. Peachy has enquired if any are yet finished in brown.

Storace the musical composer, who died lately was about 33 years old. He married, Hall, the engravers daugr. & left one child; and abt. £3000 he had saved.

Lysons called in the evening, having been at Mr. Ruckers today, who is pleased with the description of his situation & means to have the ensuing Volumes of the Rivers.

The Kemble family are much pleased with Lawrences ³/₄ head of Mrs. Siddons. Sir George Beaumont had mentioned Hoppner as the proper Artist to paint it.

J. Kemble continues his engagement as *a performer* at Drury Lane, but does not officiate as Manager. Mrs. Siddons is going to York & takes Manchester on her way.

Wednesday May 18th.

Sir George Beaumonts I breakfasted with. Du Cort called on him yesterday and shewed him Antony Pasquins Critique.

Sir George told me He intended to make his congé to Parliament being not disposed to give the price which seats sell for. An offer was made him of a ministerial seat, which He would only accept on condition that He should not be bound to support all measures or be precluded from exercising his judgment. This was allowed to be a very reasonable condition, but when *principals* were referred to, the proposal was not renewed. Colchester was thought of for him, and the probable expence not more that 5 or £600: but it being in the neighboroud of Dedham made an objection. Lord Muncaster has since offered. — N Dance gave the Duke of Dorset £4000 for his election at East Grinstead; and a treat there cost him £50 more. — Lady Mulgrave had no fortune. She is one of a large family of Children. — Sir George shewed me two small pictures which He has painted: one in imitation of Wests, Ruysdael; the other of Sir Abraham Humes Rembrant. He gave me a small picture a study in which a Church is the principal object.

Mr. Philpot came in on business.

Marchi called on me. He is disatisfied with Lady Inchiquin, who is seldom contented with what is done by him. She told him before Lady Orkney that the pictures of Sir Joshua were thrown away at the sale. He has not yet been paid any part of what is due to him for what he has done since the death of Sir Joshua; and Tassaert has endeavoured to alarm him for the safety of his money. I told him I did not believe He runs any risk & recommended to him to go on as smoothly as He can.

I dined & remained at home this evening.

Thursday May 19th.

Sir Alan Gardner I went to at breakfast. He told me he had engaged to stand for Westminster. Mr. Pitt solicited him, He replied that His situation at Plymouth is secure witht. expence or trouble; but he consented. It is understood that Mr. Fox & He are to go as much hand in hand as appearances will allow. Sheridan has been with Tooke and has endeavoured to persuade him not to offer himself; but in vain. Tooke said He shd. be well supported, and that He should do good by engaging the attention of a great number of turbulent fellows who would be prevented from running over the country at this critical time.

Sir Alan is to receive deputations from the *Parishes* inviting him to stand. He seems to be a little apprehensive about the expence as if that point was not sufficiently settled. — At the Levee yesterday the King said to Sir Alan that He did not suppose He would meet any opposition for Westminster; Sir Alan replied that He understood Horne Tooke meant to offer himself.

I said Sir George Beaumont informed me yesterday that Mr. Long is so much engaged He could not be seen. "I forced *myself upon him*", said Sir Alan, though He was denied, and found him at a long table, on which, I believe, were 500 letters; He was almost overcome by this weight of business. Rose is gone into the country to look after his own election, so that the whole devolves on Long. They seem, added Sir Alan, to have made no preparation in time and to have the whole arrangement to settle at once.

Lord Hood is to be made an *English Viscount*. Twelve months ago I knew said Sir Alan, He had such a promise, but the inconvenience of making a vacancy for Westminster caused it to be postponed. Rolle is to be a peer. They seem to encrease the list with little consideration.

The King went to the House of Lords today at 3 oClock. He was attended in the State Coach by Lords Westmorland & Wentworth. — The Coach is new. The Old Coach had glasses in each of the upper compartments on the sides of the Coach. The new Coach has glass in the *Center* only in the common way. — The King talked and seemed chearful, and I think had reason to be so; as, though the park was very full of people I did not hear a single expression or observe a sign of discontent. On the contrary, as the Coach passed along, the people opposite to it, or many of them, pulled off their hats and huzza'd. I observed many of the Nobility in the Park. The Duke of Leeds, Lord Carlisle, Duke of Montrose, Lord St. Helens &c.

Steers I met. He shewed me Antony Pasquins Critique. Du Cort had sent him *two* of them.

Burch called on me & shewed me his Book of impressions. He spoke highly of their merit, and bad me attend to the Heads of Minerva & that of the Antinous; if compared with those by Marchant, his superiority would be fully felt. He wished the Academicians would subscribe to his collection; Bacon had done it. He desired me to mention again to the Council on Saturday His hope that He might have part at least of the £100 He had solicited. I told him Mr. Bacon wd. be the proper person: but I would mention it.

Westall I drank tea with. Garrard has applied to him for the drawing of the Harvest Storm for Mr. Whitbread Junr. who proposes to make a collection of the works of English Artists. He has bought Romneys Milton.

Beechy is to carry 4 or 5 pictures tomorrow morning to the Queens Palace to shew the King. He has had a very great number of commissions since the Exhibition opened. It is said that a Mandate will come from the King requiring the Academy to make Beechy an Academician. I told Westall I do not believe His Majesty will ever interfere in an election.

Friday May 20th.

Lysons, I called on this morning. He & D. Lysons were setting out on a visit to Lord Lewisham in Kent.

Steers I called on.

Horne Tooke advertised this day offering himself a Candidate for Westminster. George Smith also published a letter to the Electors of Rochester declining the offers which had been made by some to support him as a Candidate, and adds many remarks on the corrupt state of our Government. Wilberforce Bird, and Jeffries, the Jeweller, offer also for Coventry. Le Mesurier declines for the Borough, and Thelusson offers, and Thornton again.

Saturday May 21st.

Sir George Beaumont I breakfasted with and went with Him to call on Steers to see His pictures.

I called on Greenwood who is to settle his acct. with the Executors & not with Lady Inchiquin, as it would be, Metcalfe says, irregular. Greenwood thinks He ought to be indemnified for the expence of advertising the Prints & drawings this Spring, as the sale was put off, I concurred with him.

Lord Walpoles I dined at. Mr. & Mrs. Hussey, Miss Walpole, 2 Miss

Husseys & Miss Eliz: Walpole 2d daugr. of Mr. Thos. Walpole were there. — Lady Walpole told me Mrs. Bradyll called on her a few days ago & is so much altered Lady W. did not immediately know her. There seemed a consciousness of altered situation in life which affected her manner. Bradyll has already sold one good estate. When the desperate state of his affairs was known Mrs. Bradyll anxious that her Children should be properly educated wrote to Mr. Gale, Bradylls Father, for assistance for the eldest Son, but Gale refused to take any part or bear any expence.

Miss Eliz: Walpole shewed me several miniatures in Enamel of her painting. They are burnt in by another person.

The Ladies told Susan that the Princess of Wales's situation is become so uneasy, that she has written to the Chancellor, demanding either to be sent to her own Country, or to be separated from the Prince here; or to be treated with more respect in her own house. The whole Royal Family treat her with neglect; the Duke of Gloucester excepted. who presented a letter from the Princess to the King on reading which He shed tears; yet He has been so worked upon that He does not appear to notice her much. — Lady Cholmondely is steady to the Princess. The other Ladies, particularly behave shamefully to her. Lady Jersey is supposed to be at the bottom of this.

The Prince is said to have spoken of the Princess in a most unbecoming manner. The Young Princess being mentioned to him "She may or may not be mine said He".

Lady Walpole & the other Ladies were much gratified Susan told me by an offer I desired Mr. Hussey to make to take them to the Exhibition tomorrow. The Academy Council I went to at 8. Present

Mr. West

Dance — Tyler — Hoppner — Bacon

Yenn.

The accts. which had not been passed were audited.

The recpts. of the Exhibition this night amounted to £1982. At this period (a month) last year, the accts. were only £15, the balance in favor of this year is £47.

Dance proposed that Tylers name shd. be added as the 4th. Trustee for the money invested in the funds. — The paper which had been prepared by a Clerk of the Bank was then ordered to be referred to Council. Yenn told me the King wished Dance to be the 4th. Trustee.

Bacon again brought forward Burchs petition. West proposed that it be postponed till the Exhibition accts. of the Season are examined, which was agreed to.

I requested the attention of the Council to the consideration of establishing a provission for members of our Society who may be in a state of necessity. It appeared to me that we might encrease our Charity fund, and suspend adding to the Solid fund, as the interest of that at present, would be more than sufficient to make up defficiencies in any year when the rects. of the Exhibition shd. not amount to more than £1900. What I said was listened to as being of sufficient weight to require consideration.

Hoppner went home with me & sat an Hour. He has heard that West is much straitened for money, & that his Bills remain long unpaid. Lord Mulgrave has told him that Sir George Beaumont said He ought to make studies for his whole length portraits, and not take the chance of a thought for an attitude after the Head is painted. This applied to a picture begun of Lady Mulgrave. — He read me a letter which He proposed to send to Beechy in case He went on puffing by making comparisons with Hoppner in the public prints in his own favor.

Sunday May 22nd.

G Dance I called on early, and talked with him about the Academy, and of encreasing the Charity fund, which He agreed to. He shewed me his improved designs for new Docks & Warehouses, which I like much. I gave him my opinion that a long even line of 200 f. interrupted by the Center which rises higher, is preferable to having it broken with pediments; the latter gives a meanness to it.

N. Dance came in and agreed with me. He is to go out of town on Wednesday to East Grinstead to be reelected.

The Academy I went to at Eleven. Lord & Lady Walpole, Miss Walpole, Mr. & Mrs. Hussey, 2 Miss Husseys, & Miss E. Walpole, came & staid 2 Hours. Humphry & Westall were there, & a few persons with Mr. & Mrs. Richards.

Westall took down his harvest storm and carried it into Richards room to trace it. Last night He sent to me at the Council to request me to solicit that He might have it home for the day following. I sent him word that I knew the request could not be granted.

Humphry I went with to Smirkes, who went out today for the first time after having been confined three weeks by a complaint in one eye.

At Humphrys I met Brettingham and we three went to Lawrences to see his portrait of Mrs. Siddons: it is like but not well coloured; and too much manner in the painting of it; as there is in all the portraits He has begun since he finished his Exhibition pictures. Humphry had been very lavish in praise of his pictures at the Academy, but on coming away from his house He said, "However the Exhibition pictures might induce him to sit to Lawrence, the pictures in his house would deter him". Brettingham gave me his card.

Sir George Beaumonts I dined at. West, Lysons & Barrow, who went to China with Ld. Macartney, there. We did not sit down to dinner till ½ past 6, when West came.

Sir George & West this morning saw that part of the Orleans collection which has not yet been produced to the public. He spoke of the Elevation of the Cross by Rubens, in rapturous terms. West said He would rather have been the painter of that picture than of any work of art he knows in the world. He thinks it was prepared by Rubens for the Engraver to work from, as some spaces are filled up with figures, which, in the large picture of this subject are occupied by frame work or decorations. They also mentioned the 3 Marys by Annibal Carach, as a work of extraordinary merit.

We staid till near 12 oClock. On our way home I conversed with West on the Charity fund of the Academy, and He expressed great willingness that something more should be done. He thought that if the solid fund is encreased to £10,000 it then might be left, and all over-plus rects. be applied to encrease the Charity fund.

He told me Paul Sandby has obtained from Lord Cornwallis the appointment of Drawing Master to Woolwich for his Son, and that a pension of £100 a year has been granted to him. Lord Harcourt was requested, & did apply to the Duke of Richmond, while He was Master General of the Ordnance, for this exchange, but in vain. — Tyler wrote to me on the subject of the Charity fund &c.

Monday May 23rd.

Miss Coe from Norwich dined with us. Mr. Randal only gave her 10 guineas when she left Norwich with Her Husband after they were recd. at his house.

Westall I called on in the evening.

Tuesday May 24th.

Trent Club I went to.

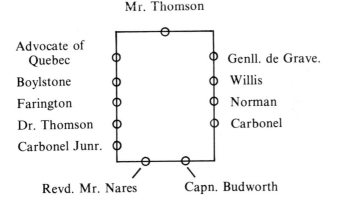

Some conversation on the merits of Authors. Willis mentioned Sharpe a•
one of the first men in the world, and that He had given as his opinion tha•
Burke, *in imagery*, excells, all moderns, at least. Willis never was please•
with Johnsons Rasselas or his Rambler; but thinks his lives of the Poets •
fine example of writing. Thomson talked much, and loosely, on severa•
subjects. When He was at Tournay, He proposed going to Fontenoy to se•
the field on which that Battle was fought; but was discouraged by bein•
told that the circumstances in the neighbouroud were so much altered h•
would no longer be able to judge of it. That of the wood *De Barri* only •
single tree remained.

Mr. Boylstone is of opinion that nothing serious will take place betwee•
England & America. The Commercial poeple are entirely for Peace, an•
are willing to have the treaty with England ratified on every point: the•
only expect not to have their trade to the West Indies interrupted.

Mr. Boylstone never knew money so difficult to be obtained as it wa•
this day in the city. There have been instances of more than 60 per cen•
being given for a *short* accommodation; and for accommodations for tw•
months eleven per ct. has been paid.

Mr. Norman asked me if, witht. indelicacy, Downman could be applie•
to know if He would part with his drawing of the Angel & Hagar. He wa•
doubtful as it was not marked in the Catalogue to be sold. I told him man•
works painted purposely for exhibition are not marked in the Catalogue•
and that there is not the least impropriety in proposing the Question to a•
Artist: but that I would ask Downman who is my neighbour & let hin•
know. He said a friend of his desired to purchase it.

Wednesday May 25th.

Banks called on me to mention his desire that the Members of the Counc•
should call on him to see his *plaister* model of Lord Cornwallis, before H•
begins to work it in marble. I recommended to him to send a circular lette•
to the members of the Council to request them to come to his house o•
Monday morning next: He would thus avoid the interruption of severa•
separate visits: This He agreed to do. He told me He thought He shoul•
compleat the marble figure by next Christmas twelvemonths.

Shakespeare Gallery I went to & obtained Reptons Landscap•
gardening for Mr. Erskine. — Tyler called on me to express his opinion o•
the business of encreasing the Charitable fund of the Royal Academy. H•
thinks it will be most proper if a member will move at a general meetin•
that the sums of money to be distributed should be limited, to prevent an•
one person, by the assistance of his friends, from obtaining too much•
suppose that widows & Children of Academicians be limited to £10, &•
Academicians who may require it to £20, and a further law that no perso•
holding any permanent place of profit in the Academy, shall be entitled t•
such benefit. He approved entirely of proceeding to encrease the Charit•

fund after the Solid fund is made £10,000 net. I told him the conversation have had with Dance & West & He agreed that we had best have a private meeting to consider the best mode of proceeding.

Offleys I dined at. Outram there. C. J. & Wm. Offley I went with to Drury Lane, to a benefit for the widow of Mr. Storace. A new musical Romance called Mahmoud, (a very foolish unexplained business) was performed. Braham, the celebrated new singer appeared in one of the Characters.

At the end of the first Act the Dancers of the Opera House performed "The new favorite Ballet in the Scots stile, called Little Peggy's Love". "The pantomime, and principal *steps* composed by Monsr. Didelot." Monsr. Didelot, Signor Genlili, Mesdames, Vida, Bossi, Barre, Parisot, Hillisburg, and Rose, danced in the Ballet.

Parisot particularly excelled. Her motion was more floating and easy than any I remember. Didelot & Bossi danced a Minuet. The House was crowded.

The Princess of Wales's situation is strongly hinted at in the papers: and Lady Jersey pointed at as the cause of the breach between the Prince & Princess.

Wednesday May 26th.

Bestland called on me this morning. He has nearly *etched* his plate of the Academicians; but still wants a portrait of Wyatt, and Yenn has not sat. I told him the model in Wax of me by Mount-Stephen, is considered a better likeness than Singletons, on looking at it. He thought so too, and I lent it to him, to copy on the plate.

Downman I called on at the request of Mr. Norman. The drawing of Hagar &c. in the Exhibition is not sold of which I informed Mr. Norman.

Downman bought the whole length portrait of Mr. Lee by Sir Joshua at the sale for 5 guineas. He has cut out the lower part of the Landscape which makes a picture, and is an excellent specimen of Sir Joshuas Landscape painting.

Lord Orford I called on. He was in great spirits, but still seated on his sofa bed. Miss Berry was with him. She spoke with much praise of my Landscape in the exhibition painted for C Offley. On acct. of her delicate health I offered to take her to the Exhibition on a Sunday with her sister & Mrs. Damer. Lord Orford expressed a desire to go as He may be carried upstairs; we fixed for next Sunday week.

After Miss Berry went away, Lord Orford began to express his satisfaction at the issue of the late trial for the Houghton estate in favour of Lord Cholmendely. With Coll. Walpoles conduct He is much displeased, but entirely acquitted Lord Walpole, who He said would not contribute to the expence of the Law suit. The estate annexed to Houghton is not £3000 a year. The *unsettled estates*, Great Massingham &c. are at Lord Orford's disposal. Lord Orford sent for Lord Cholmendely the other day, & they conversed together, and Lord C. declared his intention to make Houghton his residence, as he does not like his other situations.

Lord Orford described the late Lord Walpole (Horace) as a very indifferent character, which He said He had told him. Sir Robt. Walpole certainly did, when the prospect was in favor of his brother Horace propose to him that they should mutually agree to settle their *estates* on their Male Heirs, to the exclusion of the females of either branch. At this time Sir Robts. estate was £8000 a year; Horaces only £4000. Horace said His wife would not agree to it, to the exclusion of her daughters. After the death of Sir Robert (first Earl of Orford) and his son, the 2nd. Earl; the late Earl, the grandson of Sir Robert borrowed from his great Uncle Horace £4000, who then proposed to make a settlement similar to what Sir Robt. Walpole had proposed. Horace had then 3 Sons, two of whom were married, and had Children, whereas Lord Orford, to who He proposed the offer, was not married, and had no Brothers. Lord Orford would not make the settlement; but he made *a will to the effect*; which will is the one lately contended for by Coll. Walpole. This Will is declared to be superseded by a Codicil which alludes to another will, and of course substantiates it by a latter declaration. In lieu of this will, the late Lord bequeathed to Mrs Turk, His Mistress, the Piddlecombe Estate, and, after her death to Coll. Walpole. She dying before his Lordship, it became a lapse legacy, so that the present Lord could have bequeathed to whom He pleased: but He took no advantage of the circumstance & confirmed the bequest to Coll. Walpole; who, in several instances, has shewn little sense of the obligation. When His Lordship expressed his intention to present Great Massinghan to Horace Hamond, the Coll. seemed surprised, and on his Lordship asking him what He thought of it, He replied, coldly, "He supposed Mr Hamond would do the duty". He afterwards expressed a doubt to Lord Orford as to his power of giving away the living, and that the Executor meant to try the question. On enquiry His Lordship found the Executor never had such an intention.

Lord Cholmendley, 3 or 4 years ago by leave from Lord Orford, went to Houghton, to see the place. Coll. Walpole said He did not know that Lord Orford had any right to permit Lord Cholmendeley to go there.

Lord Orford expressed his satisfaction at having lived to see this question terminated, and that He had also lived long enough to know Coll. Walpole. Of Mrs. Walpole He spoke with kindness.

His Lordship is fully convinced that the late Lord Orford fell a martyr to bad management at the commencement of his last illness. Speaking of him He said He was not surprised when He first heard of his madness in 1773 as many singularities had prepared him for it. "I am well convinced," said his Lordship, "that he was not the Son of my Brother". Sir Henry Oxenden was his father, and it was *after* Lady Orford found herself with Child by Si

Henry, that she allowed Her husband to cohabit with her; which he had not done for a considerable time. I asked his Lordship what He thought of her person & understanding. He said she had a good person, and clear skin, but large bad features, and Horse teeth, set apart. She had sense. She was extremely vicious, and in several instances solicited men. She went to the Bed chamber of a Mr. Sturges, who had places under Sir Robert Walpole. She carried him abroad; He lost his places; she grew tired of him; and He returned to England, poor and unprovided for.

Sir Robt. Walpole wished much for Male succession: but had the mortification of knowing that He had little reason to believe his *nominal grandson* to be *really His descendant.*

I looked at two pictures, a whole & a half length of Sir Robt. Walpole, which His Lordship desires to have cleaned, as He proposes to send them to Houghton, the Lawsuit having terminated agreeable to his wishes.

Mrs. Fitzroy (a daughter of Mrs. Keppel) wife to Coll. Fitzroy son of Lord Southampton, came in. She is very agreeable in countenance & person. She is in the establishment of the Princess of Wales. N. Dance I met & Sir George Beaumont joined us. Dance told us He had this day paid £4000 for his seat in the new parliament. I asked him [how] He wd. be circumstanced if a new parliament shd. be called in a year or two. — He said He had no agreement, it was all upon honor, but He should think himself very ill used, if required to pay again at the end of so short a term.

Sir George has heard that a German officer having proposed to return to Brunswick, the Princess of Wales delivered letters to him for her mother. The officer having occasion to remain here, carried the letters to Carlton House to return them. Lady Jersey undertook to redeliver them to the Princess: but carried them to the Prince, who opened them, & read such a description of Lady Jersey as She merits. — He went to the Princess, upbraided Her with endeavouring to destroy the character of Lady Jersey, & said He shd. preserve appearances in public, but in private would have no communication with her.

It is said He has spoken very disrespectfully of the Princess, as to her person being unclean, with sores &c.

Philips I met. Mrs. Fryer proposes to give up her town house, and to reside at Taplow, which at first she thought wd. be too expensive.

Bryants Gallery I went to with Sir George & Dance to see the View of Rome by Wilson, which He sold to the Marquiss of Tavistock, 30 years ago for 100 gs. Bryant told me he expected to have it for 70 gs. Mr. Blundell of Ince called on me this morning.

Friday May 27th.

Lord Inchiquins I went to this morning. Coll. Hamilton purchased the picture of the Duke & Duchess of Hamilton at Sir Joshuas sale for the

Duke, who, it is said, means to have the Head of Mrs. Esten introduced in the place of that of the Duchess. It was bought for 100 Guineas.

Mrs. Pelham, is the Bedchamber woman who is said to behave disrespectfully to the Princess; she had heretofore been reckoned a good kind of woman. Lord Thurlow has been with the Prince on the subject of his quarrel with the Princess, and was treated disrepectfully. The Prince is said to have talked of a divorce, as having been married before to Mrs. Fitzherbert, but such a marriage cd. not be valid. The Princess seems conscious of her rights and that she is mother to the Heir apparent. It is said in her letter to Her mother, the Princess remarked on the conduct of the Queen which has left her no hopes from that quarter. The King & Queen say She must make the best of her situation.

A report was circulated early this morning that a gentleman had shot his Brother in a Chaise, and that they were Sons of Marquiss Townshend. I went into Oxford road & saw a crowd abt. an Apothecarys door near Argyle St. On enquiry at a Shop I learnt that Lord Charles Townshend was shot and lay dead in Mr. Brahams, Apothecary next door; and that Lord Frederick was in custody at Mr. Conants, the Police Office in Great Marlborough St. The Master of the house obtained admission for me and 2 other gentlemen to the Apothecarys, and in a little back room the body of Lord Charles lay on the ground on its back stretched out. There was no appearance of a wound, but the right eye lids which were closed were a little swelled, and a bluish blackness over them. In other respects the face was without bruise, and had the calm look of sleep. The wound was in the roof of the mouth, and the bullet had punctuated through the skull and lodged just under the skin at the top of the head, from which it was cut out by Mr. Braham. It appeared to me impossible that such a wound could have been given unless the pistol was *introduced into the mouth* and had that been *done by force*, the teeth, or, at least, the lips, would have been bruised, which was not the case in any degree: from these circumstances I was convinced the shot must have been fired by himself. The pistol was long and large. He was dressed in a brown coat, white waistcoat, yellowish coloured breeches, white silk stockings, and shoes with strings: His hair without powder. He resembled the Marquiss, had a tolerable, but not a handsome face; but a very well made person, and limbs: and was abt. 25 or 6 years old. He was the youngest Child of the first wife of the present Marquiss. Lord Pomfret was in the room with us. A gentleman came to us who said the Marquiss had just passed down the street with a Clergyman who had a book under his arm, and seemed to be in a distracted state. The Coroners Inquest was to sit upon the body this evening at 6.

Lord Walpole I called upon. He was not at home, but I saw Lady Walpole & Miss Walpole & Mrs. Hussey, and related to them the particulars of what I had seen. They told me that Lord Frederick was confined 9 months being in an insane state abt. 2 years ago. Lord Charles they said was a very amiable young man. Lady Walpole observed that the Marquiss himself was in a state like insanity a few years ago, a sort of religious phrenzy, when He wd. kneel in the streets.

Lord Orfords I went to, and found Lord Cholmendely with him. I mentioned the particulars to them.

Lawrences I called at. Lord Inchiquin was sitting for his picture, which I concurred with Lady Inchiquin in thinking it very like.

Trinity House, on Tower Hill, I went to, at Rigauds invitation through Richards, to see the ceiling He has painted in the Great room. The flat center of it is well designed and suitably coloured: The coves of the cieling are indifferent both in design and execution, & not adapted in colour to the flat part. Saml. Wyatt, as Surveyor to the Trinity House designed the building which I think beautiful. He told me Rigaud had £500 for executing the cieling, and was recomended by the late Captn. Money; who was an East India Director & an elder Brother of the Trinity House. Gainsborough Dupont, painted the whole length portraits of the 24 Bretheren of the Trinity House & the whole length portraits of the King & Queen & of Lord Howe & Mr. Pitt. Mr. Pitt recommended him.

Mr. S. Wyatt informed me that the Trinity House is a Corporation consisting of 24 Brothers; they annually elect a Master of their Company, and they have Honorary Members; but the Master & the Honorary Members have no votes, and never interfere in the election of vacancies in the number 24 who are the acting members. A dinner is provided once a week throughout the year at the London Tavern for the brethren who are officiating; and they have an annual election meeting and dinner, at which the Master presides. The present Master is Mr. Pitt. He has a Power of nominating to vacancies of *honorary* members, and appointing a Deputy master for the 24. — 2000 persons relieved by Trinity Company. At ½ past 4 we adjourned to the Coal Exchange Tavern, Billingsgate to dinner

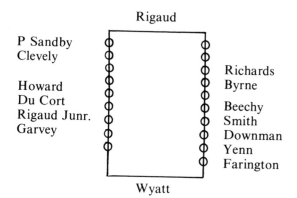

S Wyatt is about 59 years old. He had remarkable strong eye sight, but never has been able to work without glasses since within 10 days after the time when the Albion Mills were burnt. The shock He felt at that time had so great an effect on his nerves. He is convinced the Mills were not set on fire by design. It was owing to the condition of some grain which had been imported and deposited in the Mill.

S Wyatt built Heaton House (Lord Grey de Wiltons) and is now building a large house for Mr. Egerton of Tatton. He has been much employed by Mr. Coke of Holkham & spoke highly of him.

Speaking of the Westminster election He said He had formerly been applied to by the Treasury & had carried 30 votes; & thought He cd. now carry 20. He expressed willingness to vote for Fox & Sir A Gardner, & allowed me to direct them to apply to the latter.

I came away at ½ past 9 oClock, but the Company did not break up till past 12. — Yenn told me the King saw him on Windsor Terrace on Sunday evening last, and afterwards sent for him, and He remained an hour in the room with the King, Queen & Princesses. The Queen & Princesses were making purses. The King spoke abt. the Academy, & Yenn told him of the great rects. at the Exhibition.

Saturday May 28th.

Sir Alan Gardner I went to on the Hustings in Covent Garden & reccomended to him to write to Saml. Wyatt which He said He wd. do. He told me He thought that Foxs party were acting in conjunction with Tookes, and giving their 2d votes to each other. He considered himself as depending on the Gentlemen of Westminster. He desired me to speak to Mr. Booth, his Manager, at Richardsons Hotel, which I did abt. Wyatt.

Shakespeare Gallery I went to. Nicol & Ireland were speaking of the opinion held of the Prince of Wales's conduct to the Princess. In the *Times* today the unhandsome behaviour of the Prince to Lord Thurlow who offered his mediation, was properly described.

Smirke I called on in the evening. He has now been confined by the complaint in his eye 5 weeks. I told him I had mentioned the business of Anchor Smith to J. Boydell, and his answer. He concurred with me that Smith cd. not properly take any steps to obtain more money than He had verbally agreed for. I told him of our proposal to encrease the charity fund, which He much approved.

Sunday May 29th.

Lawrence I breakfasted with. We had much talk about his lowering his prices in consequence of Hoppner particularly continuing to paint ¾ pictures for 25 guineas. He said He had determined to reduce *his* to Beechy's prices, viz: 30 guineas for a ¾ &c &c. The statement which has been made in the Telegraph of the prices of him, Hoppner & Beechy is a good plea. As He does not pretend to claim superiority, if Hoppner wil not raise his price in proportion to the expences of the times, He will not give him the advantage of such a material difference. Lawrence thought it would be proper to have this signified in a newspaper but I doubted abt. it, thinking it would by degrees be generally known, if He should avoid remarks. I said, if He judged it proper to reduce his prices this would be the time, as his reputation is rising.

Lady Inchiquin I called on & apologized for Lawrence putting Lord Inchiquins sitting off till Wednesday on acct. of Lady Charlotte Stanley going out of town. Lady I. shewed me the portrait of Sir Joshua painted by himself abt. the year 1768 or 9 which she had given me.

Hughes called on me. The Bishop of Rochester had mentioned to him a Bottle conversation of the Prince of Wales, who had extolled the charms of Lady Jersey, while *Tyrwhit* expressed his admiration of the Princess of Wales.

Baker called on me. He looks ill & has been out of order some weeks.

Offleys I dined at with Susan. No company.

Sir Jos. Banks's I went to at 9. Duke of Somerset, Marsden, Dalrymple, Reynell, Dr. Garthshore, S. Lysons &c. &c. there. The Duke of Somerset is not quite of age. He seems to be a mild young man; and Dryander told me He has a turn for the Sciences; but is thought to possess but moderate parts. He is desirous of being a Member of the Royal Society, but Sir Joseph Banks does not think He can properly be elected till He is 21 years old.

Lysons told me He had been at Lord Orfords, where He met Lady Mary Churchill, who had been describing the applauding reception of the Princess of Wales last night at the Opera House.

Monday May 30th.

Flaxman called this morning.

Banks' I went to at ten to meet the members of the Council, and inspect his model of Lord Cornwallis. The model is 4 feet high; half the size of the figure as it is to be executed in marble.

Dance, Bacon & Lawrence were there. Dance thought the figure appeared too short, owing to the upper part being too large for the lower. Lawrence, that the sides of the *chest* were too narrow. Bacon made some observations. I told him I thought the figure appeared too short.

On the whole I was not pleased with the appearance of the figure altogether, neither was Dance, nor did Bacon or Lawrence commend it. The disadvantage is great of being confined to a representation of an individual person.

Lawrence told me that on reflection He thought it would be better not to take any notice in the newspapers of his altering his prices unless remarks shd. be made that may require it. He has been informed by a friend of Lord Charles Townshend that his insanity was owing to drinking, and want of rest, at a time when He was taking *mercury*.

Mr. Montgomery, Brother to Lady Townshend, has been much with Lord Frederick since his confinement, and has discovered that the two Brothers in their insane state had agreed "that they had but one Soul and two bodies", and each agreed to kill himself that they might be united, which Lord Charles did and the other attempted; but only grazed his throat.

Marchant we called on. His heads of Fox, Wyndham, and Lord Spencer, are each very *like*.

Tuesday May 30th [31st].

Sir Alan Gardner I went to before 9 and found him at breakfast. He had been kept up in Committees till 3 oClock this morning. I went with him & his little Boy to call on Mr. Hood at Lord Hoods, but He was gone, to the Hustings. We saw Lord Hood, who looked very fresh & well; Sir Alan supposes him to be 75 years old. Tooke behaves very civilly personally to Sir Alan, but in his speeches at the close of each days Poll, makes hits at his situation as being employed by Government. Sir Alan asked me to dine with him on Wednesday (tomorrow) at Richardsons Hotel, when a commemoration dinner of the First of June (Lord Howes Victory) is to be prepared. Sir Alan complains of the want of activity in Government in his support. He is no doubt of the election to his party, being attended with an expence of £5 or £6000. To himself some hundreds.

Hearne I breakfasted with, and took the size of his sketch book intended for Sir George Beaumont. The leaves 19 inches long, by 12 inches ¾.

Dr. Monro I met. He gave 70 guineas for the two Wilsons which He bought from Mrs. King. He will vote for Sir A. Gardner with Fox's permission to whom He has promised his vote.

The Hustings I went to abt. 4 oClock, a large mob assembled. Batty I met there. At the close of the Poll, Fox spoke 5 minutes; & Gardner as long: the latter could not be heard owing to a party as usual hooting. Tooke spoke 20 minutes & much clapping, & applauding. Thelwall & Jones were there. Tookes hair was tied but without powder.

Hamilton, I called on & solicited him to vote for Sir A. Gardner, which He promised to do tomorrow.

Westall I drank tea with. His Brother promised to vote for Sir A. Gardner only. Westall wrote to Porden, who came to us & said He would endeavour to get votes for tomorrow: but Lord Grosvenor has sent notice to many of his tenants &c that he takes no interest in the event of the Poll Porden will call on him tomorrow morning to learn, if he can, the cause.

Sir A. Gardner I went to after 10 oClock, to mention what Porden said abt. Ld. Grosvenor, He said He had been acquainted with it, and had written to Lord Belgrave at Chester to use his influence with his father Lord Grosvenor says He has been neglected by the Administration.

Cade called. He is to leave London tonight.

JUNE 1796

Wednesday June 1st.

Mackenzie I called on this morning & solicited a vote for Sir A. Gardner, but He spoke against a supposed coalition between Fox & Gardner & it seems to me that He is for Tooke.

Moser I called, who said He & Jackson had never voted, but if required would for Gardner towards the conclusion of the Poll.

Hamilton I called on, & went with him to Lawrence to breakfast. Bell has voted for Fox & Gardner. Lawrence went with us to Miles, who agreed to follow us to Covt. Garden. Lawrence solicited some other votes with Hamilton. I went to the Garden and met Miles who told me Lady Mary Howe came to sit earlier than he expected; but on Miles telling Her that I, Lawrence, & Hamilton, had called on him to vote she expressed her satisfaction & put off Her sitting till he should return. He gave a plumper for Sir Alan. Hamilton then came & voted for Gardner & Fox.

Yenn I called on, He has no vote.

Shakespeare Gallery I went to. J. Boydell, Nicol, & Bulmer were preparing to go & Poll. Boydell went with me to solicit two votes, we then went together to the Hustings. Nicol gave a single vote for Gardner; Boydell & Bulmer voted for Gardner & Fox. I then went upon the Hustings with Boydell & met N. Dance. Fox came in with Bradyll. Coll. Egerton was with Gardner. Devaynes came, He has lost his Election at Barnstaple. He voted for Gardner. I returned home & Hearne called on me to mention that Edridge has no vote. I went back to Covent Garden & met James Wyatt, and strongly solicited him to use his influence as Surveyor General of the Board of Works, which He said he would do; but he wished to bring this party up together: That there wld. be a Board day on Saturday, & that many of the tradesmen to the Board wd. dine together at the Freemasons Tavern; and He would take then opportunities of soliciting them and endeavour to fix them for Monday: & would write to them immediately.

Richardsons Hotel I went to & Boydell joined me. On account of the long speeches of Fox & particularly Tooke, the Candidates did not leave the Hustings till 5 o'Clock. Dinner was served up at ¼ before 6.

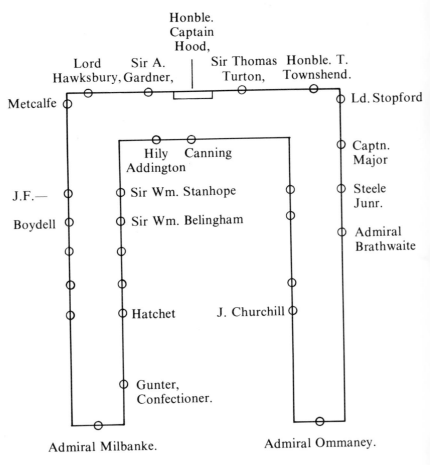

POLL this day

Gardner	1750
Fox	1616
Tooke	1192

Many appropriate toasts were given. The Company filled the room, and half a guinea was collected from each. Captn. Hood delivered the wine tickets as required. No professional Singers. Captn. Hood sung joined by everybody "God save the King", Sir Alan sung "Thursday in the morn", a little after 9 I & Boydell followed Metcalfe & Lord Hawkesbury, leaving the Company very jolly. I never saw a meeting unite better.

Booth, Sir Alan's Attorney, told me that more than 15,000 people might vote for Westminster; but the greatest number ever known was 12,200, in the contest of 1784. He expects Tooke will vote towards 3000, & is afraid of great difficulties in voting next week, owing to Tookes mob.

Tooke was very scurrilous today, made angry by the great majority of Gardner. Fox was evidently disappointed & took pains to shew he has not coalesced with Tooke.

Metcalfe told me Fox did not like the prospect of the trouble of standing again for Westminster and it is believed that He would be glad to retire from public business. Sir Alan Gardner was not well attended at his nomination, by few except naval Officers. Metcalfe & Sir George Beaumont were there. Sir Thomas Turton spoke very well previous to nominating Sir Alan, but protracted his speech too long.

After dinner Hily Addington drew up an advertisement of thanks for Sir Alan on acct. of his great success on this days Poll.

Lord Hawkesbury, I think, has a formal, speechifying manner of expression in common conversation: but He said very little.

Owing to standing before an open window to see what passed at the Hustings, I was, during dinner time, seized with a violent spasmodic attack in my shoulders, breast & face, which continued the whole evening. At night I took 4 grains of James's powders.

Thursday June 2nd.

The Cold I got yesterday caused me to continue in bed till past 12 o'Clock, — the spasmodic complaint still continuing. Westall called in the evening & told me His Brother at my request voted with 5 others plumpers for Sir Alan Gardner, & Porden has sent up, or secured near 50 votes for him.

Sir Alan I wrote to reccomending to him to write to Jas. Wyatt to thank him for his offer of service & to request He will give the preference to Monday next, also to write to Porden to acknowledge his services.

	Poll	This day
Gardner	2116	366
Fox	1978	362
Tooke	1377	185

Friday June 3rd

The Hustings in Covent Garden I went to, & spoke to Sir Alan Gardner abt. my notes sent to him last night. A hint he said was sufficient; & He had written to Wyatt & Porden. Neither Fox or Tooke were there. Each days state of the Poll is posted up in the Hustings every hour; at 10 oClock today Gardner 13 — Fox 12 — Tooke 7. Lawrence disappointed me in not coming to Woods Coffee House with his Father as He appointed. — I called on Hamilton to mention it & returned home.

Sir George Beaumont & Daniel called in the afternoon. I could not dine with Sir George on acct. of the Academy. I shewed them the little Ruysdael, and compared it with the 2 Wilsons. It was allowed that in Grandeur & stile Wilson greatly surpassed: but in strength & clearness they seemed to think Ruysdael superior. Sir George contended for the practise of Ruysdael, as Wilsons principles might be maintained equally. Daniel doubt[ed] if so much variety, so much play of tint, would attend that practise. Daniel remarked on the various distinctions of Wilson *White Lights*. — Academy Council I went to. No Council from want of a member.

West

Bacon, Stothard, Farington

Yenn.

The receipts of the Exhibition this night amount to £2668-9-0. The King asked Yenn yesterday how we went on in our receipts, and was well pleased when he saw the account.

Bacon has done what He can in favor of Sir A. Gardner. Yenn & J. Wyatt have been canvassing today, and tomorrow morning bring up a considerable number.

General Poll today		each number.
Gardner	2349	233
Fox	2275	297
Tooke	1569	192

Richold has delivered his acct. for the Annual dinner amounting to £162-16-6. I complained of the dinner as having been very indifferent, Yenn & Richards were of the same opinion. West seemed satisfied with what was at the head of the table. Altogether I am sure Richold made a job of it. The charge for servants at 2s. a head was £10-8-0. The Company were 136.

Yenn shewed me some pointed verses satirically describing Soane as an Architect destitute of merit.

Horne Tooke lodges at Bonneys during the Poll. The rabble this night drew him home.

Saturday June 4th.

Sir Alan Gardner I called on, & desired him to write a letter of thanks to Yenn, which He did. He told me that last night a mob followed his carriage to Portland Place, notwithstanding the endeavours of his Coachman to evade them. Sir Alan & Mr. Hood were pelted with mud and the Coach much broken.

Richardsons Hotel I went to, & met Wyatt & Yenn, & introduced them
to Sir Alan. They brought a considerable number of votes. Mr. Hood told
me of his escape last night, with the assistance of Mr. Thelussons servants.
We went to the Hustings, where I met Paine, and introduced him to Sir
Alan. He has been useful & is getting votes. Mr. Russell was there, and
spoke to Sir Alan. *Bush* affected to make an apology, or rather a disclaim-
ing speech, for Tookes Committee, on acct. of the insults of last night.
That mob cried out, "Tooke for ever, no Gardner". *Frend*, another of the
Committee, affected to do the same. Sir Alan made proper answers,
plainly shewing what his opinion is of the proceedings of Tookes
Associates.

	Poll	this day
Gardner	2624	275
Fox	2529	254
Tooke	1634	65

Prince of Wales, a report prevailed generally that He had shot himself.
Cooper the printer I asked for a vote. He said He had voted the first
hour, but I am sure not for Gardner.
Lord Lauderdale, stood by Fox while He made his speech from the
Hustings this afternoon.
Freemasons Tavern, I dined. Kings Birth day.

Nixon-P. Sandby-T. Sandby-Wilton-*West*-Heriot-Bourgeois-Yenn

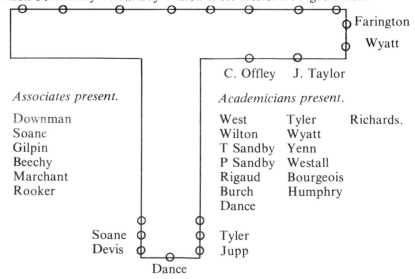

Farington

Wyatt

C. Offley   J. Taylor

Associates present.   *Academicians present.*

Downman	West	Tyler	Richards.
Soane	Wilton	Wyatt	
Gilpin	T Sandby	Yenn	
Beechy	P Sandby	Westall	
Marchant	Rigaud	Bourgeois	
Rooker	Burch	Humphry	
	Dance		

Soane   Tyler
Devis   Jupp

Dance

Muller behaved with pointed rudeness. B. West Junr. was with him, & young F. Sandby.

Du Cort & Gilpin, I had much conversation with on the different processes in painting. Du Cort held Asphaltam &c in contempt, Black alone answers the purpose on a ground properly prepared. Over a light ground, Rubens passed Oil which made a warm tint, and served as his middle colour, when glazed upon. Du Corts process is, to have his ground prepared light, this to draw his outline with Black lead pencil, then to pass Oil over it, and on that tint to glaze his shadows and embody his lights. Wilson He said had great Ideas; but no execution. Gilpin united with me & others in differing from Du Cort. I said Wilson & Claude attempted to obtain what the Flemish & Dutch Masters did not think about, "Atmospherick effects". There is little sense of Aerial tints in the works of the latter.

Daniel told me He had a conversation with Sir Geo: Beaumont who said He thought himself best qualified to paint familiar scenes. Daniel differed from him not thinking his manner of painting best adapted to such subjects. In his opinion they required a more accurate attention to circumstances, than He is accustomed to shew in his practise. — We staid till past 12 oClock. Cosway & Burch were nominated Stewards for the next year.

Sunday — June 5th.

G. Dance I called on this morning. Old Mr. Carr of York, the Architect, came to sit for a profile, He said He is between 70 & 80 years old.

Mr. Fawkes has declined standing for Yorkshire, from a prospect of contending with the Lascelles fortunes. His estate is between 7 or £8000 a year, with some incumbrance on it.

Mr. Lascelles, the Father of the late Lord Harewood, of Daniel Lascelles, and of General Lascelles killed himself, by opening the veins in his wrist. He had been in the West Indies & been guilty of extortion. The present Mr. Lascelles, (now Lord Lascelles) was a 7th. or 8th. cousin only of the late Lord, but preferred in the will of his Lordship, on acct. of General Lascelles having married Miss Catley. The grand father of the present Ld. Harewood, though a distant relation, was a servant at that time in the Lascelles family.

Old Mr. Aislibie, of Studley park, was fined £100,000 for his practises in the business of the South Sea Scheme; but had notwithstanding £200,000 left. The Heir to the Estate is Son of a Grocer at Rippon, who ran away with a Young Lady of the family. Wilberforce is supported by the trading interest in Yorkshire. They like the war which causes them to have vast orders for Cloathing both for Germany & France.

Coll. Thornton has paid the whole purchase money for the Allerton estate (formerly Lord Galways) within £20,000. Thorntons patrimonial estates had been much under let, of course in comparison with the *nominal income*, sold remarkably well, one estate which was rented for £100 a year only sold £5000. The whole produced Thornton abt. £90,000. There is an insanity in the family of Thornton, which accounts for his eccentricities. His grandfather was insane.

Exhibition I went to at 12. Mrs. Damer & two Miss Berrys, and Lysons came there, and soon after Ladies Triphina & Susan Bathurst. The observations of Mrs. Damer did not seem to me to prove that she has any exact knowledge of painting, whatever she may have of Sculpture; and she did not make inteligent remarks on the latter. I think Her manner & particularly her voice very affected and unpleasing.

At 2 Lord & Lady Beverley, and 2 daugtrs. & Sir George & Lady Beaumont came.

Miss Berry spoke with warm praise to Mrs. Damer of Sir Geo: Beaumont and wished her to know him, I mentioned this to Sir George, who desired Miss Berry to introduce him to Mrs. Damer, which she did.

Beechy came with some ladies. He told me his house was robbed on Friday night, owing to a front window over the door being left open. He lost abt. £60 worth of Plate &c.

Mrs. Wheeler, of Bengal, & her 2 daugrs. & Lady Glynn & Her Son Sir Stephen, came with Lady Chambers. Lysons told me Sir Stephen is to take orders, & is to hold His own living of Hawarden.

Lord Beverlys I dined at. Sir George & Lady B, only there.

Mr. Pitts deportment has rendered him very unpopular among the nobility, & his neglect of their applications disgusted many. Lord Beverly said, His education had been confined, and his associations of a common kind, which had given a turn to his mind, that made him unfit to conciliate the affections of people of rank as well as others.

Revd. Mr. Dutens, came to tea.

Lysons was at Court yesterday. When the Princess of Wales first appeared in the outer rooms a clapping commenced, which was with difficulty suppressed. Cookson & Hughes called while I was out.

Monday June 6th.

Bestland called to desire Wyatt to sit for his portrait for the Academical picture. The Hustings I went to at ½ past 3. The crowd was greater today than ever. Fox gained a majority of 4 on the whole Poll, which put him in spirits, & He made a speech of some length. Gardner could not be heard. Tooke spoke long & shewed more of his seditious principles than before. Fox said the behaviour of the people proved the public sentiment (that is by ruffians mobbing Sir A. Gardner). He forgot how unwilling He was after the *coalition* to admit this proof. The Poll stood

Fox	2983	this day 454
Gardner	2979	this day 355
Tooke	1913	this day 279

G. Dance wrote to me that He had got some votes. I wrote to Wyatt & to Tyler exhorting them to exert themselves.

Tuesday June 7th.

Sir Alan Gardner I called on this morning. He was at Breakfast with Lady Gardner & Mr. Hood. Last night between 7 & 8 oClock, returning from Richardsons Hotel with Mr. Hood, His carriage was followed by a number of Blackguards one of whom gave a signal whistle in King St. when the Admiral got into his carriage. As the mob pelted the carriage with mud, the Admiral got out, and walked forward on foot, the mob was then less riotous, on which the carriage again came up & he got in; the mob then renewed the pelting, on which He again left it and proceeded on foot and was pelted with mud & a stone struck him on the back of the head, which caused him to go into a Shop. At last He got home. Mr. Hood was also assaulted.

Richardsons Hotel I went to, and recd. several of J. Wyatts voters; He was prevented from attending by a rheumatic complaint in his legs. Paine came, and continues his exertions.

The Hustings I went to & staid till ½ past 3 oClock. Horne Tooke came to the Hustings abt. one, & Fox a little sooner. Tooke spoke to the Admiral expressing his concern at the assault on the Admirals person, and said He would concur in anything to prevent the like. The Admiral said such *personal* attacks were unknown at a Westminster election in which Tooke agreed. He told the Admiral that He felt it not to be fair, that He should always be heard, & the Admiral never, & said if the Admiral would not speak, He wd. not speak, unless the people were willing to hear both. The Admiral replied that He desired nothing more than to return thanks.

I talked some time to Tooke. He said that He had been generally unpopular but that He did not apprehend much from one [attack?]; He had never received injury though He had been shoved & hustled. He thought an English mob good natured. I remarked how little good it could do to a cause to have it stated that a mob professing approbation of it were guilty of great outrages. He agreed with me, and said undoubtedly government could produce a power to quell any attempts, so the mob would have the worst of it, therefore it was imprudent to tempt that power. Tooke had white woollen stockings on and a stuff shoe. He remained the whole time uncovered. I asked him if He was not afraid of catching cold. "I use myself to go bareheaded, said He, because I hate the Hat Tax, & mean to go without one".

Lord Bingham voted for *Fox* and Gardner.

J. Wyatt wrote to me to desire me to call on him and to know if some friends of his could dine with Sir Alan at Willis' room tomorrow.

Westall called to tell me that Porden had been canvassing today, and recommended that certain persons shd. be applied to.

J. Wyatt I drank tea with: Mrs. Wyatt, His 2 eldest Sons & 2 Ladies present. Sir Alan Gardner passed through the street with a large mob *huzzaing.*

Wyatt proceeds with his canvassing; and hopes to bring up several on Thursday. Westmacot senr., Armstrong, and Wigstead, wish to dine with the Admiral tomorrow.

Sir Alan I called on. Lord Bridport was there. After his Lordship went away I gave Sir Alan the names Porden sent me, recommending to him to write to them, which He said He would do. Fox this afternoon made a speech strongly recommending a peaceable conduct to the people, and describing the Admiral to be a respectable Gentleman & a brave Officer. Tooke did the same.

	Poll today	this day
Fox	3332	349
Gardner	3321	342
Tooke	2078	155

The Admiral mentioned to me how negligently Government had behaved to him in regard to this election. The Duke of Portland wrote to the Admiral late the night before his nomination proposing to him to go to Mr. Meux, the *Brewer,* to nominate him. The Admiral went at Eleven at night and was told Mr. Meux had been in bed three Hours; it being his custom to go to bed at 8 & rise at 4 in the morning to superintend his vast concerns.

Marchant called this eving. Lord Lucan voted for *Fox* & Gardner.

Wednesday June 8th.

Richardsons Hotel I went to this morning, & saw Sir Alan G: who wrote to Vidler &c., Paine came; with him I went to Mr. M [arnel], an Attorney in Salisbury [St.] who is coming forward with his interest for Sir Alan; but wishes to have a nephew appointed to the Royal Academy at Woolwich. we observed that *this is not a time to apply*, to which He agreed.

I returned home to painting.

Hustings I went to at ½ past 3. Fox spoke shortly, so did Sir Alan, Tooke long but with little point, & concluded with saying Pitts oath is a bad security.

	Poll today	this day
Fox	3665	333
Gardner	3605	284
Tooke	2215	137

Willis's rooms I went to, to dinner. Wyatt & Paine there. The Admiral Sir Alan came on foot from Richardsons Hotel, Dinner on the table at 6 — Tickets 7s.—.

Geo: Berkley ·Mr. Hood – Devaynes – Sir Alan – Genl. ₁Lewis -T. Steele

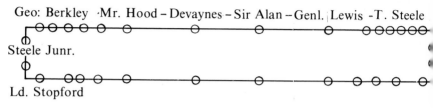

Steele Junr.

Ld. Stopford

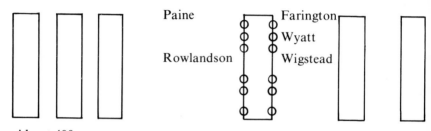

Paine   Farington

Rowlandson   Wyatt

                        Wigstead

About 400 persons were assembled. The day went off admirably. Sir Alan gave "The King & Constitution — Then "The worthy & independent electors of Westminster".

He then in an audible voice said, "Gentlemen, as I wish my sentiments to be publicly known on every subject without disguise,

I give you,
Mr. Pitt

This Toast was very well recd.

Mr. Devaynes gave,

"Admiral Gardner & success to his Election." Other toasts were *drank*. The Admiral then Said he shd. propose a song and though an indifferent singer, "would set them going".

He then sung,

"Thursday on the morn, the famous 92". This delighted the company.

Many toasts & several songs followed the two best from a Mr. Adderton.

George Berkleys health being drunk, He addressed the meeting and observed that "if Mr. Tooke were elected instead of the Hustings of Covent Garden they would find the Guillotine". Thos. Steeles health being drunk, He made a suitable acknowledgement.

The Admiral sang "Last Valentines day" and led "God save the King". At ½ past nine He left the Chair & went home in his Coach with Mr. Hood, a great concourse of people huzzaing. Some attempted to unharness the horses & to draw the carriage but were prevented by friends. The whole company broke up at that Hour.

Wigstead brought with him some impressions of a caricature print, which He has designed, Fox's Head off, & the Devil hawling Tooke, Thelwall, & Hardy, into Hell. He gave me one but I did not think it proper to shew it to the Admiral at that time.

Thursday June 9th.

Sir Alan Gardners I went to, to breakfast. Mr. Hood & Lady Gardner present. I gave Her Ladyship Wigstead's print, and an Advertisement.

Sir Alan & Mr. Hood did not think General Lewis judged well in sitting on the left hand of Sir Alan at dinner yesterday, as He is not an Elector of Westminster; and Sir Alan was obliged to repress His attempts to make ill-judged speeches.

Mr. Hood concurred with me in thinking many of the *near* friends of government had judged ill in giving a vote to Fox, as it placed him at the head of the Poll, which He certainly wd. not have been by a great number witht. such an addition to his interest.

We went in Sir Alans Coach to Richardsons Hotel & they called by the way on Milingtons in Golden Square, who had spoken of his interest but had said that "Votes not worth asking for, were not worth giving." He told them that He had formerly been ill used by the other party, & had quitted them; & wd. now serve Sir Alan.

Wyatt came to Richardsons. we went on the Hustings with Sir Alan. Mr. L. Long came & gave a plumper for Sir Alan.

Sir Alan received a letter from Captain Bedford, of the Queen, expressing his concern at the ill usage the Admiral has received from the mob, & stating it to be the wish of every Officer & Seaman in the Ship to come up & guard his person. Mr. Miller, the first Lieutt. & the Doctor came up express & brought this letter to the Hustings.

Wyatt & I went to canvass. We met Lord Grey de Wilton. He said Horrocks is likely to carry his election at Preston. Horrocks was in town some time ago, and at Lord Greys it was proposed that for a very reasonable Sum to be paid by Tom Tarleton of Liverpool, Horrocks would support the general expence, & Tarleton shd. be joined with him. This Tarleton agreed to, but afterwards declined, which He was now very sorry for.

We called on Shelley. Yenn had been with him. He expressed unwillingness to vote at all; but at last said He probably shd. for Admiral Gardner.

Bone we called on, who agreed to Poll for Gardner & Fox tomorrow. — Adamson, House painter, we called on. He has voted Gardner only. We desired his interest.

We called at other places, & lastly at Jackson & Mosers. Moser we spoke to; He behaved in a very paltry manner & we both came away with a similar opinion of him.

The Hustings we returned to. Fox, spoke 8 minutes. The Admiral, as long. Tooke, 25 minutes, very indifferent his matter, & He did not catch the multitude. He described the progress of William Grenville, enumerating the places of profit He had successively enjoyed, and said that the *domestic* enemies so much talked of are the people, who are to be plundered by placemen.

Thelwall stood near him. Fox was attended by Genl. Tarleton.

Fox in his speech made strong assertions against the Ministry, and of the opinion of the people. Sir Thomas Turton loudly & repeatedly, said *No No,* and was joined by others.

I returned home to dinner. Cade having returned from Portsmouth, went down again this evening.

	Poll today	this day
Fox	3961	296
Gardner	3884	279
Tooke	2303	88

Friday June 10th.

Wyatt I called on. Went with him to Richardsons Hotel and met Paine. Inspected the Books to see who had voted. Mr. T. Steele, Angerstein, & Hood doing the same. I called on English, glass man. He resolves not to vote. called on Mackenzie & went with him to the Broadway Westminster, at Mr. Royals, a Brewer. went up from Richardsons with two Voters. Met Young Barry, & Humphry. went to the Hustings. Fox spoke shortly, the Admiral also. Tooke spoke 20 minutes. Frend applauded much. Tooke was drawn by the mob to Bonneys. Genl. Tarleton was with Fox.

Sir Alan Gardners I dined at.

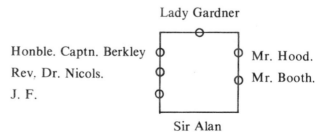

Lady Gardner

Honble. Captn. Berkley   Mr. Hood.

Rev. Dr. Nicols.   Mr. Booth.

J. F.

Sir Alan

Captn. Berkley told me Lord Berkley paid £42,000 on acct. of expences at Gloucestershire election. Captn. B. will be 43 years old in August. It is near 33 years that He went first to Sea. Had his promotion not been stopped by political differences, He wd. have had 33 Admirals under him, and wd. have been next to Elphinstone. He lost 4 years. Captn. Hood will be 43 in September. He was intended for the Sea. Sir Alan shewed me a snuffbox which belonged to his grandfather by the mother. He said the Heralds Office had quartered his mothers (the Faringtons) Arms, with those of his Father.

Mr. Booth said the newspaper proprietors take great advantages of the election advertisements. The prices they charge are very great. We staid till 12 oClock.

	Poll to day	this day
Fox	4233	272
Gardner	4174	290
Tooke	2407	104

Saturday June 11th.

Wyatt I called on; then on Mackenzie; then called on Hearne who thought I might apply to Henderson for his vote. I went to Richardsons & met Paine & inspected books for names. Westmacott brought 6 Voters. Went with Mr. Hood to canvass in Bedford St. & the Strand; and called at Hendersons who told us He had voted yesterday. He was married to Miss Keate on Thursday morng. He said He had run away with a Lady, & did not think proper to deny himself as He did not know who of her friends might call. went to Warwick lane & I brought a lame milkman in a Coach to vote.

Hustings I went upon and had a little dispute with a Mr. Robinson, an inspector for Fox, who has been remarkable for his violence. It was in consequence of his seizing a Mr. Lee, inspector for Sir Alan. Sir Alan spoke warmly to Robinson. My dispute with him was soon over. Bonney spoke afterwards of me to him. Bonney told me that He understands Sheldon proposes to move for his losing his situation of Clerk to the Pancrass, paving &c. and wished me to state if necessary, his behaviour at the Hustings, which I said I wd. do.

Much Company today on the Hustings with Fox, Tarleton, Erskine, Wm. Adam, &c. &c. Tierney was there. On the other side, Coll. Stanley, Mr. Smith, Ld. of Treasury Steele Junr., N & G. Dance, Sir Wm. Turton &c. David Hartley also there.

Fox spoke 13 minutes: very violently against administration: called on the people to meet notwithstanding the Law lately passed for regulating popular meetings &c. &c.

While Fox described that law, He so misrepresented it so much, that Sir Thomas Turton called out loudly "no, no, that is not the Law", This caused great confusion and I apprehended personal quarrels with him, "turn him out" was vociferated. at last it subsided. Sir Alan only said a few words, Tooke as few, Fox's violence having rendered it unnecessary.

After the speaking was over, Sir Thomas Turton was violently attacked by Thelwall, and many others, by words, Thelwall said He would expose his conduct.

In going to Richardsons Hotel, the Mob, as usual, hooted Sir Alan, and one fellow for insulting a Constable was taken into Custody. Richardsons I dined at. 35 at dinner.

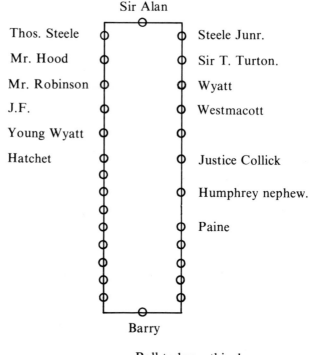

	Poll today	this day
Fox	4635	402
Gardner	4486	312
Tooke	2560	153

Jones, the Constable, came up for Sir Alan, between 7 & 8, to go with him to Portland Place, a precaution which has been judged necessary since attacks were made on his person.

Wyatt, Westmacott, & myself called at a few places to canvass for votes. At ½ past 9 I got home.

Sunday June 12th.

G. Dance I called on. He gave me some particulars of Mr. Carr of York, the Architect, who is 75 years of age.

 Richardsons Hotel, I went to & saw Mr. Richards, & the young Man his partner, Sir Alan's agents, & inspected the Books for names. Paine called on me at 5 & we went together to dinner at Sir Alan Gardners. Paine had seen Soane today who said He had not been applied to on acct. of the election. I shewed Paine Soanes answer to my application of May 31st.

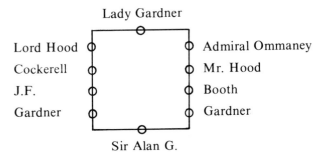

Booth told me that £98,000 was paid by one Candidate (the Ministerial) for the election in 1780. The expences for St. Martins Parish were £12000. £70 a day was charged for table expences. It has been proposed by the Committee that Sir Alan Gardner shall not be *chaired*. He said He leaves it to them to determine; & is willing to be chaired if they think proper.

 Lady Hood came in with another Lady. She is a little, lively woman.

 Mr. Hood told me Lord Hood is 71 years old. Owing to a bowel complaint he once lived 3 years on pudding only; & it was believed that his life was saved by sending him to the Meditteranean for the benefit of that Climate. He now eats heartily & generally, and drinks a pint or bottle. — Mr. Hood married a Miss Wheeler, daugr. of Counsellor Wheeler.

 It was the opinion of the company that Charles Fox is much altered in appearance; not so healthy in look. Came away at ½ past 10.

Monday June 13th.

Richardsons Hotel I went to this morning and met Paine and Wyatt. We inspected the books & sent after several persons. Wyatt wrote in the name of Sir A. Gardner to Jackson & Moser.

 The Hustings I went to. The mob greater than on any former day. The Duke of Norfolk presented himself in the front of the Hustings to Poll, claiming the right of a Citizen to Poll, though, as a Nobleman, not a right to interfere at an election. Mr. Manby, the Deputy Bailiff, conversed with the Duke, and finally refused His vote; a minute of the refusal was entered in the Poll Book. On my mentioning this to Sir Alan, who was in the *lower*

Hustings, He said Lord Pomfret had before offered to Poll *for him* & had been refused. It was said by Mr. Hall, Secretary of the Whig Club, that Lord King had voted; and that other noblemen had also voted in different places; but that in Westminster He believed such votes had not been admitted. It seems there is no law against it only a resolution of the House of Commons, and some of the Lords have refused to give up the privilege.

Fox came on the Hustings abt. one: but Tooke did not appear at all, though Bonney told me He expected him.

At 3 the Poll finally closed, when Fox advanced to the front of the Hustings; but Sir Alan remained behind. Mr. Hood went out to see if the Constables were prepared to secure Sir Alan a safe passage, and returned and reccomended to him to quit the place before the numbers were declared, when the confusion attending the pulling down the Hustings would commence. Sir Alan said He wished to receive a paper of the numbers on the Poll before He went away: but on the request being repeated by Mr. Hood, He descended from the Upper Hustings and advancing forward supported by friends, was powerfully surrounded by Constables at the door, & to His Coach, into which He & Mr. Hood went, and it proceeded escorted by the Constables and a great mob huzzaing,

I made the best of my way to Macclesfield St. where I took a Coach & drove to Portland Place where I arrived at ½ past 3, & found Lady Gardner; & gave her assurances that Sir Alan was coming home safe &c.

About 4 oClock Sir Alans Coach drove into Portland Place, with a vast concourse of people huzzaing; and preceded by abt. 16 or 20 Butchers in white Frocks ringing their Marabones & Cleavers. They formed a line before Sir Alans door, through which He passed with Mr. Hood, and coming upstairs adressed the multitude, thanking them for their services.

Mr. & Mrs. Cornwall Junr. came: the latter for a short time was much affected. Lord Hood came, and some others: after compliments paid, all, except the family, went away.

Offleys I went to to dinner. Susan & Mrs. Hamond, & Philips there. Charles & Outram were gone to Fox's dinner at the Shakespeare.

John Offley said a paper was delivered to Fox with the numbers of the Poll, which He had scarcely repeated to the multitude before He heard the Hustings was tearing in pieces by the Mob, on which He descended and was put into a Chair at the door, & carried abt. Covent Garden &c. The Hustings was completely pulled down in 15 Minutes.

Westall I called on in the evening.

The Poll at the final close was —   this day

Fox	5160	525
Gardner	4810	324
Tooke	2819	259

Majority, Fox over Gardner 350, Gardner over Tooke 1991.

June 14th.

Lord Hood on Sunday last said that in his opinion if Horne Tooke should live long enough to stand the Poll at 2 or 3 more elections He would succeed, as at each election He encreased his numbers and would continue to do so.

Shakespeare Gallery I went to. Boydell of Hawarden dined yesterday at the Shakespeare Tavern, Fox in the Chair. In the course of the evening a dispute happened between Counsellor Robinson, & Counsellor Danzey, during which a companion of Robinsons threw a glass at Danzey which struck him in the forehead & cut him very much. Great confusion ensued; at last Fox obtained a hearing and said, He lamented the effects of such a disturbance; it would give Mr. Pitt & his supporters cause to represent the meeting in a very unfavourable manner &c &c. Fox left the room soon after.

John Ireland was at the Gallery. He told me He was partly educated at Bolton in Lancashire, by his uncle, Mr. Holland, a dissenting Minister.

At the late Poll, the names underneath voted as follows.

Artists.	Fox.	Gardner.	Tooke.
Pocock		o	
Tresham	o	o	
Bogle		o	
Miles		o	
Hamilton	o	o	
J. Boydell	o	o	
Brettingham	o	o	
Northcote	o		o
Beechy	o	o	
Cooper		o	
Wm. Adam, Archt.	o	o	
Jean		o	
Shelley		o	
Lawrence	o	o	
Crunden	o	o	
Wm. Reeves	o	o	
Philips Surgeon	o	o	
Adamson		o	
Wyatt, frame maker		o	
Nicol		o	
Bulmer	o	o	
Lawrence Senr.	o	o	
Cooper, printer	o		
Drew		o	
Middleton colourman	o		o

John Barrett	○		○
Wm. Barrett		○	
Harraden	○		○
Dr. Monro	○	○	
Flaxman Senr.	○		○
Batty			○
Henderson		○	
Chappelow	○	○	
Angerstein		○	
Tierney	○		○
Daniel, Colourman	○	○	
Dr. Osborne		○	
Wilkinson, apoth,		○	
Cox, Coal Mercht.	○	○	
Thelwall	○		○
Este	○		○
Sheridan	○		○
Geo: Byng	○		
Sir G. Beaumont		○	
Sir John Leicester	○		
Honble. Edwd. Bouverie	○		
Lord Fred: Cavendish	○	○	
Lord Clermont	○	○	
Sir John Trevallyn		○	
Sir H Englefield	○		
Honble Col. Walpole	○	○	

Thelwall appears to me to be waspish, and ill tempered, and has a vulgar mind. Sir Alan Gardner yesterday while Thelwall stood before him, good humouredly adressed him, as he had occasionally done once or twice before, and observed that his countenance was not alarming & threatening to occasion apprehension. Thelwall sourly replied, "I am not so like a Tyger as you are". On the contrary Horne Tooke always preserved his good humour, in His repartees with Sir Alan.

Wednesday June 15th.

Hearne I breakfasted with. Paine called on me. He had just been with Sir A. Gardner to congratulate him on His election, and had told him He might always depend on *his* services.

Marchi called on me. Lord Inchiquin this morning desired him to carry his Bill of what is due to him to Mr. Metcalfe who will pay it.

C Offley called on me. He dined with Fox at the Shakespeare Tavern on Monday. The Duke of Norfolk spoke, & informed the Company of the event of the Herefordshire contest. He said Sir George Cornwall had lost the election & Mr. Biddulph was chosen: That the Gentlemen of the country from Personal motives had adhered to Sir George: but the *Yeomanry* had on acct. of the change in Sir Georges political principles, voted against him.

Thursday June 16th.

Marchi called this morning, & I made out his acct. to deliver to Mr. Metcalfe. He returned & said Mr. Metcalfe wished him to shew the account to Lord & Lady Inchiquin, as He could not, without their approbation, pay it.

Poggi called in the evening. He wishes to settle with Lord & Lady Inchiquin for the trouble He has had in preparing their drawings for sale, viz: an allowance for those which they have recd. back from Bond Street and pay for 7 weeks nightly attendance, in Leicester Fields, to regulate the remaining part of the drawings. He is not satisfied with the manner in which Lord & Lady I. have behaved to him. I told him that if his resolution is to have no future concern with the drawings & prints, He should immediately acquaint Lord & Lady I. with his determination or they would have ground of complaint against him when the next season approached for having allowed them to expect his assistance. This He admitted & desired me to give him my opinion of the charge He ought to make. This I declined as not being a competent judge. I thought He had best reckon up his time & calculate what it is worth, & having made his estimate consult Mrs. Poggi who knew the pains He had taken & the time He had spent. He agreed to all this, and said He would immediately do it.

Poggi told me that Buonaparte, the Commander of the French Armies in Italy, is a Corsican by birth, & of a Gentlemans family. General Paoli is godfather to him & told Poggi that He thinks Buonaparte is abt. 29 yrs. old. — When General Marbeuf was in Corsica He was supposed to have an intrigue with Buonapartes mother, and took an interest in the Children she had by her husband. Buonaparte was sent to France by Marbeuf, and received his education there. He is, in large companies, silent; but ardent in his temper and in circles where in which He is disposed to act, full of energy & free of communication. He is not at all tainted by the *modern philosophy;* and does not act on that principle, but merely as a soldier.

Marchant called. Beechy is going to Windsor to paint the Royal family, and is to have apartments in the Castle. — Marchant & Beechy are not satisfied with the portrait Lawrence has painted of me.

Friday [June 17th].

Sir Alan Gardner I called on this morning, to ask him if He would authorize me to say that Bonney had conducted himself well & with moderation on the Hustings, which He assented to.

Bonneys I went to at 12. A meeting of the Commissioners for paving, lighting & watching. Mr. Sheldon was not present, & no notice was taken of Mr. Bonneys conduct at the election.

Sir Alan Gardners dinner at Willis's rooms I went to. Tickets 7s. 6d. The room today was not so full as at the last dinner.

Mr. Penneck told me that Dr. Carmichael Smyth has interceded with Mr. & Mrs. Keate for conciliation, but, as yet, in vain. They declared that they should consider themselves as never having had a Child. She left their house at 10 o'Clock on Thursday morning last; and at 12 sent them a letter that she was married.

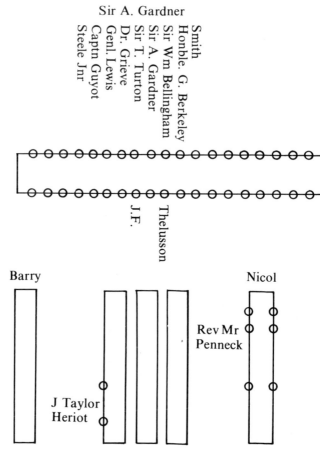

Dinner Table

Sir A. Gardner

Smith
Honble. G. Berkeley
Sir Wm Bellingham
Sir A. Gardner
Sir T. Turton
Dr. Grieve
Genl. Lewis
Captn Guyot
Steele Jnr

J.F. Thelusson

Barry

Nicol

Rev Mr Penneck

J Taylor Heriot

Col. Stanley & Jas. Stanley were in the room before dinner. The dinner was on the table at 6. Sir Thos. Turton spoke with great fluency. Sir Alan sang "Thursday in the morn", "Last Valentine's Day", and "God save the King" twice. A little after 10 Sir Thos. Turton took leave of Sir Alan, which caused me to speak to Sir Thos. across the Table, to request him not to leave Sir Alan. He took the hint; and I went round the table and whispered to Sir Thomas to make a flashy speech and bring Sir Alan off, which He did, after a bumper. The whole company broke up and the crowd went down stairs with Sir Alan who got into his Coach & I jumped in after him. He was pretty forward & I congratulated myself on having effected his departure so well.

Notice was given that the Committee for managing Sir Alan's Election had resolved to give *him* a dinner on Friday next. Booth afterwards told me that it is the first instance of such a compliment being paid. That the scheme is to make the Tickets half a guinea; and that 40 or 50 Gentlemen shall give a guinea each for his ticket, which will support the expence.

George Berkley & Smith went away after the health of Sir Thos. Turton was drank, probably from the former expecting a similar compliment.

Saturday June 18th.

Plott I called on early. He knew of the intended marriage of Henderson with Miss Keate. Mr. & Mrs. Keate have sent her cloaths &c. even including her Dolls, & childish playthings. I told him I thought this a good sign, as it was too silly to have been done but in passion, which would subside. Henderson has abt. £1600 a year, and offered when Keate admitted him to pay his addresses, to settle £500 a year on Miss Keate. Under the circumstances attending his marriage He has honorably done the same. Keate talked of giving Miss Keate £5000 down.

Sir Alan Gardner I went to at breakfast and found only him and Lady Gardner.

Yesterday, at Court, the King spoke to him a second time which is not usual. Sir Alan was standing near the Princesses, when the King coming up said to them "Sir Alan & I know what few have experienced, what it is to be pelted in a Coach".

Lady Hugh Seymour told Lady Gardner that the Princess of Wales is to have a new establishment of her own choosing, but the Prince has insisted that Lady Jersey & Mrs. Pelham shall be admitted to visit her, this the Princess has refused.

The utmost income recd. by a First Lord of the Admiralty, Sir Alan said, does not exceed £3000 a year. A Lord of the Admiralty only received clear £750 a year, and has an allowance of £90 a year for Coals &c.

Lady Hyde Parker, who has been indiscreet with Major Bailey during the absence of Sir Hyde in the West Indies, is upwards of 40 years of age, very plain, & has a harelip. She has 3 Children. Her maiden name was Botteler.

Lady Rancliff, whose indiscretion is become public has 7 or 8 Children. She was Miss James, daughter to the late Sir Wm. James.

Sir Alan told me the situation of a Commander of a Fleet on the Leward Islands Station is very teazing, as whichever of the Islands He makes his occasional Station the others press him with their anxieties to induce him to be with each of them.

Marchi called on me. He has settled with Lady Inchiquin. She had deducted £40 of the £52:10 He had charged for washing: but as she had given him £40 recd. from Greenwood on acct. of what He had done at the sale, it makes up an equivalent. He receives £532.

Sir George Beaumont called & I went with him to Grosvenor Square. The two pictures by Smirke we think look better than they did in the Exhibition: the fault is that the shadows are too brown.

Plott dined with me.

Sunday June 19th.

Du Cort called on me today and staid two hours. He was originally intended to profess as a lawer, and was placed for education in the University of Louvain. He was 30 years old before He seriously devoted himself to study painting as a profession. I shewed him my two small pictures by Wilson, which He admired very much; and the pictures by Smirke.

Sir Alexander Hamilton called on me, he leaves Town tomorrow.

Offleys I dined at. Mrs. Offley, Mrs. Hamond, John & William at home. William is recovering but looks ill.

Monday June 20th.

Richardson, the Architect, called on me to desire I would recommend his continuation of Vitruvius Brittanicus, to the Royal Academy, and his designs for Villas lately published. He has spoken to Yenn who did not seem inclined to propose them to the Academy. I told him I would speak to Dance on the subject.

Flaxman called on me, to enquire if Mr. Long had obtained permission for British artists to import their collections of studies duty free, I told him I supposed the business had been suspended owing to Mr. Longs engagements in what relates to the new Parliament.

Marchi I went with to Lord Walpoles to shew him the pictures He is to touch upon. Also to Lord Orfords to shew him the pictures to be cleaned.

Lord Orford I found seated on his sofa bed as before. He has been at Strawberry Hill, but was not so well while absent from his surgeon, therefore returned to town. He was in good spirits. Thomas Walpole Junr. (the Envoy) came in. Lord Abercorn was mentioned. It is said He considers himself as the lawful Duke of Hamilton, being the eldest *Heir Male* of that family. On the Coffin of His Uncle, the late Earl He is said to have entitled Him Duke of Hamilton. T Walpole said his salary is 6 quarters in arrear.

Miss Agnes Berry came in, & T Walpole went away; after she left us Lord Orford continued a long conversation. He said Lord & Lady Cholmendely had been a week at Houghton, and are delighted with the place, and are to pass two months there in the Autumn. Lord Orford has told Lord Cholmendely that while He lives He will keep the house in as good repair as He found it in, and that any alterations or additions which Lord Cholmendely may be disposed to make, He is welcome to begin them as soon as He pleased, — I may drag on said Ld. Orford a year or two longer, but that time I would not have an interruption to any schemes your Lordship may have formed.

I asked Lord Orford if there is no longer a probability of Col. Walpole further contesting the reversion of Houghton, He said No, for in two days the allowed time for objections will expire, after which the Chancellor will finally confirm the decision. Coll. Walpole did intend it, but has not proceeded to act. — Lord O. again spoke with great dislike of his Uncle Horace, whose meanness and selfishness were uncommon. When He was created a Peer, He said He wd. not take the same motto as His Brother, Lord Orford, had done, as his nephew Horace (the present Lord) would translate it for him ironically. That I will do whatever motto He may choose. He adopted [Sibi constat] — said Horace. Equally mean was Lady Walpole the wife. Some Members of the House of Commons, walking past her House adjoining the Treasury, Whitehall, smoke happened to issue from a window. What, does that dirty B— Horaces wife, ever wash Her Linnen said one, "No," said Old Earle, a member patronized by Sir Robt. Walpole, "but she takes in the linnen of others".

Sir Robert Walpole gave Her a Horse for Her son to learn to ride upon. She turned it into Richmond Park and there it run some years unused, and Sir Robert being Ranger she did not pay anything. A Horse being required for Sir Roberts grandson, the late Lord, He bid them take this horse, on which she sent a demand to him of 5 guineas for the Horse, which Sir Robert willingly paid for such a proof of her disposition.

Lord Clermont is a foolish fellow, but knows his own interest. He advised the late Lord Orford to pull down the steps at the front of Houghton, and then begged the stones to make use of at a House of his own.

The Duchess of Gloucester came in. She looked better than I expected to have seen her.

Humphry called on me in the evening. He thinks we should not fill more than one Associate vacancy this year. Flaxman having only exhibited a sketch can hardly be elected on the credit of so unfinished a performance. De Cort has not put his name down before. Daniel He particularly wishes shd. succeed. Wyatt is strongly interested for Bonomi, if an Architect be elected. Hodges expects soon to be Head partner in the Banking firm, He proposes to exhibit next year.

Tuesday June 21st.

Sir Alan Gardner called on me. He was yesterday in Hendon Church, with Young Mr. Cornwall, and found a monument of the memory of —

Gardner, Citizen & Joiner, a merchant of London, whose arms His Father, Coll. Gardner had adopted, & amongst his papers He mentioned his descent from Him.

Humphry called to tea. He is apprehensive that Daniels interest in the Academy will not be strong enough to secure his election if there are not many vacancies. He does not think Daniels pictures made much impression in the Exhibition.

Marchant called.

Wednesday June 22nd.

Lysons called this morning. He dined the other day with the Margrave of Anspach. The Margrave sat at the bottom of the table as usual with English gentlemen. He does not speak English well, and preferred to speak in French.

The Margravine told Lysons that she is sitting to Romney who told Her she is a better subject for a picture than when He before painted Her; for that what she has lost by being older, is amply made up in the additional strength of expression in Her countenance.

The Margravine never sees any of the Children she had by Lord Craven. She says she should like to see the second Son, as she hears he is a Young man of good disposition and abilities. Her Brother, Lord Berkley has refused to permit her to see these Children, nor has his Lordship held any intercourse with her, which formerly she regretted; but now says she is perfectly indifferent about.

Marchi called in the evening. The Duchess of Rutland has reccomended him to the Duke of Beaufort, to clean & restore the pictures by Sir Joshua Reynolds at Belvoir Castle. Marchi is desired to mention his terms, & I proposed to him to ask 6 guineas a week, and his travelling expences, and that He shall be maintained at Belvoir Castle, while employed.

Thursday June 23rd.

Marchi called. Tassaert has recommended to him to ask a guinea a day & his expences borne.

Friday June 24th.

Westall called this morning to desire me to look at a second picture of the "Storm in Harvest" which He has painted in Oil. Young Mr. Whitbread has, through Garrard, desired to have the refusal of it. Garrard says Mr. Whitbread says he proposes to make a collection of the works of English Artists. His father lately dead is said to have left him a million of property.

Fuseli called on me last night and sat till 12 o'Clock. He mentioned Blake, the Engraver, whose genius and invention have been much spoken of. Fuseli has known him a great many years, and thinks He has a great deal of invention, but that "Fancy is the end, and not a means in his designs". He does not employ it to give novelty and decoration to regular conceptions; but the whole of his aim is to produce singular shapes and odd combinations.

He is abt. 38 or 40 years of age, and married a maid servant, who has imbibed something of his singularity. — They live together witht. a servant at a very small expence.

Blake has undertaken to make designs to encircle the letterpress of each page of "Youngs night thoughts". Edwards, the Bookseller of Bond Street employs him, and has had the letter press of each page laid down on a large half sheet of paper. There are abt. 900 pages. Blake asked 100 guineas for the whole. Edwards said He could not afford to give more than 20 guineas for which Blake agreed. — Fuseli understands that Edwards proposes to select abt. 200 from the whole and to have that number engraved as decorations for a new edition.

Fuseli says Blake has something of madness abt. him. He acknowledges the superiority of Fuseli but thinks himself more able than Stothard.

Sir George Beaumont & Coombes called on me.

Coombes saw Lord & Lady Jersey, and Edward Jerningham with them, at Uxbridge lately, where they had been five or Six days. From what He cd. learn she seemed perfectly easy.

The behaviour of the Prince and Lady Jersey towards the Princess is spoken of as having been most scandalous. They sometimes mixed brandy with her wine intending to affect her, and then would laugh on the Stein (the walk) at the Princess being drunk. It is apprehended that the Queen during the intercourse she had with Lady Jersey has communicated so far with her as to be afraid of what she may divulge, which prevents Her breaking with Her. The King is steady to the Princess, such were the reports of the day.

Sir Alan Gardner sent me a Ticket to dine at Willis' rooms today at a dinner given to him & Lord Hood — but I was prevented by a Lumbago complaint which has troubled me for a week past.

Saturday June 25th.

Mrs. Thelwall Salisbury & Mrs. Hamond called this morning.

Sir Alan Gardners I went to with Susan, and introduced her to Lady Gardner. — Yesterday passed with great festivity at Willis's room. Sir Thos. Turton in the Chair. Sir Alan staid till one oClock.

While Lord Chatham presided at the Admiralty there was great complaint against him for not answering letters. Sir Alan said a principal cause of this neglect was his Lordships dislike to say "No", to those who applied. Lord Spencer on the contrary answers everybody, and in this is assisted by a Mr. Harrison, an Alderman of St. Albans, who has a situation at the Admiralty & makes his hand writing very similar to that of Lord Spencer, who has only to assent or dissent to the request and when the letter is written to sign it. Lord Spencer carries himself in his official capacity with great hauteur. When Sir Alan, or others of similar rank, attend his Lordship He never asks them to sit down. Lord Chatham was much more condescending.

It is now generally understood that the new Parliament is not to meet till November. One motive for postponing the meeting is supposed to be, that the Alien and other Bills must be renewed when the new parliament assembles, so that Pitt would have to combat all the difficulties which could be thrown in his way by Opposition, at this season. — Mr. Hood is the only Child of Lord Hood, and has four Children, 2 boys & 2 girls. The eldest Son will be a Viscount from his grandfather, the second Son a *Baron* from His great uncle, Lord Bridport, who having no Children the title is made to descend in this manner.

Sir George Beaumont sent me the little picture of a Church which He has given me. He called this afternoon. West has given him a painted Sketch which He has just finished of "Cicero discovering the tomb of Archimedes".

Sunday June 26th.

Plott called. Keate is very ill disposed towards Henderson. Henderson has £1600 a year.

Sir George Beaumonts I dined at. West has seen a picture in Labordes (the Orleans) collection, painted by S Piombo from a design of Michl. Angelo, which is exquisitely coloured; and it is in Wests opinion the finest picture in the world. It is thought Laborde will reserve the collection in order to make his peace in France when matters are settled.

Monday June 27th.

Mrs. Playfair called on me to reccomend Mrs. Barrett as a very necessitous person. She stated to me that Mrs. Barrett had recd. £300 from a Sister respectably situated in Ireland to enable her to set up in business as a Milliner, which she did in Bryanston Street, but did not succeed. She has 9 children living. One Son, George teaches drawing, but has bad health and is married and has a family. Two other Sons are House painters, one a Journey man, the other just set up in business; both imprudently married. One daughter is Housekeeper to Lady Lucan; two others support themselves by needlework. Mrs. Barrett is now lodging in a single room, and in absolute want of necessaries. Joe Barrett, Brother to the late George, injured his circumstances by his protection of his Brothers family.

Mrs. Wheatley called on me. She stated that Dr. Pitcairne has given it as his opinion that the only chance of restoration of health or use of limbs will be from the use of the Bath waters, I told her I had been informed of this by Mrs. Farington, and in consequence had called on Dance & Tyler to engage them to support a proposal that Wheatley should be assisted with a

Sum of money by the Academy. I recommended to her to draw up a representation of his case for the Council to be presented at the next meeting. She told me she had mentioned the Academy to Wheatley, but He thought no one could be assisted but the relatives of deceased members, and in consequence He proposed to receive subscriptions of 5 guineas each from 20 persons, and in the course of a year to paint pictures of 100 guineas value to be raffled for by the subscriber. Eliza and Will arrived this evening from the Isle of Wight. Dick sailed this morning at Eleven with a Convoy. Captn. Colpoys, Commodore.

Humphry & Marchant called.

Tuesday June 28th.

Marchi, I called on to see the pictures He has cleaned for Lord Walpole & Lord Orford & Mr. Walpole.

Shakespeare Gallery I went to. Steevens & G. Nicol there; we talked abt. Miss Keates marriage & I told them how well Henderson, as I Had been informed, had behaved. Nicol said Hendersons Father kept a pamphlet shop under the Royal Exchange.

J. Boydell told me His Uncle said but few of the Subscribers to the Rivers put their names down to go on. J. Boydell thinks it will be prudent to *suspend* the preparations for a continuation of the work this year. I told him I should be advised by him.

Prince of Wales, reconciliation is said to have taken place yesterday. — Will came to dinner. Dick told him on Sunday that he felt an uncommon and unaccountable depression of spirits, and that it seemed almost as if it were ominous. To Liddel He said the same. I remarked upon it that the constant apprehension of Elizas uneasiness had preyed upon his spirits, and at last made the parting so impressive.

Wednesday June 29th.

Plott I called on this morning to assure myself that Henderson had, previous to his marriage, settled upon Miss Keate £500 a year.

Nicol I met at the Shakespeare Gallery and repeated to him the above, as a proof of Hendersons disposition.

Mr. & Mrs. Henderson Susan & I called upon: they were not at home. Mrs. Roberts called on me to desire Me to write in her favor to Mrs. Rawstorne to intercede with Miss Atherton. Mrs. Rawstorne has not answered Mrs. Roberts letter & I told her I could not determine to write to Mrs. Rawstorne. Her Husband is dead. I told Her I wd. write to Her nephew John Bissell.

Tyler I met in the eving. He has been at Derby with G Dance & Soane; but did not go to Chester to see a relation a boy of 5 years old, who after the death of his sister He has, excepting a few legacies made his Heir. The mother is daugtr. to a Clergyman. Tyler will support Wheatleys application.

Marchant called in the evening.

Thursday June 30th.

Wheatly I called on this morning. He will set off for Bath as soon as the Academy has paid him the £100 we propose to move for. Dr. Pitcairne recommends to him to take a House within a mile or two of Bath & make that his residence.

Malone I called on. Lord Inchiquin is not in the new Parliament. Douglas, a Clergyman & some others are supposed to have a concern in fabricating the "Ireland manuscripts".

Sir George Beaumont called on me. He was yesterday at Hampton Court, with West, to see the pictures.

Plott dined with me. J. Offley called in the evening. Tookes meeting at the Crown & Anchor on Tuesday last was most tumultuous. A third of the company sat at dinner with their hats on. Bosville was in the Chair and had such a defect in his utterance as to be scarcely understood. George Smith was a Steward.

JULY 1796

Friday July 1st.

Susan & Eliza left London this morning at ½ past 7, and by way of Uxbridge went to Oxford to dinner on their way to Lancashire.

Steers I went to at breakfast in his new rooms. De Cort is gone to Lord Howards to make drawings for two pictures views of Audley end.

Lysons called on me. Lord Orford is gone to Strawberry Hill. He is much mortified that Col. Walpole [is] going on for a new trial with Lord Cholmondely for the Houghton Hall & Estate.

Offleys I dined at. Thelwall Salisbury, & the Revd. Mr. Royle, there. Mrs. Offley, Mrs. Hamond, Mrs. Salisbury, John & William, and an Irish young man.

Flaxman called on me this afternoon, and brought with him Mr. Sandys, an Architect; a young man who left Rome the beginning of April, and is now employed, as He says in building a Palace at Ickworth for Lord Bristol. I promised to go to the Custom House to pass his drawings etc. when they arrive.

Saturday July 2nd.

Lawrence I breakfasted with. Bone there. I shewed Lawrence Wheatlys petition, the subject of which He told me had been mentioned to him by Hamilton at Mrs. Wheatlys request. He will attend the Council on Saturday next to support it. — Smirke called in the eving. His two Sons have presented Edward a drawing of a figure, & Robert a design in Architecture, for the inspection of the next Council in order to be admitted Students.

Mackenzie called to desire me to lend him the model by Mount Stephen, of my Head, as He cannot procure a sufficient number of models of the heads of deceased Academicians to keep him employed.

Humphry called in the evening.

Sunday July 3rd.

Marchi called this morning. He has cleaned and *glazed* the picture of Lady Sarah Bunbury, Lady Susan Strangways, & Chas. Fox, painted by Sir J. Reynolds and now at Holland House. It had become almost white.

Byrne called on me. He has a good deal of intercourse with French Emigrants & with Swiss residents here. The national characteristick of the French, vanity & insolence, has nothing abated by the distresses which have happened. Driven from their country the French here are elated at the victories of their countrymen & depressed at their defeats. When their spirits are raised in Company they will sing the popular songs of the Armies &c. and in this the Swiss readily join them, most of them being determined Democrats.

Lady Gardner called on Susan.

Offleys I dined at. Mrs. Offley, Mrs. Hamond, Mr. & Mrs. T. Salusbury, John & William Offley and Mr. Crosbie Junr. of Liverpool there.

Mr. Crosbie related several particulars of what passed at Brest, Quimper &c. when He was there prisoner. He repeated what his father, some months [ago], at Offleys had told me.

Lady Ann Fitzroy and Her Brother, the Honble. Mr. Wesley, were confined in the same prison. Lady Ann was very good to the prisoners, both by giving them money &c. and by making Shirts &c. for them. She kept up her spirits wonderfully, and preserved Her spirits so as to raise those of others.

At Quimper, for about 3 weeks, many of the English prisoners were in the town on their parole, during which time, the French Officers gave Balls to them, at which the French woemen treated the English with great civility, and would always dance with them in preference.

I asked him what He thought of the sentiments of the French people as to their political situation. He said they were tired of the war and disliked the Convention, yet did not seem at all inclined to monarchy. — After the Victory which the English fleet obtained on the 1st. June 1794, He said the French published a quite contrary account, making themselves victorious. The Commissary of the prison at Quimper said 7 English Ships had been taken, on board of one of which He had been. At Paris there were illuminations — At Lyons He staid two days. The streets were solitary and the people melancholy and desponding.

Marseilles He described as at that time abounding with poeple. The streets inconveniently crowded and the great majority firm democrats.

Monday July 4th.

G Dance I called on to mention Wheatlys situation. He complained to me that He has lately been much troubled with a depression of spirits, which He thought his excursion to Derby would have removed, but He still continues the same as before He went. I told him how much I had suffered formerly from the same cause and reccomended to him amusements and association with friends.

Garvey came in to solicit a letter of introduction to the Lord Lieutenant (Lord Camden). He is going to Ireland for three months.

Stadler drank tea with me.

Tuesday July 5th.

Tyler called on me. I asked Him if West had shewn him the paper He (Tyler) had drawn up on the subject of the Charity Fund proposed by me at the Council to the King. He said West called on him some days since & stated that He had shewn the paper to the King & that His Majesty greatly approved of the proposed plan.

Tyler said that Richards had informed him that Burch, from what He hears, is not in bad circumstances. Dance has also been told the same.

Tyler thinks that Gilpin ought to be the Academician in the room of Sir Wm. Chambers.

The Prince has of late been very attentive to the Queen at Windsor, & has gone to Church with her.

Stadler drank tea with me, and brought some plates with grounds laid for etching.

Wednesday July 6th.

J Boydell & Bulmer called on me this morning and met Stadler. Boydell came to shew me some impressions from Plates of the Rivers taken off in brown by his direction. Wyatt he says can touch up such as are too faint. He has directed 25 sets to be taken off.

Dance I called on. He was going with the City members to wait on Mr. Pitt on the business of proposed Docks on the River. He thinks the *City* will eventually have the preference over the merchants to conduct the improvements.

Lysons, T. Taylor & Dance dined with me.

Jerningham has heard that Coombes has ridiculed him frequently in various places at a time when they were very much acquainted with each other. In consequence Jerningham wrote to Coombes acknowledging that the latter had praised his works far above their merit, but that as he had balanced this commendation by much personal ridicule, the account between He thought might be fairly considered as even. Coombes made no reply.

Taylor met S. Ireland the other day, who mentioning his Son frequently, always called him Sam, though his name is given out in the publication to be William Henry. Ireland said Sam had left his House without notice, & had imposed upon him throughout the whole of the Shakesperian manuscript business.

Glynn Wynn, Son of Col. Wynn and nephew to Lord Newborough, married a sister of Marchioness of Abercorn. His Brother the Revd. Dr. Wynne has closely attended Weston, the young Irishman convicted of forgery. Mr. Kirby, the Keeper of Newgate, told Dance that Dr. Wynne had requested to have a bed for himself placed in Westons room. The singularities of Dr. Wynnes character renders this remarkable, Sheriff Liptrap conversed with the Dr. as Taylor is informed and put some *home* questions to him, & refused the request. Another brother of Glynn Wynnes is now Chamberlain to the Margrave of Anspach. — Weston was executed this day. — A Gentleman, A particular friend of Lady Jersey, and who sees Her almost every day, Taylor dined with lately. He endeavoured to excuse Lady Jersey for Her attachment to the Prince, as it is certainly very flattering, at Her time of life, to be preferred to all the Youth and Beauty of the time: But while He thus apologised for Her Ladyship, He spoke of the Princess with respect as a blameless character.

Paine called on me today. Marnel the attorney of Salisbury St. has written to him to press an application to Sir Alan Gardner to obtain for Marnels nephew, a Cadets situation at Woolwich. Marnel says He obtained 23 votes for Sir Alan. Paine desired me to shew Marnels letter to Sir Alan.

Thursday July 7th.

Wheatly I called on this morning. He is much emaciated, and unable to attend as Visitor at the Academy this evening. I called on Fuseli to desire him to officiate which He said He wd. do during the remainder of the week but no longer. I then called on Rigaud who said He would take Wheatlys month, & should Wheatly recover would give up his month (the next) to Wheatly. Informed Fuseli that Rigaud wd. commence *this evening*, & take the whole time.

Willis called on me. He has dined twice in company with Sir F. Bourgeois, at Yenns & another place, and is much pleased with him, and proposes to offer to introduce him as a Member of the Trent Club. West dined at Yenns, and was a little too prosing. Willis remarked that the conversation of West is too much like delivering lectures.

Willis called on G. Smith to assure him there was nothing personal to him in Willis withdrawing his name from the Trent Club after the Toast given by Smith, but His situation under the King rendered it necessary for him to avoid any appearance of sanctioning opinions which seemed to have a democratic tendency. Smith recd. Willis very ungraciously; kept him waiting nearly half an hour, and behaved with much hauteur.

Friday July 8th.

Offleys I dined at. Mrs. Hamond, Mrs. Offley, Mrs. T. Salisbury, John, Charles, Outram & a Mr. Briggs from Dalkeith, who was at Cadiz the end of May last. He said Richerys squadron had then been blocked up by Admiral Mans squadron 9 months, though Richerys fleet is rather larger than Mans. The French Officers He said were a set of the most shabby contemptible looking fellows He ever saw. The Poeple of Cadiz shew them no respect and on many occasions insult them by bidding them go out and meet the enemy. Richery has made his situation more despicable, as previous to the arrival of Admiral Mans squadron, He had gasconaded much of what He would do with the British fleet. The Fleet of Admiral Man manouveres in sight of the Town, and frigates sometimes run close in with the Harbour; but the Officers and Men never land: The Fleet is daily served with provisions & necessary from the shore.

Cadiz is a most beautiful town but not of large extent. Mr. Briggs could walk round the Walls in 40 minutes: Yet He says it contains 100,000 inhabitants. He says the poeple are very well affected towards the English; but the *Prince of Peace* and the Court are supposed to be inclined to French, yet He does not believe there will be a war with England. He says the Inquisition is now little more than a *name*; and that the poeple detest the Friars.

Humphry called on me in the evening to remind me of Morlands application for Charity. He had been with Stubbs who is preparing a work of comparative Anatomy. At 72 Stubbs is forming Plans with as much resolution as might be expected at 40.

Saturday July 9th.

Wheatly I called on this morning, & recd. from Mrs. Wheatly his petition to the Academy. She said He was very low last night at the thought of applying for money. The small upright drawings He has made for Dr. Monro He had for each only 5 guineas; for the large ones from Dr. Pitcairne & Mr. Chamberlain 30 guineas each. A large drawing employs him a fortnight.

Fuseli I called on. He shewed me some of his pictures from Milton. One of them "Eve bringing the Apple to Adam" He said He was not satisfied with; I told him it is much inferior in conception and execution to his other designs; that there is a littleness about it. He determined at once to give it up.

To do anything considerable in painting He said it must be followed up by unremitting practise. He feels himself at times without common powers; and said that he always feels in some degree timid on given subjects which He is employed to paint. His best exertions are when He has only to consider how He shall satisfy himself.

Through Mr. Roscow of Liverpool, He has been lately employed by Mr. Wilson, who suceeds the late Mr. Rogers in the concern with Macklin, to paint a picture from the Apocalypse for their Edition of the Bible. It is a little larger than a half length upright and contains two figures. He is to have 80 guineas for it. Mr. Rogers died worth £30,000.

He alluded a little to his own circumstances, as having no profitable employ. I mentioned to him the proposed Fund for the support of distressed Academicians & their relations.

Flaxman expected that the Academy would have taken up his letter published in the morning Chronicle on decorating Churches with works of Art, and have addressed the King on the subject.

Burch called on me. I told him that his holding an Office in the Academy of profit (Librarian) & being capable of holding other offices, rendered his application in the opinion of many improper. Also that a supposition existed of his circumstances not being unfavourable. He said that He had advanced £900 in a concern from which He had withdrawn himself; and that He recd. £45. a year on acct. of the money He had advanced. That He had lost £400 by [Jefferys] the Prince of Wales's Jeweller, having only recd. from the effects 6d. in the pound. That He had also lost £100 in Barbadoes. He has lately had two commissions of 10 guineas each, one for Lady Mansfield, a seal of a favourite Cow; the other a Head of Shakespeare. He has two Sons, both were brought up to his profession: but the eldest turned Miniature Painter; the Younger continues in the line of his Father. He said in His present situation He shd. be glad of the money by way of Loan on interest if the Academy could not *give* him the £100.

Westall called on me. Mr. Knight of Whitehall has purchased his *picture* in oil of the "Storm in Harvest" for 100 guineas, and says He likes it better than the drawing.

The Academy Council I went to. Tyler & Dance audited Yenns accounts up to Midsummer. The Council then sat.

Mr. West.

Dance, Tyler, Farington, Hoppner, Stothard, Lawrence, Bacon.

Yenn laid his accts. before the Council, but as the manner in which they were made out is not agreeable to the order proposed, they were not passed, but are to be produced at the next Council. The distribution of the Charity was next considered.

Wheatleys letter was read. On which I moved "that 100 guineas be given to him to enable him to take the benefit of the Bath waters". This was voted unanimously by those present, viz: all the above named except Bacon who came in just after the Vote had passed, and *seemed* much disatisfied with it. He refused to read Wheatlys letter; and by many expressions and hints, marked his discontent.

P. Sandby applied for Mrs. Serres. Serres had placed abt. £600 in the funds which before his death He was obliged to sell out & part of it was expended in his last illness and to pay for his funeral. — Part afterwards went to relieve Jack Serres, and now nothing is left. The 4 daughters propose to keep a school, and each to take a department in teaching. Mrs. Barrett applied in great distress. She proposes keeping a day school. — Francis Barrett, the eldest daugr. of Geo. Barrett, has endeavoured to maintain Herself by needle work but the prices are so lowered in consequence of French emigrant woemen working at a very cheap rate that a maintenance can scarcely be obtained. She is in debt for lodgings &c. near 5 guineas, but if relieved does not mean to apply again.

Gilpin, through Hoppner, recommended [T.] Gooch, who has by a paralytic disorder scarcely had the use of his right hand.

Elizabeth Lowe, widow of M. Lowe, has two Children; She is now servant to Paul Sandby who permits one of the Children to be in his house.

John Wilson I recommended. It is judged prudent that I shd. receive the money given to him & apply it as may seem most for his advantage.

Charles Gill, formerly pupil to Sir Joshua Reynolds, reccomended by Northcote. He is married, has two Children and is extremely poor.

Sums granted.	£		£
Francis Barrett	21. 0.0.	Mary Vispre	4. 4.0.
Eliz: Baker	10.10.0.	Leand: Beastall	4. 4.0.
Henry Morland	10.10.0.	Hanah Eichall	3. 3.0.
John Cozens	10.10.0.	Chrit: Kitchingman	3. 3.0.
Ann Carver	10.10.0.	John Wilson	6. 6.0.
Eliz: Lowe	8. 8.0.	Thornethwaite	10.10.0.
Ann. Fournier	6. 6.0.	Mrs. Serres.	26. 5.0.
Pris: Todderick	6. 6.0.	Charles Gill	10.10.0.
Mary Tomkins	6. 6.0.	Francis Barrett, Junr.	10.10.0.
Ann Seest	4. 4.0.	[T.] Gooch.	10.10.0.
M:A: Picot	6. 6.0.	Alefounder	5. 5.0.
Fra: Seeman	4. 4.0.		
Eliz: Roberts.	5. 5.0.		£208.19.0.
Jane Smith	4. 4.0.	Wheatley	105. 0.0.
Brought over	£114. 9.		£313.19.0.

Added afterwards E. Roper   3. 3.0.

In 1774.

	£	s	d
Mrs. Ravenet	21	----	
Mrs. Finllayson	21	----	
— Crone	21	----	

1791.

Sir G. Chalmers	21 ----

1793.

Mrs. Rigg	21 ----
Mrs. Barrett	21 ----

In 1774   £181-13-0 was given.

Thornthwaite, the Engraver, was reccomended by Mr. Cruikshanks, Surgeon, to Fuseli, & by *him* to me. He is married, has two Children, and by a paralytic stroke, from which He is recovering, has been unable to provide for himself & family.

Burchs application was next considered. Bacon spoke for him; & I stated the conversation I had had with him this morning; I represented the difficulty He said He shd. be under if disappointed of the money, which He even requested on loan. Mr. West remarked on the danger of setting a precedent of *lending* money to Members of the Society, & after much conversation, West related the circumstances of Burchs being appointed Librarian, and made it fully understood that granting the £100 would not have the Kings approbation: On *this hint* Bacon said He shd. press the matter no further.

A vote was passed that Mrs. Hadriel, the Housekeeper, should have her salary encreased from £42 a year to £50 which passed unanimously.

	s d.
Exhibition receipts this year were	£3141-15-0.

which is more by £72 than the receipts of the year 1780.

General state of the finances.

	£ s d.
Rects. of Exhibition	3141-15-0.
Expenditure of 1796 to Midsummer	1099-18-6.
	2041-16-6.

Balance in hand of Banker including £162-8-4. recd. from Executors of Sir Wm. Chambers.	s d £2117-1-3½.

	£ s d.
Consolidated Fund reduced 3 per cents	9800.
Charity do.	4000.
	£13800.

Printers Bill	474. 2.9.
Advertisements	65 - -
Dinner	164-18-6.
Singers	10-10-0.

Yenn has applied to Wilton for a room to make into an Office for him as Treasurer; but finding some difficulty, has desired the Council will make it their act.

The Council did not break up till near one o'Clock.

Sunday July 10th.

Yenn I called on at the Mews, and had a conversation with Him about the room He requires for an Office and about accomodating the Housekeeper. We agreed that Tyler & myself, with West, should go to the Academy & inspect the rooms & make our report.

I strongly stated to Yenn the necessity for giving Wheatley the assistance He requires even from a motive of oeconomy. If the Bath waters cause a recovery of his health, the Academy will be at no further expence: On the contrary, shd. He become a Cripple, the Academy must allow him an Annuity for He must not be left to starve.

Wheatley I called on & told him what passed last night, & that I hoped that He might be enabled to leave London on Saturday next.

Tyler I called on, & represented to him that it seemed to me prudent that some members of the Academy should sign a voucher of the reality of Wheatleys distressed situation; which voucher should be presented to his majesty along with the petition. This will convince his Majesty that we do not witht. due consideration give away so large a Sum as 100 guineas. Tyler agreed with me, & fixed to accompany me to Wests tomorrow morning, to state to him our opinion.

Baker called on me. He says Edridge is fully employed by poeple of fashion, to make black lead pencil drawings. For whole lengths 8 gs. half lengths 5 gs.

Paines I went to, to dinner.

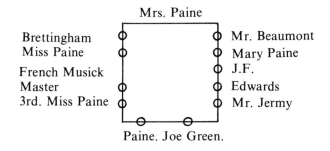

Mrs. Paine

Brettingham			Mr. Beaumont
Miss Paine			Mary Paine
French Musick			J.F.
Master			Edwards
3rd. Miss Paine			Mr. Jermy

Paine. Joe Green.

Mr. Beaumont told me that Wilberforce lost much popularity by his motion for Peace, and had He not made a popular speech at York, in December last, His election wd. have been uncertain. — He said that Mr.

Fawkes holds Republican principles. — The Lascelles family are quite Aristocrats.

The late Sir John Kay did not leave his fortune to His Brother, now Sir Richard, but to natural Children, who bear his name. The title will be extinct.

Yenn shewed me today a printed inscription for a monument to the memory of Sir William Chambers in which the bad & corrupt taste of Soane in his works at the Bank were strongly described. Yenn said that to G Dance is imputed this whimsical deviation of Soane from the examples of good taste. Dance in the Library at Shelburne House, & at Guildhall, has set Soane his example. Newgate is allowed to be a specimen of propriety in Architecture; Yenn in this is repeating the opinions of others.

Monday July 11th.

Edwards called on me this morning & mentioned that He & Paul Sandby had conversed abt. T. Sandbys not being able to deliver his Lectures in the Royal Academy, & P Sandby proposed that Edwards should read them for him, which Edwards said He should be willing to do provided He might be allowed to make alterations where He thought fit.

Lysons came in & prevented further conversation.

Tyler called on me & we went together to West who concurred with us in thinking it would be proper to sign a *voucher* for the fidelity of Wheatleys situation, that His Majesty might be convinced we did not give away the Academy money, but on well considered, and necessary occasions. West proposed that it should be done by letter addressed to him & signed by Dance, Tyler & myself, which we agreed to.

I then mentioned the further establishing a Charity fund. West said the King is well convinced of the propriety of doing it, & West expressed a hope that we may accomplish it before the King goes to Weymouth.

West was painting a small picture on a dark, mouse coloured, prepared ground, which He finished as He goes on.

The Tears came twice into Wests eyes while He was speaking of the proposed Charity fund.

Mr. More, Secretary to the Society for the Encouragement of Arts &c." came in. West is painting his portrait. Tyler told me afterwards that More was formerly an Apothecary and has now £150 a year, & a House &c. as Secretary.

I observed to West & Tyler how necessary it now is that we should be very cautious who we admit as Members of the Royal Academy, as inferior Artists wd. most probably become burdens of expence to it. We agreed to go to the Academy tomorrow eving. to inspect the rooms below stairs.

Tyler went with me to the Academy where we communicated to Mrs. Hadriel, that Her salary is raised from £42 to £50 a year.

Sir George Beaumont called on me. He is going out of town on Wednesday. G. Dance came in and we went together to Gains: Duponts to see His Uncles pictures. I was struck when I went into the room with the general colour of them as strongly resembling the pictures of *Wootton,* in which remark Sir George concurred. These pictures were painted at Bath, and have not so good a taste of colour as his latter pictures.

Marchi called on me. He goes this evening to Belvoir Castle. He has seen Lord Holland, who He found in a House at Brompton, as is supposed with Lady Webster.

Westall called on me in the evening. Young Ireland now declares Himself to be the Author of the Shakespere forgeries. Old Ireland abuses his Son & says He has not half sense enough, but that he stole or procured them somewhere. — I went to Westalls & drank tea. Sir George Beaumont in the evening sent me the book of subscriptions for Poor Cozens, and 30 guineas which He had collected.

Names of Subscribers.

		£	s	
	R P Knight	2.	2.	
Column 1	Chas. Townley	2.	2.	
10.10	C: Cracherode	2.	2.	
	Earl of Powis	2.	2.	
	Mr. Robt. Markham	2.	2.	
	B. West	2.	2.	
Column 2	John Campbell	2.	2.	
10.10	Sir G. Beaumont	2.	2.	
	C. Long	2.	2.	
	J. Windham	2.	2.	
	Sir A Hume	2.	2.	
Column 3	Lord Clive	2.	2.	
10.10	Mr. Edwd. Knight	2.	2.	
	Sir H Englefield	2.	2.	
	Mrs. Palmer	2.	2.	

	£30.10.	[£31.10.]
Royal Academy.	10.10.	

£41. 0.	[£42.0.]

July 12th.

Edwards breakfasted with me, and I undertook to speak to Dance, Tyler & West on the subject of his reading T. Sandbys Architectural Lectures. As to any payment Edwards wished that to be left to Sandby & himself.

Tylers I went to & met West, & Dance, and with Tyler we proceeded to the Royal Academy and inspected the lower rooms. It was their joint opinion that the long room with two windows in which Mr. Wilton now models should be divided into 2 rooms; one of which shd. be given to the Housekeeper, and a door made from Her Kitchen passage. The small room, with one window should be given to Yenn for a Treasurers office, and the little room opposite to Richards to him.

We then took into consideration where to place the Cast of the Farnese Hercules; and it was resolved to place it on the left hand of the steps of the Vestibule, between the Pillars and on the other side to answer it, the Apollo. The Lamps to swing from the cieling of the Vestibule.

I read a letter which I had prepared to be signed by Dance, Tyler & myself, directed to West and intended to be shewn to the King, that His Majesty may be convinced we do not grant the Academy money witht. due attention to the case. Wheatley is the object of it.

I then mentioned that Edwards, & Paul & Thomas Sandby, Had conversed about T. Sandbys lectures being read by Edwards. West said that the King had asked him lately whether Sandby proposed to resign or what was to be done in consequence of lectures not being read by him. West was not prepared to answer his Majesty. West, Dance & Tyler entirely concurred that there can be no possible objection to permitting Edwards to read the Lectures which I am to state to him, & when He has settled the business with T. Sandby we shall propose it in Council.

Fuseli called on me in the evening. He spoke very highly of drawings made in Italy by William Lock of the poeple of the country of various classes. — Mr. Lock Senr. is 65 years of age. He seldom goes out of the House, and complains of cold feet, in so much so, that He sits on thick carpet & close to the fire, at this Season.

Wednesday July 13th.

Smirke called on me this morning. I desired him to sketch outlines only of two groups of figures on plain Canvass. — Wm. Hardman & His Son called, going to Lancashire. He looked at His picture by Watteau, and proposed to have it cut down to a small size. West sent the following letter to.

Sir,

Mr. Wheatley having proposed to apply to the Council of the Royal Academy for pecuniary assistance, we, the undersigned, declare that we are convinced that He has given a faithful description of his situation. His constitution is so impaired by repeated attacks of the Gout, as to render it probable that He will in a little time be totally incapable of following his profession; unless the Bath waters, which Dr. Pitcairne urgently recommends, restore the use of his hands. Should that be their happy effect, His ability, as He is well disposed to be industrious, will enable him to provide for a wife and four small Children, which for some time past has not been in his power. We therefore hope the Council will be induced to consider his Case and to represent him as an Object that merits his Majestys Gracious favor. We are, Sir, Your most Humble servts. Geo: Dance, William Tyler, Jos: Farington. July 13th. 1796.

Edwards called, and I told him that I have communicated the proposal for him to read Sandbys Lectures in the Royal Academy to Mr. West, Dance & Tyler who approved it. I also mentioned that His Majesty had asked a question on the subject. I said it now remained for him to settle the business with T. Sandby, who must by letter addressed to the Council, express his wish that Edwards may act as his Deputy, whenever He is unable to attend, and that we thought He shd. pay Edwards £10 a year for his trouble. To all this Edwards agreed & said he would go to Windsor to T. Sandby to settle the business. I said He might make use of Mr. West, Dance, Tyler & my name as thinking it a proper measure.

H Hamond came to Town to consult Maule, on account of a trouble-some deafness. Sir John Wodehouse is to be created a Peer by the Title of Lord Agincourt. His eldest Son is to be married to Miss Norris, of Whitton, an Heiress with £100,000.

Horace dined with Mr. Coke at Mr. Everitts at Lynn, who with others in that town, determined to support Mr. Cokes election, contrary to his expectation, as He thought He had lost that interest by the part He took relative to Paving &c. the town of Lynn. Sir Edwd. Astley & His Eldest Son, also declared for Mr. Coke.

Thursday July 14th.

Richardson called on me this morning abt. his architectural publications. I told him that Mr. Dance had undertaken to mention them at a Council.

Wheatley I called on. I told him West had promised to go to Kew this morning to lay the vote of the Council in his favor before his Majesty. In his anxiety abt. this business He had apprehended that his Majesty may have noticed that *His* name owing to a neglect of Richards had not been signed to an adress. I told him not to entertain any doubt on that account.

Sir George Beaumont has bought a small picture from him which He prized at 6 or 7 guineas. Sir George gave him a £10 note. He felt that this purchase is an accommodation under his present circumstances.

Hamilton called on Him last night, & mentioned that Tyler had an apprehension that the intention of the Academy might be defeated, if His creditors knew of his receiving £100 from the Academy. He said He had accepted a Bill which He must pay but shd. have enough left to support him at Bath 3 or 4 months.

Yenn I called on at the Mews, He shewed me the statement of his Quarterly accounts made out agreeable to direction.

Total Exhibition Expence   £859.15.9½.

Some Particulars.

Cooper for printing Catalogues	£469.17.3
Smith the Carpenter for Exhibition expences only	63. 9.6

Advertisements.

True Briton	£12.17.6.
Oracle	11.14.0.
Herald	6. 6.0.
Times	6. 6.0.
Morng. Chronicle.	7. 4.0.
Telegraph	6. 6.0.
Daily Advertiser	4.19.0
	£55.12.6.

£ s.d.

Loss on bad gold and silver   −.12.6.

Paid True Briton in all from Sept. 29th 1795 to June 14th. 1796 – £17.15.0.

I then stated to Yenn that West, Dance Tyler & myself, had visited the lower apartments at the Academy, and were of opinion that He shd. have the small room under Wiltons office; that the long room in which Wilton models, should be divided, & the Housekeeper have one half with a door broke through to her Kitchen; and that Wilton should give up the small room opposite Richards' apartments to Richards. Yenn did not like this arrangement. He thinks the Housekeeper should be allowed to sit in the little room on the Hall floor excepting during Exhibition time. That He (Yenn) should have the long room in which Wilton models for his papers; and Wilton retain the little room under his office. Finally I proposed to meet him at the Academy at ½ past 6 on Saturday, and with Dance & Tyler to have further conversation on the subject.

Yenn was at Windsor on Monday. The King told him that Beechy had painted the Queen, and Yenn saw the picture. The King, Queen &c &c. are delighted with the picture. While the Queen was sitting, Yenn heard, Beechy had talked in his odd way.

Offleys I dined at. H. Hamond & Mrs. Ball there.

Friday July 15th.

Tyler I called on, and we considered the plan for establishing an Academical provission for decayed Members of the Academy & their widows. I told him I thought it would not be prudent to make any regular provission but for Members of the Academy & their widows. That his proposal of allowing Annuities to Exhibitors &c wd. lay the Academy open to innumberable Claims, and encourage people, bad artists, to endeavour to exhibit for the sake of having such a claim. That this, & all other descriptions of relations to the Arts, should be left to the discretion of the Council for the time being. On reflection He allowed the force of these objections. We agreed in thinking that an Academician should not be excluded if the Sum allowed should make up his income with what He before possessed £100 a year — and a Widow £60 a year. Associates to be on the footing of Widows; and the widows of Associates to have half the Sum of the Widows of Academicians.

We talked abt. appropriating the rooms of the Royal Academy; and He proposed that Wilton should give up the little office below stairs to Richards & Richards give up the *Porters room*, to the House Keeper.

Mr. Beaumont, Paine & Humphry dined with me. Joe Green, & Mr. Jermy, they left at Salt Hill this morning and *they* did not come agreeable to appointment. Mr. Jermy, Son to Commissioner Proby has bought late Sir Joshua Reynolds House, on Richmond Hill.

Saturday July 16th.

Dance I called on & stated to him what passed in my conversation with Yenn abt. the rooms at the Academy.

Council I went to at ½ past 6 with Dance & Tyler.
Present
West, Dance, Tyler, Farington, Bacon, Yenn.

Yenns accounts having been made out in the manner prescribed by the Committee were passed.

The expenditure of 1796 is calculated at	£2037.2.2½
Charity including Wheatley	317.2.0
	£2354.4.2½.

Total income of 1796	£3718. 3.4.	
Total expenditure	2354. 4.2½	
remains to be placed in the funds.	£1363.19.1½	

It was then resolved that Mr. Yenn be desired to purchase £200, 3 per cents to make the solid fund £10,000. Also resolved to purchase £2000 in the 3 pr cents reduced, to make the Charity Fund £6000. As the funds are now reckoned at £60, the Treasurer will have remaining £43.19.1½. Mr. West then stated that He had laid the charity list before his Majesty who approved it; also stated Wheatleys case which His Majesty considered such as justified the Academy in voting him £100 guineas.

Mr. West further stated that for the accomodation of the Treasurer, & the Housekeeper, some new arrangements in the disposal of the rooms must take place; to this His Majesty gave his consent leaving it to the Council to do what is proper.

List of names of Candidates to be Associates we then read.

Christopher Pack, Painter.
Henry Barnard Chalon,
Arthur W. Devis, Painter
Joseph Barrett, Landscape & Animal Painter
Henry de Cort of Antwerp, Painter.
Thomas Daniell, Painter
Francis Towne, Painter.
Henry Bone, Enamel Painter.
Daniel Turner, Painter.
Henry Spicer, Painter.

Charles Rossi
— Sculptor.
Ignace Jos: Vanden Berg
from Antwerpe,
Engraver.
Anker Smith,
Engraver.

Mr. Richards observed that the Engravers not being eligible He shd. not include them in the printed list. The following were then proposed to be Students of the Royal Academy & their drawings were produced.

Architects

Robert Smirke	admitted	Alexr. Jameson	No
Jos: Dixon	do.	William Macgaven	do.
William Atkinson	do.	Daniel Riviere	do.
Richard Smirke	do.	Samuel Stump	do.
Joseph Sutton	do.	William Whiting	do.
John Dadley	No		

Mr. West proposed that Mr. Laborde, Brother to the Paris Banker, be admitted to draw in the Plaister Academy, *not as a Student,* but by leave of Council. It was granted, Mr. West produced a drawing.

Left the Academy at ½ past 10.

Wheatley I called on & communicated the information that His Majesty had confirmed the vote in his favor, at which both He & Mrs. Wheatley were much affected.

Hamilton is only to have £400 for the Picture of the Prince of Wales' marriage of which Tomkins has only paid £100 & does not seem urgent to have the picture finished. Hamilton complains much of the times. He has some years expended £900. Hoppner last year expended £1100. They both have Children at School.

Sunday July 17th.

Smirke I called on & communicated to Richard & Robert their being made Students of the Royal Academy. I told Smirke I thought Daniells election might be secured by proper exertions. He said Bourgeois had promised to vote for him.

Yenn I called on & recd. a draft for 100 guineas for Wheatley. Yenn is strenuous for Bonomi being elected Academician, to fill Sir Wm. Chambers' vacancy. I told him I did not think an Architect wd. be elected. Wyatt is for him. He told me the King has a favorable impression of Bonomi.

Wheatley I called on & paid him the draft for £100 guineas. He mentioned that his eye sight is not so good as formerly, that is he cannot touch small parts witht. glasses.

Mrs. Playfair I called on No. 42 Howland St. and gave her Yenns direction in the Mews, to forward to Mrs. & Miss Barrett.

Captn. Westcote called on me. He came from Portsmouth yesterday and has only 4 days allowance of absence. He gives a very favorable acct. of the conduct of His late Admiral Lafferey [Laforey], whose attention to His duty in the West Indies was unremitting, notwithstanding the reports to the contrary. Admiral Lafferey was in tolerable health when He left the West India Islands; but in a few days the weather was sensibly felt by the Ships Crew to be very cold. Admiral Lafferey, abt. 68 years of age, was more particularly sensible of the change. He wore flannel waistcoats & Westcote recommended to him a great coat & a fire; the former He made use of. One day Westcote went to him in the Stern gallery & finding him apparently much indisposed & very pale, the Admiral told him that without any previous sense of their approach He had fainted 3 times: but that He did not apprehend anything from it, as He once, in the same manner fainted at Bath. He continued however unwell, with spasms in his Stomach, and died about 4 days before they reached England; as they thought, owing to a sudden change of climate. His Son was on board. He was a man of agreeable manners, as a Commander.

Bakers I dined at. Hearne & Edridge there.

Monday July 18th.

Tyler I called on this morning and shewed him my preparation of a Plan for providing for necesitous members of the Academy & their Widows. He shewed me some provissions which had occurred to him.

Mrs. Macquery called on me. She was 79 years old the 20th. of last April. She is in St. Martins Alms House, a room is allotted to two woemen and they receive on the 21st. of every month 20 shillings each. No person is admitted under 60 years of age; & they must be parishioners. Her niece is 47 years old whose only child, a Son, abt. 19 years old is with Captn. Burt in the Duke of Montrose, Indiaman.

Lysons called on me. Lady Willoughby has accepted the situation which Lady Jersey held under the Princess of Wales, for 6 months. Lord Jersey has not resigned his situation.

Sir Joseph Banks has recd. His Majestys order to introduce Lysons on Thursday 28th. inst. to the King, Queen & Royal Family at Kew, where

Lysons is to shew them his drawings of the Roman pavement.

Lysons has agreed with the Carpet maker to let him have the patterns & Lysons is to have 10 pr. cent on the sale of them.

Poggi called on me. Mrs. Poggi thinks it will be most prudent to keep to the terms proposed of having a share of the per centage on the sale of Sir Joshuas drawings than to insist on an immediate settlement.

Smirke called to see two little pictures which I have finished, and strongly recommended to me to persevere in the same practise.

Daniell I drank tea with: Smirke there. We looked over two Portfolios of drawings. Those of Madura are particularly interesting. In one of the buildings [pillars] of granite 35 feet long, & 5 feet square, were raised to the height of 40 feet & placed in a part of the building.

I spoke to Daniell abt. the ensuing election of Associates, and mentioned several names of those who will vote for him. I recommended to him to apply to a few persons who He is acquainted with, and told him I had little doubt of his being elected if some attention is paid to the business. Smirke to go with him to Bartolozzi.

Wheatleys I called at & saw Mrs. Wheatley. The Children being ill she cannot go with him to Bath.

Tuesday July 19th.

Lord Jerseys letters &c. in defence of Lady Jersey were published today.

Edwards called on me this morning. He went to Windsor on Saturday & saw Thos. Sandby, who is much pleased that Edwards will read his Lectures for him, and has promised to write to the Council before Saturday to express his wish that Edwards may be appointed his Deputy. No terms were mentioned between them, I therefore proposed, to prevent any difficulties, that the Council shall propose that Edwards do receive £10 and T. Sandby the remaining £20. Edwards much approved this proposal.

I read to Him some heads of the Scheme for providing for Members of the Academy &c. all which He approved.

Talking of the power of different men, He observed at what different [times] of life men shewed their talents & felt their strength. Sir Joshua Reynolds painted his best pictures after 60. Gainsborough when dying commented that He was quitting the world when He began to feel his strength in art. He mentioned that the pictures I last Exhibition produced were remarked by everybody as very superior and different to what I had before painted; but the fact is, said He, the materials have been collecting through life, and are now producing.

Dance I drank tea with & met Tyler. We employed ourselves till Eleven oClock in forming a Plan for relieving necissitous members of the Academy & their Widows. The mode of proceeding I had sketched out was adopted, viz: To state the situation of the finances of the Academy, and thereby to shew that at this period they are so circumstanced as to justify the application of all surplus money to establish a fund for pensions. All my propositions & the Sums to be granted were adopted. Dance being engaged in preparing His Plans for Docks on the Thames which must be laid before the City Committee on Wednesday next, I agreed to dine with Tyler tomorrow & to finish the remainder of the Plan.

Dance remarked on the violent manner in which the architects are attacking Soanes professional character.

Wednesday July 20th.

Edwards called this morning, and brought his collection of Catalogues of Exhibitions. Edwards has made a large collection of Anecdotes of Artists.

Mrs. Payne called & Mary Payne, who sat in my painting room near 3 hours, while I painted on some trees to shew her the manner of finishing them.

Smirke & Chas Offley dined with me: we had some conversation on the present state of Europe: they were of opinion that we should make peace with the French even upon the condition of our surrendering all the places we have taken from them in addition to their keeping possession of all the countries they have conquered. I differed from them.

Daniell called. He told me He yesterday called on Zoffany, and asked Him for his vote at the next election of Associates. Zoffany promised him, and added that Had He seen Daniells name on the list He should have voted for it. Loutherbergh also promised him; & said He would speak to Cosway, who He thought Daniell shd. call upon.

Wheatley I called on. He has taken places for himself and Mrs. Wheatley in the night Coach which sets off for Bath tomorrow evening at 4 oClock & gets there at 10 next morning. Dr. Pitcairne recommended this Coach as being more roomy than the Mail coach. Dr. Pitcairne reccomended Dr. Frazer of Bath. He advised Wheatley to begin by drinking two glasses of water in the morning, and if He chose it, one glass at one oClock; at the Kings Bath. Also to Bathe. *This* He said is the Season when the waters have ten times the power, though the place is not visited as at other Seasons. Dr. Pitcairne refused fees from Wheatley; and having a balance of £15 to pay him, gave him a £20 draft. They are only lately acquainted, the Dr. having ordered some drawings from seeing those at Dr. Monros.

Wheatley proposes to remain at Bath through the winter. I told him I have no doubt but He will find the Waters & Climate such as will induce him to make it a permanent residence.

Wyatt I called upon this morning, and He promised to sit to Singleton for His portrait for the Academy print on his return next from the Country. I shewed him the list of Candidates to be Associates, and asked him to vote for Daniell, and that one vacancy only would probably be filled. He said He was a principal cause of Daniell going to India, having spoken to George Hardinge, at a time when persons *not appointed* were refused leave to go. Daniell was with Haig a Coach painter in Queen Ann St. east, and had either served an apprenticeship to him, or was a Journeyman. Haig, had been apprentice to Catton. Wyatt concluded by saying He knew De Cort, & Rossi, but thought Daniell had the best claim & would not oppose him. Wyatt thinks Academicians shd. speak to each other on the subject of Elections: but He does not approve of Candidates soliciting.

Wyatt is going to Font Hill to Mr. Beckfords, who after an absence of 3 years, is lately returned to England. Wyatt shewed me the Plan & Elevation of a Tower, which He is going to build for Mr. Beckford. It is to be situated on a Hill, about 3 miles from Fonthill. At the foot it is to be 175 feet Square. The height is to be 175 feet. The Story on which He is to live is to be 60 feet from the ground. The Upper Story is to be one room occupying the square of the Building; and to [be] lighted by a lanthorn from the top. It will be upwards of 70 feet high. Mr. Beckford proposed this scheme some four years since, and said, but Wyatt thinks witht. any serious contention, that He would direct that He would be buried at the top of the lanthorn. Mr. Wildman, his agent, startled at the apprehension of such singularity after what had been said of Mr. Beckfords conduct, has hitherto thrown obstacles in the way of it. — Mr. Beckford asked how He shd. get up to his first floor 60 feet high. Wyatt said He should have a Stair Case to a Hall with 4 fire places in it, up which staircase He might drive a Coach & 4 & turn in the Hall. The heigth from the Hall to the first story wd. be trifling.

Mr. Beckfords income is £70,000 all which He expends, and sometimes overdraws His agent. He has two daughters, who are with his mother at West end, Hampstead.

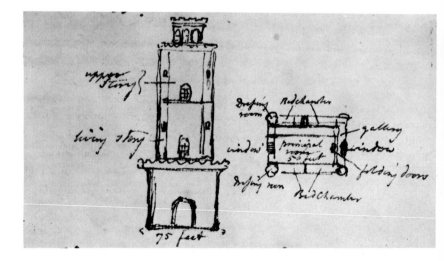

Wyatt told me that his professional Journies are so many that He computes that he travels 4000 miles in a year.

Smirke called on me & I read him the corrected proposals I have drawn up for establishing a fund for the relief of members of the Academy & their widows. He approved of them entirely, & thought it would be imprudent to make the Annuities too high as it would encourage idleness in the Academy and intrigue out of it.

We agreed to go together to Bath in abt. a fortnight.

Yenn I called on, for the money due to Cozens and J. Wilson, but Richards pays this day the Academy Charity.

Tyler I dined with. In the evening we looked over the Pension fund proposal, and I added the precautions to prevent future Councils from giving away the pensions witht. due enquiry into the situation & circumstances of each individual. Also the reasons why the Fund shd. be ultimately limited to £26,000, 3 pr. cents, yielding an interest of £780 which will admit of Pensions to

per annum

4 Academicians	at £70 —	280
5 widows of do.	at 50 —	250
3 Associates	at 50 —	150
3 widows of do.	at 30 —	90
		£770

Here the fund shd. be closed. To encrease the annuities would be holding out an encouragement which eventually might induce relaxations in the professional exertions of the members; and a want of due attention to the interests of those who may be dependent upon them. "The surplus savings after this fund is closed to be added to the solid fund, and the Academy will thereby be enabled to make such additions to its collections, and in other respects adopt such measures as will encrease the advantages and add to the splendour of the Institution".

Dick I recd. a letter from by the Post; dated Latitude 37 North, 13 West, July 7th. Admiral Colpoys had left them before under the Convoy of two Ships of 74 guns, which had then just made a signal for letters for England. They had a most pleasant passage so far. 28 sat down at his table daily, & the Crew & passengers well behaved; & the superior officers gentlemanlike men.

Tyler mentioned to me today that he is *occasionally* troubled with a Diabetes complaint; a sudden flushing of urine. This has caused him for some time past to give up tea, & to drink Cocoa to breakfast, and to avoid weak liquors, wine & water &c. This He has done by advice.

Tom King, He told me, was Clerk to an Attorney, before He entered on the stage. Though remarkable for representing impudent characters on the Stage, in private life he has always been considered a modest well-behaved man. Garrow, the Council, who in *his profession* is as impudent as any of his brethren, in private is modest & reserved. Lord Stormont (now Mansfield) was at Westminster School when Tyler was there. He was a very heavy Lad, but reckoned a fine Scholar.

Friday July 22nd.

Dance I called upon this morning & read to him the whole of the regulations for the Academy Pensions — limiting academicians to 70, Associates & widows of academicians to 50, and Widows of Associates to £30 pr. annum which He approved.

Lysons called in the evening. The Morning Post is the paper in which Lady Jersey publishes her reflections on the Princess &c. This paper on Thursday made a false assertion that Dr. Randolph never delivered the parcel, or that it was not booked. Yesterday the paper submissively retracted.

Lysons is to have from Morley the carpet maker at Chelsea 10 per cent upon the whole sale of carpets made in imitation of the drawings of the Roman floor for the first twelvemonths. Lysons thinks He shall make £500 by it; but in drawing up the agreement He must take care that He does not make himself liable to partnership.

Saturday July 23rd.

Dance I called on this morning. He thinks with me that it will be prudent to limit the Pension Fund to £26,000, 3 per cents, and to apply all surplus money afterwards to the Solid Fund, to advance a sum sufficient to yield an interest that will defray the Annual Expences of the Academy witht. Exhibitions. So that should they fail the Academy wd. not sink.

Smirke I called on & read to him the regulations for the Pension Fund, which He approves of entirely & the limitations of Annuities, to Academicians £70, Associates, £50, widows of academicians £50 widows of associates £30.

Council at Academy went to in the evening. Present

West

Tyler, Dance, Hoppner, Westall, Farington.

Read letter from Thomas Sandby requesting that Edwards may read the Architectural Lectures for him next Spring, if He is not, as He has not been, well enough in the last two years to read them; also read a letter from Edwards offering his services. It was agreed by the Council that Edwards may read the Lectures. — It was resolved at the motion of Dance that the cast of the Farnese Hercules be placed in the Hall of the Academy between the pillars next to the window; and that the Apollo be placed between the opposite pillars.

I then read the Plan, which in conjunction with Dance & Tyler, I had prepared for establishing a pension fund for the support of necessitous Academicians & their widows. Much conversation took place, in which all present agreed to the proposals for establishing such a plan, & West expressed how fully it met the Kings approbation. Finally Dance made a Motion —

"That Mr. Farington having produced a Plan for establishing a Pension Fund for the relief of necessitous Members of the Royal Academy & their widows, Resolved that a Plan for so laudable a purpose be taken into Consideration at the next Council".

This was unanimously agreed to & entered on the minutes, and it was resolved that a Council for the purpose should be held this day fortnight.

At half past 10 Council broke up. I went home with Westall, who told me He thought dependent relatives, viz, Sisters, or Children, should be included, to which I agreed, but did not know how they cd. be so described as to prevent objection. It must be considered.

Sunday July 24th.

Lysons I breakfasted with. He is preparing patterns of his Roman floor for Morley.

Lysons name is now placed at the Royal Society as a Candidate for election. Marsden, Dalrymple, & Major Reynell, were the three first that signed and carried it in. The election will not be before January next, as they now keep the names up a long time.

Strawberry Hill we went to by way of Richmond in the Stage, which was full. Lysons got into a long conversation with a passenger about Methodists &c. and entertained the other passengers much by his description of the strange behaviour of some of their preachers.

Lord Orford we found in good spirits, but He told us He had been in as He thought a very critical state the day & night before. Throughout the day He had been so lightheaded as to talk in a very confused manner, and in the night was seized with so violent a palpitation of the heart that at two o'Clock He rung up the servants, and being placed in a Chair, began to vomit. This relieved him; At 3 He went to Bed again, & slept till near Eleven. He accounted for this attack as proceeding from having disordered his stomach by eating Strawberrys & Cream.

We found Lord Clifden & his Brother & Sister, Mr. & Miss Agar there, & Mr. Williams, who went away immediately. Lady Jersey had been the subject of conversation, & Lord Orford seemed fully convinced of her having intercepted the letter. Lord Jersey has been with the King to complain of the Princess of Wales having endeavoured to take away Lady Jerseys Character, The King made no reply but bowed him out of the room. Mrs. Pelham had said before the Princess "that all crooked poeple stunk".

Lord Orford desired me to look at a miniature which hung over the

Chimney piece. It was the portrait of a gentleman. He asked me what I thought of the expression, I said, the countenance was sensible & penetrating. That it ought to be replied His Lordship, for it is the portrait of Mr. Roscow, Author of the Life of Lorenzo de Medici, who is the best Historian and Poet of this age. — Gibbons first Volume is enamelled; but the succeeding Volumes are very inferior. Hume, wrote with ability the lives of James 1st. & Charles 1st. and his object was to undervalue Elizabeth, — His other parts of the English History were written for sale, and carelessly. — Roscows life of Lorenzo is impartial, modest & equal; and His translations of the poetry of Lorenzo, notwithstanding the disadvantage of language, is better than the originals. His Lordship said He wrote to Mr. Roscow requesting him to send him his portrait, as he coveted to have a portrait of the best poet of the age. Mr. Roscow replied that great as was the compliment which his Lordship paid him, there would be more affectation in *refusing* than in complying with His Lordships request.

Lord Orford then mentioned Dr. Darwin, & wished for a portrait of him as a man of great genius, and a poet of the first order. — "While reading his Poem" said His Lordship, "one does not well know what it is about, the subject is so singular, but it contains admirable passages; and about twelve lines on the creation, one more exquisite than any others that I remember.".

"I cannot go to Mr. Knights to see his Antique bronzes, which I excessively admire, because I have abused his literary works. I think him as an Author arrogant and assuming; His matter is picked up from others having little originality. The absurdity of his making Lucretius his model is a proof of bad taste. — His dictatorial manner is very offensive, and His placing Goldsmith in the rank which He has done is a proof of want of judgment. Goldsmith in his Deserted Village had some good lines, but his argument 'that Commerce destroys villages', is ridiculous. There are occasionally smooth lines, among a great number of very bad ones, in Knights publications, but pretending to a great deal, He has little power".

"History," said His Lordship, "is little to be depended upon. Even the publications of the day are perpetually misleading the readers. — When the Duke of Gloucester was so created, the newspapers stated that He was created Duke of Lancaster. At a future period if they were to be read, it would be supposed that He had been first created Duke of Lancaster & that the title was afterwards changed."

Of Miss Burneys (now Mrs. D'Arblay) new Novel, Camilla, He said, "I have a great regard for her. She seems to have exhausted her mind in her former works so as to have little left to produce; This novel is too long & inferior to the others."

He commended very much a Poem which lay on the table on the subject of the Law, entitled [blank].

The originality of Ossian, He observed, is now generally disbelieved.

Since the death of Hume it appears He did not believe the poems to be original.

Lord Leicester is a very remarkable instance of possessing a passion for Ancestry. When He was only 22 years old, He applied to Lord Orford for his opinion, whether He should not take the title of Lord Bassett, being descended from Margery eldest daugr. of a Peer of that tittle; another Peerage He could claim from the same female ancestor; and also to be *Champion of England,* as she was the *eldest* daughter, whereas, Mr. Dymock claimed from a younger daughter. — "My claim *I did* put in, in the reign of Elizabeth" said His Lordship.

Lord Leicester when His father was to be created a Marquiss, offered to join in a settlement of £12,000 if He would make *Leicester* the tittle and not Townshend. Which His Father refused to do, and added His Son might choose any *second* title but *Townshend.*

Lord Lyttleton, the Statesman, was a very absent man, of formal manners, who never laughed. — In conversation He would frequently forget propriety in regard to the subject of it before the Company He happened to be in. — At Lady Herveys, one evening when Lady Bute & Her daughter, afterwards Lady Macartney, were present, He began to relate a conversation which He that day had with Mr. Wildman, on the subject of Bees, & proceeded to describe the *generation* of Bees, with many particulars, which put the Ladies into some confusion.

At another time Lord Orford met him at Lady Herveys, when with a tea cup in his hand, He advanced towards the table & returning back talking solemnly and moving backwards, before He reached his chair, He crossed His long legs and sat down, not on his chair, but on the floor; the wig went one way, and the tea cup another, while his Lordship with unmoved gravity continuing his conversation recovered himself.

Before Lord Lyttleton was married he was supposed to be much attached to the sex, and it was said of Him that He went to the Tavern with a Whore in his hand & an Horace in his pocket.

Though made Chancellor of the Exchequer, Lord Lyttleton was unqualified for the office, being so deficient in knowledge of figures that He often made a jumble in his reports to the House mistaking halfpence for guineas. — He was formal & singular in his dress. Lord Orford once called on him when he was recovering from an illness and found him dressed in a Brocade coat, with a Nightcap on.

Mr. Winnington, was a man of superior wit. It was equal to the best of George Selwyns and more constant. — It is a trifle which I mention said His Lordship; but once passing along a street with him near Drury Lane, we saw over a door — "Young Ladies educated & boarded", — "*Boarded* it should be," said Winnington, "before educated."

"The Diary of Gibbon, gave me a better opinion of his heart," said His Lordship, "than I had before". "It exhibits some weaknesses, but *Vanity* is *not vice*". — Lord Sheffield for the sake of £3000 treated the memory of his deceased friend ungenerously; for the sake of swelling out the work, He published many things which should not have been included. I had not patience to read the second Volume."

"I have a doubt of Johnsons reputation continuing so high as it is at present. I do not like his Ramblers".

Mr. Cambridge has many singularities. He is about the same age with Lord Orford. — Abyssinian Bruce, being to dine with Lord North, Cambridge requested to be invited to meet him. Bruce as usual told many strange stories; He said He had sent Camels to America. Cambridge was struck with this, and wrote to his acquaintance Soame Jenyns, then at the board of trade requesting to know if any information of Camels being imported to America had been recd. by the Board. Jenyns, delayed his answer a few days & then wrote to him that many had arrived in America but their names were spelt differently, *Campbells*. — A fine Child of his eldest Son, of 7 or 8 years old, which lived with him, died. — It is a great loss said He to Lord Orford, but as it answers no purpose my wife and I have determined not to grieve about it.

Cambridge has been acquainted with a succession of great men, and with men in great power; but He never got anything by it. His acquaintance has been general, but He has not fixed a freind. — Of his old wife He still speaks as if she were a Venus; "Yet with all this admiration," said His Lordship, "He sees as little of her as possible, for He is as seldom at home as He can be."

He has a passion for knowing every person who is in any degree remarkable and solicits eagerly an opportunity to be with such. — Lord Orford on some occasion saying He felt little inclination to see poeple who were talked about, "That" replied Cambridge, "is exactly my case".

Lord Orford said Mrs. Cosway once brought General Paoli to visit me. I returned his visit by leaving a Card at his door without asking for him. I always despised his conduct. A man is not obliged to be a Hero; but if a Man professes himself to be one He should die in the last ditch. Paoli to secure his person fled from his country, and left many of his freinds to be sacrificed.

"I am more gratified by the ornamental part of Art," said His Lordship, "than by the dry & scientific. Harmony delights me. I prefer the art of Bologna to that of Rome."

"England is the country in which variety of Character is to be found. A thousand Frenchmen smile, & bow, & think & talk alike; but Englishmen vary as much in mind as in person. Here is a Seward, a Pennant, a Dalrymple, a Cambridge, and every name that may follow is attached to a distinct character. Dalrymple, a Geographer, a Sailor, afflicted with scurvy, & lame with gout, employs his hours in reading wretched Novels & analysing them, and is vain of his person & adress. Pennant, Seward, & Cambridge have equal oddities."

His Lordship regretted that the Houghton Estate cause should be still in suspense. He is apprehensive that His death is waited for, after which a claim of £20,000 will be made on those estates, being a Sum borrowed by the late Earl of Orford, and which ought to have been paid out of the estate which the present Lord *permitted* to go to Col. Walpole.

"Mr. Berry spoke very handsomely of Tresham to me; and asked if there is not to be an election at the Academy." — Tresham, while at Rome, wrote some verses which bore hard upon Jenkins & Byers, the Antiquarian dealers. Byers was sulky upon it, but Jenkins meeting Tresham lamented that He should have decribed unfavourably a Man who had a great regard for him. "If you have such," said Tresham, "lend me a Hundred Crowns", "That I will" replied Jenkins, & immediately gave him an order for the money. We sat with Lord Orford till near 12 o'Clock.

Monday July 25th.

Strawberry Hill I left this morning, & walked with Lysons to Sheene, where we breakfasted with Mr. Peach, & Mrs. & Miss Peach.

Lord Orford said yesterday that He felt great compassion for the wretched state of Johnsons mind in his last illness. The relation one can scarcely read without horror. — Lord Orford never was acquainted with Johnson; Sir Joshua Reynolds offered to bring them together, but Lord Orford had so strong a prejudice against Johnsons reputed manners, that he would not agree to it.

To day I observed to Lysons that age had not weakened the prejudices of Lord Orford, and that his feelings on all occasions seemed to be as quick as they could have been at an early period of his life. His resentments are strong; and on the other side his approbation, when He does approve, unbounded. Lysons agreed with me fully: but it is not now a time to contest any point.

Mr. Peach told us that He heard Mr. Mainwaring, the Member for Middlesex, a few days ago say, that in the last three years, the newspaper called the Times had cleared to the Proprietors £24,000. It is in 16 shares, of which Walter has Eleven. — Harris, the Proprietor of Covent Garden Theatre, pays Walter an Annuity of £100 that His Play House may be well recommended in that paper.

Mr. Peach saw General Walpole yesterday, who is arrived from Jamaica. — There were about 70 Dogs employed or intended to be employed against Maroons in that Island; concerning which General Macleod made his motions in the House of Commons. — Genl. Walpole said the Maroon men were so active that the Dogs would have had but little effect on them, but the woemen & Children wd. have been at their mercy. — Genl. Walpole saw Lord Balcarres' letter in the Jamaica newspaper, although the original had not reached Mr. York in England; so that Genl. Macleod was so far on good ground as to its authenticity. At a solemn meeting with the Maroons Genl. Walpole pledged himself to the two Chiefs, who were intelligent men, that the Maroons if they submitted shd. not be sent out of the Island; but contrary to this engagement they had been put on board Ships. Genl. Walpole had been offered a Sword as a testimony of respect for his services by the Jamaica Assembly, but had declined accepting it while the engagement He had made with the Maroons remained unfulfilled.

John Wilson called on me today after my return, & I paid him some money on acct. of the Academy. He got a violent cold the last winter, which appears to me to have brought him in to a consumptive state. He told me Charles, the puffing, advertising miniature painter, had been kind to him, and that He saved Charles from being drowned near Chelsea many years ago. Charles' real name is [blank].

Westall I called on in the evening, and we had some conversation about Academy Pension fund, and of extending the annuities to other relatives besides Widows.

Westall has completed his drawings for Boydells edition of Milton. They are 28 in number & He had 40 guineas each for them.

Thursday July 26th.

Westall I called on. — It has been stated in the news paper that a spurious Print of his "Storm in Harvest" is preparing.

Humphry called on me in the eving: We talked about an election of Associates. I represented to him that Englishmen ought to have a preference over foreigners provided the abilities of the Candidates are equal: and that I thought there were English Men of equal powers to Mr. De Cort. He said De Cort had very respectable connexions among the nobility &c., and understood the Flemish manner of painting profoundly, and that He only wanted a little more feeling in his art to be a distinguished character in his profession, and that He had brought to England a new mode of practise.

Mrs. Flaxman says that Flaxman is lately so much disgusted with the conduct of an Academician, for his oppressive proceeding in a money affair for rent due, that He seemed to be much cooled in His wish to belong to the Society.

Wednesday July 27th.

Plott, I called on this morning. He gave me some Catalogues & many papers, relative to the Incorporated Society of Artists.

Mr. Keate still continues to go about describing Henderson & His daughters conduct in the most unfavourable manner.

C. Offley I dined with. Smirke & Mr. Barrow of Hull there.

C. Offley has recd. a letter from his correspondent Mr. Sealy of Lisbon, who states, that there had been an addition made of Members to the State Council, and a report strongly prevailed of the French having demanded of Spain a passage to Portugal for 80,000 troops; and that the Portuguese may purchase Peace by paying 40, Milions of Crusade (4 milions sterling) and shutting their Ports against England. A meeting of the Oporto merchants is to be held tomorrow in consequence of this information. — Sealy did not give much credit to it.

Smirke told me Rossi, the Sculptor, was with the Prince of Wales today modelling a small head of him in the Uniform of the 10th. regt. of Dragoons. Rossi waited 3 hours today before He was admitted, during which time the Prince was entirely engaged by a Shoemaker, and two Taylors who succeeded each other. — The Shoemaker carried in at least 40 pair of Boots, — and was with the Prince an Hour while He was trying them. The first Taylor that was admitted, after many trials of patterns, & cuttings, was dismissed, not having given satisfaction: The other was then sent for. Rossi, yesterday waited 5 hours in vain.

The Prince told Rossi that *His Mother* (The Queen) had noticed Rossis model of Eleanor & Edwd. 1st. in the Exhibition.

Smirke went with Daniell to Bartolozzi at North end last Friday & found him at home much indisposed, and looking very ill: At His age [he] over works himself, rising at 5 in the morning and continuing his application till late at night. He promised Daniell his vote cordially.

Thursday July 28th.

Lysons called on me at noon. — He Breakfasted this morning at ½ past 5 with Sir Joseph Banks at his House near Hounslow. At half past 6 got to Kew with Sir Joseph, and waiting a little time, with several others in the Biliard Room, the King came to them, and entered into conversation successively with each. — As the Queen was not come down, the King said He would walk with Sir Joseph into the Botanic Gardens and would see Lysons drawings when the Queen came down. — About 8 the Queen, Princess Royal, Princesses Elizabeth & Augusta appeared and walked with the King into the Breakfast room, followed by Sir Joseph, Col. Digby, & Lysons; who shewed his drawings of the Roman floor, which pleased them much, and they observed how beautiful the patterns would be for work. — The King said to Lysons, "Let me give you one piece of advice. Do not publish till you have fully explored all that can be discovered". His Majesty observed that it is to be lamented that others had not formerly endeavoured to preserve memorials of antiquities which have been discovered in various places. — The Princess Royal took notice of the Asphaltum Outline, & Lysons explained how it is prepared.

The King spoke warmly of the Country & the poeple of the Clothing country in Gloucestershire. — Understanding that Lysons had been bred to the Law, the King talked to him of Special pleadings &c. He said Lord Kenyon had done some good among the Attornies and would do more. He mentioned Austen, the Clerk of Crossley, now in Newgate under sentence of death for forgery; and said though Crossley & the rest had escaped He believed Austen was the least guilty of any of them, and that the execution of his sentence is postponed as it is expected He will make some discoveries relative to the others. Lysons observed that the King has a defect in or rather hurry of utterance; but His observations were well understood, and his expression correct.

Humphrys, I dined with. Giffard and Daniell there. Burns, the Scotch Poet who died lately was mentioned. Giffard spoke highly of his powers, saying He thought, Burns, had more of the true spirit of Poetry than any man of his time.

Giffard thinks Knight has good lines & ability; but writes too confidently; and in his last work the Progress of Society does not seem to have fully considered his subject. He says, and unsays. His manner is too dictatorial & assuming.

Giffard has been informed by a Mr. Ireland, a friend of his, that Roscows Life of Lorenzo is a work of superior merit.

Giffard has had little use of his right eye, since He had the small pox 25 years ago; and at present has a nervous complaint in his left eye owing to reading much, and probably the nervous system has been weakened by his inordinate use of tea, which He has till lately, been accustomed to drink 3 times a day, and basons of it.

Daniell cannot see near without glasses. He perceived his eyes lose something of their power while He was in India, and imputed it to drawing much in the open air in that hot climate, and to working by Candle light.

Daniell mentioned to me that Bartolozzi has promised him his vote.

Friday July 29th.

Edwards called on me, and I told him that the Council had agreed to his acting as Deputy for T. Sandby in reading his Lectures.

Byrne called. Mr. Keate has been with him, and had a long conversation about Miss Keate marrying Mr Henderson, and said that 3 years ago He would have consented, but then she seemed to have little disposition towards him. In what He said on the subject Keate seemed influenced by the same prejudice which has caused him in the opinion of his friends to act very improperly. — Plott is condemned for having known of the proceeding and not having mentioned it. If Byrne calls at Keates He is not to mention the name of Mrs. Henderson before Mrs. Keate, such is the way in which two poeple of their age conduct themselves on this occasion.

Byrne strongly expressed his belief of Henderson being a respectable man. He recommended to Keate to consider the case comparatively. Suppose, said Byrne, she had married a man of indifferent character and of no property, "such a thing might have been". — Byrne thought Keate was struck with some part of the conversation, & is of opinion that were Mrs. Keate out of the Question He would soften.

Miss Byrne called & I lent her some drawings to copy.

Smirke drank tea with me. — Daniell is abt. 48 years of age. He was apprentice to Mr. Mansfield, a Coach Painter in Little Queen St, Lincolns Inn fields, who had been Cattons Master, and was afterwards Journeyman to Catton. — The Climate of Calcutta affected his health, and obliged him to quit the place; on which giving up the Idea of making money in India, He resolved to explore different parts of India, and to endeavour to bring to England a large collection of views which He might there turn to some account. Being disappointed of his intention of coming to England over-land, He crossed the Sea to China. — The expences attending his return to England were £1400 and on his arrival here He found He had lost some hundred pounds by a Mr. Hague, a former acquaintance.

Smirke speaking of his own progress in art lamented that He had not at an early period had an opportunity of copying good pictures, which would have eradicated those habits of painting which He had contracted during his education as a Coach painter. — He also regrets that He has not drawn more figures from the life, as He has been too much in the habit of trusting to his memory. His proficiency under his Master, a Coach painter was such that, while He was apprentice He was sometimes borrowed by Catton to execute particular things. At that time Daniell was Journeyman to Catton.

Smirke is much gratified by the ardent desire his Younger Son, now under Soane, is filled with to excell in his profession. His improvement has been extraordinary for the time. Soane does not conciliate the regard of his pupils, by a liberal conduct.

Saturday July 30th.

Dance called this morning, to borrow a drawing of the Tower, as He is to prepare regular drawings of his design for the new Docks. — It is now pro-posed to make Docks & Wharfs at St. Catherines below the Tower, for the *export* trade only, of certain articles of Commerce, Tobacco &c. &c. — Dance much approves this proposal as it may soon be executed, and by thus separating from the general mass of business now done on one spot several branches of business, the convenience to all will be very great. — The Commissioners have desired him notwithstanding to make complete drawings of his grand design, though He said to me it would be a work of such magnitude as to be like undertaking to erect a Palmyra or Balbeck.

J. Boydell called. He is going to Mr. North at Hastings.

Sunday July 31st.

Hoppner I called on this morning, to have his opinion of his Plan for the pension Fund. He said two remarks He had to make viz

That there should be a distinction between the annuities granted to Academicians of superior & inferior merit, and

That provision should be made for the Academy educating a Son of an Academician who should incline to study the Art.

On the first I observed that no distinction could be made among the Academicians on the score of merit without great jealousies attending it. — That we ought to be careful in our future elections, but those who are chosen we must consider as having equal rights.

To the second, were such an establishment made, Boys with little or no talent for the sake of the encouragement would pursue the Art, to their own loss in the end and the discredit of the Society. In cases where there shall seem sufficient reason to give such assistance the Academy can at discretion do what may seem prudent. — Hoppner admitted that the consequences in both cases might be dangerous.

Hoppner has been 9 or 10 days at the Duke of Dorset at Knowle, painting the 3 children. — The Duke is become very unpleasant in his temper, anxious and saving. At Cassino He lost 15 shillings to Hoppner and during the Play was fretted when the cards He wished for were taken up. — He cannot bear to hear other places described as beautiful, Knowle, He considers as possessing everything.

The Duchess is a woman of most excellent temper, and is unmoved by the Dukes peevishness; never seeming to be discomposed.

The Duchess of Gordon was mentioned, and her behaviour to Mrs. Mills, who now possesses Egremont House. The Duke appeared to justify the impertinence of the Duchess, who had said She wd. look in at Mrs. Mills' rout to laugh at them. — Hoppner reprobated the conduct of the Duchess, & said Her ignorance, & ill manners He shd. be sorry to see match'd by her inferiors in situation. — The Duke had hinted, He knew not why such poeple as Mrs. Mills shd. affect to give routs. — This passed at dinner before the servants, one of whom afterwards told Hoppner He was alarmed at the conversation though He wished people would more often speak their minds; it might do the Duke good. Hoppner thought the Duchess was frightened.

The Duke continually shews his value for family. — Speaking of Necker,. "but" said the Duke "He is a man of *no family*". — At Paris the Duke had mentioned that Hailes, his Secretary, was a man of no family; this being circulated Hailes felt the inconvenience of being in much less request than He would otherways have been from his situation.

Dr. Moseley came in to see one of Hoppners children.

Paines I went to with Hoppner.

Humphry is quite out of favor at Knowle. He went to Knowle when the Duke was not there, after the Dukes marriage, and took possession of a room without previously shewing a proper attention to the Duchess. This has lost him her favor. The Duke is equally disgusted on some account. One charge is that He painted copies of Portraits at Knowle, & demanded payment for them as having been ordered by the Duchess, which she denied.

The Duke has asked Hoppner for his portrait, which He says is still in the room but has been removed [moved].

At Paines we found Marlow, and Humphry. — It is 8 years since I last saw Marlow. He now resides at or near Twickenham. He told me he had not for many years past slept in London; and that His Health was not so good while He continued there.

Marlow said He went as a Pupil to Scott about the year 1756 and was with him 5 years. — Scott resided in Covent Garden, on the South side. — He had much business and gained by his profession 7 or 800 pounds a year. He had for a picture of 6 feet by 4 feet, 60 or 70 guineas. — For a half length 40 guineas, and for a Kitcat 25 guineas, & so on in proportion. — He was much afflicted with the gout, but applied to his profession, and in the Summer time would begin to paint at 6 oClock in the morning, and in the Winter would have his pallet set early. Scotts expenses might be about £500 a year. He died at the age of 70 at Bath.

Sir Edward Walpole was a great patron of Scott. It was his custom, when in London, to sup every Tuesday evening at Scotts House, and with him usually came a Mr. Martin, who when Sir Edward was made a Knight of the Bath, was one of his Esquires. Sir Edward was pleasant in his manner, and joked with those about him. — Gilpins name (the other pupil of Scott) being Sawrey, Sir Edward called him *Sorry* & to contrast it called Marlow, *Glad.*

Gilpins inclination to painting Horses arose accidentally from his liking to sketch from groups in Covent garden, of which Carts & Horses made a part. — Scott painted a view of Covent Garden, and Gilpin assisted him. Scott had 150 guineas for the picture.

We looked at two pictures by Wilson. Hoppner admired the *colour* but thought the handling of the trees very deficient. — We also looked at a picture by Gainsborough, painted while He imitated the Flemish Masters. Some parts are like nature, but the whole is heavily arranged, badly formed and poorly executed. I remember formerly admiring this picture much & making it a sort of Model, — induced perhaps by the great praise bestowed on it by others.

I told Paine I had not had an opportunity of shewing Marnels letter to Admiral Gardner, and that I did not believe we should succeed, but that if He thought proper I would write to the Admiral at Portsmouth. Paine declined this.

Hoppner mentioned that Lord Grosvenors affairs are in a very bad condition. — That He has for several years continued to borrow money on his estates till at last He has no good security to offer. — On an examination made in consequence it appears that Lord Belgrave is likely to inherit but a small part of what the world has supposed that Lord Grosvenor would be able to leave him.

Hoppner told us that the Duke of Dorset had informed him that De Cort waited on his grace with a letter of introduction; and with ostensibly only a desire to be permitted to make studies in Knowle Park. De Cort continued several days in Sevenoaks & made several drawings in the Park, & selected those points of view which the Duke was known to approve. — The Duke said He saw through De Corts Scheme, but did not fall into it, and did not invite him to his table.

On our return to Town I called at Hoppners, where we found Giffard & Dr. Amyatt, a Physician. — Mrs. Hoppner told us that Mrs. Banks had informed her of the death of Cosways daughter, a little girl of 6 years and a half old, of a putrid fever and sore throat, thought to have been occasioned by the Child being exposed to the air improperly after having taken James's powders. Cosway is said to be much affected, but Mrs. Cosway is thought not likely to suffer much.

AUGUST 1796

Smirke drank tea with me.

Collins called with Humphry. He mentioned that from his apartments in Pallmall, he saw the Prince of Wales, on the day of his reconciliation with the Princess of Wales, go to Lady Jerseys: and this day He came out of that House Arm in Arm with Lord Jersey — Collins had several times observed that when the Prince visited Lady Jersey, she was accustomed to drop the linnen blinds of the windows.

Humphry was a considerable time with the Margravine of Anspach (Lady Craven) yesterday at Brandenburgh House. — She spoke of Lady Jersey, and allowed her beauty, but said she had thick legs. — The Margravine added that the Prince had denied the Child being his; but that would be sufficiently proved to be untrue as the Princess during Her passage to England, was *very unwell,* on which account a Lady who was with her wrote to the Queen, shewing the necessity of postponing the marriage, which was accordingly done & the Princess came up the River to make the interval on shore shorter. "The child," said the Margravine, *"was born to an Hour".*

The Margravine said the Prince was not induced to marry by Lady Jersey; it was in consequence of violent quarrels with Mrs. Fitzherbert, and with her He wd. have been glad to have been on terms again but she refused.

Humphry asked how the Margrave was affected at the accounts from Germany. "Not at all," said the Margravine, "He has formed his Plan, & lets things take their course".

Mary Paine came this morning & sat in my painting room some hours, while I shewed her how to begin a picture.

She mentioned to me that Green by his excess in drinking is very much altered; has little appetite, and in general his spirits are very bad.

Fuseli, Smirke & Offley dined with me.

Fuseli, said, Roscow, Author of the Life of Lorenzo, is an Attorney;

627

about 41 or 2 years old. — He was born in Yorkshire. His Father in a low line of life, having kept a little Inn. He has 6 Sons.

The Medicis, said Fuseli, were the Tyrants of Florence. They got money; and with it they employed the poor, bribed the necessitous; and by degrees oppressed the rich. — Roscow in describing the Medici family has forsaken his principles. He is here the advocate of Tyranny; though He has been always ready to sign any parchment of remonstrance against encroachment on liberty.

Roscow was 12 years preparing the life of Lorenzo. He was assisted by Mr. Clarke Son of a banker at Liverpool, who collected for him at Florence such materials as were necessary; a part of these Fuseli said are extremely valuable.

Lord Orford has done the business for Roscow with the world. His warm panegerycks drew the attention of fashionable collectors. The first Edition was published for Roscow. It consisted only of 450 copies; & being put at 2 guineas, a high price, made a handsome profit. The credit of the work is now so high that Cadell & Davis have given Roscow 1200 guineas, and 50 copies on fine paper, for the 2d. edition.

The History of Lorenzo might have been comprised in one Volume. Roscow is as ready at versification as Hayley. "The Literary men are in arms about its claims; but Lord Orford has done the business". — Miss Burney for her new Novel of Camilla, had 1100 guineas subscription, and sold the copy of the work afterwards to Cadell for 1000 guineas. — The novel is so indifferent, it renders the genuineness of her former works suspected.

Cadell has got 1000 guineas by Sewards Collection of Anecdotes. Seward nothing.

Edwards, the Bookseller, is gone to Italy to purchase books. He is son to a bookseller at Halifax in Yorkshire, who has made a good deal of money. He is a master of his business.

Anderson, of the India House, who died lately prepared the Indian Budgets for Mr. Dundass, who on acct. of his death before the Budget was finished could not bring it forward. — Anderson was born in Aylesbury in Buckinghamshire, of low extraction, having been at Plough. His talent for calculations caused him to be noticed, and in time to be recommended to Lord Grenville, who recommended him to Mr. Dundass. He had before this written an answer to a Pamphlet by Tierney on India affairs, in which He over set Tierneys arguments & calculations.

Anderson had £500 a year allowed him. — He had been rather a free thinker on religious matters, but about a fortnight before his death He told Fuseli that He had read the Bishop of Landaffs book against Paine, and thought it contained much conviction. — Fuseli remarked that there was something like presentiment & preparation in this, though at the time He was in good health. — He died of a Brain Fever, and was about 36 years old. He was much devoted to society and good fellowship, and extremely respected by his acquaintance. *Holcroft* was mentioned. He behaved in a cruel manner to his daughter, as He had before done to his Son. His daugtr. He turned out of doors. — She is since married to Tooke Harwood. — Holcroft is a disagreeable companion, being addicted to dispute on all subjects. — *Godwin* has the same disagreeable manner. — Smirke said Godwin had spoken highly of Lawrence.

Offley told us He had recd. a letter from Oporto, informing him that the people of that Town, Fidalgos (Gentlemen) and Hidalgos (Tradesmen) had been singly called to a private council & by order of government sworn to secrecy on some as it is supposed political account. The conjecture is that subscriptions are to be levied either for the purpose of national defence, or to purchase peace from the French.

Wednesday August 3rd.

Shakespeare Gallery I went to. Bulmer there. He thinks if we proceed with the publication of the Rivers we should not have so much letter press. 40 or 50 pages might do for each River. The work will not answer if there are more.

Lysons called & read his agreement with Morley, the Carpet manufacturer.

Offleys I dined at.

C. Offley

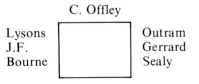

J. Offley

Much talk of Spanish War. Offley shewed 2d. note from Pitt desiring to see him tomorrow at 4.

Lysons has no high opinion of Groses Antiquary accounts; they are collated with very little trouble from 3 or 4 known books. Humour was the Forte of Grose.

Outram I desired to mention to Machell that I did not write to him, because having ommitted to do it, from low spirits, when I recd. his letter, I afterwards could not.

Lysons told me that yesterday He dined with Berwick, Roberts, & Hornyhold, money is extremely scarce in the City. The advantages of the first loan are but equivalent to the losses on the 2d. loan. Pitt wd. not be now able to obtain a loan.

Lysons hears that if Pitt does not make Peace before Novr. He must go out. — War ill managed. — Bank Directors much out of humour with Pitt.

— West India expenses enormous. St. Domingo cost 2 milions more than expected.

Thursday August 4th.

Lysons I breakfasted at with Smirke. Morley was there & Smirke & I witnessed the agreement between them.

Morley spoke of the very high price of the articles used in his business of manufacturing floor Cloths. — Linseed oil from Holland which sold for £26 now sells for £53 or 4. — Flax from Russia which sold for £32 or 3 now sells for £63 or 4. — He has made floor Cloths of *one piece* 7 yards wide. It is manufactured with Shuttles which run on Castors.

Morley has been employed by Church, late Member for Wendover. Church lives upon a great scale of expence having upwards of 30 Horses. He does not allow any servant to wear powder. He was formerly agent for the French in America, & married a daughter of Genl. Stirling. He is very violent against government and talks of going to America. — Smirke told me that Wyatt has not put forward the young men & others who have been educated or employed under him. He will not allow Dixon to exhibit, as He says the designs are borrowed from His drawings.

Will came to town & brought George, who went to School.

Byrnes I dined at.

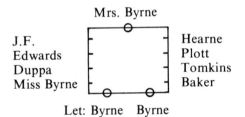

Plott told me that Duppa breakfasted with Keate lately and was desired by him to carry a message to Plott, which was, that Mr. Keate never desired to see him within his doors again, or to see his face. Plott shewed me a letter which He proposed to send to Keate, but I recommended an alteration. — Duppa informed me that He proposes leaving England on Monday next from Gravesend, in a vessell for Hamburgh. — He is to pay 8 guineas for his passage. — He proposes to proceed from Hamburgh to Vienna; and from thence to Dresden; where He expects to find an English gentleman, Dr. Kingslake, and they mean to travel together, probably to Constantinople, & to Egypt, and to return by the way of Italy. He does not propose to make a long residence anywhere for the purpose of studying his art (engraving &c). — At Constantinople He shall enquire into the state of Arts & Sciences in that Capital. — He has lodged £1000 in the hands of Sir

Robt. Herries whose Bills He carries out, and thinks of being absent about 3 years.

Byrne told me J. Boydell had ruined publications by his manner of managing the Shakespeare work, which had been sacrificed to a narrow economy; That the subscriptions to it had fallen off near two thirds. Alderman Boydell is excused, the blame is imputed to J. Boydell. I told him He heard only one side of the question.

Plott came home with me, and after some conversation I advised him not to write to Keate but to pass his extravagant conduct over with contempt. He said He would do so.

Friday August 5th.

Lord Orford told me when I was last at Strawberry Hill, that Queen Caroline, when Regent, visited his Father, then Minister, at his house at Chelsea, and dined there. The etiquette was that the Queen sat at the top of the table, with Lady Walpole (His mother) on her right hand, and Frederick, Prince of Wales, on Her left Hand. — Sir Robt. Walpole stood behind her chair, and handed her Majesty the first glass of wine, after which He retired to another room, where He dined with many distinguished persons of the Court. — In the evening there was a Ball.

Tyler I called on. — He met West on Friday last on his return from Kew, where He had been with Yenn, & stated the proceedings of the Academy to his Majesty; and thinks it most proper to carry on the business of the Academy in that way by going to the King attended. — The King leaves all to the Academy and was shewn that the proposed Plan of a Pension fund wd. not affect his Majestys Purse. — I desired Tyler to call on Bacon & inform him of the Proposed Pension fund Plan, & to request him to attend the Council.

Will called & I wrote to Dick.

Offleys I dined at. No company.

C. Offley waited on Mr. Pitt yesterday. Thomson, Webb, Waye, and a Mr. Harris went with him. — They were shewn into an Anti-room, and in a few minutes into the room where Mr. Pitt was standing at the window, He bowed to the Gentlemen and they took their Seats on Chairs which had been placed.

C. Offley first spoke, as Chairman, & stated the alarm which was felt in consequence of advices from Oporto & Lisbon, and requesting to know if there were sufficient grounds for apprehension, and whether the merchants would be assisted by government as in 1762 with Transports to bring their property over, to be placed under the care of Government here and the duties on it paid as it should be taken out.

Mr. Pitt, half smiling said it was impossible to say what a people who acted in so extraordinary manner as the French had done might attempt, but He thought there was not cause for taking measures to remove the property immediately, as there wd. be sufficient time to do that when the intention of the French is less doubtful. That of course government would give the merchants all proper assistance and indulgence in case of need. — He asked what quantity of wine there may be at Oporto, & was told abt. 40,000 pipes, & that it wd. take a month to ship that quantity on board transports. — That of this quantity shd. there be no pressing occasion to remove it not more than 5000 pipes are expected to be brought to England before Christmas next; instead of 15 or 20,000 pipes on acct. of the *duty*. At Lisbon there are abt. 8,000 pipes.

Pitt had Boots & Spurs on. — They were with him abt. 20 minutes. — He said of the intention of *Portugal* there was no fear: That He wished they would draw up a regular statement of their situation & wishes; and hinted that they would not make much noise about it. — The value of the 40000 pipes of Port to the Merchants is abt. £800,000. — Of the 8000 pipes of Lisbon &c abt. 130,000.

Offley remarked to me that there is no fashion about Pitts person & manner: That He appeared like a man come from a College: That He has a habit when attentive of pushing up his under lip, & drawing down the corners of his upper lip in the form of Whiskers.

The gentlemen were very much satisfied with his reception of them.

Saturday August 6th.

Hearne I called on this morning, and looked over his Exhibition Catalogues. — A female relation of Cozens has left him £40 a year, which must be enquired abt.

Will called to examine acct. of my expences for George, to make out a statement for Bob.

Academy Council I went to at 7.

Yenn told me the King was much pleased with Lysons drawings, and mentioned that Lysons had said the people who have the care of Tewkesbury Church, had whitewashed the antient Monuments. — His Majesty much approves the Pension fund scheme.

Council present.

West,
Bacon,
Tyler,
Farington,
Dance,
Yenn.

Took the placing the Hercules into consideration. — Yenn, & Richards did not approve placing it between the pillars next the window on acct. of disproportion to the Architecture &c. The rest of us contended that the first object of the Academy shd. be to afford subjects for study & to place them in proper lights. Dance at last proposed that the figure shd. be placed

in the Center where the stairs now are & fix the stairs between the pillar on the right & left of it. — This Idea was warmly recd. and West recommended that the figure shd. be placed during the vacation, we strongly urged him as *we went home* to direct Yenn to place the figure in that situation.
A Letter from Mr. Long of the Treasury was read.
Copy.

Sir,
Having laid before the Lords Commissioners of His Majestys Treasury, the representation of the President & Council of the Royal Academy requesting that the Casts, Prints, and Drawings, the property of British Artists returning to England may be imported Duty Free on affirmation being made by Deputies from the Council of the Royal Academy that they have inspected the Articles and believe them to be intended for the private use and study of the Artists who may solicit the indulgence and not for sale. I am commanded by their Lordships to acquaint you for the information of the President & Council that in order to encourage the Arts, They are of opinion the Casts, Prints and drawings the property of British Artists returning to England should be admitted to be imported free of duty subject to the same regulations as are required by the Minutes of this board of the 16th. January 1794 respecting works the performance of artists so returning from their studies, and my Lords trusting that the inspectors to be appointed as proposed by the said minutes will be as careful as far as depends on them not to permit to importation free of duty any articles intended for merchandise.

I am, Sir,

Your most Humble Sent.

Chas. Long

Treasury Chambers.
29th. July 1796.
John Richards Esqr.

After the above letter had been read resolved that at the next Council a proper letter of acknowledgement be sent to the Lords of the Treasury & to Mr. Long, and Resolved that the 4 Senior Council, 2 for each half year should *alphabetically* be appointed inspectors. — We talked abt. the election of Associates. West said He thought we should leave a vacancy or vacancies.
We then proceeded to the business of the evening.
Dance moved that Mr. Farington should read his Plan for a Pension fund and move his resolutions.

I then read them through, and Bacon who had not before heard them read, very much approved the Plan, and thought the limitations in the amount of annuities in the different classes judicious. — He proposed that some notice should be taken of cases where there might be a family of young Children, or where the particular necessities of an Academician who might merit great attention urged him to apply for relief that the Council should not be considered as precluded from giving assistance beyond the limited annuities. I observed to him that such cases had been allowed for in a passage in the plan but it might be expressed still more decidedly: but that all sums advanced on such occasions must be considered as *temporary*, and be carried to the current expenses of the year. The Resolutions were then read and amounted to 14 in number, and passed *unanimously*.

Richards then requested that I would write them out fairly, and He would transcribe them into the Journal of Council.

Mr. West proposed that he might have a Copy of the Plan as now agreed to, which He would privately shew to the King after his Majesty returns from Weymouth; and He shd. then be able to communicate to the next Council, any remarks his Majesty may make, so that there shd. be no danger of His Majesty crossing his Pen through a part after it has passed & been confirmed by a general meeting. — This was agreed to, and the next Council fixed to be on Monday Octr. 3d. and that the general meeting shall be on Friday Octr. 7th. Richards stated that T. Malton had called on him, & complained that He had not recd. a letter of notice from Richards of the time for putting his name down to be a Candidate for Associate. On this representation it was agreed to allow him to put his name down, though it is believed that He must have known the time specified.

Yenn went away before the Pension fund business was brought forward. The Council did not break up till past 12 oClock.

On our way home Dance told me He went this morning with Soane to Mr. Pitts at Holwood House. The situation of ground is beautiful, but the House very indifferent indeed, & scantily furnished. — There are about 500 acres of ground annexed to it. They saw Mr. Pitt, who was there witht. company. Lord Hawkesberry had come over for an Hour upon business. Mr. Pitt was going to dinner to Mr. Longs. Dance was much pleased with his deportment which was quite free from Hauteur.

Sunday August 7th.

At home all day.

Monday August 8th.

Flaxman I called on this morning, and gave him an extract of Mr. Longs letter to the Academy, for him to communicate to the British Artists at Rome.

He told me that Metz brought Caleb Whiteforde to his house a few days ago, when Metz saying He did not bring Drawings, & Prints &c. from abroad on acct. of the duty, Flaxman mentioned that objection for British Artists would be removed and was now before the Lords of the Treasury, a Member of the Academy having interested himself to obtain it. Whiteforde asked who it was. Flaxman replied Mr. Farington. "Why, Mr. — Farington," answrd. Whiteforde, "because Mr. West when I proposed the matter to him declined it; on which, Mr. Farington going with me to pass my articles through the Custom House, as an Inspector from the Academy, I mentioned it to him, who readily offered to give every assistance in his power."

I know added Flaxman that Whiteforde is much with West & will carry what I said to him.

I remarked to Flaxman on the impertinence of Whiteforde pushing himself forward on business of the Royal Academy & told him what passed between Whiteforde & me relative to the last election of Associates.

Flaxman expressed his great surprise on finding the time for putting down Names of Candidates has elapsed, as He understood from Humphry, on the Kings Birth day, that names wd. be recd. any time in 3 months, & He meant to have put down his name this week. I asked him if He had not recd. a notice from Richards of the limited time. He declared He had not. I said an application had been made by an Exhibitor to have his name receivd. He not having recd. a notice from Richards. — Flaxman seemed much disturbed about it, I recommended to him to speak to Humphry, and said I would also mention it to him.

Flaxman shewed me some designs for the proper decorations of Churches so that the parts might every where make a whole, and preserve symetry. — He had heard of the proposed *Academy Pension Fund*; and He thought general advantage to the Arts would arise if the Academy wd. be at the expence of decorating one window of St. Pauls with Painting & under it Bass reliefs. Such an example would probably be generally followed. — I told him that nothing could well be undertaken till the Pension Fund is established; after which the institution being secured in main points the overplus money might be applied in the best way to raise the Arts of the Country.

He told me He had seen my etching of Hernes oak, at Lysons Chambers, and thought it admirable, superior to Waterlo's.

I asked him if the lines which he had pasted in the Bishop of Landaffs

"Apology for the Bible" were wrote by Hayley. He said they were.

"To Mr. Flaxman
with the Bishop of Landaffs apology for the Bible".
"Freindship! whose hands the purest gifts dispense,
"Soothing with tender light the vapor vexed earth,

"Present this Group, Truth, Sanctity, & Sense,
"(Remembrancers of Love) to Genius and to Worth!

"Stadler I called on & He called on me in the evening. Prestel, Son to the late Mrs. Prestel, has recd. a letter from a freind at Franckfort, who, though an Aristocrat, writes that the French have behaved with the greatest decorum since they obtained possession of that City: exacting nothing but the Contribution first demanded, amounting to 600,000 Livres in Money; and 200,000 Livres in Goods, making together about £320,000 sterling, — and that they pay for every article which they require. They have declared that they overlook all former behaviour of any part of the Inhabitants towards the French. While the town was bombarded the shot were pointed to that part of the town where the rich resided, and abt. 150 Houses were damaged. — At present the people of Frankfort rather dread the return of the Austrians — than the continuance of the French.

Tuesday August 9th.

Hearne I called on this morning, with Catalogues of Exhibitions to make up his Set.

Flaxman I drank tea with. Mrs. Flaxman & his sister & Young Hayley there.

He read me 3 or 4 pages of his introduction to observations on the Arts & proposals for encouraging them. — He remarks that Arts are natural to Man, Hence the Indian decorates His Bow & His Spear &c &c. and urges the necessity for turning this disposition to the best account.

He has given the extract from Mr. Longs letter to Howard, who is to send it to Gavin Hamilton at Rome.

I mentioned that I yesterday wrote to Humphry desiring to see him on acct. of Flaxmans name not having been put down; but Humphry was engaged. He said Howard had not recd. a notice from Richards. Nothing more passed on this subject.

He shewed me the Prints from Ghibertis gates at Florence, and two of his own Sketch Books.

Banks will be able to make a profitable job of the Statue of Lord Cornwallis. The Marble, including the Pedestal, will not cost him more than £200. — He may clear 12 or £1300 by the Statue.

Banks returned from Italy well stored with just Ideas of his Art, and was well qualified for great works, — but was not encouraged — I observed that his conduct with regard to Politicks had done him harm — Flaxman thought his indiscretion in that respect both in Italy & in England had hurt his interest, added to which the bluntness of his manners had disgusted many.

Wednesday August 10th.

Humphry I called on this morning. He was in great spirits on having recd.

advices from His agents in Bengal who have got the Bond for 42000 Rupees, given to him by the Nabob of [Oudh]. This Bond, or order on his Treasurer, is dated 1786 and bears interest. Humphry has full hopes of obtaining payment by means of the interest He can make with political poeple here. Humphry told me He has £200 a yr. now in England, and made by his profession last yr. £570.

I related to Humphry what Flaxman had said relative to his understanding that 3 months was the allowed time for receiving names of Candidates to be Associates. — Humphry thinks Flaxman must have misunderstood him. He thinks it will be best for Flaxman under the present circumstances, to postpone putting His name down till next year.

Smirke I called on. He has mentioned to Daniell Flaxmans situation; who thinks Flaxman must have known the time, from the conversation Humphry had with Mrs. Flaxman.

Humphry drank tea with me, and called on Flaxman, who was not at home, and then returned to me. We cannot help thinking there is something odd in this business: either that Flaxman expected to have been solicited to put his name down, or as Mrs. Flaxman hinted to Humphry, was so disgusted with a Member as for a time to have no wish to belong to the Society.

The Miss Hickeys have written from Bath where they are with Mr. Burke, that He is in a very bad state of Health, & they are apprehensive of a decline.

C. Offley called on me today, and wrote a second letter to Mr. Campion. £14000, Port House, £7600 Lisbon.

Thursday August 11th.

Richards I called on this morning & delivered to him a fair Copy of the Pension Fund Plan. — He suggested that to prevent disputes after "Widows," should be added, "while they remain such", which I agreed to, and made the addition.

Stadler called this eving. to look over Plate of Hernes oak, and outline for view of Greenwich Hospital for frontispiece to D. Lysons 4th. Vol:

Friday August 12th.

Humphry I called on this morning & found Flaxman there. — We had a long conversation on the subject of Flaxmans name being added to the list of Associates. I told him that as there would not be a Council till October I should have no opportunity of representing the nature of his disappointment; and that if He desired to add His name to the list, He must apply *personally*. Flaxman in a handsome manner said He should choose to postpone putting his name down to the next year; & Humphry observed that as He had only exhibited a Sketch & that not of any *finished work*, it would be most becoming for himself & for the Academy, to postpone offering his name to next year. — We told Flaxman of the probability that several vacancies would remain open. He remarked that if Rossi, a Sculptor, shd. be elected this year, probably it would be an objection to a Sculptor being elected next year. We gave him to understand, as our opinion, that this should not from the danger of it, affect his resolution. After He had determined to postpone, I told him I should certainly have voted for him; and Humphry did the same.

Nollekens was mentioned. Flaxman gave him credit for some Busts & single Figures which He had executed. The Bust of [blank] and of Mr. Robinson He particularly remarked. His figure of Venus is beautiful; but whether from accident or no, is in the same attitude of a figure in a Bass relief found in Herculaneum. His monument to the memory of the Captains, in Westminster Abbey is a very moderate performance, much inferior to Bacons Lord Chathams monument.

Nollekens has shewn a very narrow disposition in supporting an execution in a House in Charles St. belonging to Mrs. Nollekens; where, the landlord being defficient in his rent, an inventory was taken of the goods, and amongst them of certain pictures of *Howard,* a lodger, who had always paid his rent regularly. Howard *went to* Mr. & Mrs. Nollekens, who said the Law must take its course, & represented that it would answer to Howard to pay the difference as He wd. not be able for £40 a yr. to get such good lodgings elsewhere. Howard paid 15 guineas. — As a contrast to this account, Flaxman mentioned that He had been told that when Nollekens was at Rome, happening to play at Biliards with a Scotchman, He won every game. The Scotchman in warmth threw down his purse & challenged Nollekens to play against it, which He did & won it. The Scotchman was much distressed; but Nollekens on finding the amount of the contents declared had He supposed it contd. so much He would not have played against and therefore returned it to the Scotsman.

Sturt, the engraver, who has published the English dresses, was mentioned as being in difficulties. He was Pupil to Ryland.

Baker, Hearne & Edwards dined with me.

Soanes architecture at the Bank was described to be affected and contemptible.

Edwards speaking of Old Rooker, remarked how extraordinary it was, that He who in the morning was employed in engraving the fine plate of the Inside of St Pauls, should in the evening play Harlequin on the Stage. Hearne did not think it extraordinary. The engraving of that Plate was a mechanical process, ruling lines &c, it was not to be considered *as an effort of mind,* but a dexterity of hand in ruling lines &c. It required no sentiment, no elevation, such as would actually raise a man above the other practise.

Saturday August 13th.

Lindoe called today and told me He proposed to remove his things in a few days, as the time for my going into the Country approaches: and his own health is now from a nervous cause, not perfect, He is not inclined to set down to work at present having finished his Copy from Rembrandt. Mr. Barclay, his uncle, has recommended Kennion to him to teach him Architecture & Perspective.

Dance I drank tea with and proposed that we shd. call on West and encourage him to give directions to place the Hercules where the steps now are. — I told him of Flaxmans proposal to put the busts of Castor & Pollux on each side the Hercules. All this Dance agreed to.

N. Dance is returned from a visit to the Duke of Dorset. He found him what Hoppner described Humoursome & uncomfortable not suffering the dinner to be all placed on the table. — The Duchess *feels* the inconvenience of it but prudently submits.

Lord Liverpool, He also visited, who gave him an acct. of his life. — N. Dance thinks him a common kind of man, whom luck & perseverance have made. — G. Dance thinks the money N. Dance is saving will go to Mr. Brudenell nephew to Mrs. Dance, who will be Earl of Cardigan.

Criticisms on Exhibition, 1796.

Oracle
April 25th. Nos. 152, 192. Landscapes. Sir G. Beaumont,
"To be mentioned with the first works of the Modern School".
Ditto
April 26th. Sir G: Beaumont is unquestionably at the head of the Landscape. Of the 2 pictures He exhibits no. 152 is the richer subject; and possesses all that display of the pallets treasures, which was once to be observed in the Landscape of the elder Catton.
Free Briton & Sun.
April 30th. Sir G.B.
"The exquisite taste of this gentleman has long been the theme of admiration and praise in the extensive circle of fashion. When we view him as an Artist we have equal scope for eulogium on the delicacy & power of his pencil. The Landscape before us must afford the most unqualified pleasure to the liberal & tasteful Connoisseur".
St. James's Chronicle.
April 30th. Landscapes. Sir G.B.
No. 152 & 192 "are rather sketches, than finished Landscapes. Last year Sir George exhibited the best picture in the Exhibition. There are masterly strokes, and fine colouring, in the present Landscapes, but they are not finished".
Morning Post
May 5th. No. 152. "A Landscape, Sir G. Beaumont.
This picture is deserving the most minute inspection. The colouring, as usual, strictly accords with the subject of which He treats. The trees start from the Canvass as if they assumed the character of reality, and the light

and shade are managed with great art and effect. This picture is finely finished and highly glazed".

Morning Herald.
April 27th.
Sir George Beaumont Bart.   "We have much satisfaction in recording the progressive excellence of this Amateur pencil: its honorary productions this year are two Landscapes pure nature charmingly designed and wrought up with all the magic glow of the Flemish School. No. 192 possesses the brilliant beauties of Ruysdael, without his formalities".

Este	Telegraph	
	April 25th.	"Farington 4 Landscapes of much merit".
	ditto. 28th.	"They who love pretty Landscapes, should look at Sir George Beaumonts, Faringtons & Freebairns.
Boaden	Oracle ⎫ April 25th. ⎭	"Mr. Farington has a number of exquisite Landscapes, which will be fixed upon by every visitor to the room".
	do. April 26th.	"Farington considerably advanced in the colour of his pictures, claims the next rank of praise after Sir George Beaumont and probably Freebairn succeeds him".
Ireland	True Briton April 25th.	"Farington has 4 beautiful Landscapes, one of which exhibits the gleams of the declining Sun, and the rising of the Moon".
	Morning Chronicle April 27th.	"Ibbetsons & Faringtons Landscapes are extremely fine".
	Morning Herald April 30th.	"In the simple scenes of rural nature, this Artist is, perhaps, without a rival. His Landscapes generally display a superior glow of harmony. Evening No. 181 is peculiarly brilliant; but the figures in No. 178 *(the Mill)* are unworthy a situation in scenery so beautifully picturesque".
Taylor	True Briton & Sun April 27th.	No. 178. A Landscape, J. Farington R.A "The chasteness & delicacy which characterize the works of this Artist are consistently displayed in the work before us. The scene is rural, and happily chosen; The colouring & execution of the best kind. Mr. Westall has become the envied possessor of this charming piece".
	True Briton & Sun April 30th. No. 168.	"Lodore Waterfall, J. Farington R.A. A very pleasing scene, very charmingly executed".

St. James's Chronicle
April 30th.

J. Farington, R.A.

No. 156. "A Landscape. A pleasing picture highly finished. The front "trees are beautifully pencilled. If the water had been a little more limpid and more illumined, the effect would have been charming".
No. 168 & 178, "want force & effect".
No. 181 Evening. The last gleam of the Sun.
"The truth and correctness, in the lights & shadows of this landscape, are imagined in a masterly manner. The light catches the tops of the Rocks, and shews the situation of the Sun; and the moon rises in the opposite Hemisphere, with astronomical exactness". "The whole effect is natural and beautiful".

Times.
May 5th.

"Though we cannot speak of that rapid improvement in Landscape painting which we noticed in our first observation on this years exhibition, with respect of portraits, the least we can observe is that the pieces in this department have not fallen off in merit. The bathing of Horses, by Sir Francis Bourgeois ranks very high. He has, in this picture, contrived to execute with uncommon success the greatest difficulties. For solidity and luxuriance of science it takes the lead of all his other pieces, but it may not be amiss to notice, that the figures of the horses are better than those of the riders. *If Farington possessed an energy of colouring equal to his other merits, there would indeed be little to blame.*"
"Freebairns pieces are natural and Walmsley has given a view of the eagles nest at the Lake of Killarney taken on the spot; this Landscape could be a still more striking resemblance if it possessed a still more lively state of colouring".

Ledger and
London Packet.

May 6th. "178 A Landscape (The Mill), J. Farington, R.A.
"Here the Academical character is again vindicated; the solidity of touch and general management of this picture is admirable. The same may be said of its companion at a little distance which will be easily found in the Catalogue".

1796.

Dinners.

March 16th.

Wilton
Tyler
Hoppner
in all 7

Total expence
wine included £1.18.10.

4 Port   s   d
1 Sherry 10-6.

April 9th.

Mr. Malone
Hughes
Lysons.
in all 7

Total expence
wine included £1.8.1.

     s
3 Port   6 } 0.9.0.
1 Sherry 3.

May 15th.[5th]

Sir A. Hamilton
Lady Hamilton
Marchant
Liddel
in all 8.
Total expence
wine included £1.8.1.

     s
3 Port   6 } 0.9.0.
1 Sherry 3.-

May 13th.

Mrs. Offley
Mrs. Hamond
C. Offley
J. Offley
W. Offley
Outram
H. Hamond

in all 11

Total ex-
pences,
wine included
£1.18.3.

5 Port   0.10.0.
1 Sherry 0. 3.0.
_____

£0.13.0.

July 6.

G. Dance.
Lysons.
J. Taylor.
in all 4.

Total expence
wines included   0.13.4.

3 Port   6.0
pint Sherry 1.6.   0.7.6.

July 15th.

Mr. Beaumont.
Paine
Humphry

Total expence –
wine included   0.15.1.

2 Bottles, }   s
1 pint Port } 0.5.0.

August, 2nd.

Fuseli   Total
C. Offley   expence 0.11.8
Smirke
   2 Port   0.4.0.
   1 Sherry 0.3.0.

Sunday August 14th.

Paines I went to, to dinner with Humphry & His Nephew. — Joe Green there. Mary Paine has begun a Landscape in Oil very well.

The Duke of Devonshires manner of living while He is in London is singular. He seldom rises before three o'Clock in the afternoon; breakfasts & then rides out; dines, and at night goes to Brookes's; where He remains till two or three oClock in the morning. — Mr. Trebeck, the Vicar of Chiswick, having prevailed upon the Duke to engage to vote on some occasion at St. Georges, Hanover Square, The Duke was startled on being informed He must attend at two oClock in the day. This, to the great surprise of His servants, He did and voted. — Mrs. King & Mrs. Foxcroft called at Paines.

Hookhams rooms, in Bond St. I went to in the eveng. with Humphry.

Monday August 15th.

Flaxman called on me this morning, and read a letter adressed to Gavin Hamilton at Rome, stating that the Lords of the Treasury have granted permission for British Artists to import Casts, Prints, & drawings purchased for their use & study, duty free. — He mentions that to Mr. Long & Mr. Farington this indulgence is principally owing as they have exerted themselves to obtain it.

Flaxman proposed to adress a letter to the President & Council of the R. Academy to recommend the propriety of decorating the inside of St. Pauls, Covent Garden, now rebuilding, in such a way as to preserve a general *uniformity,* and not to allow monuments to be placed at random. — Hardwick is the Architect employed. Flaxman is now preparing a monument to the memory of Mr. Bellamy, founder of the Whig Club, which Perry, editor of the Morning Chronicle, caused him to be employed to execute. In the Morning Chronicle He intends to publish his letter.

On the subject of decorating Churches, The Bishop of Durham offered to Flaxman to propose it to the Bench of Bishops.

Smirke I called on in the evening, He suffers much from the complaint in his stomach. — He was at Windsor, a few days ago, and is delighted with the beauty of St. Georges Chapel. — He found it difficult to reconcile Himself to the Cartoons, — The dryness which prevails over them, the weakness, in many instances, of the drawing, the puerile littleness of design in the landscape, and general want of relish in these pictures, as to effect, were obstacles which He could scarcely overcome — though He felt that the draperies were admirably contrived, — the colours as to situation, & contrast well chosen, and [blank: passage unfinished].

Richard Smirke who was with him, was not prepared to regard them with pleasure.

Bowyer has lost his only Child a daughter abt. 18 years old, of a decline. Her parents were attached to her in the strongest degree.

Tuesday August 16th.

Edwards called on me this morning and brought a manuscript Volume of Sketches of lives of Modern Artists written by himself. He read a few of them as specimens. He does not mean that they shall be published during his life time.

Humphry called in the evening. He waited on Lady Spencer yesterday at Devonshire House, and had a long conversation with Her Ladyship on the disorder in her eyes with which the Duchess of Devonshire is afflicted. — One of the Duchesses eyes is in such a state now that she can only distinguish light from darkness. An opening below the eye has been made to draw of the blood & humours. Humphry strongly recommended Mrs. Marshall, but Lady Spencer said the first of the faculty were employed and as the Duchess was better, they could not be dismissed.

Lady Spencer called on Humphry today & said she would sit for her picture, & wished she could afford to have all her grandchildren painted.

Through Humphrys reccomendation the Duchess of Newcastle has been under the care of Mrs. Marshall 4 months, and her eyes are surprisingly recovered.

Mrs. Marshall is upwards of 70 years of age. She was born at the Devises, and happening about 40 years ago to have a complaint in her eyes to which she was applying remedies, a Gipsy woman told her *she* would cure her, which she did; & communicated to her the remedy, with which Mrs. Marshall has continued to relieve Her friends & acquaintances who have stood in need of it. At Mrs. Linleys, Humphry met Mrs. Marshall, who told him, while she examined his eyes, that the disorder was the effect of a scorbutic habit, which she perceived from his breath. She gave him an Anti-scorbutic medicine to take internally, & she applied her preparation to his eyes. He felt benefit from it after the first application. She strongly urged him not to use his eyes by Candle light, to read or draw, — and not to use spectacles which will produce a change in the power of seeing. "The medicine I took to remove the scorbutic humour operated upon me violently for several months witht. weakening me." He added "that it removed the taint on his breath". (This is a remarkable proof that those who have a tainted breath do not perceive it).

Humphry this evening, related to me the particulars of his becoming an Artist, and of his early professional life.

Wednesday August 17th.

The weather has been bright & dry for several days, but a cold easterly wind has rendered it unpleasant. I have been at home today.

Smirke is very indifferent again with his Stomach complaint. Batty has today brought Dr. Ainslie to him.

David Alans death an account of I saw in this days paper. He died near

Edinburgh on the 6th. of this month. He was of a weakly constitution. I became acquainted with him at Lord Hopetouns in 1788; and afterwards saw him at Edinburgh in 1792. — He had been in Italy, and had some ingenuity in drawing: but did not seem capable of making any considerable progress in the Art.

Thursday August 18th.

Montgomery Campbell died at Steyning in Sussex, on Tuesday last after 24 hours illness — in consequence of eating fruit. He was on his way to Brighton.

Lindoe came today and took away his painting apparatus. — He complains much of a nervous habit, and seems full of fancies. — He has something of talent; but no steadiness of application; flying off after every novelty.

Smirke I called on, he is better. Dr. Ainslie talks of Antimonials as proper for him to strengthen his stomach & bowels, — and produce regularity. — I plead for Bath waters producing that effect.

Humphry called in the eving. — Singleton, his former Pupil has just finished a small head of J. Wyatt, engraved in the dotting manner; for which He is to have only 12 guineas. — Humphry proposed to Wyatt that to the name, the tittle of Surveyor General of the Board of Works should be added, but Wyatt would not consent, as He said it would appear as if He had the Head engraved to publish the title. It is a private plate for Wyatt.

Friday August 19th.

Lindoe I called on this morning & left a note at his Lodgings No. 30 East St. — to desire him to call on me any day before Wednesday next that I may shew him how to use the camera.

Offleys I dined with. C. J. & Wm. Offley only.

Mr. Angerstein, is the natural Son of a Mr. Thomson, a Russian merchant, (the firm Thomson and Peters) who had also other natural Children. One of his Thomsons daughters married Mr. Ibbetson, Son to the late Archdeacon of St. Albans. Mr. Thomson died a few years ago, as did Mr. Ibbetson.

The news today from France of the victories of their Armies in Italy, over General Wurmser, almost exceed belief for rapidity and the effects which have followed. — It seems to be the opinion that the Germanick Constitution will undergo a total alteration, in which the sovereign power of the House of Austria will be sunk.

John Offley dined lately at Greenwich. To the same House the Duke & Duchess of York — Lady Ann Fitzroy & [blank] came & dined in a private manner. — The Duke is much altered in appearance. John Offley thought He looked liked a man of 50 years of age, though only 34 — His conduct in a domestic capacity does him great credit.

Saturday August 20th.

Trumbull I met this morning. He is lately returned from the Continent. He complained much of the delay of the Publication of the Prints from His picture of Gibraltar, & actions in America. Sharp is now 3 years over the time He engaged to complete His work in — Trumbull says He is in consequence at a stand, for He cannot think of preparing more subjects till He knows how these Prints will answer. — "Better Play for nothing, than work for nothing", said He, & "I know not whether I am to be a gainer or not till the Prints are published."

I asked him what He thought of the disposition of the French whose victories are so universal and extraordinary. "Peace, said He, is the wish of the poeple, and of the Army". They are induced to fight with such astonishing ardour because they are persuaded it is the only way to procure a peace soon. — Their armies consist of abt. 600,000 men, half of whom are of the respectable Class of Citizens who languish to be at home with their families & friends. — I asked Him if the government of France is not averse from Peace from an apprehension of the Consequences of the return of the armies. He replied, "There is nothing to apprehend, The numerous garrisons &c. will employ 300,000 men which will include the blackguards and dangerous part of the troops; the other half have homes to go to and a maintenance there." — He said it is true that the French in making up their Armies have not paid attention to uniformity of size in selecting their men, nor have regarded the Cloathing, — but their arms are good and bright; and their discipline is admirable. — In the Towns which they take they become peaceable inhabitants while they stay. |

I expressed the satisfaction I felt that there seemed to be a good understanding between England & America. He angrily replied He did not know how long it may continue, if the Commanders of English Vessels are permitted to insult the american Ships as they do. He was stopped on his passage and notwithstanding He shewed all the papers required by the regulations, yet His Ship was kept an Hour in Custody, & threatened to be carried in as a prize. The Captain of the English Ship at last let her go, on Trumbull stating that when He landed He would make it a public affair.

Lindoe I called upon. He is so well pleased with his Copy of Rembrandts "Daniels Vision", that He did propose to ask 100 guineas for it; but He means to put it at 70 guineas.

I drank some Porter which He had from Thrales Brew House, He said it was a sort brewed for the use of the Empress of Russia, and would keep fine 7 years. He told me that the Cause of the Colour of Porter being so deep & the taste peculiar, is owing to *that part* of the Barley used in making it, which is burnt so that each grain is throughout a Black brown. This operation on the Barley is done in Hertfordshire, chiefly abt. Saffron Waldon, and the manner in which they burn it is the cause why no Country Porter has the flavour of London Porter.

Offleys I dined at. Mrs. Ball there. She speaks with great regard of the Portuguese, among whom she lived with her Husband many years. A great change in manners took place while she knew Portugal. When she was first in Lisbon it would have appeared monstrous for a man and woman to walk side by side, even the Husband, *followed* his *wife,* if they went out together; but now they appear as in England, arm in arm etc.

Dance I called on in the eveng. He goes tomorrow to Hampshire on a visit to his Brother.

Sunday August 21.

At Church. — Mr. Mathew preached.

Plott I called on & desired him to give me what particulars He knows relative to the late Mr. Hone.

Keates servant has called on Plott, and told him that Mr. Keate had called him into a room and given him a charge never to admit Plott should He come to the House.

Offleys I dined at. — L. Salisbury — John & Wm. Offley set off today for Margate.

Campion married to his 2nd. wife in 1774 a Miss Page at Oporto, daugtr. to Mr. Page with whom He had been apprentice. — Her Brother was then, and is now, settled at Oporto. — He had one Son by his first wife; and two daughters by a Mrs. Booth who is now living. — The eldest of these daugtrs. is married to a Mr. Charlton, a principal clerk in Coutts's Banking House, — the 2nd. daugtr. is lately married to a Son of Mr. Sass, who keeps a [Colourman's] Shop, the Corner of King street, Holborn. Campion gave them £1300 stock each; abt. £1000 sterling.

Monday August 22.

Smirke I called on this morning & we fixed to go to Bath on Tuesday 30th. — Lindoe called on me & I shewed Him how to use the Camera.

Offleys I dined with. Mr. Thomson, a friend of the Ibbetson family there. — Mr. Thomson, the Father of Mr. Angerstein, had one Son and four daughters also, which bore his name. — The eldest daughter married Charles Boone M.P. The Second Sir [Joshua] Vanneck. — The 3rd. Mr. Hankey, from whom she fled with Col. Straubenzee, and went with him to India, where she died in Child bed, — The 4th. daughter married Ibbetson, — who she became acquainted with at Bath, from whence they run up to town and were married at St. Clements Church. — Ibbetson was very much attached to Her; but she did not like him, and she went to Lisbon under pretence of bad health, but in fact it was believed, because She thought He wd. not follow her there. — being pressed by accts. of his dying state she did come to England, and arrived in London the day after He was buried. She had been much blamed, as having been privy to the amour going on between Her Sister, Mrs. Hankey, and Col. Straubenzee.

Dr. Ibbetson, Archdeacon of St. Albans had 9 Children. Three Sons & 6 daugrs. The eldest daughter married Mr. Boscawen, a Commissioner of the Victualling Office, — by whom she has 8 children. The 2nd. daugr. married Mr. Madan, only Son of Dr. Madan, author of Thelypthora. — Lieut. Ibbetson, an officer, married well at Peterborough. — Captn. Hartwell, now a Commissioner of the Navy, married a daughter of Admiral Elphinston. He was a Commissioner of the Victualling Office, but obtained his present situation because the widows of Commissioners of the Navy have £400 a yr. Pension, and those of the Victualling Office have only £200 a yr.

Harry called in Charlotte St, this evening having come up to Town today.

Tuesday August 23rd.

C Offley I went with to Regnard the Statuarys, at Mrs. Offleys desire to see an advertised monument which is ill executed & not worth purchasing.

Harry I dined with at the London Coffee House, C. Offley there. Harry was on the Grand Jury at the Assizes at Lancaster: Mr. Gwillym made a very respectable appearance. Miss Athertons were there.

G. Smith pleaded a cause at the Sessions at Manchester, having before asserted that He wd. bring his client off; but He failed in his promise and got no credit by his attempt. Jem Topping said afterwards I thought this fellow had some brains till he exposed himself in this business.

Hulton of Park, has injured his estate, and is destroying his constitution by drinking.

Wednesday Augst. 24th.

Harry dined with me today. — A Handsome dinner was given by Gentlemen of the Town of Manchester the [blank] of May, — to Mr. Stanley & Mr. Blackburn the two County Members; who were met by a procession at Pendleton Turnpike, from whence they were drawn into the town. It happened that Blackburns carriage was first, so He had most of the attention of the Mob. — Stanley was not in Spirits, He was anxious abt. the event of the Election for Preston, & hinted that shd. not Lord Stanley *succeed there, He* must expect to lose *his seat* (for the County) — Blackburn said *No,* you wd. be safe, but *I should go.* — Bamford read a letter which He had recd. from Lord Derby, who declared that He had no intention of interfering with the present County Members who were approved by their constituents; that He had never expressed any displeasure at Coln. Stanley having lately held different political sentiments, and was satisfied that the Col. voted according to his conscience.

Coln. Stanley spoke on this occasion & said His Lordship had truly stated that nothing disagreeable had taken place between them in consequence of their difference in political opinions.

It is supposed that the Preston election did not cost Horrocks more than £3000; but that it cost Lord Derby and Sir Harry Houghton at least £20,000 — The Houses which Horrocks opened were careful of his interest and only gave Ale, while those of Ld. Derby were profuse of everything.

Entwhistles, is the first trading House in Manchester. Wm. Barrows, probably the second. — Barrow is supposed to be worth £80,000. He has one Son & 2 daugrs. The Son is to be married to the eldest Miss Hardman after Christmas.

Jos: Marriott, and Tom Boardman, allow Will Boardman £20 a month, and Mrs. Rooke proposes to allow her sister £50 a yr. — who replied that "Her situation obliged her to accept it".

Lord Derby did not approve the proposed marriage of young Mr. Hornby & Lady Charlotte Stanley, and said they had better see more of the world &c &c. but at last consented. — Lord Stanley is so deaf as to be obliged to use a Trumpet.

Smirke shewed me a letter this morning, which he had recd. from Thomson, Secretary to the Society established at Edinburgh for the improvement of Arts & Manufactures &c — proposing to him to apply for the place held by the late David Alan, of Teacher to draw to abt. 25 youths — salary £120 a year, — if not agreeable to him, to offer it to Hamilton or Westall.

Thursday August 25th.

Marchant I called on this morning. He has had a severe attack of a disorder in his bowels; occasioned as He supposes by his having got cold at Vauxhall. — He shewed me the letter He recd. from Lord Spencer of which the following is a Copy.

"Dear Marchant,

The inclosed is for Your Homer, which I assure you I consider as very basely paid by it. I hope you will not forget that it is only the first of many of your works which I hope to have.

Yours very sincerely,

Spencer.

Wimbledon Park.
   4th August 1796.
     N Marchant Esqr.
      at Mr. Perigals — Bond street."

Inclosed was a draft for 100 guineas. — Marchant told me that a little time before He recd. the letter Lord Althorp called on him and *sounded him* abt. the price. — One Hundred Guineas was what Marchant expected for it. Abt. a week before He recd. the letter Lady Spencer told him that Lord Spencer meant to give him 100 guineas, — Marchant said He should be glad to have it soon as the Funds were low, and He wd. purchase in.

Marchant was acquainted at Rome with David the French Artist. One side of his face is much larger than the other and appears as if swelled. When He left Rome He told Marchant that He was going to Paris at the entreaties of his wife; but wd. soon return, as Rome was the only place for an Artist to reside in. — Little was it then expected that He wd. become the bloody Companion of a Robespierre. At his House in Paris Young men to the number of abt. 20 assembled to study. They were not engaged to him but made him presents of Coffee, Tea &c &c as an acknowledgement.

C. Offleys I dined at, Harry there. Offley has recd. letters from Lisbon in which great apprehension of a Spanish War is expressed.

Lewis, the Apothecary came in. He is a native of a place near the Severn abt. 14 miles above Shrewsbury. — He spoke of Mr. Probart who resides abt. 3 miles from that town. Mr. P. is abt. 65 years of age. He was originally a Shoe cleaner in the family of Sir Watkin Williams Wynne; from whence He became a stable assistant at Lord Powis's, by degrees having learnt to read & write, He was advanced, till He became a surveyor and to be employed in valuing land. He has had the care of many estates, of Lord Powis's, Lord Clives &c. and with a fair character, is supposed to be worth £100,000. — Lord Clives affairs are now in a very prosperous state. Lord Powis is not married, has indifferent health, — and keeps a woman in his house, therefore not being likely to marry; Ld. Clive who married his sister may probably be His Heir.

Friday August 26th.

Daniell I called on this morning and requested him to look at the picture painted by George [Farington] for Sir John D'Oyley, which He did, and from what He recollected of the picture which Pott got possession of He is certain *this* is the picture intended for Sir John D'Oyley. — Daniell went to Devis and brought him to see the picture. They both agreed that so far was the picture which was in Potts possession from being *finished* as Grainger described it to be, that parts of the canvass were not covered. — Daniell said that Pott told him "Farington had given up an intention of finishing *that picture* as He thought He could improve the composition", and therefore began another. — Devis & Daniell agreed that Potts picture is *smaller* than that which I have, and *does not contain so many figures,* — That the composition is not so good. That there were figures of Sepoys in Potts picture which appeared too tall and were not so judiciously introduced. — Devis recollected parts of the picture which I have, particularly some figures of the Nabobs Court; He was shewn the picture by the Nabob, It was then in a Biliard Room. Devis saw the picture which was at Potts in 1793, also a study a little larger than a Kitcat of the same subject, which is an additional proof of the pains George had taken to make the picture for Sir John compleat. Daniell & Devis readily agreed to answer in writing any queries I may put to them relative to these pictures.

Devis said Pott was shy of letting him see any of the drawings which He had purchased at the sale of Georges effects.

Harry dined with me. — He is desirous of knowing what Will is inclined that Harry should be brought up to, — as it is time to determine.

Saturday Augst. 27th.

Daniell I called on this morning, & read to him Graingers letter to me. He is convinced it was written without any real knowledge of the picture, but evidently to suit Sir John D'Oyleys wishes to get rid of the business. — He drank tea with me, also William Daniell, and He mentioned having seen Renaldi, an Artist lately arrived from Calcutta, who has seen the pictures which were at Potts. They were, with other articles, brought down to Calcutta after the death of Pott and sold there very cheap.

Humphry also drank tea with me.

C Offley called. The Oporto Merchants have again been with Mr. Pitt who will grant the indulgence of bonding any wines which may be brought over in consequence of the apprehension of the Spanish War. — Mr. Pitt declared that the experience of *two or three* years would not be sufficient to induce him to take off the last tax laid upon Portugal wines.

Sunday August 28th.

Daniell called on me this morning, and I read to him my correspondence with Sir John D'Oyley, and my letter to Pott. He plainly saw that Sir John wished to shuffle off the business. He went from me to Renaldi, who is confined to the House today by some symptoms of the gout.

Harry called on me & we went together to Dine with Paine.

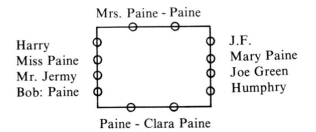

Mary Paine has copied the picture Her first attempt in Oil very well. Joe Green told me that the Revd. Thomas Carwardin was born in Herefordshire. His Father possessed a small estate, and had one Son and 3 or 4

daughters. The daugr. who afterwards married Mr. Butler was some time with Spencer the Miniature painter who taught her that art and she instructed Her Brother. Another Sister Mrs. [blank] kept a boarding school in Essex where Carwardine found his present wife, then a girl of 13 or 14 years old. — Having secured Her growing affections, He married Her abt. the year 1771 or 2. She had £3000 and the reversion of an estate which she told Green produced abt. £420 a year clear. Carwardine also holds a living of £200 a year which was also the property of his wife and for which He took orders. He has also one or two other livings and is a Prebendary of St. Pauls but His Church preferment together does not produce him above £500 a year. They have eight Children. The eldest a Son of 23 years old intended to be an Attorney. The second Son is designed for the Church. The eldest daugr. is abt. 19 years old. There is no provission made for the younger children. The estate of the Mother being entailed on the eldest Son.

Marlow brought the two Prints He has lately published to Paine. The Price was two guineas, Paine took them concluding that so shy a man as Marlow wd. not have offered them had not the money been desirable.

Monday August 29th.

Daniell called this morning, and Renaldi with him, who saw the picture of the Durbar, and declared, as Daniell & Devis had before done that it is larger, more finished, and much better composed than that was which Pott purchased & which Renaldi saw in Potts House in 1789, and *last January* in Calcutta, at Mr Solvins, a Flemish artist, who purchased it at the sale of Potts effects. — Renaldi wrote his opinion adressed to me, and this afternoon Daniell sent me a letter containing his opinion; and Devis called on me while Daniell & Renaldi were with me & brought a letter to me containing his opinion.

Will called on me & was here while the above Artists were with me.

Smirke I called on & carried several of my drawings for his eldest daugtr. to copy at his Desire.

Susan wrote me that Jodrell has been very ill at Chester, something like a stroke.

Harry & Will I dined with at the London Coffee House.

Harry has been told by a person very well informed that £30,000 was settled on the younger Children of the Earl of Derby, the disposal of it subject to his Lordships pleasure, who has given Lady Charlotte £28,000 and £20000 to *Lady Elisabeth*, the latter the supposed daugr. of the Duke of Dorset. — Lord Derby has agreed to pay Young Hornby 4 per cent on the £28,000 during his life.

Tuesday August 30th.

Mr. Metcalfe I called on this morning, and gave him a draft for the pictures bought by Westall at Sir Joshuas sale.

He told me that Ralph Kirkley is not yet paid the whole of his demand.
Lady Inchiquins £15,000 which she advanced to liquidate Lord Inchiquins
Bonds, will be replaced in two years. — Metcalfe remarked on the risk she
run. Had Lord Inchiquin died soon after the marriage she would have lost
all the money.

Metcalfe is treasurer of the money subscribed for Dr. Johnson's monument. Bacon charges £1100 for it: of which by agreement between them
signed by each Bacon & Sir Joshua Reynolds engaged mutually to bear all
the expences of placing the statue in St. Pauls instead of Westminster
Abbey, — which might *exceed the subscription*, which amounting only to
£900, Sir Joshuas Estate & Bacon are responsible for each £100. Metcalfe
has the signed paper in which I signed my name as a subscriber to that
monument, & paid the money to Sir Joshua.

Sir Wm. Chambers	£10.10.	Wm. Hodges	£3.3	John Webber	£3.3
J. Farington	3. 3	Thos. Banks	3.3	Richd. Cos-	
Geo. Dance	3. 3			way £3.3	

These subscriptions had not been put in the printed list.

Greenwood I called on & shewed him Mr. Metcalfes rect. — Moriss's I
dined at with Will & Harry & several others. Daniell called on me, and I
read him the letter I have written to Sir John D'Oyley, which He approved
of.

Wednesday August 31st.

Lane of Lynn, I wrote to, on the subject of his Son, giving it in my opinion
that He ought to allow him time to shew the extent of his natural talent
which his many disadvantages prevent our judging of at present.

Col. Wemyss I wrote to & sent his "History of Fife".

Sir John D'Oyley I sent a Packet to by the Post, inclosing my letter , —
Daniells, Devis's, & Renaldis letters.

Will called. He told me George is strongly bent to go to Sea, I observed
to him that Sir Alan Gardner reccomends that Boys intended for the Sea
shd. be put on board Ships at 10 years old.

Reading I went to this afternoon with Smirke, who has been very indifferent last night.

Mrs. Otway was a passenger, She told us she was daugtr. to a Captn.
Smith who had an East India Companys Ship from Bombay, and was lost
at Sea. She has a Sister and a Brother or two. Mr. T. Otway Her Husband
is a native of Kendal and nephew to Captn. Otway of the Navy. He was a
Bankers Clerk and married to Her by stealth when He was 33 years old &
she 17. Her mother was a *Native* of India. — She has been much at Dumfries & told me that Wat Riddel married to His first wife a Scotch Lady
who had property in the West Indies. She died & He went over to look

after Her estates, and there married one of the daugrs. of Governor Wood-ley. He then returned to Dumfries and purchased a seat near it, and kept a Coach & four. — The West India Estate not turning out well, the Scotch estate was sold, & the Coach laid down; and He now lives in Dumfries privately.

Robert Riddel died suddenly in the night. His full habit and free living made this very likely to happen.

Burns, the Poet, was a violent Democrat, and often offended Company by his improper expressions, and prevented his friends from reccomending him for some place, which they were inclined to have done. — He was addicted to woemen much notwithstanding He was married and had children. — He died very poor.

Mr. Otway joined us at supper, to which we had invited Mrs. Otway. — He told us the Crops in this Country are greater than has been remembered, and have been got in without interruption from the weather. — He said many poeple in this part are much alarmed at the apprehension of a French invasion, and talk of packing up their goods.